# ANNUAL EDITIONS



# Nutrition 02/03

*Fourteenth Edition*

**EDITOR**
**Dorothy J. Klimis-Zacas**
*University of Maine, Orono*

Dorothy Klimis-Zacas is associate professor of clinical nutrition at the University of Maine and cooperating professor of nutrition and dietetics at Harokopio University, Athens, Greece. She teaches undergraduate and graduate classes in nutrition and its relation to health and disease for students of dietetics, nurses, and physicians.

Her current research interests relate to basic investigations in the area of trace mineral nutrition and its role in the development of atherosclerosis and to applied investigations that utilize nutritional interventions to reduce cardiovascular disease risk in adolescents both in the United States and in the Mediterranean region.

A Ph.D. and Fullbright Fellow, Dr. Klimis-Zacas is the author of numerous research articles and the editor of two books, *Manganese in Health and Disease* and *Nutritional Concerns for Women*. She is a member of Sigma Delta Epsilon, The American Society of Nutritional Sciences, The International Atherosclerosis Society, the American Dietetic Association, The Society for Nutrition Education, and The American Heart Association.

*McGraw-Hill/Dushkin*
530 Old Whitfield Street, Guilford, Connecticut 06437

Visit us on the Internet
***http://www.dushkin.com***

# Credits

1. **Nutrition Trends**
   Unit photo—© 2002 by Sweet By & By/Cindy Brown.
2. **Nutrients**
   Unit photo—© 2002 by PhotoDisc, Inc.
3. **Diet and Disease: Through the Life Span**
   Unit photo—© 2002 by Cleo Freelance Photography.
4. **Obesity and Weight Control**
   Unit photo—© 2002 by PhotoDisc, Inc.
5. **Health Claims**
   Unit photo—McGraw-Hill/Dushkin photo.
6. **Food Safety**
   Unit photo—© 2002 by Sweet By & By/Cindy Brown.
7. **World Hunger and Malnutrition**
   Unit photo—United Nations photo.

# Copyright

Cataloging in Publication Data
Main entry under title: Annual Editions: Nutrition. 2002/2003.
1. Nutrition—Periodicals. 2. Diet—Periodicals. I. Klimis-Zacas, Dorothy J., *comp.* II. Title: Nutrition.
ISBN 0–07–250684–9 613.2'.05 91–641611 ISSN 1055–6990



Fourteenth Edition

Cover image © 2002 PhotoDisc, Inc.
Printed in the United States of America 1234567890BAHBAH5432 Printed on Recycled Paper

# Editors/Advisory Board

Members of the Advisory Board are instrumental in the final selection of articles for each edition of ANNUAL EDITIONS. Their review of articles for content, level, currentness, and appropriateness provides critical direction to the editor and staff. Wethink that you will find their careful consideration well reflected in this volume.

### EDITOR



### ADVISORY BOARD



# Staff

### EDITORIAL STAFF



### TECHNOLOGY STAFF



### PRODUCTION STAFF

# To the Reader

In publishing ANNUAL EDITIONS we recognize the enormous role played by the magazines, newspapers, and journals of the public press in providing current, first-rate educational information in a broad spectrum of interest areas. Many of these articles are appropriate for students, researchers, and professionals seeking accurate, current material to help bridge the gap between principles and theories and the real world. These articles, however, become more useful for study when those of lasting value are carefully collected, organized, indexed, and reproduced in a low-cost format, which provides easy and permanent access when the material is needed. That is the role played by ANNUAL EDITIONS.

Since nutrition is an evolving science, it necessitates updating *Annual Editions: Nutrition* annually to keep up with the plethora of topics and controversies raised in the field. The main goal of this anthology is to provide the reader with up-to-date information by presenting current topics of information based on scientific evidence. *Annual Editions: Nutrition* also presents controversial topics in a balanced and unbiased manner. Where appropriate, international perspectives are presented. We hope that the reader will develop critical thinking and be empowered to ask questions and seek answers.

Consumers are thoroughly confused with the food choices that they have to make when they walk into a supermarket or visit a restaurant. Additionally, there is conflicting information on several nutrition topics that appear on the news, popular magazines, scientific journals, and over the Internet. "Nutrition experts" and "health advisers" seem to sprout everywhere. We are at the pinnacle not only of a revolution in information technology but also of nutritional research. Information is distributed at a very fast pace, across continents, and without consideration of country borders. Thus, informing the consumer regularly with reliable and current nutrition information is the duty of the professional.

*Annual Editions: Nutrition 02/03* is to be used as a companion to a standard nutrition text so that it may update, expand, or emphasize certain topics that are covered in the text or present a totally new topic not covered in a standard text.

To accomplish this, *Annual Editions: Nutrition 02/03* is composed of seven units that review current knowledge and controversies in the area of nutrition. The first unit describes current trends in the field of nutrition in the United States and the rest of the world, including the new dietary guidelines for the United States. Units two, three, and four include topics that focus on nutrients and their relationship to health and disease, the changing nutrient needs and concerns through the life cycle, and weight control. Units five and six cover topics on health claims and focus on food safety, including subjects about which consumers are misinformed and are thus vulnerable to quackery. Finally, unit seven focuses on world hunger and malnutrition, including environmental sustainability and biotechnology. A *topic guide* will assist the reader in finding other articles on a given subject, and *World Wide Web* sites will help in further exploring a particular topic.

Your input is most valuable to improving this anthology, which we update yearly. We would appreciate your comments and suggestions as you review the current edition. Please complete and return the postage-paid *Article Rating* form at the end of this book.

D. Klimis-Zacas

Dorothy Klimis-Zacas
*Editor*

# Contents

## UNIT 1
## Nutrition Trends

Eight articles examine the eating patterns of people today. Some of the topics considered include nutrients in our diet, eating trends, portion size and servings, and how the food industry is making Americans overweight.



The concepts in bold italics are developed in the article. For further expansion, please refer to the Topic Guide and the Index.

# UNIT 2
## Nutrients

Eight articles discuss the importance of nutrients. Topics include the role of proteins, fats, carbohydrates, and vitamin and mineral supplements in our diet.



The concepts in bold italics are developed in the article. For further expansion, please refer to the Topic Guide and the Index.

# UNIT 3
## Diet and Disease: Through the Life Span

Eight articles examine our health as it is affected by diet throughout our lives. Some topics include the links between diet and degenerative diseases, cholesterol, the human genome project, and nutrition for the elderly.



The concepts in bold italics are developed in the article. For further expansion, please refer to the Topic Guide and the Index.

# UNIT 4
## Obesity and Weight Control

Seven articles examine weight management. Topics include the relationship between dieting and exercise, the effects of various diet plans, and a new approach to binge eating disorders.



The concepts in bold italics are developed in the article. For further expansion, please refer to the Topic Guide and the Index.

# UNIT 5
## Health Claims

Six articles examine some of the health claims made by today's "specialists." Topics include misconceptions about herbs, energy bar claims, and nutrition myths and misinformation.

# UNIT 6
## Food Safety

Seven articles discuss the safety of food. Topics include food-borne illness, mad cow disease, food additives, and food irradiation.



The concepts in bold italics are developed in the article. For further expansion, please refer to the Topic Guide and the Index.

# UNIT 7
## World Hunger and Malnutrition

Seven articles discuss the world's food supply. Topics include global malnutrition, nutrition and infection, agricultural biotechnology, and a sustainable world food supply.



The concepts in bold italics are developed in the article. For further expansion, please refer to the Topic Guide and the Index.

The concepts in bold italics are developed in the article. For further expansion, please refer to the Topic Guide and the Index.

# Topic Guide

This topic guide suggests how the selections in this book relate to the subjects covered in your course. You may want to use thetopics listed on these pages to search the Web more easily.

On the following pages a number of Web sites have been gathered specifically for this book. They are arranged to reflect the units of this *Annual Edition.* You can link to these sites by going to the DUSHKIN ONLINE support site at *http://www.dushkin.com/online/.*

**ALL THE ARTICLES THAT RELATE TO EACH TOPIC ARE LISTED BELOW THE BOLD-FACED TERM.**

# World Wide Web Sites

**The following World Wide Web sites have been carefully researched and selected to support the articles found in this reader. The easiest way to access these selected sites is to go to our DUSHKIN ONLINE support site at *http://www.dushkin.com/online/*.**

# AE: Nutrition 02/03

**The following sites were available at the time of publication. Visit our Web site—we update DUSHKIN ONLINE regularly to reflect any changes.**

## General Sources

**American Dietetic Association**
*http://www.eatright.org*
This consumer link to nutrition and health includes resources, news, marketplace, search for a dietician, government information, and a gateway to related sites. The site includes a tip of the day and special features.

**The Blonz Guide to Nutrition**
*http://www.blonz.com*
The categories in this valuable site report news in the fields of nutrition, food science, foods, fitness, and health. There is also a selection of search engines and links.

**CSPI: Center for Science in the Public Interest**
*http://www.cspinet.org*
CSPI is a nonprofit education and advocacy organization that is committed to improving the safety and nutritional quality of our food supply. CSPI publishes the *Nutrition Action Healthletter,* which has monthly information about food.

**Institute of Food Technologists**
*http://www.ift.org*
This site of the Society for Food Science and Technology is full of important information and news about every aspect of the food products that come to market.

**International Food Information Council Foundation**
*http://ific.org*
IFIC's purpose is to be the link between science and communications by offering the latest scientific information on food safety, nutrition, and health in a form that is understandable and useful for opinion leaders and consumers to access.

**U.S. National Institutes of Health**
*http://www.nih.gov*
Consult this site for links to extensive health information and scientific resources. Comprised of 24 separate institutes, centers, and divisions, the NIH is one of eight health agencies of the Public Health Service, which, in turn, is part of the U.S. Department of Health and Human Services.

## UNIT 1: Nutrition Trends

**Food Science and Human Nutrition Extension**
*http://www.extension.iastate.edu/nutrition/*
This extensive Iowa State University site links to latest news and reports, consumer publications, food safety information, and many other useful nutrition-related sites.

**Food Surveys Research Group**
*http://www.barc.usda.gov/bhnrc/foodsurvey/home.htm*
Visit this site of the Beltsville Human Nutrition Research Center Food Surveys research group first, and then click on USDA to keep up with nutritional news and information.

**U.S. Food and Drug Administration**
*http://www.fda.gov/default.htm*
This is the home page of the FDA, which describes itself as the United States' "foremost consumer protection agency." Visit this site and its links to learn about food safety, food and nutrition labeling, and other topics of importance.

## UNIT 2: Nutrients

**Dole 5 A Day: Nutrition, Fruits & Vegetables**
*http://www.dole5aday.com*
The Dole Food Company, a founding member of the "National 5 A Day for Better Health Program," offers this site to entice children into taking an interest in proper nutrition.

**Food and Nutrition Information Center**
*http://www.nal.usda.gov/fnic/*
Use this site to find dietary and nutrition information provided by various USDA agencies and to find links to food and nutrition resources on the Internet.

**Nutrient Data Laboratory**
*http://www.nal.usda.gov/fnic/foodcomp/*
Information about the USDA Nutrient Database can be found on this site. Search here for answers to FAQs, a glossary of terms, facts about food composition, and useful links.

**NutritionalSupplements.com**
*http://www.nutritionalsupplements.com*
This source provides unbiased information about nutritional supplements and prescription drugs, submitted by consumers with no vested interest in the products.

**University of Pennsylvania Library**
*http://www.library.upenn.edu/resources/websitest.html*
This vast site is rich in links to information about virtually every subject in health and nutrition studies. Its extensive population and demography resources address concerns such as nutrition in various world regions.

**U.S. National Library of Medicine**
*http://www.nlm.nih.gov*
This site permits you to search databases and electronic information sources such as MEDLINE, learn about research projects, and keep up on nutrition-related news.

## UNIT 3: Diet and Disease: Through the Life Span

**American Cancer Society**
*http://www.cancer.org*
Open this site and its various links to learn the concerns and lifestyle advice of the American Cancer Society. It provides information on alternative therapies, tobacco, other Web resources, and more.

**American Heart Association**
*http://www.americanheart.org*
The AHA offers this site to provide the most comprehensive information on heart disease and stroke as well as late-breaking news. The site presents facts on warning signs, a reference guide, and explanations of diseases and treatments.

**The Food Allergy Network**
*http://www.foodallergy.org*
The Food Allergy Network site, which welcomes consumers, health professionals, and reporters, includes product alerts and updates, information about food allergies, daily tips, and links to other sites.

**Go Ask Alice! from Columbia University Health Services**
*http://www.goaskalice.columbia.edu*
This interactive site provides discussion and insight into a number of issues of interest to college-age people and those younger and older. Many questions about physical and emotional well-being, fitness and nutrition, and alcohol, nicotine, and other drugs are answered.

**Heinz Infant & Toddler Nutrition**
*http://www.heinzbaby.com*
An educational section full of nutritional information and meal-planning guides for parents and caregivers as well as articles and reviews by leading pediatricians and nutritionists can be found on this page.

**LaLeche League International**
*http://www.lalecheleague.org*
Important information to mothers who are contemplating breast feeding can be accessed at this Web site. Links to other sites are also possible.

**Nutrition and Kids**
*http://www.nutritionandkids.net/1227*
This Web site takes a positive, fun approach to the more serious issues that affect children, including poor eating habits, obesity, and inactivity.

**Vegetarian Pages**
*http://www.veg.org*
The Vegetarian Pages Web site offers information on everything of interest to vegans, vegetarians, and others.

## UNIT 4: Obesity and Weight Control

**American Anorexia Bulimia Association/National Eating Disorders Association**
*http://www.edap.org*
The AABA is a nonprofit organization of concerned people dedicated to the prevention and treatment of eating disorders. It offers many services, including help lines, referral networks, school outreach, support groups, and prevention programs.

**American Society of Exercise Physiologists (ASEP)**
*http://www.css.edu/users/tboone2/asep/toc.htm*
The goal of the ASEP is to promote health and physical fitness. This extensive site provides links to publications related to exercise and career opportunities in exercise physiology.

**Calorie Control Council**
*http://www.caloriecontrol.org*
The Calorie Control Council's Web site offers information on cutting calories, achieving and maintaining healthy weight, and low-calorie, reduced-fat foods and beverages.

**Eating Disorders: Body Image Betrayal**
*http://www.geocities.com/HotSprings/5704/edlist.htm*
This extensive collection of links leads to information on compulsive eating, bulimia, anorexia, and other disorders.

**Shape Up America!**
*http://www.shapeup.org*
At the Shape Up America! Web site you will find the latest information about safe weight management, healthy eating, and physical fitness. Links include Support Center, Cyberkitchen, Media Center, Fitness Center, and BMI Center.

## UNIT 5: Health Claims

**Consumer Information Center--Fraudulent Health Claims**
*http://www.pueblo.gsa.gov/cic_text/health/fraudulent-health/frdheal.htm*
"Don't be fooled" by frudulent health claims! This site presents information on how to spot false claims, why health faud schemes work, medical problems that attract health fraud schemes, dietary supplements precautions, reporting problems to the Federal Trade Commission, and how to obtain more information from other sources.

**Federal Trade Commission (FTC): Diet, Health & Fitness**
*http://www.ftc.gov/bcp/menu-health.htm*
This site of the FTC on the Web offers consumer education rules and acts that include a wide range of subjects, from buying exercise equipment to virtual health "treatments."

**Food and Drug Administration**
*http://www.fda.gov/default.htm*
The FDA presents this site that addresses products they regulate, current news and hot topics, safety alerts, product approvals, reference data, and general information and directions.

**Healthcare Reality Check**
*http://www.hcrc.org*
Science-based information on alternative and complementary medicine is available on this Web site. Some anti-quackery sites that are available address scientific review of alternative medicine, "Quackwatch," "Chirobase," multi-level-marketing watch, a skeptical dictionary of alternative medicine, FTC facts for consumers on alternative medicine, and others.

**National Council Against Health Fraud**
*http://www.ncahf.org*
The NCAHF does business as the National Council for Reliable Health Information. At its Web page it offers links to other related sites, including Dr. Terry Polevoy's "Healthwatcher Net."

**QuackWatch**
*http://www.quackwatch.com*
Quackwatch Inc., a nonprofit corporation, provides this guide to examine health fraud. Data for intelligent decision making on health topics are also presented.

## UNIT 6: Food Safety

**American Council on Science and Health (ACSH)**
*http://www.acsh.org/food/*
The ACSH addresses issues that are related to food safety here. In addition, issues on nutrition and fitness, alcohol, diseases, environmental health, medical care, lifestyle, and tobacco may be accessed on this site.

**Centers for Disease Control and Prevention**
*http://www.cdc.gov*
The CDC offers this home page, from which you can obtain information about travelers' health, data related to disease control and prevention, and general nutritional and health information, publications, and more.

**FDA Center for Food Safety and Applied Nutrition**
*http://vm.cfsan.fda.gov*
It is possible to access everything from this Web site that you might want to know about food safety and what government agencies are doing to ensure it.

### Food Safety Information from North Carolina

*http://www.ces.ncsu.edu/depts/foodsci/agentinfo/*

This site from the Cooperative Extension Service at North Carolina State University has a database designed to promote food safety education via the Internet.

### Food Safety Project (FSP)

*http://www.extention.iastate.edu/foodsafety/*

FSP's site contains food safety lessons, 10 steps to a safe kitchen, consumer control points, and food law.

### Gateway to Government Food Safety Information

*http://www.foodsafety.gov*

Links to news and safety alerts, consumer advice, illness reporting and product omplaints, foodborne pathogens, industry assistance, national food safety programs, federal and state government agencies, and other topics addressing food safety are available on this Web site.

### National Food Safety Programs

*http://vm.cfsan.fda.gov/~dms/fs-toc.html*

Data from the Food and Drug Administration, U.S. Department of Agriculutre, Environmental Protection Agency, and Centers for Disease Control and Prevention expanding on the government policies and initiatives regarding food safety are presented on this site.

### USDA Food Safety and Inspection Service

*http://www.fsis.usda.gov*

The FSIS, part of the U.S. Department of Agriculture, is the government agency "responsible for ensuring that the nation's commercial supply of meat, poultry, and egg products is safe, wholesome, and correctly labeled and packaged."

## UNIT 7: World Hunger and Malnutrition

### Population Reference Bureau

*http://www.prb.org*

A key source for global population information, this is a good place to pursue data on nutrition problems worldwide.

### World Health Organization

*http://www.who.ch*

This home page of the World Health Organization will provide you with links to a wealth of statistical and analytical information about health and nutrition around the world.

### WWW Virtual Library: Demography & Population Studies

*http://demography.anu.edu.au/VirtualLibrary/*

A multitude of important links to information about global poverty and hunger can be found here.

**We highly recommend that you review our Web site for expanded information and our other product lines. We are continually updating and adding links to our Web site in order to offer you the most usable and useful information that will support and expand the value of your Annual Editions. You can reach us at: *http://www.dushkin.com/annualeditions/.***

# UNIT 1

# Nutrition Trends

## Unit Selections

1. **The 2000 Dietary Guidelines for Americans: What Are the Changes and Why Were They Made?** Rachel K. Johnson and Eileen Kennedy
2. **Picture This! Communicating Nutrition Around the World**, *Food Insight*
3. **The New American Plate**, *American Institute for Cancer Research*
4. **Food Portions and Servings: How Do They Differ?** *Nutrition Insights*
5. **Americans Ignore Importance of Food Portion Size**, *Medical College of Wisconsin Physicians & Clinics*
6. **In the Drink: When it Comes to Calories, Solid Is Better Than Liquid**, *Nutrition Action Healthletter*
7. **Food Industry Is Making America Fat**, *USA Today Magazine (Society for the Advancement of Education)*
8. **Supermarket Psych-Out**, *Tufts University Health & Nutrition Letter*

## Key Points to Consider

- Discuss the dietary guidelines suggested for Americans in the 2000 report. What changes would you make in your own eating habits as a result of reading this article?
- What sort of similarities are there among the diets in communities around the world?
- How do serving sizes differ from portion sizes?
- What are some of the techniques that marketers use to influence your food-buying decisions?

**Links: www.dushkin.com/online/**
These sites are annotated in the World Wide Web pages.

**Food Science and Human Nutrition Extension**
*http://www.extension.iastate.edu/nutrition/*

**Food Surveys Research Group**
*http://www.barc.usda.gov/bhnrc/foodsurvey/home.htm*

**U.S. Food and Drug Administration**
*http://www.fda.gov/default.htm*

Consumers worldwide are bombarded daily with messages about nutrients and health. They are presented with "new" food products at the supermarket and in restaurants and it is up to them to distill the sometimes controversial reports and make their own decisions. The first unit describes current trends and developments in the field of nutrition, reports on how the American diet is evolving and on the nature of the "new" dietary guidelines and dietary allowances, explains differences about food portions and servings, and addresses the paradox of nutrition knowledge and eating behavior. Communicating global concepts about nutrition through food guides that have been adopted for different cultures makes the reader aware of the commonalties and interrelatedness of different cultures. New advances in research and the role of nutrients in health and disease have enabled the food industry to develop functional foods whose safety and role in health are questioned. Finally, the reader will be able to read about the foods that are powerhouses of vitamins, minerals, and phytochemicals and be aided in the attempt to make wise food selections.

Focusing on building a healthy base, choosing sensibly, and, for the first time, advising the population to aim for fitness are the basic goals of the New Dietary Guidelines featured in the first article. Keeping foods safe is also added for the first time to the 2000 Dietary Guidelines.

Communicating nutrition information and guidance around the world is discussed in the next article, which makes it clear that nutrition messages travel far and fast and that different countries use pictorial presentations to communicate similar themes of dietary guidance. Even though there is diversity, the common message is balance, variety, and moderation in food choices.

The New American Plate is a new approach to eating that concentrates on the intake of plant- versus animal-based foods and their portion sizes. It helps you control your weight as well as reduce your risk of getting cancer.

Large portions of food are the norm in many eateries. The incidence of obesity in the United States is on the rise and consumers are thoroughly confused about food guide pyramid servings, food label servings, and food portions. The next article explains the differences and offers guidance to educators to help consumers understand the concept of servings and portions.

It seems that the message of professionals to reduce fat calories has been misinterpreted by Americans. Most Americans think that eating certain types of food while avoiding others is more critical to weight management than reducing their portion sizes and, thus, caloric intake. Again the theme of "quick-fix" remedies reemerges. Portion sizes are getting larger and larger in restaurants and other food establishments. Plates have increased from 10-inch to 12-inch sizes and most Americans are unaware of this change. The total daily intake for Americans has increased by 184 calories per day over the last 20 years.

Is there a connection between huge portion sizes and the increasing number of Americans who are overweight? Health experts say yes. Value marketing, which is selling more of a product for less money, has a definite downside. As Dr. J. L. Stantar says, "it shifts the pressure from our wallets to our waistbands." This leads to obesity, heart disease, diabetes, high blood pressure, and other degenerative diseases. Consumers should demand food of higher nutritional value in smaller portions for less money from the food industry.

Another problem is that consumers are not aware of the large number of calories that are added to their daily calorie consumption from the beverages they drink. Americans are drinking more and more, thus consuming more calories then they ever did before, and they are not aware of it. Beverages are high in "hidden" calories, and liquids do not fill us up. That is a bad combination. So think before you drink!

The last article of the unit reveals some of the secrets that supermarkets use to influence the consumer's buying decisions. Colors, shapes, and sizes are carefully designed to increase purchases. You can be ready, though, with some countertricks of your own.

# The 2000 Dietary Guidelines for Americans: What are the changes and why were they made?

*RACHEL K. JOHNSON, PhD, MPH, RD; EILEEN KENNEDY, DSc, RD*

The Dietary Guidelines for Americans form the foundation of US federal nutrition policy. Each federal nutrition program in the United States uses the Dietary Guidelines as one part of the nutrition standard. Therefore, every day the guidelines directly impact 21.4 million Americans receiving food stamps, 26 million children who participate in the school lunch program, 7 million children participating in the school breakfast program, and approximately 7.4 million women, infants, and children receiving benefits under the Special Supplemental Program for Women, Infants, and Children (WIC). The Food Guide Pyramid (1), the most widely distributed and best-recognized nutrition education device ever produced in the United States, is based in part on the US Dietary Guidelines.

The National Nutrition Monitoring and Related Research Act of 1990 (2) mandates that the guidelines be reviewed by the US Department of Agriculture (USDA) and the US Department of Health and Human Services (HHS) every 5 years. Hence, in 1998 the secretaries of USDA and HHS appointed an 11-member committee (Figure 1) to review the 1995 Dietary Guidelines for Americans and recommend what changes, if any, should be made in the 2000 guidelines. The Dietary Guidelines Advisory Committee was charged by the secretaries with answering the following question: "What should Americans eat to stay healthy?" The committee rigorously reviewed the peer-reviewed scientific literature, found that substantial new knowledge was available, and agreed that revision of the 1995 guidelines was needed. The aim of this paper is to discuss the changes in the 2000 guidelines and present the scientific rationale for these changes. The final Dietary Guidelines for Americans were released by the President on May 27, 2000.

## GENERAL

Major revisions were made in the presentation of the guidelines using 3 basic messages: Aim for fitness, Build a healthy base, and Choose sensibly for good health (ABC). The committee recommended increasing the number of guidelines from 7 to 10 and believed the ABCs for good health would help organize the guidelines in a memorable, meaningful way. The guidelines are intended for healthy children (aged 2 years and older) and adults of any age.

1. **A**im for fitness
- Aim for a healthy weight.
- Be physically active each day.

2. **B**uild a healthy base
- Let the Pyramid guide your food choices.
- Eat a variety of grains daily, especially whole grains.
- Eat a variety of fruits and vegetables daily.
- Keep foods safe to eat.

3. **C**hoose sensibly
- Choose a diet that is low in saturated fat and cholesterol and moderate in total fat.
- Choose beverages and foods to moderate your intake of sugars.
- Choose and prepare foods with less salt.
- If you drink alcoholic beverages, do so in moderation.

## SPECIFIC RECOMMENDED GUIDELINES

### Aim for fitness

**Aim for a healthy weight** The change in this guideline was aimed at improving the clarity of the wording. The word "balance" in the 1995 guideline (Figure 2) was interpreted by some focus group participants to mean that it was acceptable to be overweight as long as physical activity and energy intake were balanced. The word "improve" was construed by some to mean to increase weight and by others to decrease weight (3). The committee believed the new guideline combined the message into one actionable phrase.

The new guideline contains easy-to-use information on how to evaluate body weight. This includes a nomogram to simply calculate body mass index (BMI) (Figure 3) and gives instructions on how to measure waist circumference. Using the 1998 National Institutes of Health National Heart, Lung, and Blood guidelines for the identification, evaluation, and treatment of overweight and obesity, consumers are guided through a process of using their BMI, waist circumference, and other risk factors to determine if they are at a healthy weight (4).

Although the evidence that overweight and obesity lead to adverse health outcomes is indisputable (5), there is less agreement about the management of obesity. This is especially true with regard to whether the emphasis should be on weight maintenance or weight loss. The committee recommended that if people are overweight, they should aim for a loss of about 10%

**Chair**
Cutberto Garza, MD, PhD., Cornell University, Ithaca, NY

**Vice-Chair**
Suzanne Murphy, PhD, RD, University of Hawaii, Cancer Research Center of Hawaii, Honolulu, Hawaii

Richard J. Deckelbaum, MD, Columbia University, Institute of Human Nutrition, New York, NY
Johanna Dwyer, DSc, RD, Tufts University, Frances Stern Nutrition Center, Boston, Mass
Scott M. Grundy, MD, PhD, University of Vermont, Burlington
Rachel K. Johnson, PhD, MPH, RD, University of Vermont, Burlington
Shiriki K. Kumanyika, PhD, RD, University of Pennsylvania School of Medicine, Philadelphia, Pa
Alice H. Lichtenstein, DSc, Tufts University, Jean Mayer USDA Human Nutrition Research Center on Aging, Boston, Mass
Meir Stampfer, MD, DrPH, Harvard University, Channing Laboratory, Cambridge, Mass
Lesley Fels Tinker, PhD, RD, Fred Hutchinson Cancer Research Center, Seattle, Wash
Roland L. Weinsier, MD, DrPH, University of Alabama, Birmingham

*FIG 1: Year 2000 Dietary Guidelines for Americans Advisory Committee*

of their weight over 6 months. This is based on evidence that weight reductions of 5% to 15% reduce risk factors for obesity-associated conditions (6), and that people's initial goal should be to lose 10% of their weight over a period of about 6 months (4). Emphasis is placed on consumption of foods that are low in energy density as a means to control energy intake. This recommendation is based on a group of studies that demonstrated the energy density of foods plays a role in daily energy consumption (7–9). Hence, consumers are urged to make grains (especially whole grains), fruits, and vegetables the mainstays of their diet. People are urged to choose sensible portion sizes and cautioned that if a food is labeled low-fat, it does not necessarily mean the food is low in energy.

The number of children in the United States who are overweight has more than doubled over the past decade (10), and parents are advised to see a health care professional for evaluation and intervention if they are concerned about their child's weight. Parents are also urged to limit the time children spend in sedentary activities like watching television or playing video and computer games. One-fourth of all children in the United States watch 4 or more hours of television each day, and hours of television watched is positively associated with increased BMI and skinfold thickness (11).

**Be physically active each day** A new guideline on physical activity was added because the benefits of physical activity go well beyond energy balance and weight management (12). Over the past 5 years, 9 national position papers or reports have been published documenting the importance of moderate physical activity for good health (4,12–19). These reports indicate that being physically active for 30 to 45 minutes per day reduces the risk of developing heart disease, hypertension, colon cancer, and type 2 diabetes mellitus. These conditions are major contributors to morbidity and mortality in the United States. Furthermore, physical activity is related to improvements in flexibility, bone mass density, risk of hip fractures in women, depression and anxiety, and health-related quality of life. In children, physical activity improves aerobic endurance and muscular strength as well as BMI, blood lipids, blood pressure, and bone health (13,20).

The committee also recommended the addition of this guideline because physical activity levels in both US children and adults have declined and are much lower, on average, than what is recommended for good health and weight management (4,13,18,19). Hence, improvements in physical activity levels are needed in every age group. The committee followed standards supported by the Centers for Disease Control and Prevention and the American College of Sports Medicine (12) and recommended that adults be physically active at least 30 minutes most days-preferably all days of the week. Children are urged to be physically activity at least 60 minutes per day (13,21).

## Build a healthy base

**Let the Pyramid guide your food choices** The wording of the 1995 guideline "Eat a variety of foods" was changed to the new wording based on 3 lines of evidence. First, a critical concept to be conveyed by this guideline is nutritional adequacy. Choosing foods from all the Pyramid food groups improves nutrient adequacy (22,23). Thus, the committee felt that the recommendation to use the Food Guide Pyramid was better justified than simply a broad recommendation to eat a variety of foods. The second issue confronting the committee was that guidance to consume a variety of foods might promote overconsumption of energy. A limited number of controlled feeding studies demonstrated that more food is eaten at a meal if a variety of foods are available than if the selection is more limited (24). In addition, a 1999 analysis of nationwide food consumption data suggested that a wide variety of sweets, snacks, condiments, entrees, and carbohydrates, coupled with a small variety of vegetables, was positively associated with increased energy intakes and body fatness (25).

The last consideration by the committee was that the 1995 guideline was unclear to consumers. Focus group participants responded that variety in the 1995 guideline was too vague to guide consumers to take specific actions. There was no definition of variety, or of a desirable level of variety (3). On the other hand, many focus group respondents stated that the Food Guide Pyramid was the most useful part of the US Dietary Guidelines (26). The overall literature on effects of variety in the diet was viewed by the committee as mixed. Revised wording stressing the Food Guide Pyramid better reflected the goal of this guideline.

**Choose a variety of grains daily, especially whole grains** The 1995 guideline "Choose a diet with plenty of grain products, vegetables, and fruits" was split into 2 separate guidelines. These separate guidelines were recommended for several reasons: increasing attention to grains as distinct from vegetables and fruits, simplification of the messages, and clarification that there are distinct advantages to the 2 broad categories of plant foods. The committee added the important phrase "especially whole grains" for 2 major reasons: a) some research has shown that consumption of whole grains lowers risk for cardiovascular disease and some forms of cancer (27), and b) intake of whole grains is very low in the United States, with intakes averaging only half a serving per person per day (28). The committee considered whether increasing the intake of whole grains at the expense of enriched, folate-fortified refined grains would decrease the intake of some micronutrients (iron, folate, and zinc) to undesirably low levels. An analysis of dietary intakes using data from the 1994–1996 USDA Continuing Survey of Food Intakes of Individuals data demonstrated that substituting 3 servings of whole grains for enriched, folate-fortified refined grains did not adversely affect nutrient intake levels.

**Choose a variety of fruits and vegetables** Very few Americans meet intake recommendations for these 2 food groups (29). Fruits are purposely listed before vegetables because fewer people meet the recommended intake of fruits. The revised wording of this guideline focuses on the importance of variety within the fruit and vegetables groups and avoids the use of the word "diet" which many consumers considered to be suggestive of restrictions (26). Numerous ecological studies, prospective studies, and case-controlled studies showed an association between fruit and vegetable intake and decreased risk of cardiovascular disease. In addition, several case-control studies indicate that intakes of selected fruits or vegetables are associated with lower incidence of some cancers. Increased intake of fruits and vegetables has also been associated with decreased blood pressure (30).

**Keep food safe to eat** The committee added this guideline because it promotes actionable measures that can be taken by consumers and public officials to keep Americans healthy. The 1995 guidelines did not mention food safety (Figure 2). The proposed new guideline covers the following topics: a) healthful eating requires that food be safe, b) foodborne illness is a major preventable public-health problem in the United States, and c) consumers can apply simple food-handling practices to minimize their risk of foodborne illness. The proposed new guideline emphasizes 7 simple messages that consumers can apply whenever they are preparing, serving, and storing food:

- Clean.
- Wash hands and food surfaces often.
- Separate. Separate raw, cooked, and ready-to-eat foods while storing and preparing.
- Cook. Cook foods to a safe temperature.
- Chill. Refrigerate perishable foods promptly.
- Follow the label.
- Serve safely.
- If in doubt, throw it out.

Each of these messages is consistent with well-founded principles of microbiology and sanitation (31,32). The first 4 messages (clean, separate, cook, chill) are, in essence, identical to the Fight BAC! messages of the Partnership for Food Safety Education (33). The last 3 bullets in the guideline provide additional advice to consumers to ensure that food will be safe and wholesome.

### 1995: Dietary Guidelines

- Eat a variety of foods
- Balance the food you eat with physical activity—maintain or improve your weight
- Choose a diet with plenty of grain products, vegetables, and fruits
- Choose a diet low in fat, saturated fat, and cholesterol
- Choose a diet moderate in sugars
- Choose a diet moderate in salt and sodium
- If you drink alcoholic beverages, do so in moderation

### 2000: Dietary Guidelines

Aim for Fitness
- Aim for a healthy weight
- Be physically active each day

Build a healthy base
- Let the pyramid guide your food choices.
- Eat a variety of grains daily, especially whole grains.
- Eat a variety of fruits and vegetables daily.
- Keep foods safe to eat.

Choose sensibly
- Choose a diet that is low in saturated fat and cholesterol and moderate in total fat.
- Choose beverages and foods to moderate your intake of sugars.
- Choose and prepare foods with less salt.
- If you drink alcoholic beverages, do so in moderation.

***FIG 2: The 1995 and the recommended 2000 Dietary Guidelines for Americans.***

## Choose sensibly

**Choose a diet low in saturated fat and cholesterol and moderate in total fat** The wording of this guideline was changed from the 1995 guideline to emphasize the importance of reducing intake of saturated fat and cholesterol. There is robust evidence that diets high in saturated fat and cholesterol contribute to the development of coronary heart disease. It is now well accepted that lowering serum low-density lipoprotein (LDL) cholesterol levels will reduce the risk for coronary heart disease (34). The guideline text also emphasizes the importance of reducing *trans*-fatty acid intakes. *Trans*-fatty acids are included because of an impressive body of evidence indicating

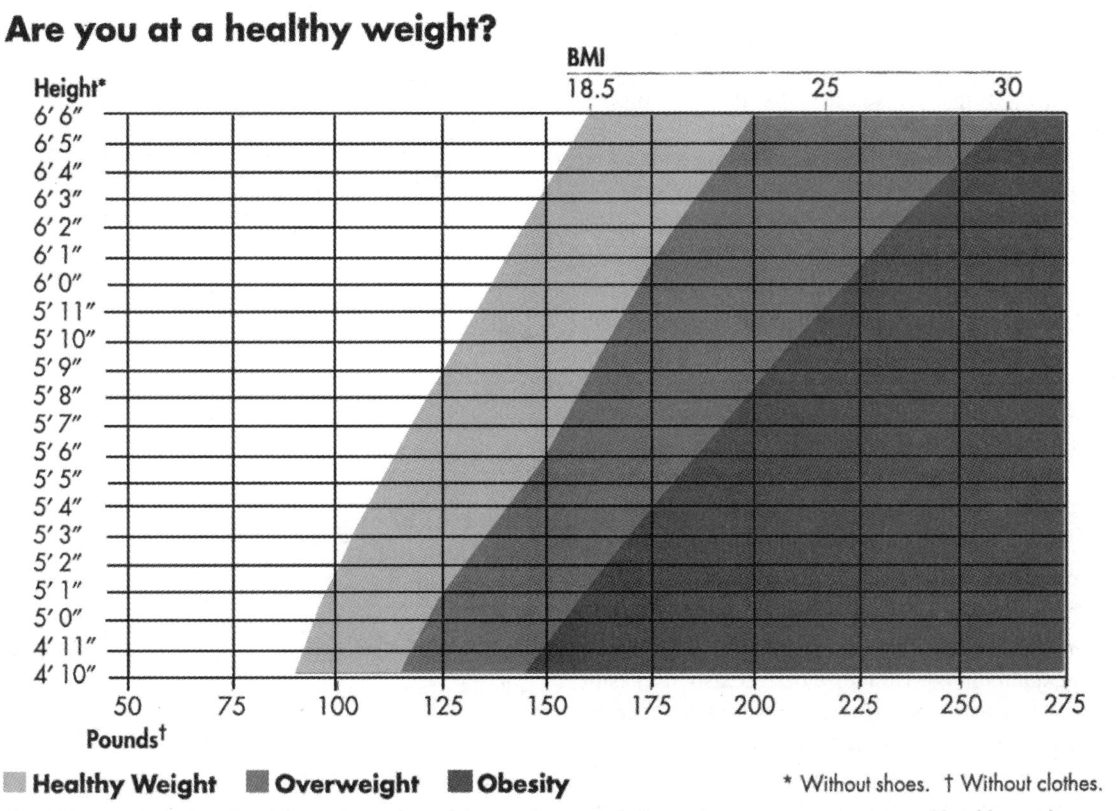


that they raise serum LDL cholesterol levels as well as lower serum high-density lipoprotein (HDL) cholesterol.

An important change in this guideline is the placement of total fat after saturated fat and cholesterol. In addition, the wording recommends a diet termed "moderate" in total fat.

Although the guideline continues to recommend a diet with 30% or less of energy from total fat, the committee believed the phrase, "moderate in total fat" best reflects this concept.

Research in laboratory animals, short-term studies in humans, and some epidemiological evidence suggest that high-fat diets contribute to obesity. More recently, however, data from both experimental and population studies question the strength of the relationship between dietary fat and body weight. Indeed, the committee was concerned that emphasizing low-fat diets for weight control had left the erroneous impression that low-fat diets, without energy reductions, would lead to weight loss. This belief may have led to overconsumption of total energy. In fact, although the percentage of fat in the US diet has fallen, total fat intake is not lower than in the recent past because of apparent increased intakes of energy (37).

The committee emphasized that all the guidelines, including the fat guideline, apply to children beginning at age 2 years. Current recommendations for adults do not need to be modified for children who are 2 years of age or older. Studies support the safety for children of diets that are low in saturated fat and cholesterol and moderate in total fat, as long as energy needs are met (38–40).

**Choose beverages and foods to moderate your intake of sugars** The Dietary Guideline for sugars emphasizes moderating the intake of sugars for 2 reasons. First, the focus group research indicated that consumers understand the word "moderate" to mean some but not too much (26). This, in fact, is the intent of the guideline. Second, the concept of a moderate intake is consistent with the theme of moderation in the fat and alcohol guidelines.

The principle diet and health association for the sugars guideline continues to be dental caries. The Dietary Guidelines Advisory Committee report emphasized that there is no compelling evidence that sugars affect children's behavior. In addition, there is little evidence linking sugars with the etiology of noninsulin dependent diabetes. Finally, there is little evidence that diets high in sugars are associated with obesity. However, this lack of association may be confounded by the pervasive problem of underreporting of food intake (41), which is more prevalent and severe among overweight and obese people (42–44). To further complicate the issue, the intakes of food high in added sugar are known to be underreported to a greater extent than other foods (45). Thus, it is difficult to draw conclusions about associations between self-reported sugar intake and BMI. Because the data on total sugars, added sugars and nutrient density, and sugar intake and obesity provided ambiguous patterns, the advisory committee strongly advised the government to pursue more research in these areas.

For the first time, however, the word "beverages" was added to the wording of the guidelines to emphasize that they are a major source of sugars in the US diet. There is also discussion in the text distinguishing added sugars from naturally occurring sugars. This was done because focus group participants found it confusing when the 1995 guideline promoted the consumption of fruits and low-fat dairy products—which are high in the naturally occurring sugars fructose and lactose—while at the same time promoting a diet moderate in sugar. Added sugars are defined as all sugars used as ingredients in processed and prepared foods such as bread, cake, soft drinks, jam, and ice cream, as well as sugars eaten separately. Sugars occurring naturally in foods such as fruit and milk are excluded (46). The most important source of added sugars in the American diet is nondiet soft drinks, which account for one third of all intake of added sugars (47). Nondiet soft drinks, sugars and sweets (such as candies), sweetened grains (cakes, cookies, pies), fruit aides and fruit drinks, flavored milk and other sweetened milk products (ice cream) provide more than three fourths of the total intake of added sugars (47). Soft drink consumption is associated with lower intakes of several "shortfall" nutrients (folate, vitamin A, and calcium) (48) and may be inversely associated with intakes of calcium-rich beverages, such as milk (49–51). Hence, the guideline text cautions consumers not to let soft drinks or other sweets crowd out other foods needed to maintain health, such as low-fat milk or other good sources of calcium.

**Choose and prepare foods with less salt** The intent of this guideline is unchanged from the 1995 guideline. However, the new wording is framed in terms of choosing foods rather than a diet. This is meant to convey a clearer meaning and to avoid the erroneous interpretation that the guideline refers to either prescribed "special diets" or to weight-reduction diets. Reference to food preparation ("choose and prepare foods") was proposed to highlight the particular importance of food preparation practices in determining the sodium content of foods. "Less" is substituted for "moderate" because of its greater clarity for consumers who find the term "moderate" difficult to interpret. "Sodium" was dropped from the guideline for simplicity; salt is the more familiar term.

**If you drink alcoholic beverages, do so in moderation** The committee recommended retaining the 1995 wording of this guideline. The text now places more emphasis on the adverse effects of excess alcohol intake and adds information on the increased risk of breast cancer associated with alcohol intake. Moderate drinking is clearly defined as one drink per day for women and 2 drinks per day for men, and the text is reworded to make it clear that the different limits are based on both metabolism and body size. The guideline strengthens the language concerning pregnant women by saying "women who may become pregnant or who are pregnant" should not drink.

The principal benefit of moderate alcohol intake is the lowered risk of cardiovascular disease. However, the text now clarifies that this benefit occurs mainly in men older than age 45 and women older than age 55. Moderate consumption provides little, if any, benefit to younger people. This age specificity is based on the age- and sex-specific rates of coronary heart disease (52) and on the age-specific relative risks related to moderate alcohol consumption obtained from prospective cohort studies of men and women in the United States(53–55).

# CONCLUSION

The impact of the Dietary Guidelines for Americans is wide ranging. Not only are the Dietary Guidelines used as the basis of nutrition standards for the federal government's food and nutrition programs, but the guidelines also form the basis for nutrition education messages for the general public. Each edition of the Dietary Guidelines continues to reflect the overwhelming consensus of science to answer the question posed at the beginning of this commentary: "What should Americans eat to stay healthy?"

A systematic campaign to promote the Dietary Guidelines will also be launched by USDA and HHS. Consumption patterns based on the Dietary Guidelines for Americans will lead to major improvements in public health and nutrition for the United States. Dietetics professionals have a key role to play in promoting the Dietary Guidelines as one component of healthful lifestyles.

## References


1. Welsh S, Davis C, Shaw A. Development of the Food Guide Pyramid. *Nutr Today*. 1992;27:12–23.
2. Federation of American Societies for Experimental Biology, Life Sciences Research Office. Third Report of Nutrition Monitoring in the United States, vol 1. Washington, DC: US Government Printing Office; 1995.
3. *Dietary Guidelines for Americans Focus Group Study: Final Report*. Washington, DC: ILSI Human Nutrition Institute; 1998.

4. National Institutes of Health, National Heart, Lung, and Blood Institute. *Clinical Guidelines on the Identification, Evaluation, and Treatment of Overweight and Obesity in Adults.* Washington, DC: US Dept of Health and Human Services, Public Health Service; 1998.
5. National Institute of Diabetes and Digestive and Kidney Diseases. National Task Force on Prevention and Treatment of Obesity. Obesity and Health Risk. *Arch Intern Med.* In press.
6. Goldstein DJ. Beneficial health effects of modest weight loss. *Int J Obes Relat Metab Disord.* 1992;16:397–415.
7. Bell EA, Castellanos VH, Pelkman CL, Thorwart ML, Rolls BJ. Energy density affects energy intake in normal-weight women. *Am J Clin Nutr.* 1998;67:412–420.
8. Rolls BJ, Hill JO. Carbohydrates and weight management. ILSI North America. Washington, DC: ILSI Press; 1998.
9. Stubbs RJ, Ritz P, Coward WA, Prentice AM. Covert manipulation of the ratio of dietary fat to carbohydrate and energy density: effect on food intake and energy balance in free-living men eating ad libitum. *Am J Clin Nutr.* 1995;62:330–337.
10. Troiano RP, Flegel KM. Overweight children and adolescents; description, epidemiology, and demographics. *Pediatrics.* 1998;101:497–504.
11. Andersen RE, Crespo CJ, Bartlett SJ, Cheskin LJ, Pratt M. Relationship of physical activity and television watching with body weight and level of fatness among children: results from the Third National Health and Nutrition Examination Survey. *JAMA.* 1998;279:938–942.
12. Pate RR, Pratt M, Blair SN, Haskell WL, Macera CA, Bouchard C, Buchner D, Ettinger W, Heath GW, King AC, Kriska A, Leon AS, Marcus BH, Morris J, Paffenbarger RS, Patrick K, Pollack ML, Rippe JM, Sallis J, Wilmore JH. Physical activity and public health—a recommendation from the Centers for Disease Control and Prevention and the American College of Sports Medicine. *JAMA.* 1995; 273:402–407.
13. Centers for Disease Control and Prevention. Guidelines for school and community health programs to promote lifelong physical activity among young people. *MMWR.* 1997:46:1–34.
14. Mazzeo RS, Cavanagh P, Evans WJ, Fiatrone M, Hagberg J, McAuley E, Startzell J. Exercise and physical activity for older adults. *Med Sci Sports Exerc.* 1998;30:992–1008.
15. National Institutes of Health Consensus Development Panel on Physical Activity and Cardiovascular Health. Physical activity and cardiovascular health. *JAMA.* 1996;276:241–246.
16. Pollock ML, Evans WJ. Resistance training for health and disease: introduction. *Med Sci Sports Exerc.* 1999;31:10–11.
17. Pollock ML, Gaesser GA, Butcher JD, Despres J-P, Dishman RK, Franklin BA, Garber CE. The recommended quantity and quality of exercise for developing and maintaining cardiorespiratory and muscular fitness, and flexibility in healthy adults. *Med Sci Sports Exerc.* 1998:30:975–991.
18. *Physical Activity and Health: A Report of the Surgeon General.* Atlanta, Ga: US Department of Health and Human Services, Centers for Disease Control and Prevention, National Center for Chronic Disease Prevention and Health Promotion; 1996.
19. *Healthy People 2010 Objectives: Draft for Public Comment.* Washington, DC: US Department of Health and Human Services, Office of Public Health and Science; 1998.
20. Ulrich CM, Georgiou CC, Snow-Harter CM, Gillis DE. Bone mineral density in mother-daughter pairs: relations to lifetime exercise, lifetime milk consumption, and calcium supplements. *Am J Clin Nutr.* 1996;63:72–79.
21. Health Education Authority. Young and active? Young people and health-enhancing physical activity—evidence and implications. In: Biddle S, Sallis J, Cavill N, eds. *Health Education Authority.* London, England: Trevelyan House; 1998.
22. Kant AK, Schatzkin A, Block G, Ziegler RG, Nestle M. Food group intake patterns and associated nutrient profiles of the US population. *J Am Diet Assoc.* 1991;91:1532–1537.
23. Krebs-Smith SM, Smicklas-Wright H, Guthrie HA, Krebs-Smith J. The effects of variety in food choices on dietary quality. *J Am Diet Assoc.* 1987;87:897–903
24. Rolls BJ. Experimental analyses of the effects of variety in a meal on human feeding. *Am J Clin Nutr.* 1985:42:932–939.
25. McCrory MA, Fuss PJ, McCallum JE, Yao M, Vinken AG, Hays NP, Roberts SB. Dietary variety within food groups: association with energy intake and body fatness in men and women. *Am J Clin Nutr.* 1999;69:440–447.
26. Report of the Initial Focus Groups on Nutrition and Your Health: Dietary Guidelines for Americans. 4th ed. US Dept of Agriculture, Center for Nutrition Policy and Promotion; 1999.
27. Jacobs DR, Meyer KA, Kushi LH, Folsom AR. Whole grain intake may reduce the risk of ischemic heart disease death in postmenopausal women: the Iowa Women's Health Study. *Am J Clin Nutr.* 1998;68:248–257.
28. Albertson A, Tobelmann R. Consumption of grain and whole-grain foods by an American population during the years 1990–1992. J Am Diet Assoc. 1995:95:703–704.
29. Krebs-Smith SM, Cook A, Subar AF, Cleveland L, Friday J. US adults' fruit and vegetable intakes, 1989 to 1991: a revised baseline for the Healthy People 2000 objective. *Am J Public Health.* 1995;85:1623–1629.
30. Appel LJ, Moore TJ, Obarzanek E, Vollmer WM, Svetkey LP, Sacks FM, Bay GA, Vogt TM, Cutler JA, Windhauser MM, Lin PH, Karanja N. A clinical trial of the effects of dietary patterns on blood pressure. DASH Collaborative Research Group. *N Engl J Med.* 1997;336:1117–1124.
31. Council for Agricultural Science and Technology. Foodborne pathogens: Risks and consequences. Task Force Report No 122. 1994; 18.
32. Institute of Medicine. *Emerging Infections: Microbial Threats to Health in the United States.* Washington, DC: National Academy Press; 1992.

33. Partnership for Food Safety Education. Fight Bad Keep Food Safe from Bacteria. Available at: http://www.fightbac.org. Accessed May 3, 2000.
34. Gould AL, Rossouw JE, Santanello NC, Heyse FJ, Furberg CD. Cholesterol reduction yields clinical benefit: impact of statin trials. *Circulation*. 1998; 97:946–952.
35. Grundy SM. Overview: 2nd International Conference on Fats and Oil Consumption in Health and Disease: How we can optimize dietary composition to combat metabolic complications and decrease obesity. *Am J Clin Nutr.* 1998;67(suppl):497S–499S.
36. Krause RM. Triglycerides and atherogenic lipoproteins: rationale for lipid management, *Am J Med.* 1998;105(suppl):58S–62S.
37. Anand RS, Basiotis PP. Is total fat consumption really decreasing? *Nutr Insights*. USDA Center for Nutrition Policy and Promotion: April 1998.
38. Lauer RM, Obarzanek E, Kwiterovich PO, Kimm SYS, Hunsburger SA, Barton BA, van Horn L, Stevens VJ, Lasser NL, Robson AM, Franklin FA, Simons-Morton DG. Efficacy and safety of lowering dietary intake of fat and cholesterol in children with elevated low density lipoprotein cholesterol: the dietary intervention study in children. *JAMA*. 1996;273:1429–1435.
39. Niinikoski H, Viikari J, Ronnemaa T, Helenius H, Eero J, Lapinleimu H. Regulation of growth in 7–36 month old children by energy and fat intake in the prospective, randomized STRIP trial. *Pediatrics*. 1997:100:810–816.
40. Obarzanek, E, Hunsberger SA, van Horn L, Hartmuller VV, Barton BA, Stevens FJ. Safety of a fat reduced diet: the Dietary Intervention Study in Children. *Pediatrics*. 1997;100:51–59.
41. Black AE, Prentice, AM, Goldberg GR, Jebb SA, Bingham SA, Livingstone BE, Coward AW. Measurements of total energy expenditure provide insights into the validity of dietary measurements of energy intake. *J Am Diet Assoc.* 1993:93:572–579.
42. Bandini LG, Schoeller DA, Cyr HN, Dietz WH. Validity of reported energy intake in obese and nonobese adolescents. *Am J Clin Nutr.* 1990:52:421–425.
43. Lichtman SW, Pisareka K, Berman ER, Pestones M, Dowling H, Offenbacher E, Weisel H, Heshka S, Matthews DE, Heymefield DB. Discrepancy between self-reported and actual caloric intake and exercise in obese subjects. *N Eng J Med.* 1992;327:1893–1898.
44. Prentice A, Black A, Coward W, Davies H, Goldberg G, Murgatroyd P, Ashford J, Sawyer M, Whitehead R. High levels of energy expenditure in obese women. *BMJ*. 1986;292:983–987.
45. Poppitt SD, Swann D, Black AE, Prentice AM. Assessment of selective underreporting of food intake by both obese and non-obese women in a metabolic facility, *Int J Obesity*. 1998:22:303–311.
46. Cleveland LE, Cook DA, Krebs-Smith S, Friday J. Method for assessing food intakes in terms of servings based on food guidance. *Am J Clin Nutr.* 1997:65 (suppl): 1254S–1263S.
47. Guthrie JF, Morton JF. Food sources of added sweeteners in the diets of Americans. *J Am Diet Assoc.* 2000;100:43–48.
48. Harnack L, Stang J, Story M. Soft drink consumption among US children and adolescents: nutritional consequences, *J Am Diet Assoc.* 1999:99:438–441.
49. Guenther PM. Beverages in the diets of American teenagers. *J Am Diet Assoc*. 1986;86:493–495.
50. Skinner JD, Carruth BR, Moran J. Houck K. Coletta F. Fruit juice intake is not related to children's growth. *Pediatrics*. 1999;103:58–64.
51. Guthrie JF. Dietary patterns and personal characteristics of women consuming recommended amounts of calcium. *Fam Econ Nutr Rev*. 1996:9:33–49.
52. *Health, United States, 1999 with Health and Aging Chartbook.* National Center for Health Statistics: Hyattville, Md; 1999.
53. Fuchs CS, Stampfer MJ, Colditz GA, Giovannucci EL, Manson JE, Kawachi I, Hunter DJ, Hankinson SE, Hennekens CH, Rosner B, Speizer FE, Willett WC. Alcohol consumption and mortality among women. *N Engl J Med.* 1995;332:1245–1250.
54. Rimm EB, Giovannucci EL, Willett WC, Colditz GA, Ascherio A, Rosner B, Stampfer MJ. Prospective study of alcohol consumption and risk of coronary disease in men. *Lancet*. 1991;338:464–468.
55. Thun MJ, Peto R, Lopez AD, Monaco JH, Henley J, Health C, Doll R. Alcohol consumption and mortality among middle-aged and elderly US Adults. *N Engl J Med.* 1997;337:1705–1714.

*Every member of the Year 2000 Dietary Guidelines Advisory Committee (Figure 1) contributed countless hours to the report upon which this manuscript is based. We are indebted to them. We thank the dedicated staff members from HHS (Linda Meyers, PhD; Kathryn McMurry, MS; and Joan Lyon, MS) and USDA (Shanthy Bowman, PhD; Carol Davis, MS, RD; and Alyson Escobar, MS, RD) who assisted with the preparation of the report. We are grateful to Carol Suitor, PhD RD, for her expert editorial assistance throughout the process of preparing the report.*

---

*R. K. Johnson is associate dean of research at the College of Agriculture and Life Sciences and professor of nutrition at the University of Vermont, Burlington. Eileen Kennedy is the Deputy Under Secretary for Research, Education, and Economics at the US Department of Agriculture.*
*Address correspondence to Rachel K. Johnson, 108 Morrill Hall, Burlington, VT 05405.*

# PICTURE THIS!

## Communicating Nutrition Around the World

What picture comes to mind when you think of a healthful diet? The U.S. Departments of Agriculture (USDA) and Health and Human Services hope you think of their Food Guide Pyramid. Since 1992, the Pyramid has served as a visual adaptation of the *U.S. Dietary Guidelines for Americans*, the seven basic dietary recommendations to promote wellness and prevent chronic disease. Today, the Pyramid can be seen not only in nutrition education materials for children and adults, but also on grocery bags, food packages and in the media.

Food guides, such as the USDA's Food Guide Pyramid, are tools used to communicate complex scientific information in a consumer-friendly way. For the most part, government agencies use graphic depictions to communicate dietary guidance messages that provide population-wide recommendations for eating to promote health.

A previous issue of *Food Insight* (March/April 1998) featured various countries' dietary guidelines and noted how cultural norms influence the guidelines. This issue will highlight the evolution of the American food guide as well as visual depictions of dietary guidance used around the world.

### A Photographic History

Food guides are not new educational tools. The first United States food guide was developed in 1916 by the USDA and consisted of five food groups—milk and meat; cereals; vegetables and fruits; fats and fat foods; and sugars and sugar foods. By the 1940s, the food guide listed *ten* food groups, including water and eggs. Vegetables and fruits were split into three individual groups—leafy green and yellow vegetables; citrus, tomato and cabbage; and other vegetables and fruits. Ten food groups were difficult for consumers to remember, so these groups were trimmed to *four* food groups by the late 1950s.

Previous versions of the United States food guide were tools used to promote a diet containing essential vitamins and minerals. School children were often the educational target for the simple illustrations used to depict the optimal diet. One of the most familiar food guides of the past is the "Basic Four," containing four food groups—milk, fruit and vegetable, bread and cereal and meat groups—which was used for nearly 25 years. The emphasis of the "Basic Four" food guide was to help Americans get a foundation diet, meaning, it was intended to meet only a portion of caloric and nutrient needs.

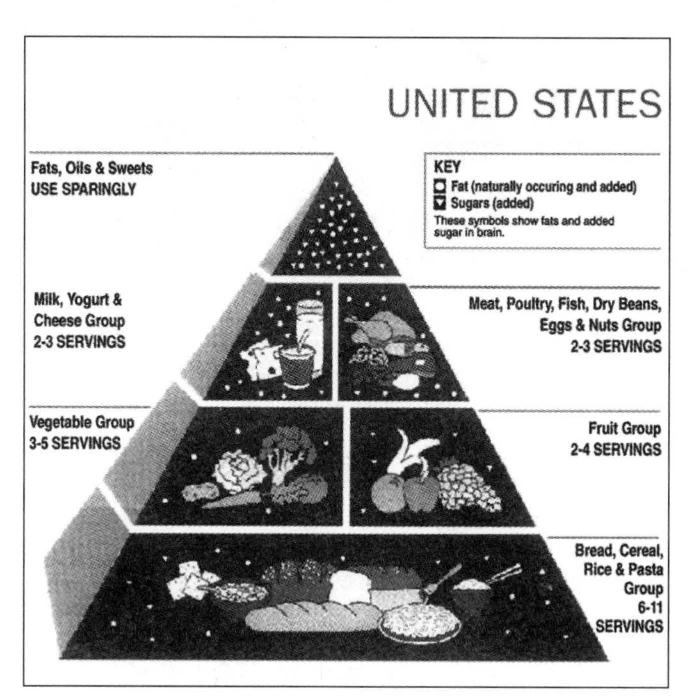


After the publication of the first *Dietary Guidelines for Americans* in 1980, work began on a new food guide graphic to reflect the latest science on diet and health. In addition to a review of existing research, government agencies conducted extensive quantitative and quali-

tative research with American consumers to ensure the resulting graphic communicated key dietary guideline concepts. The pyramid design proved most useful in graphically communicating the intended messages across various socioeconomic groups.

**Food guides,** such as the USDA's Food Guide Pyramid, are tools used to communicate complex scientific information in a consumer-friendly way.

No single adaptation of the pyramid graphic can depict all of the eating practices of the diverse American populace. However, because of the simplicity and understandability of the pyramid shape, the U.S. Food Guide Pyramid can be translated to reflect the customs of numerous ethnic and cultural groups within the United States. The pyramid concept has been adapted to Asian, Mexican, vegetarian and Mediterranean diets by various organizations. For instance, to better serve their state population, the Washington State Department of Health created materials using the pyramid shape to depict diets for Russians, Southeast Asians and Native Americans. The pyramid concept has also been adapted to communicate other health-promoting activities. For example, a physical activity pyramid, developed by a private organization, promotes ways to stay active in everyday life and a "life balance" pyramid by the same group offers ideas to build and maintain emotional well-being.

### Pictures From Around the World

The use of the pyramid has been very successful in the United States. The pyramid shape appears to easily convey the concept of variety and the relative amounts to eat of the various food groups. However, because of cultural differences in communicating symbolism and other cultural norms, the pyramid is not necessarily the graphic of choice for food guides worldwide. No single graphic can portray the dietary guidelines of various countries around the world. Rainbows, circles, pyramids, and even a chalice are used to represent the "optimal" diet. The different graphics used reflect cultural norms and symbols as well as the emphasis of the dietary guidelines of each country. In developed countries, food guides tend to promote a diet that prevents chronic disease. In developing countries, however, the goal of the food guide is to promote a diet that provides nutrients to safeguard against malnutrition.

Yet, despite the different pictorial representations, different countries communicate similar themes. Food guide graphics from countries as diverse as Italy and South Africa convey a common message—balance, variety and moderation in food choices. While the number of food groups displayed in the graphics varies from country to country, most guides attempt to illustrate the food groups' optimal proportion of the total diet, as does the U.S. Food Guide Pyramid. For instance, based on the *Dietary Guidelines for Americans*, grains should comprise the largest proportion of the diet. Therefore, grains are depicted at the base of the Pyramid—the largest part of the pyramid shape. Breads and grains, fruits, vegetables, dairy foods and meats are included in all the various guides.

**The primary role** of food guides, whether in the United States or around the world, is to communicate an optimal diet for overall health of the population.

The wheel or dinner plate design is a popular graphic that represents the total diet, with each section depicting a food group and its relative proportion to the total diet. This design is used in the United Kingdom, Germany and Norway, among other countries. Many of food guide graphics used are unique to their respective countries. Japan depicts its "optimal" diet through the use of the numeral six as the basis of its food guide to remind consumers of the six food categories. The Japanese government has since developed new dietary guidelines. However the same food guide is still used by many as a reference since a new food guide has not been developed.

Canada's Food Guide to Healthy Eating is a four-banded rainbow, with each color representing one of its four food groups. The rainbow shows that all food groups are important but different amounts are needed from each group. The larger outer arcs of the rainbow are the grain products and fruits and vegetables. According to Canada's dietary guidelines, these foods should make up a larger part of a healthy eating plan. Similarly, the smaller inner arcs make up the milk products and meat and meat alternatives that should make up a smaller amount of a healthy eating plan.

Many of the food guides around the world emphasize the bread, cereals and grain foods as the largest part of the diet. Israel's chalice graphic illustrates the importance of water for overall health by placing "water" at the top and largest section of the chalice. Israel has one of few food guides that characterize water as a principal part of the diet.

South Africa's food guide graphic contains the least number of food groups and organizes foods in a unique way—according to the foods' "function" in the body. Group 1 contains "Energy Food," and includes margarine, grains, porridge and maize. The second group is entitled "Body Building Food" and includes chicken, beans, milk and eggs. The third group is "Protective Food," to protect your body from illness and includes cabbage, carrots, pineapples and spinach.

## A Picture Paints a Thousand Words

You've undoubtedly heard the phrase "a picture paints a thousand words" numerous times. Nutrition education has long proven this idiom to ring true through the use of food models and pictures to depict such things as portion sizes. Likewise, symbols such as a heart, checkmark or apple are often used on restaurant menus to denote choices that meet specific nutrition or health guidelines.

The primary role of food guides, whether in the United States or around the world, is to communicate an optimal diet for overall health of the population. Whether a star, a chalice, a square or a pyramid graphic is used, all are meant to improve quality of life and nutritional well-being in a simplified and understandable way.

# The New American Plate

## Meals for a healthy weight and a healthy life

Studies show that more than half the adults in this country are overweight. About one in five are classified as obese and at special health risk. And this problem continues to grow, even though as many as 25 percent of American men and 40 percent of American women are on a diet at any given time. It's become apparent that diets don't work. What's worse, they distract us from the larger issue of overall health.

### The New American Plate

#### What is the New American Plate?

It's not a short-term "diet" to use for weight loss, but a new approach to eating for better health. The New American Plate emphasizes the kinds of foods that can significantly reduce our risk for disease. It also shows how to enjoy all foods in sensible portions. That is, it promotes a healthy weight as just one part of an overall healthy lifestyle.

A large and growing body of research shows that what we eat and how we live have a lot to do with our risk of developing cancer, as well as heart disease, adult onset diabetes and many other chronic health problems.

At the center of the New American Plate is a variety of vegetables, fruits, whole grains and beans. These plant-based foods are rich in substances that help keep us in good health and protect against many types of cancer. They are also naturally low in calories. When plant-based foods are on our plate, we're able to eat larger, more satisfying meals—all for fewer calories than the typical American diet. Switching to the New American Plate and the healthy lifestyle it reflects does not require deprivation. There is nothing you have to give up, and you will not go hungry. The New American Plate may not be overflowing, but it is full of great tasting food for better health.

#### Advice That's Scientifically Sound

The New American Plate is based on recommendations set forth in a landmark research report, *Food, Nutrition and the Prevention of Cancer: A Global Perspective,* published in 1997 by the American Institute for Cancer Research. The report was written by an expert panel of scientists who reviewed more than 4,500 research studies from around the world. It remains the most comprehensive report ever done in the area of diet, nutrition and cancer. Estimates from the AICR report show that 30–40 percent of all cancers could be prevented through changing the way we eat and exercise. Eliminating tobacco would raise that figure to 60–70 percent. These simple action steps represent the best advice science currently offers for lowering your cancer risk.

#### Diet and Health Guidelines for Cancer Prevention

1. Choose a diet rich in a variety of plant-based foods.
2. Eat plenty of vegetables and fruits.
3. Maintain a healthy weight and be physically active.
4. Drink alcohol only in moderation, if at all.
5. Select foods low in fat and salt.
6. Prepare and store food safely.

And *always* remember...
**Do not use tobacco in any form.**

## Proportion: What's on the New American Plate?

When thinking about the New American Plate, use this general rule of thumb: Plant-based foods like vegetables, fruits, whole grains and beans should cover two-thirds (or more) of the plate. Meat, fish, poultry or lowfat dairy should cover one-third (or less) of the plate. The plant-based part of the plate should include substantial portions of one or more vegetables or fruits — not just grain products like pasta or whole grain bread.

### Plenty of Vegetables and Fruits

We should all make sure to eat at least five servings of vegetables and fruits each day. Research suggests that this one dietary change could prevent as many as *20 percent* of all cancers. Vegetables and fruits provide vitamins, minerals and phytochemicals (natural substances found only in plants) that protect the body's cells from damage by cancer-causing agents—stopping cancer before it even starts. A number of phytochemicals may also interfere with cancer cell growth and reproduction.

By including fruits or vegetables at every meal, it's easy to reach five—or even more—servings a day. It's also important to eat a *variety* of these healthful foods. That way, you get the widest possible array of protective nutrients and phytochemicals. Be sure to include vegetables that are dark green and leafy, as well as those deep orange in color. Also include citrus fruits and other foods high in vitamin C. Juice does count towards your "five or more" goal, but most of your servings should come from solid fruits and vegetables.

### Other Plant-based Foods

In addition to fruits and vegetables, AICR recommends eating at least seven servings of other plant-based foods each day. This includes grains (such as whole wheat bread, pasta, oatmeal, barley and brown rice) and legumes (dried beans and peas, including kidney, garbanzo and black beans, lentils and green peas).

Make sure to include whole grains in your meal choices each day. They are higher in fiber and natural phytochemicals than refined grains like white bread and rice.

### When is a Vegetable a High-calorie Food?

When it's covered in cheese sauce, gravy, regular salad dressing, full-fat sour cream or any other high-fat topping. The way you cook also makes a difference. Frying in oil or butter adds a hefty dose of fat and calories to food.

Keep your vegetables—and fruits, whole grains, beans and lean meats—healthy as well as tasty. Bake, steam, microwave or stir-fry in a small amount of oil. Cook with fragrant herbs and spices. Sprinkle with a few chopped nuts, or a strong-tasting cheese like Parmesan or extra-sharp cheddar. Choose flavorful and lowfat toppings such as marinara sauce, salsa, mustard, reduced-sodium soy sauce and flavored vinegar. Even a simple squeeze of lemon works wonders.

## Meat on the Side

If you eat red meat like beef, pork or lamb, choose lean cuts and limit yourself to no more than a 3 ounce cooked (4 ounce raw) portion per day. That's about the size of a deck of cards. Findings from AICR's expert report show that diets high in red meat probably increase the risk of colon cancer.

Research on the impact of poultry, fish and game is not as extensive, so no specific limits have been set. Just keep portions small enough that you have room to eat an abundance of vegetables, fruits, whole grains and beans.

Reverse the traditional American plate, and think of meat as a side dish or condiment rather than the main ingredient. It can be as simple as preparing your favorite, store-bought brown rice or grain mix and topping it with steamed green beans, carrots, yellow squash and an ounce or two of cooked chicken.

## Making the Transition

When adjusting your meals to include more plant-based foods, even the smallest change can provide real health benefits. Every new vegetable, fruit, whole grain or bean that finds its way onto your plate contributes disease-fighting power. And all the fat and calories you save may make a real difference on your waistline.

Many other benefits come from increasing the amount of plant-based foods on your plate. Learning about new foods, tasting new flavors, trying new recipes—the New American Plate allows you to enjoy an endless combination of nutritious foods that leave you well satisfied.

As you make the transition towards the New American Plate, it helps to evaluate your current eating habits. Just how close is the plate in front of you to a New American Plate? Take a look at the following examples.

### STAGE 1: The Old American Plate

The typical American meal is heavy on meat, fish or poultry. Take a look at this plate. Fully half is loaded down with a huge (8–10 oz.) steak. The remainder is filled with a hearty helping of buttery mashed potatoes and peas. Although this meal is a home-style favorite, it is high in fat and calories and low in phytochemicals and fiber. A few changes, however, will bring it closer to the New American Plate.

### STAGE 2: A Transitional Plate

This meal features a more moderate (4–6 oz.) serving of meat. A large helping of green beans prepared with your favorite herbs and the addition of a filling whole grain (seasoned brown rice) increase the proportion of nutritious, plant-based foods. This plate is on the right track, but doesn't yet take advantage of all the good-tasting foods the New American Plate has to offer.

### STAGE 3: A Better Plate

The modest 3 ounce serving of meat (red meat, poultry or fish) pictured here fits AICR's guideline for cancer prevention. This plate also features a wider variety of foods, resulting in a diverse assortment of cancer-fighting nutrients. Two kinds of vegetables help increase the proportion of plant-based foods. A healthy serving of a tasty whole grain (brown rice, barley, kasha, bulgur, millet, quinoa) completes the meal.

### STAGE 4: The New American Plate

A one-dish dinner like this stir-fry is just the kind of meal that belongs on the New American Plate. It's bursting with colorful vegetables, hearty grains and cancer-fighting vitamins, minerals and phytochemicals. Red meat, poultry or seafood is used as a condiment, adding a bit of flavor and substance to the meal. Plates like this one show the delicious possibilities—the new tastes, colors and textures—that can be found on the New American Plate.

## Standard Serving Sizes

| Food | Serving | Looks Like |
|---|---|---|
| Chopped Vegetables | ½ cup | ½ baseball or rounded handful for average adult |
| Raw Leafy Vegetables (such as lettuce) | 1 cup | 1 baseball or fist of an average adult |
| Fresh Fruit | 1 medium piece | 1 baseball |
| | ½ cup chopped | ½ baseball or rounded handful for average adult |
| Dried Fruit | ¼ cup | 1 golf ball or scant handful for average adult |
| Pasta, Rice, Cooked Cereal | ½ cup | ½ baseball or rounded handful for average adult |
| Ready-to-Eat Cereal | 1 oz., which varies from ½ cup to 1 ¼ cup (check label) | |
| Meat, Poultry, Seafood | 3 oz. (boneless cooked weight from 4 oz. raw) | Deck of cards |
| Dried beans | ½ cup cooked | ½ baseball or rounded handful for average adult |
| Nuts | ⅓ cup | Level handful for average adult |
| Cheese | 1 ½ oz. (2 oz. if processed cheese) | 1 oz. looks like 4 dice |

Source: U.S. Department of Agriculture

## Portion Size: The Forgotten Factor

It began slowly, beneath the notice of most Americans. Decades ago, fast food chains started competing for consumer dollars by offering larger portions. Soon, "value meals" and "super sizes" became commonplace. In the meantime, modestly sized bagels and muffins disappeared from American cafés, replaced by creations three or four times their size. Even table-service restaurants started using larger plates laden with more food to assure customers they were getting their money's worth. At the same time, portion sizes began expanding in the American home.

Central to the New American Plate is a recognition that it's not just *what* we eat that matters, but also *how much* we eat of each food. According to statistics from the U.S. Department of Agriculture (USDA), the average number of calories Americans eat each day has risen from 1,854 to 2,002 over the last 20 years. That significant increase—148 calories per day—theoretically works out to an extra 15 pounds every year.

### Learning About Servings

A good way to figure out the actual amount of food on your plate is by becoming familiar with the serving sizes standardized by the USDA.

Standardized serving sizes provide accepted measurements for calories, fat, cholesterol, carbohydrates, protein, vitamins and minerals. Referring to serving sizes allows us to speak the same language as health professionals and food manufacturers.

The chart (Standard Serving Sizes) lists standard serving sizes for a variety of foods. But one look makes it clear that these servings are smaller than most people think. For example, AICR recommends seven or more servings of grains, beans and other starches per day. If this sounds like a great deal of food to you, consider the following:

## Fad Diets and the New American Plate

You've probably noticed a new wave of fad diets flooding the American marketplace. Behind these quick-fix plans lies the notion that certain kinds of foods—such as sugar, bread and carbohydrates in general—are "bad" or "fattening" and must be avoided.

But it's not an effective or healthy idea to start changing your meals according to the theory of a best-selling diet book. Most of these plans call upon you to abandon the disease-fighting benefits of a diet rich in vegetables, fruits, whole grains and beans. In fact, plates that feature healthy portions of plant-based foods tend to be lower in calories and fat than plates recommended by many fad diets. And when it comes to weight management, it is *total* caloric intake that counts, not any kind of magic "protein vs. carbohydrate" formula.

- The two cups of spaghetti covering your dinner plate equals not one, but four grain servings.
- Those small bagels found in grocery store freezer aisles equal about two grain servings. The jumbo bagels commonly served in shops and cafés are closer to four or five.
- The full bowl of whole grain cereal you pour yourself in the morning may amount to two or three grain servings—a good head start on what you need for the day.

## Familiar Foods and the New American Plate

The New American Plate can be as familiar or as adventurous as you like, and it works with any kind of meal. Just combine your usual foods in new proportions, or make one or two switches.

| Old American Plate | New American Plate |
|---|---|
| **Lunch** | |
| Sandwich with<br>4 oz. of meat<br>Snack crackers<br>Cookies | Sandwich with 2 oz. of meat, sliced tomato, cucumber and fresh spinach<br>Piece of fresh fruit<br>1 cookie if desired |
| **Italian Restaurant** | |
| Veal parmigiana<br>Pasta<br>Salad | Large bowl of minestrone soup<br>½ portion pasta with marinara sauce<br>Salad |
| **Barbecue** | |
| 2 hamburgers or hotdogs<br>½ cup potato salad<br>Chips<br>Brownies | 1 burger (preferably lean meat or veggie)<br>1 cup marinated vegetable salad<br>2 melon slices or ½ cup fruit salad<br>1 brownie if desired |

### "Eyeball" What You Eat

In many cases, the serving sizes listed on "Nutrition Facts" food labels are equivalent to USDA standardized serving sizes. You can use the "Nutrition Facts" labels to develop an important weight management skill. It takes only a few minutes to learn, and it's a tool you will use many times.

At your next meal, check the serving size listed on the "Nutrition Facts" label. Fill a measuring cup or spoon with that amount and empty the food onto a clean plate. Now take a good look. Make a mental snapshot of how much of the plate is covered by a single serving.

Do the same thing with some of your other favorite foods. You will only have to measure once or twice, and in no time you'll develop a real-world sense for serving sizes. Why is this helpful? Once you know how a standard serving is supposed to look on your plate, you can use this information at future meals. You'll also understand exactly how many servings of certain foods you've been eating all along—and have a clearer picture of the calories and nutrients you've been taking in. This knowledge can help you make some important changes for health.

*Start reshaping your diet by looking at your plate. Is the greater proportion of your meal plant-based? Are your portion sizes appropriate to your activity level?*

### Servings vs. Portions

Serving sizes may have been standardized by the government, but each individual has very different caloric needs and weight management goals.

That's why it's important to distinguish between a *serving*, which is simply a general unit of measure, and a *portion*, which is the actual amount of a food appropriate for a specific person.

For example, those who sit at a desk all day may need only one cup of cereal (the standard serving size) in the morning. Others who run five miles a day may need two or three cups (servings) for their portion.

The portion sizes you eat depend on your needs as well. Do you exercise regularly? Is your body experiencing an increased energy demand, as happens during puberty or pregnancy? Are you trying to cut back on calories in order to work towards a healthy weight? Then your plate should feature portions that reflect these needs.

### Portions and Weight Loss

Looking to lose weight? Remember that the New American Plate features more food and fewer calories than a traditional meat-based meal. That's why it's possible to feel satisfied eating a meal built around vegetables, fruits, whole grains and beans and still work towards a healthy weight. Add some regular physical activity, and you have a safe, effective way to manage your weight for the long-term.

But what if the problem persists? You make the switch to a healthy diet, but still can't seem to maintain a healthy weight. There may be many factors at play here, but consider the obvious ones first. Are you exercising regularly? Are your portion sizes too large?

AICR recommends one hour a day of brisk physical activity and one hour a week of more vigorous exercise. That's the recommendation for reducing cancer risk. But any exercise you do is better than none at all. In working towards this activity level, you will burn more calories, which will help lower your weight. Always check with your doctor before starting or changing your exercise program.

As for portion size, it may be time to "eyeball" those standard servings once again. Using the previously presented table (Standard Serving Sizes), take a moment to measure out the standard serving of foods like potatoes or cereal on an empty plate or in a bowl. How many of these servings go into the portions you eat regularly? Are you eating three standard servings of potatoes when you're full after only two? Are you pouring two standard servings of cereal when your activity level requires only one?

Gradually cut back on the number of servings you include in your regular portions. Even small changes add up to a substantial difference. Choosing the regular burger instead of the quarter-pound burger saves you about 160 calories. Stopping after just one cup of pasta on a three-cup platter saves almost 300 calories. Once you suit your portions to your needs, you will find it easier to maintain a healthy weight for life.

A fad diet that has not stood up to rigorous scientific testing is not the way to go. Obesity became an epidemic in this country at the same time portion sizes grew enormous. It is likely that you can reach a healthy weight on your own by simply reducing the size of the portions you eat and exercising more. If you still do not see your weight gradually moving in a healthy direction, contact your doctor or a registered dietitian for a more individualized plan.

## Final Message

What's new about the New American Plate? It's the idea that eating for a healthy life can also mean eating for a healthy weight. There is no need to follow the latest diet trend—most don't have our health in mind. We just need to keep an eye on the knids of food on our plate, and the size of the portions we eat.

A diet based mostly on vegetables, fruits, whole grains and beans can help prevent cancer, heart disease, adult onset diabetes, stroke, hypertension and conditions like cataracts and macular degeneration. It can also keep your weight in a healthy range. And because eating form the New American Plate is as pleasurable as it is beneficial, you will soon find it becomes a permanent part of your life.

From *American Institute for Cancer Research Newsletter,* November 2000, pp. 3-22. 

# FOOD PORTIONS AND SERVINGS
## How Do They Differ?

Consumers appear to be confused about serving sizes—what they mean and how to use them. Complicating the problem are large portions of food that are becoming the norm in many eating establishments, which differ from the servings in the Food Guide Pyramid (FGP) and on the Nutrition Facts Label on food packaging. For example, a large deli bagel might weigh 6 ounces (about 6 FGP servings of bread) while the 1/2 medium bagel listed on the Food Guide Pyramid weighs 1 ounce (about 1 serving of bread). With so much variation in portions of foods, it's easy for consumers to become confused about what serving sizes mean and how to use them.

### *What's a Food Guide Pyramid Serving?*

The Food Guide Pyramid serving is a unit of measure used to describe the total amount of foods recommended daily from each of the food groups. Criteria for selecting the serving sizes are identified in the box. Larger portions count as more than one serving; smaller portions count as partial servings. The Pyramid shows a range of servings for each of the five major food groups. The number of servings an individual requires depends on how many calories he or she needs. For example, the Pyramid suggests 6 to 11 servings of grain products each day. An individual consuming 1600 calories would eat 6 servings of grains while an individual consuming 2800 calories would need 11 servings of grains. Additional information on what counts as one food guide serving unit and the suggested number of servings for various calorie levels is reported in *The Food Guide Pyramid (1).*

### *What's a Food Label Serving?*

A food label serving is a specific amount of food that contains the quantity of nutrients listed on the Nutrition Facts Label. The 1990 Nutrition Labeling and Education Act (NLEA) specified reference serving amounts for almost 200 product categories to be used on labels. To make food label servings consumer-friendly, the serving sizes are expressed in household measures, such as cups, ounces, or pieces, as well as grams, and generally reflect the amount an individual might reasonably consume each eating occasion.

**Serving Sizes in the Food Guide Pyramid are based on four criteria *(2,3)*:**

1. Amount of foods from a food group typically reported in surveys as consumed on one eating occasion;
2. Amount of foods that provide a comparable amount of key nutrients from that food group, for example, the amount of cheese that provides the same amount of calcium as 1 cup fluid milk;
3. Amount of foods recognized by most consumers (e.g., household measures) or that can be easily multiplied or divided to describe a quantity of food actually consumed (portion);
4. Amount traditionally used in previous food guides to describe servings.

### *Food Label vs. Food Guide Pyramid Serving Sizes—How Do They Differ?*

For many food items, the serving size in the Food Guide Pyramid and on the food label are the same (e.g., 1/2 cup canned fruit or vegetables). However, some serving sizes differ because the Pyramid and the food label serve different purposes. The Pyramid describes serving units for each food group (e.g., 1/2 chopped or cooked vegetables and 1 cup raw leafy vegetables) so that they will be easy to remember and help consumers select a healthful diet. The food label serving unit is specific for each product category and designed to help consumers compare nutrient information on a number of food products within a category. The food label serving units cover mixed dishes (e.g., frozen entrees) as well as simple items (e.g., canned fruits). Pyramid serving units are primarily for simple food items, such as fruits, vegetables, and plain grain products.

Additionally, the Pyramid serving size specifies the amount of food that provides a designated amount of key nutrients from that food group; for example, 3/4 cup fruit juice and 1 cup milk. Some food label product categories such as "beverages" specify the same serving size (1 cup), regardless of the food group in which the beverage (fruit juice, milk, or soda) belongs.

## Amounts of foods reported at each occasion,[1] 50th percentile, by age and gender

| Food | FGP[2] serving sizes | 20-39 years Men | 20-39 years Women | 40-59 years Men | 40-59 years Women | 60+ years Men | 60+ years Women |
|---|---|---|---|---|---|---|---|
| | | *Number of FGP serving sizes* | | | | | |
| Apples, raw | 1 medium | 1.0 | 1.0 | 1.0 | 1.0 | 0.9 | 0.9 |
| Orange juice | ¾ cup | 1.3 | 1.3 | 1.3 | 1.1 | 1.1 | 1.0 |
| String beans, cooked | ½ cup | 1.5 | 1.0 | 1.0 | 1.0 | 1.4 | 1.0 |
| Broccoli, cooked | ½ cup | 1.3 | 1.0 | 1.6 | 1.3 | 0.8 | 1.1 |
| Fluid milk | 1 cup | 1.0 | 0.9 | 1.0 | 0.7 | 0.8 | 0.7 |
| Cheese[3] | 1-½ oz | 0.7 | 0.6 | 0.7 | 0.7 | 0.7 | 0.7 |
| White bread | 1 slice | 2.0 | 1.8 | 1.9 | 1.7 | 1.8 | 1.5 |
| Rice, cooked | ½ cup | 1.7 | 1.5 | 1.6 | 1.3 | 1.4 | 1.2 |
| RTE cereals | 1 oz | 2.1 | 1.5 | 1.8 | 1.3 | 1.7 | 1.2 |
| Pasta, cooked | ½ cup | 2.2 | 1.5 | 2.0 | 1.5 | 1.7 | 1.5 |
| Muffins | 1 oz (approx.) | 2.3 | 1.9 | 2.1 | 1.8 | 2.0 | 2.0 |
| | | *Number of 1-ounce meat equivalents*[4] | | | | | |
| Beef steak, cooked | 1 oz | 5.7 | 4.9 | 5.3 | 4.3 | 4.9 | 3.8 |
| Ham, cured cooked | 1 oz | 1.9 | 1.5 | 2.0 | 1.6 | 2.0 | 1.9 |
| Eggs, fried | 1 large | 1.8 | 1.4 | 1.8 | 1.0 | 1.6 | 0.9 |
| Dry beans, cooked | ½ cup | 1.9 | 1.0 | 1.5 | 1.0 | 1.3 | 1.0 |

[1]Data calculated from CSFII 1989-91, NFS Report No. 91-3.
[2]FGP (Food Guide Pyramid).
[3]Includes all cheeses, other than cream or cottage, regardless of fat content.
[4]Serving sizes of meats and meat alternates are listed in 1-ounce equivalents because serving amounts vary by type of food (steak, roast, ground meat, beans, eggs, or peanut butter). The Food Guide Pyramid suggests 2 to 3 servings of meat or meat alternates for a total of5 to 7 ounces each day.

In both cases—the Food Guide Pyramid and the food label—the "serving size" is a unit of measure and may not be the portion of food an individual actually eats at one occasion.

### What's a Portion?

A "portion" can be thought of as the amount of a specific food an individual eats for dinner, snack, or other eating occasion. Portions, of course, can be bigger or smaller than the servings listed in the Food Guide Pyramid or on a food label. Many factors affect food portions, such as the individual's age, gender, activity level, and appetite and where and when the food is obtained and eaten.

### How Do Food Guide Pyramid Serving Sizes Compare With Portions Typically Reported?

Recently, the Center for Nutrition Policy and Promotion (CNPP) reviewed data on quantities of some foods commonly eaten in the United States that individuals reported consuming at each eating occasion in the USDA 1989–91 Continuing Survey of Food Intakes by Individuals (CSFII) *(4)*. The table presents typical amounts of selected foods expressed in food guide serving units, that were consumed by three age groups of adult men and women. Results are similar to data on typical portion sizes obtained from a study using the USDA 1977–78 Nationwide Food Consumption Survey *(5)*. Consistent with their greater calorie need, men's portion sizes (number of food guide servings at each eating occasion) are larger than those for women; for both genders, portion sizes decrease with age, especially for foods such as meats and grain products.

**Amounts of selected foods reported per eating occasion,[1] 50th percentile, by age and sex**

| Food | FGP[2] serving sizes | 20-39 years Men | 20-39 years Women | 40-59 years Men | 40-59 years Women | 60+ years Men | 60+ years Women |
|---|---|---|---|---|---|---|---|
| | | *Number of FGP serving sizes* | | | | | |
| Apples, raw | 1 medium | 1.0 | 1.0 | 1.0 | 1.0 | 0.9 | 0.9 |
| Orange juice | ¾ cup | 1.3 | 1.3 | 1.3 | 1.1 | 1.1 | 1.0 |
| String beans, ck | ½ cup | 1.5 | 1.0 | 1.0 | 1.0 | 1.4 | 1.0 |
| Broccoli, ck | ½ cup | 1.3 | 1.0 | 1.6 | 1.3 | 0.8 | 1.1 |
| Fluid milk | ½ cup | 1.0 | 0.9 | 1.0 | 0.7 | 0.8 | 0.7 |
| Cheese | 1-½ cup | 0.7 | 0.6 | 0.7 | 0.7 | 0.7 | 0.7 |
| White bread | 1 slice | 2.0 | 1.8 | 1.9 | 1.7 | 1.8 | 1.5 |
| Rice, ck | 1 oz | 2.1 | 1.5 | 1.8 | 1.3 | 1.7 | 1.2 |
| Pasta, cooked | ½ cup | 2.2 | 1.5 | 2.0 | 1.5 | 1.7 | 1.5 |
| Muffins | ~1 oz | 2.3 | 1.9 | 2.1 | 1.8 | 2.0 | 2.0 |
| Crackers | 6-8 crax | 1.0 | 0.8 | 0.9 | 0.7 | 0.7 | 0.6 |
| | | *Number of 1 ounce meat equivalents[3]* | | | | | |
| Beef, ground | 1 oz | 2.5 | 2.0 | 2.5 | 2.1 | 2.8 | 2.3 |
| Beef steak | 1 oz | 5.7 | 4.9 | 5.3 | 4.3 | 4.9 | 3.8 |
| Pork, chops, rst | 1 oz | 3.8 | 3.0 | 3.6 | 2.8 | 2.8 | 2.4 |
| Ham | 1 oz | 1.9 | 1.5 | 2.0 | 1.6 | 2.0 | 1.9 |
| Eggs, fried | 1 large | 1.8 | 1.4 | 1.8 | 1.0 | 1.6 | 0.9 |
| Dry beans, ck | ½ cup | 1.9 | 1.0 | 1.5 | 1.0 | 1.3 | 1.0 |
| Peanut butter, | 2 Tbsp | 0.9 | 0.6 | 0.9 | 0.5 | 0.8 | 0.5 |

[1]Data calculated from CSFII 1989–91, NFS Report No. 91-3.
[2]FGP (Food Guide Pyramid).
[3]Serving sizes of meats and meat alternates are listed in 1-ounce equivalents because serving amounts vary by type of food (steak, roast, ground meat, beans, eggs, peanut butter). The Food Guide Pyramid suggests 2 to 3 servings of meat or meat alternates for a total of 5 to 7 ounces per day.

### *What Is the Challenge for the Grain Products?*

As in the earlier study *(5)*, individuals' typical portion sizes for grain products in the 1989–91 CSFII equaled 1 1/2 to 2 food guide serving units, for example, 2 slices of bread or a cup of cooked pasta. However, the Food Guide Pyramid retains the grain serving size units of 1 slice of bread or 1/2 cup of cooked pasta, etc., used in previous food guides, in part because the serving units are familiar and easy to use. This may have caused some confusion among consumers who are unaware of the specified serving unit—they may either perceive 6 to 11 servings of grain products suggested by the Pyramid to be far more than can be eaten or may alternatively interpret this as permission to consume more than they should of these foods, often with added fats and sugars. However, changing the *serving unit* to the more typically reported 2 slices of bread or 1 cup of cooked pasta would *reduce* the *number* of servings suggested by the Pyramid to 3 to 5 and might give an appearance of a conflict with the Dietary Guideline to include plenty of grain products in the diet.

## *How Can Educators Help?*

Educators can help consumers better understand the concepts of servings and portions by:

- ***Explaining that Food Guide Pyramid servings are units of measure that are easy to use and understand. They are not prescribed portions to eat as a meal or snack.***
- ***Explaining that the number of servings suggested in the Food Guide Pyramid are related to the caloric needs of the individual—the higher the caloric needs, the higher the suggested number of servings.***
- ***Providing tips on how to visually estimate serving sizes.***
- ***Explaining why Food Guide Pyramid servings and food label servings differ.***
- ***Explaining how serving sizes differ from portion sizes.***
- ***Showing individuals how to evaluate their diets to determine if changes are needed to achieve a healthful diet. One way to evaluate an individual's diet is to total the number of Food Guide Pyramid servings eaten daily and compare them—based on caloric need—with the number of servings suggested by the Food Guide Pyramid.***

## *References*


1. U.S. Department of Agriculture. 1996. *The Food Guide Pyramid*. Home and Garden Bulletin No. 252.
2. Cronin F.J., Shaw, A.M., Krebs-Smith, S.M., Marsland, P.M., and Light, L. 1987. Developing a food guidance system to implement the dietary guidelines. *J. Nutr. Educ.* 19:281–302.
3. Welsh, S.O., Davis, C., and Shaw, A. 1993. *USDA's Food Guide: Background and Development, USDA*. Miscellaneous Publication No. 1514.
4. Krebs-Smith, S.M., Guenther, P.M., Cook, A., Thompson, F.E., Cucinelli, J., and Udler, J. 1997. *Foods Commonly Eaten in the United States: Quantities Consumed Per Eating Occasion and in a Day, 1989–91*. USDA ARS NFS Report No. 91-3.
5. Krebs-Smith, S.M., and Smiciklas-Wright, H. 1985. Typical serving sizes: Implications for food guidance. *J. Am. Diet. Assoc.* 85:1139–1141.


---

**Authors**: Myrtle Hogbin, R.D., Nutritionist; Anne Shaw, Ph.D., Nutritionist; Rajen S. Anand, Ph.D., Executive Director, Center for Nutrition Policy and Promotion, USDA.

# Americans Ignore Importance of Food Portion Size

**Medical College of Wisconsin Physicians & Clinics—Milwaukee, Wisconsin**

Most Americans believe the kind of food they eat is more important for managing weight than the amount of food they eat, according to a new survey.

In the survey, a surprising 78 percent of respondents said that eating certain types of food while avoiding others was more central to their weight management efforts than eating less food. The survey was commissioned by the American Institute for Cancer Research, a private cancer charity.

This finding troubles nutrition experts, who have long suspected that messages about "low-fat" eating may cause the public to lose sight of a more pressing concern: total calorie intake. They stressed that effective weight management strategies place equal focus on both the kind and amount of food consumed. They added, however, that there is an increasing American trend to ignore the issue of portion size.

Indeed, the survey suggests that Americans are seizing on 'quick-fix' strategies with little regard for how much food they actually consume. "People are eating more and wondering why they're getting fatter, " said Melanie Polk, M.M.Sc., R.D., Director of Nutrition Education at the Institute. "One big reason is that their focus is too narrow."

Americans, she said, are concentrating too exclusively on cutting fat, or going on fad diets that restrict carbohydrates, sugar, or some other factor. Too often, such strategies fail to address the larger picture of total calories consumed, not to mention good nutrition.

## Portion Size Linked to Weight Management

Almost 62 percent of those responding to the survey said they were currently above their ideal weight. Half of those who were above their ideal weight said they needed to lose six to 20 pounds, and another 13 percent said they needed to lose 21 to 30 pounds. Ten percent of those who said they were above their ideal weight reported being over by 50 pounds or more.

These numbers are in accordance with recent figures from the National Institutes of Health attesting that for the first time in history, the majority of Americans—an estimated 55 percent—are clinically overweight, while one in every four Americans is obese (severely overweight). This means that most Americans are now at increased risk for obesity-related diseases like cancer, coronary heart disease, stroke, diabetes, high blood pressure, gallbladder disease and osteoarthritis.

Anecdotal evidence from several sources illustrates the steady increase in U.S. portion sizes over the past few decades. Foreigners coming to this country express amazement at the amount of food served up in American homes and eateries. Foods adopted from foreign countries like croissants and bagels have grown to double or triple their original size, and the native muffin has ballooned from a standard ounce-and-half to as much as eight ounces today.

Meanwhile, fast food outlets feature gigantic "value meals" and "supersizes." Even table-service restaurants have swapped 10-inch plates (once the industry standard) for 12-inch sizes.

USDA statistics show that American total daily caloric intake has risen from 1,854 kcal to 2,002 kcal over the last 20 years. That significant increase—148 calories per day—theoretically works out to an extra 15 pounds every year. (Ironically, the same studies show that the average American has lowered the percentage of fat in his or her diet from 40 percent to 33 percent over the same amount of time.)

According to the survey, however, most Americans are unaware that portions they consume have increased in size. Six in ten (62 percent) of survey respondents said that the portions served in restaurants are the same size or smaller compared to 10 years ago. Eight in ten said the portions they eat at home are the same or smaller. Americans under 35 years of age were more likely to recognize that their food portions have grown compared to baby-boomers aged 35 to 54 and Americans 55 or older.

---

Each year, Medical College of Wisconsin physicians care for more than 180,000 patients, representing nearly 500,000 patient visits. Medical College physicians practice at Children's Hospital of Wisconsin, Froedtert Memorial Lutheran Hospital, the Milwaukee VA Medical Center, and many other hospitals and clinics in Milwaukee and southeastern Wisconsin.

---

# In the Drink

## When it Comes to Calories, Solid is Better than Liquid

"What would you like to drink with that?" asks the waitress. Think twice before you answer.

Your body may not register the calories you *drink* as well as it does the calories you *eat*. So when you down a soda or other liquid calories before or with a meal, you may not eat less food later in the day to compensate. Making matters worse: serving sizes for beverages are ballooning… as are Americans.

"Beverages are huge contributor to obesity," says Richard Mattes of Purdue University in West Lafayette, Indiana. "They're major players that often get overlooked."

### Stealth Calories

In one study by Mattes, people were asked to consume 450 calories' worth of jelly beans every day for four weeks and 450 calories' worth of soda every day for another four weeks.[1] On days they ate the jelly beans, the participants compensated by eating roughly 450 fewer calories of others foods. So they ingested no more calories than usual.

But on days they drank the soda, the participants didn't compensate. They ended up eating roughly 450 *more* calories than usual.

"Liquid calories don't trip our satiety mechanisms," says Mattes. "They just don't register."

More evidence that liquid calories go unnoticed: Short-term studies show that if you drink a calorie-containing beverage with a meal, you'll wind up consuming more calories at that meal than if you drink a calorie-free beverage.[2]

But what about the long term? Researchers at the Monell Chemical Senses Center in Philadelphia gave 20 men and women about 40 ounces a day of either regular or diet cola (made with the artificial sweetener aspartame).[3] After three weeks, the women who drank the regular cola gained an average of two pounds; the men's weight didn't change. On the diet soda, the men lost one pound and the women's weight didn't change.

"It doesn't matter if you drink them with a meal or before a meal," says Barbara Rolls of the Pennsylvania State University, author of *Volumetrics: Feel Full on Fewer Calories* (HarperCollins, 2000). "The calories from most drinks add on to—rather than displace—food calories."

And that has added on to the nation's obesity epidemic, argues Mattes. "Over the last 20 years, we've gotten fatter, but what's really changed is that we're drinking a lot more calories than we ever did before."

### The Bottomless Cup

In the 1950s, a "family size" bottle of Coke was 26 ounces. Now soft drink sizes at McDonald's *for one person* range from 12 ounces (for children) to 42 ounces. A "Double Gulp" at 7-Eleven convenience stores holds 64 ounces. That's eight cups—a huge serving even if you get it with ice. And the soft drinks you get at movie theaters like Loews and some AMCs (which can hit 44 ounces) often come with free refills.

"Sweetened soft drinks add more calories to our diet than any other beverage," notes Rolls.

America's appetite for soft drinks is at an all-time high, with no signs of slowing down. Soda pop dwarfs all other beverages we consume. Even if you subtract diet sodas—about a quarter of the market—it's still the number-one beverage (see "Sweetened Soda Rules").

And it's not just soft drinks. A "venti" Caffè Latte at Starbucks is 20 ounces. A large shake at McDonald's or a Dunkin' Donuts Coolata is 32 ounces. And a single-serve bottle of just about any beverage—Arizona Iced Tea, Gatorade, Fruitopia, you name it—can run as high as 20 ounces.

Look at the "Nutrition Facts" labels on those bottles and you'll see calories listed for an eight-ounce (one-cup) serving (as if people split the bottle into 2 ½ servings).

But other than children who get an eight-ounce carton of milk with their school lunch, it's hard to know who

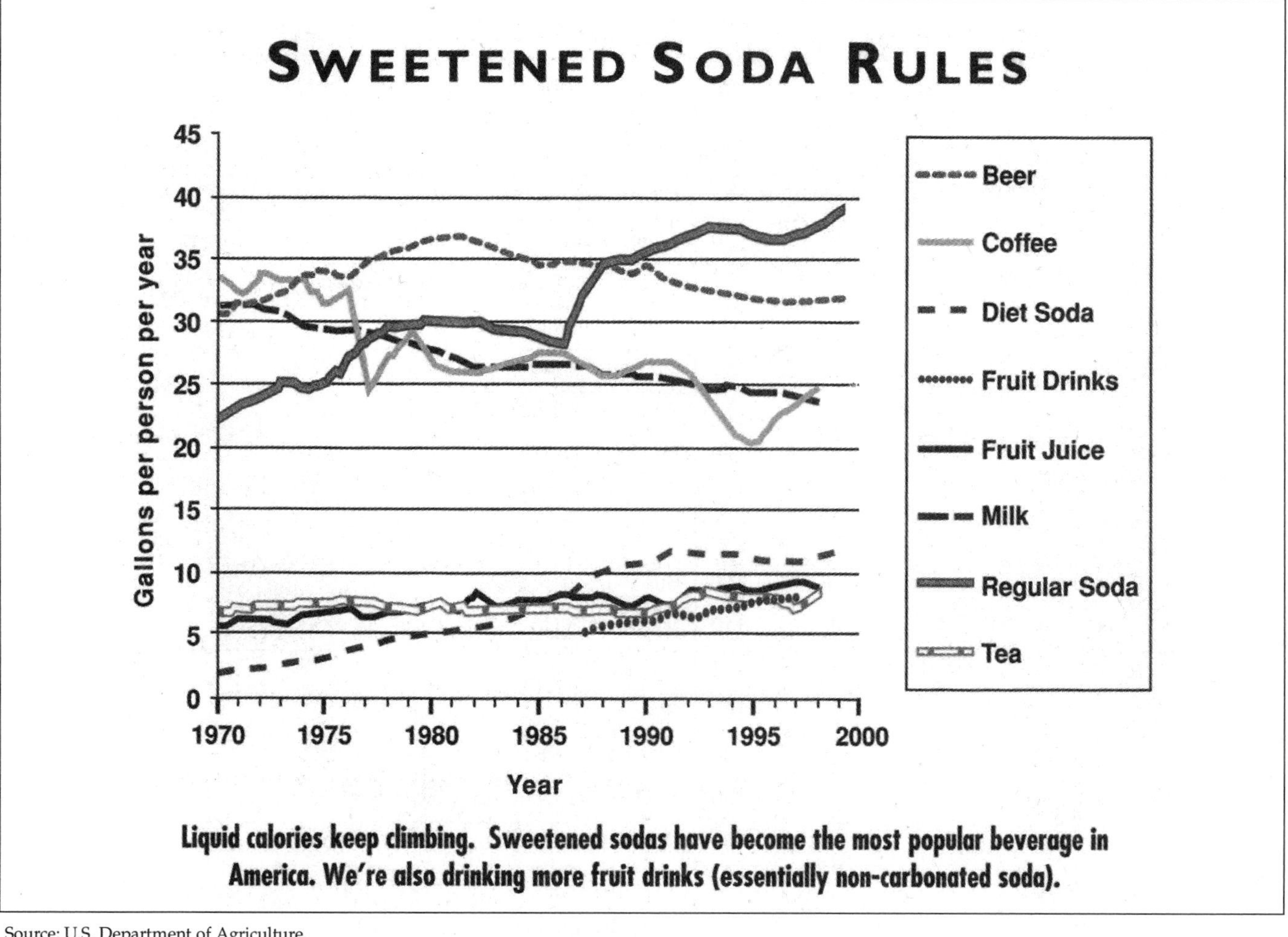


**Liquid calories keep climbing. Sweetened sodas have become the most popular beverage in America. We're also drinking more fruit drinks (essentially non-carbonated soda).**

Source: U.S. Department of Agriculture.

stops at one cup any more. You can't even buy an eight-ounce drink at many restaurants. A "small" drink at McDonald's is 16 ounces. And large sit-down restaurant chains like Applebee's, Chili's, Denny's, Olive Garden, Outback Steakhouse, and T.G.I. Friday's start you off with 14 to 22 ounces of soda... and offer free refills.

Even alcoholic beverages are ballooning. T.G.I. Friday's sells 18-ounce cocktails like the Ultimate Daiquiri, Hawaiian Volcano, Long Island Iced Tea, Margarita, or Mudslide.

Restaurants like Applebee's, Olive Garden, and T.G.I. Friday's offer either 16-ounce or 22-ounce draft beers. And at restaurants like Romano's Macaroni Grill and Buca di Beppo, two Italian sit-down chains, a serving of wine can be ten ounces.

(When the *Dietary Guidelines for Americans* and health authorities advise men to stop at two drinks a day and women to stop at one, they're talking about a five-ounce serving of wine, a 12-ounce serving of beer, or 1.5 ounces of liquor. Do patrons who drink alcohol at some restaurants know that each glass may contain two servings?)

And as mugs and glasses grow, so grow our bellies and bottoms. Twenty ounces of most beverages—even juice or milk—mean 200 to 450 calories. A 32-ounce large shake at McDonald's means 720 calories. A 32-ounce large Dunkin' Donuts Coolata means 820.

## Good to the Last Drop

Do people drink more just because they're served more?

"Serving sizes have a tremendous effect on everyone, but a much more dramatic effect on males," says Brian Wansink, director of the Food and Brand Research Lab at the University of Illinois at Urbana-Champaign.

In a new (still unpublished) study, he gave free Coke or Sprite to 372 teens and adults who were eating at McDonald's, Burger King, or Hardee's restaurants. Roughly half were given a child-size (12-ounce) drink, while the others got a large (32-ounce) drink.

"The girls and women drank 17 ounces when they got the large size, but only 9 ounces when they got the small drink," says Wansink.

"The differences were even more extreme for the boys and men. They consume anything you give them—about 28 of the 32 ounces in the large drink and 11 of the 12 ounces in the small drink."

## DRINK TO ME ONLY

All beverages are not created equal. Here's a selection of popular drinks, ranked from least number of calories to most. Some serving sizes may seem large, but we didn't make them up. All are available in bottles, in cans, or at restaurants. Restaurant drinks will have even more calories if you get no ice.

| **Beverage** *(size)* | **Calories** | **Beverage** *(size)* | **Calories** |
|---|---|---|---|
| Water or seltzer | 0 | Snapple Lemonade (*16 oz.*) | 240 |
| Diet soda (*20 oz.*) | 5 | 7-Up, Coca-Cola, or root beer (*20 oz.*) | 250 |
| Coffee, with one liquid creamer (*8 oz.)* | 30 | Beer, regular, draft (*22 oz.)* | 280 |
| Tea, with two packets of sugar (*8 oz.*) | 50 | Margarita (from mix), on the rocks (*8 oz.)* | 290 |
| V8 (*11.5 oz.*) | 70 | 7-Eleven Big Gulp, Coca-Cola (*32 oz.)* | 300 |
| Milk, fat-free (*8 oz.*) | 90 | Fruitopia, The Grape Beyond (*20 oz.)* | 300 |
| Beer, light (*12 oz.*) | 100 | Hawaiian Punch (*20 oz.*) | 300 |
| Milk, 1% (*8 oz.)* | 100 | Orange soda (*20 oz.*) | 300 |
| Starbucks Cappuccino, short ( *8 oz.*)1 | 100 | Sunny Delight (*20 oz.*) | 300 |
| Apple or orange juice (*8 oz.*) | 110 | McDonald's Coca-Cola, large (*32 oz.*) | 310 |
| Irish coffee, w/out whipped cream (*8 oz.*) | 120 | Eggnog (*8 oz.*) | 340 |
| Nestea Iced Tea, sweetened (*16 oz.)* | 120 | Starbucks Caffé Latte, venti (*20 oz.*)[1] | 350 |
| Gatorade (*20 oz.*) | 130 | Tropicana Twister Fruit Punch (*20 oz.*) | 350 |
| Cranberry juice (*8 oz.)* | 140 | McDonald's Chocolate Shake, sm. (*16 oz.*) | 360 |
| Starbucks Caffe Latte, short (*8 oz.*)1 | 140 | Odwalla Future Shake, Vanilla Al'mondo (*16 oz.*) | 380 |
| Beer, regular (*12 oz.)* | 150 | McDonald's Coca-Cola, super size (*42 oz.*) | 410 |
| Grape juice (*8 oz.)* | 150 | Dairy Queen Misty, large (*32 oz.*) | 440 |
| Mimosa (*8 oz.*) | 150 | McDonald's Hi-C Orange Drink, super size (*42 oz.*) | 460 |
| Martini (*2.5 oz.*) | 160 | Nestlé NesQuik Chocolate or Strawberry Milk (*16 oz.*) | 460 |
| Wine, white (*8 oz.)* | 160 | Jamba Juice, Strawberries Wild Smoothie, Power Size (*32 oz.*) | 560 |
| Gin & tonic, on the rocks (*7.5 oz.*) | 170 | 7-Eleven Double Gulp, Coca-Cola (*64 oz.)* | 600 |
| Wine, red (*8 oz.*) | 170 | Burger King Vanilla Shake, large (*32 oz.*) | 630 |
| Milk, whole (*8 oz.*) | 180 | McDonald's Chocolate Shake, lg. (*32 oz.*) | 720 |
| Ginger ale (*20 oz.*) | 200 | Dunkin' Donuts Coolatta, large (*32 oz.*)[2] | 820 |
| Starbucks Cappuccino, venti ( *20 oz.*)[1] | 200 | Baskin-Robbins Chocolate Milkshake, large (*24 oz.)* | 1,130 |
| Starbucks Coffee Frappuccino, tall (*12 oz.*) | 200 | Smoothie King, Strawberry Hulk (*40 oz.*) | 1,920 |
| Dairy Queen Misty, small (*16 oz.*) | 220 | | |
| Ultra Slim-Fast, canned (*11 oz.)* | 220 | | |
| V8 Splash (*16 oz.*) | 220 | | |
| Arizona Iced Tea (*20 oz.*) | 230 | | |
| Sobe Orange Carrot Elixir 3C (*20 oz.)* | 230 | | |

[1]Prepared using whole milk.
[2]Prepared using cream.
Source: Manufacturers and U.S. Department of Agriculture (USDA).

And what's remarkable, says Wansink, is that "people don't perceive that they're consuming any more calories with a large drink than with a small."

When asked how many calories they drank, most people had no clue, he says. "But even when we looked at people who said they could estimate calories well—usually females—they said they had consumed about 100 calories, whether they drank 9 ounces or 17 ounces."

## Take Charge

Don't get us wrong. It's not just 300-calorie beverages that are making Americans pudgy. It's also 670-calorie Cinnabons, 800-calorie tuna salad sandwiches, 1,000-calorie Big Macs and Fries, 1,200-calorie orders of Stuffed Potato Skins, 1,600-calorie platters of General Tso's Chicken, and 2,400-calorie plates of Cheese Fries.

But at least some people think twice before gulping down 1,000 calories of food. They may not question the "hidden" calories in beverages.

Yet they're so easy to avoid. Dieters may have trouble eating less food over the long term. But surely they could get used to drinking noncaloric beverages with and between meals.

"People have two options," says Mattes. "Either they start consuming non-caloric beverages like water, tea, coffee, or diet soda. Or they can drink whatever they want, but compensate by eating less food."

Here are some other strategies for avoiding beverage bloat:

- Order "kiddie" or "small" sizes. At McDonald's (and many other restaurants), a child's serving is 12 ounces. And a "small" at most fast food restaurants is 16 ounces (two cups).
- Ask for ice in your drink. You'll get less beverage... and fewer calories.
- Get an empty cup or glass and split a beverage with a friend. If the waiter offers a free refill, ask for water.
- Don't have a caloric beverage as a snack to stave off hunger before a meal. It won't curb your appetite as well as solid food. Try baby carrots, slices of melon, or orange wedges instead.
- You don't have to eliminate healthy beverages like orange juice and low-fat milk. Mix OJ with seltzer for a refreshing drink with half the usual calories. And the calcium, protein, and other nutrients in that glass of milk may be worth its 100-or-so calories.
- Diet soft drinks are better than regular soda. But if you guzzle caffeinated soda, coffee, or tea all day, it may leave you jittery and unable to sleep.

## Notes


1. *Internat. J. Obesity 24*: 794, 2000.
2. *Physiol. Behav. 48*: 19, 1990.
3. *Am. J. Clin. Nutr. 51:* 963, 1990


## Acknowledgment

The information for this article was compiled by Jackie Adriano.

# Food Industry Is Making AMERICA FAT

The American Institute for Cancer Research (AICR) is asking Americans to buck a food industry trend that is contributing to the nation's obesity epidemic. "Value marketing" appeals to the consumer's desire for bargains by offering more product for less money. AICR Director of Nutrition Education Melanie Polk maintains that this marketing strategy is having a measurable and unfortunate long-term effect on national health.

As "family-sized" packaging began appearing in supermarket aisles, "supersizes," "value meals," and other oversized portions became commonplace in the nation's eating establishments. AICR's Polk wants Americans to understand that this kind of targeting by food manufacturers, retailers and restaurants comes with certain health risks. "Americans have to keep in mind that getting more food for less money has an inescapable—and often overlooked—downside. It simply shifts the pressure from our wallets to our waistbands."

Today, more Americans than ever—55%, according to the National Institutes of Health—are clinically overweight, while one in every four is obese (severely overweight.) In fact, figures released this month from the Centers for Disease Control and Prevention show that the nation's obesity rose 6 percent between 1998 and 1999 alone. (To put that figure in perspective, consider that American obesity rose a total of six percent during the *seven-year period* before 1998.) Together, these numbers indicate that for the first time in history, most of the American population is at increased risk for obesity-related ailments like certain cancers, coronary heart disease, stroke, diabetes, high blood pressure, gallbladder disease and osteoarthritis.

Does the growth in portion sizes factor largely in the American obesity crisis? According to a survey commissioned by the AICR, the answer is yes. Twenty-six percent of Americans base the amount of food they consume on how much they are served. This passive approach to portions (once known as the "Clean-Plate Club") is more prevalent among overweight Americans than those who say they are at their ideal weight.

When it comes to bigger portions, representatives of the food industry insist they are only responding to consumer demand, not creating it. "Last I checked, it's the consumer who's shoveling all that food into his mouth, not the food industry," notes John L. Stanton, professor of food marketing, St. Joseph's University, Philadelphia, Pa., an industry consultant, lecturer, and coauthor of *Twenty-One Trends in Food Marketing.* "I don't think there's any question that portion sizes are getting bigger, but it doesn't make sense to hold restaurants or food manufacturers to blame for giving their customers exactly what those customers say they want. That's called customer service."

He cites consumer surveys conducted by food marketers in which respondents consistently rate "value" as one of the most important considerations when buying food at home or in restaurants. From an industry perspective, Stanton explains, it comes down to simple economics—the cheapest way to give customers extra value is to increase portion sizes. "If you're a restaurant owner, for example, you can give your customers value in one of two ways. You can either cut your prices, or you can put more food on [customers'] plates. And when it comes down to a choice between cutting your prices by a dollar, or giving people about thirty cents worth of extra food, it's pretty much a no-brainer."

The problem, argues Polk, is that Americans are eating all that extra food. U.S. Department of Agriculture (USDA) statistics show that total daily caloric intake has risen from 1,854 to 2,002 over the last 20 years. That increase—148 calories per day—theoretically works out to an extra 15 pounds gained every year. Thus, what's good for the food industry may be bad for American health. As food profits increase, the numbers on the nation's bathroom scales do so as well.

The billions of dollars spent each year to promote food products only intensifies the problem. According to the USDA, more advertising dollars are spent annually by the food industry than by any other source. Conservative estimates place the figures at $11,000,000,000 for advertising and another $22,000,000,000 on trade shows, incentives and other consumer promotions.

GENETIC ENGINEERING

## What Do You Know About Foods Made From GENETICALLY MODIFIED CROPS?

Some food companies have stopped using genetically modified crops as sources for their foods. Like many Americans, though, you may think you don't know enough about the issue to decide whether you agree with those who pressed for these changes. A survey by the International Food Information Council found that just one in five Americans consider themselves informed about foods produced with genetically modified organisms. Peter Goldsbrough, a plant scientist and expert in genetically modified crops at Purdue University, West Lafayette, Ind., has developed nine questions to test your knowledge of genetically modified foods and agricultural biotechnology:

**1**. Have you eaten foods made from genetically modified crops?

**A**. Yes **B**. No

**2**. Which foods use genetically modified organisms in their production to the largest extent?

**A**. Cheese **B**. Vegetables **C**. Meat

**3**. What are the *current* benefits of having foods made from genetically modified crops?

**A**. They improve farm profitability and make some farmers' jobs easier.

**B**. They allow farmers to increase greatly the amount of crops produced.

**C**. They improve convenience for consumers—*e.g.*, by creating foods with longer shelf lives.

**D**. They improve the nutritional quality of foods.

**E**. They cause less damage to the environment than conventional chemical-intensive agriculture.

**4**. Of the food we eat, how much contains the genetic material DNA?

**A**. Less than five percent **B**. 20% **C**. 50% **D**. 80% **E**. Nearly 100%

**5**. Most foods derived from genetically modified crops contain:

**A**. The same number of genes as food produced from conventional crops

**B**. The same number of genes as foods produced from hybrid crops

**C**. One or two additional genes

**D**. Hundreds of additional genes

**E**. No genes at all

**6**. What effect does eating genetically modified foods have on your genes?

**A**. It could cause your own genes to mutate.

**B**. It could cause your own genes to absorb the excess genes.

**C**. It has no effect on your genes.

**D**. The effects on human genetics aren't known.

**7**. Are foods made from genetically modified crops required to pass human testing?

**A**. Yes **B**. No

**8**. Are foods derived from genetically modified crops required to be tested for possible allergic reactions in people.

**A**. Yes **B**. No

**9**. Are foods derived from genetically modified crops required to be tested for possible allergic reactions in people?

**A**. They offer substantial health advantages over foods that are produced from conventional crops.

**B**. They offer some health advantages over foods produced from conventional crops.

**C**. They are neither better nor worse than foods from conventional crops.

**D**. They are slightly less healthful than foods from conventional crops.

**E**. Foods produced from genetically modified crops are a known health risk.

### ANSWERS

**1. A.** "If you live in the United States, it's almost certain that at one time or another you've eaten foods made from genetically modified crops," Goldsbrough indicates. A large percentage of the corn and soybeans grown in the U.S. comes from genetically modified plants, and the crops from them are made into common food ingredients such as high fructose corn syrup and vegetable oil, as well as other food additives. The corn syrup is used in a number of products, including soft drinks, and the vegetable oil is used to fry foods such as fast-food french fries. According to the Grocery Manufacturers of America, an estimated 70% of the foods on grocery store shelves in 2000 were made or manufactured using genetically modified crops.

**2. A.** Before the advent of genetically modified organisms, cheese was produced using an enzyme obtained from the stomachs of calves slaughtered for veal. Today, genetically modified bacteria produce that same protein. One result of this is that many cheeses are now considered kosher.

**3. A.** Genetically modified crops have made life a little bit easier for the nation's farmers who use them. However, scientists and farmers believe that soon all of the answers will be true: Genetically modified crops will create foods that are more nutritious, have longer shelf lives, contain fewer pesticides, and be produced with less damage to the environment.

**4. E.** All plant and animal cells contain DNA, so nearly all food contains genetic material, regardless of whether the food has been genetically modified. There are a few exceptions, though. "During processing of some food products, such as vegetable cooling oils, almost all of the DNA is removed," Goldsbrough explains.

**5. C.** Genetically modified crops contain one or two additional genes than either conventional or hybrid crops.

**6. C.** "Genes in foods are easily digested and there is no evidence that these new genes are going to have any effect on our genes," Goldsbrough says.

**7. B.** "There are currently no regulations that require human testing of these crops," Goldsbrough points out. "The producers are required by the Food and Drug Administration to say where the genes come from and to disclose nutritional properties, but that is as far as the requirements go."

**8. B.** There are no requirements to test whether genetically modified crops cause allergic reactions. So far, this system appears to work. When conventional new foods—such as kiwi fruit—are introduced to the U.S. market, allergic reactions are common. After three years of widespread use, however, no allergic reactions to genetically modified crops have been reported.

**9. C.** "Most of the genetically modified crops currently available are designed to reduce farmers' production costs. Under some circumstances, there may be less pesticides used, and there is some indication that genetically modified corn is less likely to be infected with fungal toxins that are natural carcinogens, but the overall health effect of these benefits is minor," Goldsbrough maintains. "In the future, these technologies hold the promise of delivering foods that are nutritionally enhances. For example, foods might provide essential vitamins or contain natural compounds that can help improve your health."

"Value marketing has confused Americans about what a normal and appropriate portion of food should look like," said Polk. "With every oversized fast food meal or 64-ounce soft drink we see, we lose perspective." Accordingly, the AICR has drawn up some simple advice for dealing with enormous restaurant and fast-food portions. Choosing the regular burger instead of the quarter-pound size saves about 160 calories. Ordering a cup of cream of mushroom soup instead of a bowl cuts the calories by a whopping 180 calories. Stopping after just one cup of pasta on a three-cup platter can save almost 300 calories.

"Say small, say half, and share," Polk suggests. "If you're given the option, order the small. It may not seem cost-effective, but it's enough food to satisfy most people." Moreover, "At table-service restaurants, ask the server to put half of your entrée in a doggie bag before bringing it to your ta-

Food

# Myths and Truths

Is it "feed a cold, starve a fever" or "starve a cold, feed a fever"? Is either one true or are they myths? One way to find out is to take the Food Myths and Truths Quiz below, designed by the American Dietetic Association to get people thinking about and reevaluating those old wives' tales they grew up believing were true about nutrition and the foods they eat. Are the following statements myths or truths?

1. A food that is labeled "98% fat-free" contains only two percent of its total calories from fat.
2. Fresh vegetables and fruits contain more nutrients than canned or frozen.
3. People are not born with a preference for salty flavors.
4. Your stomach shrinks when you eat less.
5. Brown bread has more fiber than white bread.
6. Foods grown with organic or natural fertilizers have no more nutrients than those grown with synthetic fertilizers.
7. Organically grown foods are more healthful and safer than those grown conventional ways.
8. Cottage cheese is a great source of calcium.
9. Irradiation zaps the nutrients from food.
10. Feed a cold, starve a fever or is it starve a cold, feed a fever?

### ANSWERS

**1. Myth**. The "98% fat-free" claim refers to the weight of food, not its calories. If a food is labeled fat-free, it contains .5 grams of fat or less per serving. Read the nutrition facts for grams of fat per serving.
**2. Myth**. There is little difference, depending on the handling of the produce. Canned and frozen produce are generally processed at their peak and may contain more nutrients than fresh produce. Canned or frozen produce may have added sugar or salt, though, which is something to consider when purchasing these items.
**3. Truth**. Preferences for salty food are learned. If you slowly cut down sodium intake, your desire for salt will decrease.
**4. Myth**. Your stomach expands to handle large amounts of food. As the food moves through your digestive system, your stomach returns to its normal size and stays there until your next meal.
**5. Myth**. Being brown in color does not mean a bread is high in fiber. If the bread's ingredient list states it contains whole wheat or other whole grains, it probably has fiber. The brown color is likely from caramel coloring found in the ingredient list. Check the nutrition facts label for the number of grams of fiber per serving.
**6. Truth**. Plants cannot tell the difference between types of fertilizers. Factors such as climate, crop handling, and maturity at harvest affect the nutrient content of fruits and vegetables.
**7. Myth**. No evidence has shown a difference. Organic foods are typically grown with natural pesticides and insecticides to prevent crop damage. With conventional agriculture, pesticides are carefully regulated to ensure their safe use for the environment and human health. If you prefer organic foods, they are nutritious choices in a healthful eating plan.
**8. Myth**. Cottage cheese supplies 65 mg in a half cup of calcium. If you are eating it for its calcium content, try more-calcium-dense foods, such as eight ounces of milk or yogurt, which contain 300 mg, or one ounce of cheddar cheese, which contains 200 mg.
**9. Myth**. Irradiation results in minimal nutrient loss just like other forms of food processing, such as drying, freezing, and pasteurization. Irradiation helps produce maintain quality longer.
**10. Myth**. Either way, this is a myth! To fight infection, your body needs a supply of nutrients, plenty of fluids, and extra rest. A day's eating plan with variety and balance is as important as ever.

ble. This strategy, of course, is *very* cost-effective—it provides two full meals for the price of one."

She predicts that things aren't going to get any better for the American population anytime soon. "Food makers, marketers and restaurants are going to continue to compete for the American dollar. That means that portion sizes are going to continue to get bigger, and, unless we take action, so will we. At this point, the only way to inject a little sanity back into the discussion is for consumers to stand up and demand it." She believes that if enough people call for it, restaurants could be cajoled into offering reasonable portions. "Tell them you don't want more for less. Tell them you want less for less—less food for even less money. You want to sit down and enjoy an amount of food that you can finish without feeling stuffed, at a fair and reasonable price."

# Supermarket Psych-Out

REMEMBER THE AD for Sheba cat food, the one in which the woman with the luxurious voice feeds her luxuriously furry feline from a tin that has large black lettering and a picture of a black cat? Well, it's no accident that the tin has all that black on it.

There was a time when black had a "no-frills association," explains Mona Doyle, president of The Consumer Network, a Philadelphia firm that conducts research on consumer perceptions. "It would have looked doleful" to people shopping for food products," she says. But today, she points out, black has become "a symbol of quality—a status connotation, elegant." In other words, it's associated in people's minds with high-class, expensive goods (a relevant point, since Sheba costs more than twice as much as several other brands).

Color is "a very powerful tool," notes Eric Johnson, head of Research Studies for the Chicago-based Institute for Color Research, which collects scientific information about the human response to color. A customer spends only the briefest amount of time at the supermarket deciding which products and which brands to buy, and the colors food manufacturers use to package their products are chosen with a great deal of care to sway you in what are sometimes split-second decisions.

But color is not all that's used to influence you at what marketers call the "point of purchase." The shape of a food package is meant to entice, too, as are (of course) various price promotions. Here's a look at color, shape, and a couple of other tricks of the trade that companies use to send silent messages to you when you're making choices about which products to buy.

## The color of your purchases

There has been "a longstanding understanding in industry that if you want to sell a product, package it in red and white," says The Consumer Network's Ms. Doyle. Think of Campbell's soup, Carnation Instant Breakfast, and Marlboro cigarettes, to name just a few red-and-white-packaged items. But the color field has been thrown open, so to speak. Take a look.

**Red** Red stimulates feelings of arousal and appetite. Indeed, the Institute for Color Research's Mr. Johnson explains that when the eye sees red, the pituitary gland sends out signals that make the heart beat faster, the blood pressure increase, and the muscles tense—all physiologic changes that can lead to the consummation of a purchase. (No wonder so many foods have red on their packaging.)

Red is also considered a "warm and inviting color," says Paul Brefka, a Boston-area product designer. You'll often see at least some red on boxes of pasta, he says. It evokes shared, hearty Italian meals.

**Green** "Thirty years ago, green was barf color," Ms. Doyle remarks. But then it "became associated with the environment, and that meant pro-health. It has morphed 180 degrees." Just how much green's reputation has come around has been underscored in a study conducted by Brian Wansink, PhD. The director of the University of Illinois Food & Brand Lab, which looks at how consumers make purchasing decisions at the point of sale, Dr. Wansink did a covert color switch on a popular sweet treat. He put O'Henry candy bars, normally found in yellow wrappers, into green ones. When the bars were seen in green, consumers said they had fewer calories, more protein, and fewer calories from fat than when they were in their usual packaging.

Green's effect is probably why Hershey's reduced-fat Sweet Escapes candy bars have green on their wrappers, just as Healthy Choice frozen dinners are packaged in largely-green boxes. Decaffeinated coffee tends to come wrapped in green, too, while regular coffee often comes in "robust" red.

**White** By itself, white suggests reduced calories. Sales of sugar-free Canada Dry Ginger Ale increased when its labels incorporated more white, Dr. Wansink says. Silver also means fewer calories. A bottle of Diet Coke is mostly silver; a bottle of regular Coke, mostly red.

**Yellow** Yellow is the fastest color that the brain processes, Mr. Johnson explains. Thus, he says, it's an "attention getter." There's also "a mythic thing about yellow being a happy color," he notes. For those reasons, it's not surprising that yellow is a very common color in supermarkets, appearing on everything from boxes of Cheerios to Domino Sugar to Triscuit wafers to Hellmann's mayonnaise.

**Orange** In sociologic studies, Mr. Johnson says, orange indicates affordability. It suggests, "I'm easy, I'm cheap," perhaps because it's not considered a classy color. But its suggestion of accessibility and affordability make it a good color for such "Everyman" products as Arm & Hammer Baking Soda, Burger King meals, and Stouffer's frozen entrees.

**Brown** Rich browns indicate "roasted" or "baked" says Mr. Johnson, which is why you'll often see brown as a background color on things like bags and boxes of gravy and cake mixes. Brown also suggests rich flavor—a reason it often appears on cans of coffee.

**Blue** You won't find a preponderance of foods packaged in blue. People generally want the colors on their boxes, bottles, and cans to reflect what's inside. Mr. Johnson puts it this way: "Human beings require congruency of color in order to buy the goods. People will not buy baked beans in a purple can. Beans are not purple."

Interestingly, that is not so for children, who think incongruously colored foods and food packages are "fun." That's why there has been, for instance, blue Kool-Aid, blue popcorn, and blue candies.

## The shape of things to come... into your home

Most instant coffee comes in cylindrical jars—but not Taster's Choice. It's packaged in a deep square jar. The reason: Nestle, Taster's Choice's maker, felt it would provide more of an image of a "hefty" taste if presented that way—a sort of antidote to people's assumption that freeze-dried coffee crystals can't pack a hearty flavor.

Nestle, of course, is not the only company that pays careful attention to the shape of its packaging. "Shape is probably the hottest tactic in differentiating brands," says Jim Peters, editor-in-chief of *Brand-Packaging* magazine. Ms. Doyle agrees that package shape has become an extremely important marketing tool.

Just think about the "sensuous, literally provocative shapes of today's packages," she says, giving ice cream containers as an example. They used to be "brick-like," she says—utilitarian. Now, they're "more hand-friendly, sensuous," she notes—round, oval, trapezoidal. It's thought that because ice cream is an indulgence product, she explains, it "should have an indulgent look and feel."

Even dishwashing detergent containers are "tactile, designed for the hand" today, she says. They all have "silhouette shapes—it's easy to look at them as a female form. They have a waist line. They're easy to hold." Which goes to show, she says, that "we're no longer Puritan in many ways."

## Bigger seen as better

Consumers often go for the larger size of a product at the supermarket. One reason, of course, is that bigger is generally seen as cheaper on a per-ounce basis. In addition, a larger container is thought to last longer, saving the shopper from having to schlep back to the supermarket as quickly to restock. Neither is necessarily the case.

On a recent trip to the grocery store, we found that a 40-ounce jar of Heinz Tomato Ketchup, at $2.49, cost 6.2 cents an ounce, whereas the smaller, 28-ounce bottle, at $1.49, was only 5.3 cents an ounce. It was a similar story with some cereals. A 24-ounce box of Kellogg's Corn Flakes cost 12.5 cents an ounce, but the littler, 18-ounce box came to just 11.9 cents an ounce.

That happens about 10 percent of the time, Dr. Wansink says. The way around it is simple. Simply check "unit prices" listed on supermarket shelves, which list the price by the pound next to the price for a particular-size container. That way, you can be certain that the size you take is the best buy that day. (Prices and deals change frequently from shopping trip to shopping trip.)

As for the bigger-package-lasts-longer tack, the reason it might not work is that people tend to take bigger portions from bigger containers. Dr. Wansink made the discovery when he asked 98 women in New Hampshire and Vermont to take enough spaghetti from a box to make dinner for two. When they took spaghetti from a 1-pound box, they averaged 234 strands each. When they took it from a larger, 2-pound box on a separate occasion, they averaged 302 strands each—a 29 percent increase (and a 105-calorie difference per serving).

The same thing happened with cooking oil. The women poured 3.5 ounces into a pan when they poured it from a 16-ounce bottle; 4.3 ounces from a 32-ounce bottle (a difference of 192 calories).

All packaged foods list serving sizes on the Nutrition Facts panel. But, says Dr. Wansink, "few people appear to read them."

### Some Grocery Aisle Counter-Tricks of Your Own

***To keep from buying too many supermarket products that you didn't plan to buy...***

**1. Make a grocery list before leaving the house.**

**2. Write down how many of each item you need so you won't be swayed by signs and placards to buy more than you really want.**

**3. Don't automatically reach for the largest size; it's not always the cheapest on an ounce-for-ounce basis. Check units prices (price per pound) on shelves to make sure the size you purchase is the best buy.**

## "Limit: 2 per customer" and other messages by the numbers

Sometimes it's not the package itself that does the enticing but the sign above it. A limit on how many boxes or bottles the shopper is allowed to take can be particularly effective, as Dr. Wansink demonstrated when he experimented with signs for displays of canned soup in a Sioux City, Iowa, grocery store. When consumers saw soup for 79 cents a can with no limit on how many they could purchase, they typically bought three to four cans. But when the display was changed to limit the purchase to 12 cans, they purchased as many as seven cans each, increasing sales by 112 percent.

Ironically, when supermarkets set a limit like that, they often are not trying to get consumers to buy more of a particular product; they simply are trying to make sure people don't buy too much of it. Such products are frequently loss leaders—items that are marked down so much the store loses money on them in an effort to lead people in so they will end up doing the rest of their shopping there.

"Limit" signs are not the only kind to get people to buy more of a product. Even a sign that says "4 cans for $4" as opposed to "1 can for $1" makes people buy more, Dr. Wansink explains, because it "anchors" people to a higher number. When he manipulated supermarket signs to give prices for multiple units of an item instead of the price for a single package, sales increased 32 percent in 12 out of 13 categories, including cookies, frozen dinners, and soft drinks.

Straightforward suggestions to buy a certain amount, as in "Buy 18 Snickers Bars for Your Freezer," also make people buy more than twice as much as when a sign simply says, "Buy Snickers Bars for Your Freezer." When Dr. Wansink put up a sign for Snickers Bars in a Philadelphia convenience store that did not include any suggestions on how many bars people should buy, they tended to buy one each. But when the sign suggested to people that they buy 18, they bought an average of three.

"People say, 'I'm not going to buy 18!'" Dr. Wansink explains. But they're still influenced to buy more than they would otherwise. Even signs stamped on cartons that say things like "Shipped to stores in boxes of 28 units" make people buy more, Dr. Wansink says.

Fortunately, he points out, the numbers game is very easy to get around. All you have to do is write quantities next to the items on your grocery list. That anchors you to a number of your own choosing before you even walk inside the store.

---

# UNIT 2

# Nutrients

## Unit Selections



## Key Points to Consider

- Check out several labels from foods containing fats and oils that you eat frequently. Can you tell how much trans fat each contains? Determine the percentage of your average daily calories that is contributed by total fat and saturated fat. What do your calculations tell you about potential health risks?
- Are some nutrients more important than others in maintaining health? Support your answer.
- What are the best ways to supplement your diet with vitamins and minerals?
- What kinds of interactions do some drugs have on foods?

**Links: www.dushkin.com/online/**
These sites are annotated in the World Wide Web pages.

**Dole 5 A Day: Nutrition, Fruits & Vegetables**
*http://www.dole5aday.com*

**Food and Nutrition Information Center**
*http://www.nal.usda.gov/fnic/*

**Nutrient Data Laboratory**
*http://www.nal.usda.gov/fnic/foodcomp/*

**NutritionalSupplements.com**
*http://www.nutritionalsupplements.com*

**University of Pennsylvania Library**
*http://www.library.upenn.edu/resources/websitest.html*

**U.S. National Library of Medicine**
*http://www.nlm.nih.gov*

This unit focuses on the most recent advances that have been reported on nutrients and their role in health and disease. With the onset and development of new technologies in the area of nutrition, the plethora of information on the role of certain nutrients, and the speed with which information is printed and disseminated, even the professional has a very hard time keeping up with the data. The media reports any sensational, even erroneous data, which confuses the public and creates many misunderstandings. Consumers should remember that preliminary findings have to undergo rigorous testing in animal models and clinical trials before they are accepted and implemented by the scientific community.

Additionally, how individuals will respond to dietary changes will depend on their genetic makeup along with other environmental factors. Thus, the National Academy of Sciences has a difficult task in trying to establish exact amounts of nutrients that will cover the requirements but not create toxicity in the long run for the majority of the population.

The articles of this unit have been selected to present current knowledge about nutrients resulting from state-of-the-art research and controversies brewing at the present time. Articles related to nutrient function and their effects on chronic disease such as cardiovascular disease, cancer, and osteoporosis are included. A topic that has serious implications for health, which is not given enough attention, is that of drug/nutrient interactions. Unfortunately many unnecessary deaths or organ malfunctions occur because of these interactions. It seems that the consumer is not aware of or educated about these potential life-threatening effects. Increased awareness, especially among the elderly and low-literacy individuals, should reduce their occurrence.

High protein diets have been the rage recently. People go on these diets unaware of the ill effects on the body. The American Heart Association Science Advisory Committee discusses the role of protein in the diet and criticizes these diets in that they restrict healthful foods and thus compromise vitamin and mineral intake as well as place people at risk for heart, renal, bone, and liver abnormalities.

Another area of perennial controversy concerns fats and the various types of fat. Americans have focused on single ingredients, attempting to exclude them from food. This has resulted in the proliferation of low-fat products that are not necessarily low in calories. Trans fatty acids that arise from food processing, which converts liquid oils to solid margarines, are as harmful to heart health as saturated fat. Since no labeling exists for fried foods, baked goods, and food purchased in restaurants, the consumer should avoid them, using instead soft or semi-liquid margarine or olive oil, thus limiting trans fat in the diet.

Consumers have misinterpreted the advice to choose a diet low in fat as eliminating all fat from their diet. As research notes, a diet moderate in total fat is advised, especially incorporating omega-3 fatty acids found in fish such as tuna and salmon. Omega-3 fatty acids promote heart health and eye health and have beneficial effects on the immune system.

Osteoporosis is a debilitating disease whose incidence is steadily increasing worldwide as the population is getting older and pollution gets worse in major cities around the world. Carol Coughlin updates us on the role of nutrients in osteoporosis prevention. Not only do we need optimal calcium in our diet but also a number of other nutrients (such as vitamins D, K, and B12) and minerals (such as phosphorus, magnesium, boron, and fluoride) to maintain optimal bone mass throughout life.

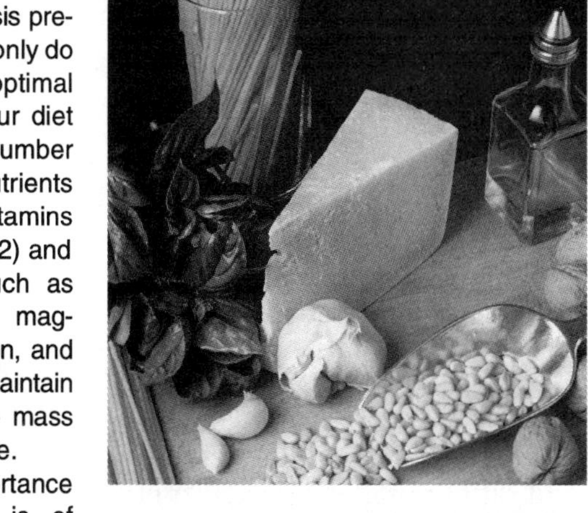

The importance of vitamins is of great interest to consumers because vitamins have been touted to cure and/or prevent disease. It is also the favorite area of many quacks and health-promotion salespeople. Recent research about vitamins provides insights into their functions but also alerts the consumer to be careful of megadosing, because vitamins may have pharmacological effects.

One common fear among aging Americans and baby boomers is memory loss. This has resulted in the increased intake of vitamin supplements. Evidence on the role of B-complex vitamins and vitamins E, K, and C on brain function and memory is still sketchy and far from conclusive. Americans in large numbers are taking supplements either to bolster their diet or protect against chronic disease, but they are not aware of when, how, and in what form the vitamins should be taken. They are also unaware of vitamin and mineral interactions that may either enhance or limit the absorption of their supplements. Practical advice offered by professionals is very important to increase consumer awareness and dispel many myths perpetuated from unreliable sources. The National Tolerable Upper Intake Levels that have been recently issued by the National Academy of Sciences protect the consumer from ingesting too much of one nutrient.

Finally, both professionals and consumers are not paying attention to the area of drug/nutrient interactions. This area becomes especially important among the elderly and people with chronic diseases who take a large number of different kinds of medications, as it may bring about primary or secondary nutrient deficiencies and lead to malnutrition. Potentially detrimental effects on body systems and compromising a person's nutritional status as well as death may result from such interactions. Educating the public as to the health problems that may be precipitated by interactions of different categories of drugs and food is crucial to public health, as the last article in this unit points out.

# Dietary Protein and Weight Reduction

## A Statement for Healthcare Professionals From the Nutrition Committee of the Council on Nutrition, Physical Activity, and Metabolism of the American Heart Association

Sachiko T. St. Jeor, RD PhD; Barbara V. Howard, PhD; T. Elaine Prewitt, RD DrPH;
Vicki Bovee, RD MS; Terry Bazzarre, PhD; Robert H. Eckel, MD;
for the AHA Nutrition Committee

***Abstract***—High-protein diets have recently been proposed as a "new" strategy for successful weight loss. However, variations of these diets have been popular since the 1960s. High-protein diets typically offer wide latitude in protein food choices, are restrictive in other food choices (mainly carbohydrates), and provide structured eating plans. They also often promote misconceptions about carbohydrates, insulin resistance, ketosis, and fat burning as mechanisms of action for weight loss. Although these diets may not be harmful for most healthy people for a short period of time, there are no long-term scientific studies to support their overall efficacy and safety. These diets are generally associated with higher intakes of total fat, saturated fat, and cholesterol because the protein is provided mainly by animal sources. In high-protein diets, weight loss is initially high due to fluid loss related to reduced carbohydrate intake, overall caloric restriction, and ketosis-induced appetite suppression. Beneficial effects on blood lipids and insulin resistance are due to the weight loss, not to the change in caloric composition. Promoters of high-protein diets promise successful results by encouraging high-protein food choices that are usually restricted in other diets, thus providing initial palatability, an attractive alternative to other weight-reduction diets that have not worked for a variety of reasons for most individuals. High-protein diets are not recommended because they restrict healthful foods that provide essential nutrients and do not provide the variety of foods needed to adequately meet nutritional needs. Individuals who follow these diets are therefore at risk for compromised vitamin and mineral intake, as well as potential cardiac, renal, bone, and liver abnormalities overall.

**Key Words:** AHA Science Advisory • diet • nutrition • protein • obesity

Because more than half of all adults in the United States are either overweight or obese[1-3] and because these conditions are associated with increased risk of heart disease, overall morbidity, diabetes, hypertension, dyslipidemia, stroke, gallbladder disease, osteoarthritis, sleep apnea, and respiratory problems, as well as some forms of cancer, effective weight reduction and maintenance strategies are needed.[4] Americans are concerned about what they are eating, as demonstrated by an overall decline in the proportion of total fat intake to ≈34% of kilocalories per day. However, there has been an apparent concomitant increase in total energy intake in the average US adult,[4] and significant weight gains have been observed over time. It is evident that weight-reduction efforts have met with limited success and that the treatment of obesity is complex and difficult. Importantly, most American adults are dieting.[5] Thus, the popularity of diet books promoting high-protein intakes with emphasis on some form of carbohydrate restriction is of concern to informed health professionals because of the lack of scientific evidence to support their claims and their long-term adverse implications for overall health.[6,7]

Although consensus exists that caloric restriction promotes weight loss, the effect of varying the macronutrient composition of the diet on weight loss has been debated. Diets with altered levels of protein, carbohydrate, or fat are frequently popular with the dieting public, which is desperate to find new strategies for successful weight loss and maintenance. Attention continues to be focused on modification of fat and carbohydrate intake, because these are the major contributors of energy in the diet. However, controversies regarding the efficacy, benefits, and consequences of high-carbohydrate and/or low-fat diets in weight-management efforts frequently pique interest in high-protein diets as alternative strategies.

**TABLE 1. Protein Intake at Various Levels of Energy Intake**

| Energy Intake, kcal/d | Low-Protein Diet (<10% kcal) | Average Diet (≈15% kcal) | High-Protein Diet (≥20% kcal) | Very-High-Protein Diet (≥30% kcal) |
|---|---|---|---|---|
| 1200 | 30 | 45 | 60 | 90 |
| 2000 | 50 | 75 | 100 | 150 |
| 3000 | 75 | 112 | 150 | 225 |

Data are from Reference 24. Protein intake is in grams per day.

This advisory provides a brief overview regarding the role of protein in the diet and reviews the recent popular high-protein diets and summarizes their limitations. This advisory also builds on and extends recommendations of the current American Heart Association Dietary Guidelines[8] to include considerations regarding high-protein intake specifically for purposes of weight reduction. New guidelines for evaluating high-protein diets are provided.

## Role of Protein in the Diet

Proteins are essential components of the body and are required for the body's structure and proper function. Proteins function as enzymes, hormones, and antibodies, as well as transport and structural components. Transamination and oxidation result in elimination of protein as water, carbon dioxide, and nitrogen.[9,10] The continual process of synthesis and subsequent breakdown of protein in the body is referred to as protein turnover. The rate of protein turnover affects organ protein mass, body size, and ultimately the body's protein and amino acid requirements.[10,11]

Amino acids[11] are the central units in protein metabolism. They are incorporated into various proteins and converted to metabolically essential compounds (ie, nucleic acids, creatine, and porphyrins). Of the ≈20 amino acids in human proteins, 12 are manufactured by the body and are known as nonessential amino acids. The remaining 8 (isoleucine, leucine, lysine, methionine, phenylalanine, threonine, tryptophan, and valine) must be obtained from the diet and are thus termed essential amino acids. Proper protein nutriture is based on proper balance and sufficient intake of essential amino acids and intake of an adequate amount of nitrogen for the body to produce the nonessential amino acids.[12] The nutritional quality of food proteins varies and depends on essential amino acid composition. Foods that contain essential amino acids at levels that facilitate tissue growth and repair are known as complete protein foods. Such foods are also classified as having high biological value, ie, a large proportion of protein is absorbed and retained. Biological value refers to an index in which all protein sources are compared with egg whites, which provide the most complete protein and have the highest biological value of 100. In general, foods with high protein quality or high biological value are from animal sources, such as eggs, milk, meat, poultry, and fish.

Conversely, a low concentration of 1 or more essential amino acids in a food lowers its nutritional quality. Although plant proteins form a large part of the human diet, most are deficient in 1 or more essential amino acids and are therefore regarded as incomplete proteins. Their protein quality can be upgraded, however, by combining them with others that are higher in protein quality or that contain whatever essential amino acids are lacking or deficient (protein complementarity).[9,10,13] For example, combining corn (limited in lysine) with beans (limited in methionine) results in a high-quality protein food combination. Thus, the requirement for adequate essential amino acids can be met in a vegetarian diet by mixing foods of complementary amino acid composition.[12-14] Only a few dietary sources of pure protein do not contain fat or carbohydrates, eg, egg white (albumin) and powdered casein from milk. Most high-protein foods contain fat (eg, meat, fish, and poultry) and/or carbohydrates (eg, milk, fruit, vegetables, legumes, nuts, breads, and cereals). Lean animal protein sources and vegetable proteins can be incorporated easily into a healthy diet plan.

An average of 102 g of protein per person per day is available in the US food supply.[15] Actual protein consumption ranges from 88 to 92 g for men and from 63 to 66 g for women.[16] Animal products provide ≈75% of the essential amino acids in the food supply, followed by dairy products, cereal products, eggs, legumes, fruits, and vegetables.[16] The recommended daily allowance (RDA) for protein of high biological value for adults, based on body weight, is ≈0.8 g/kg[17] or 0.36 g/lb. There are many conditions in which extra protein is needed, including childhood/adolescence (ie, periods of growth), pregnancy, lactation, intense strength and endurance training and other forms of physical activity, some disease states, and possibly in the elderly.[18] In the general population, however, protein intake above the required amount is inefficiently used by the body and imposes the additional burdens of metabolizing and excreting excess waste products (eg, urea and ammonia) by the liver and kidney.[19-22]

Low-protein diets (<10% of total energy) are sometimes prescribed to treat kidney and liver disorders.[23] For weight reduction, however, high-protein diets (≥20% of total energy) and very-high-protein diets (≥30% of total energy) have become popular. Protein intakes at various levels of energy intake are summarized in Table 1.[24] At high levels of total energy intake (3000 kcal/d) and very high levels of protein intake (≥30% of kilocalories), protein can exceed 225 g/d (2 to 4 times the range in the typical diet of 50 to 100 g/d). In general, diets with excess total protein raise concerns as outlined below. High-protein diets with carbohydrate restriction (as promoted for weight reduction) are generally self-limiting, and caloric intake rarely exceeds 1500 kcal/d.[7] On the other hand, low-calorie diets (1200 kcal/d) may lack sufficient protein quality and quantity and should be carefully evaluated for protein adequacy.

## TABLE 2. Compensatory Changes in the Macronutrient Composition of Various Diets

| Diet Description | Fat (% kcal) | Carbohydrate (% kcal) | Protein (% kcal) | Alcohol (% kcal) |
|---|---|---|---|---|
| Average diet | 34 | 49 | 14 | 3 |
| Moderate-fat diet | 30 | 55 | 15 | ... |
| Very-low-fat/ very-high-carbohydrate diet | 15 | 70 | 15 | ... |
| Low-carbohydrate/ very-high-protein diet | 30 | 40 | 30 | ... |
| Very-low-carbohydrate/ very-high-protein/ fat diet | 55 | 15 | 30 | ... |

## High-Protein Diets and Weight Reduction

Weight reduction is achieved if there is an energy deficit, that is, if caloric intake is reduced below the level of energy expenditure. In obese individuals, macronutrient composition of the diet has little effect on the rate or magnitude of weight loss over the short term unless nutrient composition influences caloric intake.[25-27] Importantly, however, overall caloric intake depends on the overall palatability of the diet and satiety. The current average macronutrient composition of the American diet is 12% to 16% of calories from protein, 34% from fat, and 49% from carbohydrate.[15,16,24] The majority of dietary advice has focused on the fat content of the diet because fats provide ≈9 kcal/g, whereas protein and carbohydrate provide ≈4 kcal/g. However, the essentiality and palatability of protein have led periodically to its popularity in numerous diets.[28-31]

Major shifts in the proportion of one macronutrient result in compensatory changes in the other macronutrients.[24] Variations in macronutrients in various diets are presented for comparisons in Table 2. Many of the popular high-protein diets promote protein intakes of 71 to 162 g/d, or 28% to 64% of energy, and severely limit carbohydrates to 7 to 56 g/d, or 3% to 16% of energy.[28-32]

High-protein, high-fat diets induce metabolic ketosis and are initially attractive because they may induce quick weight loss. This initial weight loss, however, may be attributed in part to the diuretic effect from low carbohydrate intake and its effects on sodium and water loss, glycogen depletion, and ketosis. As the diet is sustained, loss of appetite associated with ketosis leads to lower total caloric intake.[33] High-protein diets of ≥30% kilocalories from protein also can promote negative energy balance due to significant restriction in the type and amount of foods eaten. The structured eating plan, strict eating schedules, and limited tolerance for high-protein foods reduce overall flexibility but offer initial appeal. These characteristics may help limit caloric intake and may account for weight loss. However, neither the efficacy of these diets compared with higher carbohydrate diets in promoting weight loss nor the safety of these diets has been documented in long-term studies.

The amount of protein recommended in high-protein diet regimens exceeds established requirements[19] and may impose significant health risks. First, animal protein (rather than plant-based proteins that also contain carbohydrates) is generally advocated in these diets. A diet rich in animal protein, saturated fat, and cholesterol raises low-density lipoprotein (LDL) cholesterol levels, an effect that is compounded when high-carbohydrate, high-fiber plant foods that help lower cholesterol are limited or eliminated.[16,34-37] Furthermore, a high-carbohydrate diet that includes fruit, vegetables, nonfat dairy products, and whole grains has been shown to lower blood pressure,[38] so limitation of these foods may raise blood pressure via associated reductions in potassium, calcium, and magnesium coupled with increased sodium intake. High-protein foods such as meat, poultry, seafood, eggs, seeds, and nuts are high in purines. Purines are broken down into uric acid, so excess consumption of these foods increases uric acid levels and may cause gout in susceptible individuals.[39] A surplus of protein in the system also increases urinary calcium loss, which may facilitate osteoporosis.[40] In addition, elimination or severe restriction of fruit, vegetables, beans, and whole grains from the diet may increase cancer risk.[41] A very-high-protein diet is especially risky for patients with diabetes, because it can speed the progression, even for short lengths of time, of diabetic renal disease.[42-44] Finally, because food choices may be severely restricted on high-protein diets, healthful foods such as low-fat milk products, cereals, grains, fruits, and vegetables (which are higher in carbohydrates and contain essential nutrients) are also generally restricted or eliminated.[28-32] This can lead to deficiencies in essential vitamins, minerals, and fiber over the long term; these deficiencies can have adverse health effects if they are allowed to persist. Furthermore, when carbohydrates are severely restricted with high-protein diets, fatigue often occurs when muscle glycogen is depleted during bouts of exercise.[45] Some popular high-protein/low-carbohydrate diets limit carbohydrates to 10 to 20 g/d,[6] which is one fifth of the minimum 100 g/d that is necessary to prevent loss of lean muscle tissue.

Several high-protein diets are described in Table 3. These diets are also evaluated according to the evaluation criteria listed in Table 4. A popular premise of high-protein diets is that excess carbohydrate results in elevated insulin levels, which in turn promotes storage of body fat and other metabolic consequences. To induce weight loss, the high ratio of protein and fat to carbohydrate purportedly promotes metabolic changes that reduce serum insulin levels. However, in fact, protein intake also stimulates insulin secretion.[46] Insulin resistance or hyperinsulinemia is complex and regulated by a number of interacting factors. It occurs as a result of obesity or excess fat storage and lack of physical activity, and it can be reduced significantly by caloric restriction, weight loss, and exercise.[47-50] Changes in calorie balance over wide ranges of fat intake apparently do not influence insulin action in humans.[51]

## TABLE 3. Diet Summaries

| | Atkins[29] | Zone[30] | Protein Power[31] | Sugar Busters[32] | Stillman[28] |
|---|---|---|---|---|---|
| Diet philosophy | Eating too many carbohydrates causes obesity and other health problems; ketosis leads to decreased hunger | Eating the right combination of foods leads to metabolic state at which body functions at peak performance, leading to decreased hunger, weight loss, and increased energy | Eating carbohydrates releases insulin in large quantities, which contributes to obesity and other health problems | Sugar is toxic to the body and causes release of insulin, which promotes fat storage | High-protein foods burn body fat. If carbohydrates are consumed, the body stores fat instead of burning it |
| Foods to eat | Meat, fish, poultry, eggs, cheese, low-carbohydrate vegetables, butter, oil; no alcohol | Protein, fat, carbohydrates must be eaten in exact proportions (40/30/30). Low-glycemic-index foods, alcohol in moderation | Meat, fish, poultry, eggs, cheese, low-carbohydrate vegetables, butter, oil, salad dressings, alcohol in moderation | Protein and fat. Low-glycemic-index foods. Olive oil, canola oil, and alcohol in moderation | Lean meats, skinless poultry, lean fish and seafood, eggs, cottage cheese, skim-milk cheeses; no alcohol |
| Foods to avoid | Carbohydrates, specifically bread, pasta, most fruits and vegetables, milk | Carbohydrates, specifically bread, pasta, fruit (some types), saturated fats | Carbohydrates | Potatoes, white rice, corn, carrots, beets, white bread, all refined white flour products | All carbohydrates: bread, pasta, fruit, vegetables, fats, oils, dairy products |
| Diet composition—average for 3 days | Protein 27%; carbohydrates 5%; fat 68% (saturated 26%) | Protein 34%; carbohydrates 36%; fat 29% (saturated 9%); alcohol 1% | Protein 26%; carbohydrates 16%; fat 54% (saturated 18%); alcohol 4% | Protein 27%; carbohydrates 52%; fat 21% (saturated 4%) | protein 64%; carbohydrates 3%; fat 33% (saturated 13%) |
| Recommended supplements | Atkins supplement that includes chromium picolinate, carnitine, coenzyme Q10 | 200 IU vitamin E | Multivitamin and mineral supplement | No | Multivitamin and mineral supplement |
| Health claims scientifically proven? | No long-term, validated studies published | No. Theories and long-term results are not validated | No long-term, validated studies published | No long-term, validated studies published | No long-term, validated studies published |
| Practicality | Limited food choices. Difficult to eat in restaurants because only plain protein sources and limited vegetables/salads allowed | Food must be eaten in required proportions of protein, fat, carbohydrates. Menus plain and not appealing; vegetable portions very large. Difficult to calculate portions | Not practical for long term. Rigid rules | Eliminates many carbohydrate foods. Discourages eating fruit with meals | Extreme limitations in food choices. Very little variety |
| Lose and maintain weight? | Yes, but initial weight loss is mostly water. Does not promote a positive attitude toward food groups. Difficult to maintain long-term because diet restricts food choices | Yes, via caloric restriction. Could result in weight maintenance if carefully followed. Diet rigid and difficult to maintain | Yes, via caloric restriction. Limited food choices not practical for long term | Yes, via caloric restriction. Limited food choices not practical for long term | Yes, but loss is mostly water. Maintenance based on strict calorie counting. Very limited food choices not practical for long term |

**TABLE 4. Compliance With AHA Criteria for High-Protein Diets**

| AHA Protein Criteria | Atkins[29] | Zone[30] | Protein Power[31] | Sugar Busters[32] | Stillman[28] |
|---|---|---|---|---|---|
| Total protein is not excessive (average 50-100 g/d, proportional 15-20% kcal/day to carbohydrates and fat) | No. 1st 2 weeks = 125 g/d (36%) Ongoing weight loss = 161 g/d (35%) Maintenance = 110 g/d (24%0 | No. 127 g/d (34%) | No. 91 g/d (26%) | No. 71 g/d (27%) | No. 162 g/d (64%) |
| Carbohydrates are not omitted or severely restricted. Minimum of 100 g/d | No. 1st 2 weeks = 28 g/d (5%) Ongoing weight loss = 33 g/d Maintenance = Yes 128 g/d | Yes. 135 g/d (36%) | No. 56 g/d (16%) | Yes. 114 g/d (52%) | No. 7 g/d (3%) |
| Total fat (30%) and saturated fat (10%) are not excessive | No. 1st 2 weeks = 53% fat, 26% saturated fat per day | Yes. 29% total calories, 4% saturated fat per day | No. 54% total fat, 18% saturated fat per day. | Yes. 21% total calories, 4% saturated fat per day | No. 33% total calories, 13% saturate fat per day |
| Total diet can be safely implemented over the long term by providing nutrient adequacy and support a healthful eating plan to prevent increases in disease risk | No. Limited food choices. Diet low in fiber, vitamin D, thiamine, pantothenic acid, copper, magnesium, manganese, potassium, calcium.* High in total fat and saturated fat | No. Food must be eaten in required proportions of protein, fat, carbohydrates. Menus not appealing, vegetable portions very large. Low in copper* | No. Not practical for long term. Rigid rules. Diet low in calcium, fiber, pantothenic acid, copper, manganese.* High in total fat and saturated fat | No. Eliminates many carbohydrate foods. Discourages eating fruit with meals. Low in calcium, vitamin D, vitamin E, pantothenic acid, copper, potassium* | No. Eliminates many foods. Diet low in fiber, vitamin A, thiamine, vitamin C, vitamin D, folate, pantothenic acid, calcium, copper, magnesium, manganese, potassium* |

*Nutrients <67% RDA for women 25-50 years old.

There are very few long-term studies of high-protein diets. One randomized dietary intervention study[52] in 65 healthy overweight men and women that compared 2 ad lib diets varying in protein content (12% versus 25% of kilocalories from protein) demonstrated larger weight losses with the higher-protein diet (8.9 kg) versus the lower-protein diet (5.1 kg) over 6 months. However, another study[53] showed similar weight losses with diets of varying protein and fat composition, which indicates that total energy intake is the most important determinant for weight loss. The short-term effects of high-protein diets have been appraised mainly in terms of increased weight loss and its associated benefits. Deleterious effects on cardiovascular disease risk factors were demonstrated in a study[37] of 24 obese individuals who followed the Atkins diet for 3 months, in whom caloric intake declined but LDL cholesterol levels rose despite the weight loss. Most of the weight loss occurred in the first few weeks, which suggests the combined effects of fluid loss and potential anorectic effects of induced ketosis.

A recent review of the literature regarding the effects of low-carbohydrate (high-protein) diets reported from 1956 to 2000 concluded from 20 published studies that there is a pattern of weight loss that ranges from 2.8 to 12.0 kg within varying time frames and number and type of subjects included.[6,7] However, when carbohydrate is restricted, subjects generally reduce their overall intake of calories, and this calorie deficit is related to the weight loss. These studies raised important questions regarding the long-term effects of these diets on weight maintenance and overall health. Long-term studies are needed to determine the overall safety and efficacy of high-protein diets. In particular, benefits and potential risks beyond the initial weight loss observed should be addressed.

## Guidelines for Evaluating High-Protein Diets

In evaluating high-protein diets, it is important to ensure that eating patterns follow the AHA Dietary Guidelines[8] and incorporate primary prevention strategies for coronary heart disease, such as those outlined by the National Cholesterol Education Program,[54] especially in persons with multiple risk factors, including obesity:

1. Total protein intake should not be excessive (average 50 to 100 g/d) and should be reasonably proportional (≈15% of kilocalories per day) to carbohydrate (≈55% of kilocalories per day) and fat (≈30% of kilocalories per day) intake.
2. Carbohydrates should not be omitted or severely restricted. A minimum of 100 g of carbohydrate per day is recommended to ensure overall nutritional adequacy through the provision of a variety of healthful foods.
3. Selected protein foods should not contribute excess total fat, saturated fat, or cholesterol.
4. The diet should be safely implemented over the long term, ie, it should provide adequate nutrients and support dietary compliance with a healthful eating plan to prevent increases in disease risk.

## Summary

Scientific studies do not demonstrate that high-protein diets without concomitant decreases in caloric intake result in sustained weight loss or improved health. Most Americans consume more protein than their bodies need. Extra protein is not used efficiently by the body and may impose a metabolic burden on the kidneys and liver. High-protein diets may also be associated with increased risk for coronary heart disease due to intakes of saturated fat, cholesterol, and other associated dietary factors. When diets high in protein are severely limited in carbohydrates, food choices become restrictive, and overall nutrient adequacy and long-term palatability are also of concern. Successful weight loss occurs most frequently when a nutritionally adequate diet that allows for caloric deficits (≈500 kcal/d for each 1 lb lost per week) is tailored according to individual food preferences. A minimum of 1200 kcal/d for women and 1500 kcal/d for men should be provided. Total energy deficit has the greatest overall impact on weight reduction, especially when coupled with increased physical activity and behavior modification to maintain negative energy balance. Over the long term, diet composition should be consistent with a balanced eating plan that supports weight maintenance and lowers chronic disease risk.

## Footnote

The American Heart Association makes every effort to avoid any actual or potential conflicts of interest that may arise as a result of an outside relationship or a personal, professional, or business interest of a member of the writing panel. Specifically, all members of the writing group are required to complete and submit a Disclosure Questionnaire showing all such relationships that might be perceived as real or potential conflicts of interest.

This statement was approved by the American Heart Association Science Advisory and Coordinating Committee in June 2001. A single reprint is available by calling 800-242-8721 (US only) or writing the American Heart Association, Public Information, 7272 Greenville Ave, Dallas, TX 75231-4596. Ask for reprint No. 71-0211.

## References


1. Mokdad AH, Serdula MK, Dietz WH, et al. The spread of the obesity epidemic in the United States, 1991–1998. *JAMA*. 1999; 282: 1519–1522.
2. Flegal KM, Carroll MD, Kuczmarski RJ, et al. Overweight and obesity in the United States: prevalence and trends, 1960–1994. *Int J Obes Relat Metab Disord*. 1998; 22: 39–47.
3. Kuczmarski RJ, Carroll MD, Flegal KM, et al. Varying body mass index cutoff points to describe overweight prevalence among US adults: NHANES III (1988 to 1994). *Obes Res*. 1997; 5: 542–548.
4. National Heart, Lung, and Blood Institute, National Institute of Diabetes and Digestive and Kidney Diseases. Obesity education initiative. In: *Clinical Guidelines on the Identification, Evaluation, and Treatment of Overweight and Obesity in Adults: The Evidence Report*. Bethesda, Md: National Heart, Lung, and Blood Institute, in cooperation with the National Institute of Diabetes and Digestive and Kidney Diseases; 1998:12–19. NIH publication No. 98-4083.
5. Serdula MK, Mokdad AH, Williamson DF, et al. Prevalence of attempting weight loss and strategies for controlling weight. *JAMA*. 1999; 282: 1353–1358.
6. Kennedy ET, Bowman SA, Spence JT, et al. Popular diets: correlation to health, nutrition, and obesity. *J Am Diet Assoc*. 2001; 101: 411–420.
7. Freedman MR. *Popular Diets: A Scientific Review*. Washington, DC: USDA Office of Research, Education and Economics; 2000: 1–8.
8. Krauss RM, Eckel RH, Howard B, et al. AHA Dietary Guidelines: revision 2000: a statement for healthcare professionals from the Nutrition Committee of the American Heart Association. *Circulation*. 2000; 102: 2284–2299.
9. Kreutler P, Czajka-Narins D. Protein.In: *Nutrition in Perspective*. Upper Saddle River, NJ: Prentice Hall; 1987: 121–162.
10. Matthews D. Proteins and amino acids.In: Shils M, Olson J, Shike M, et al, eds. *Modern Nutrition in Health and Disease*. 9th ed. Baltimore, Md: Williams & Wilkins; 1999: 11–48.
11. Fuller M. Proteins and amino acid requirements.In: Stipanuk M, ed. *Biochemical and Physiological Aspects of Human Nutrition*. Philadelphia, Pa: WB Saunders; 2000: 287–304.
12. Berdanier C. Proteins.In: *Advanced Nutrition: Macronutrients*. 2nd ed. Boca Raton, Fla: CRC Press; 2000: 130–196.
13. Lappe FM. *Diet for a Small Planet*. New York, NY: Ballantine Books; 1971.
14. Committee on Diet and Health. Diet and health: protein.In: *Diet and Health: Implications for Reducing Chronic Disease Risk*. Washington, DC: National Research Council, Food and Nutrition Board; 1989: 259–271.
15. *Nationwide Food Consumption Survey: Nutrient Intakes: Individuals in 48 States*. Hyattsville, Md: US Dept of Agriculture, Consumer Nutrition Division, HNIS; 1977–1978. Report No. 1-2.
16. McDowell M, Briefel R, Alaimo K, et al. Energy and macronutrient intakes of persons ages 2 months and over in the United States: Third National Health and Nutrition Examination Survey, Phase 1, 1988–91. Washington, DC: US Government Printing Office, Vital and Health Statistics; 1994. CDC publication No. 255.
17. National Research Council, Food and Nutrition Board. *Recommended Dietary Allowances*. 10th ed. Washington, DC: National Academy Press; 1989.

18. Campbell WW, Crim MC, Dallal GE, et al. Increased protein requirements in elderly people: new data and retrospective reassessments. *Am J Clin Nutr.* 1994; 60: 501–509.
19. Rafoth RJ, Onstad GR. Urea synthesis after oral protein ingestion in man. *J Clin Invest.* 1975; 56: 1170–1174.
20. Fraser CL, Arieff AI. Hepatic encephalopathy. *N Engl J Med.* 1985; 313: 865–873.
21. Cottini EP, Gallina DL, Dominguez JM. Urea excretion in adult humans with varying degrees of kidney malfunction fed milk, eggs or an amino acid mixture: assessment of nitrogen balance. *J Nutr.* 1973; 103: 11–19.
22. Walser M, Mitch WE, Maroni BJ, et al. Should protein intake be restricted in predialysis patients? *Kidney Int.* 1999; 55: 771–777.
23. Barsotti G, Cupisti A, Barsotti M, et al. Dietary treatment of diabetic nephropathy with chronic renal failure. *Nephrol Dial Transplant.* 1998; 13 (suppl 8): 49–52.
24. St. Jeor ST, Ashley JM. Dietary strategies: issues of diet composition.In: Fletcher GF, Grundy SM, Hayman LL, eds. *Obesity: Impact on Cardiovascular Disease.* Armonk, NY: Futura Publishing Co; 1999: 233–246.
25. Hill JO, Peters JC, Reed GW, et al. Nutrient balance in humans: effects of diet composition. *Am J Clin Nutr.* 1991; 54: 10–17.
26. Golay A, Allaz A, Morel Y, et al. Similar weight loss with low- or high-carbohydrate diets. *Am J Clin Nutr.* 1996; 63: 174–178.
27. Hill JO, Drougas H, Peters JC. Obesity treatment: can diet composition play a role? *Ann Intern Med.* 1993; 119: 694–697.
28. Stillman IM, Baker SS. *The Doctor's Quick Weight Loss Diet.* New York, NY: Dell Publishing Co; 1967.
29. Atkins C. *Dr. Atkins' New Diet Revolution.* New York, NY: Avon Books; 1999.
30. Sears B. *The Zone.* New York, NY: Harper Collins; 1995.
31. Eades MR, Eades MD. *Protein Power.* New York, NY: Bantam Books; 1996.
32. Steward HL, Bethea MC, Andrews SS, et al. *Sugar Busters!* New York, NY: Ballantine Books; 1998.
33. Special Committee on Nutrition. A critique of low-carbohydrate ketogenic weight reduction regimens: a review of Dr. Atkins' diet revolution. *JAMA.* 1973; 224: 1415–1419.
34. Armstrong B, Doll R. Environmental factors and cancer incidence and mortality in different countries, with special reference to dietary practices. *Int J Cancer.* 1975; 15: 617–631.
35. Connor WE, Hodges RE, Bleiler RE. Effect of dietary cholesterol upon serum lipids in man. *J Lab Clin Med.* 1961; 57: 331–342.
36. Hegsted DM. Serum-cholesterol response to dietary cholesterol: a re-evaluation. *Am J Clin Nutr.* 1986; 44: 299–305.
37. Larosa JC, Fry AG, Muesing R, et al. Effects of high-protein, low-carbohydrate dieting on plasma lipoproteins and body weight. *J Am Diet Assoc.* 1980; 77: 264–270.
38. Appel LJ, Moore TJ, Obarzanek E, et al, the DASH Collaborative Research Group. A clinical trial of the effects of dietary patterns on blood pressure. *N Engl J Med.* 1997; 336: 1117–1124.
39. Franzese TA. Medical nutrition therapy for rheumatic disorders.In: Mahan LK, Escott-Stump S, eds. *Krause's Food, Nutrition, & Diet Therapy.* 10th ed. Philadelphia, Pa: WB Saunders; 2000: 970–986.
40. Barzel US, Massey LK. Excess dietary protein can adversely affect bone. *J Nutr.* 1998; 128: 1051–1053.
41. American Institute for Cancer Research. *Food, Nutrition and the Prevention of Cancer: A Global Perspective.* Washington, DC: World Cancer Research Fund/American Institute for Cancer Research; 1997.
42. Walker JD, Bending JJ, Dodds RA, et al. Restriction of dietary protein and progression of renal failure in diabetic nephropathy. *Lancet.* 1989; 2: 1411–1415.
43. American Diabetes Association. Nutrition recommendations and principles for people with diabetes mellitus. *Diabetes Care.* 1999; 22: S42–S45.
44. Henry RR. Protein content of the diabetic diet. *Diabetes Care.* 1994; 17: 1502–1513.
45. Costill DL, Hargreaves M. Carbohydrate nutrition and fatigue. *Sports Med.* 1992; 13: 86–92.
46. Liu Z, Long W, Hillier T, et al. Insulin regulation of protein metabolism in vivo. *Diabetes Nutr Metab.* 1999; 12: 421–428.
47. Drenick EJ, Brickman AS, Gold EM. Dissociation of the obesity-hyperinsulinism relationship following dietary restriction and hyperalimentation. *Am J Clin Nutr.* 1972; 25: 746–755.
48. Facchini F, Coulston AS, Reaven GM. Relation between dietary vitamin intake and resistance to insulin-mediated glucose disposal in healthy volunteers. *Am J Clin Nutr.* 1996; 63: 946–949.
49. Tremblay A. Nutritional determinants of the insulin resistance syndrome. *Int J Obes Relat Metab Disord.* 1995; 19 (suppl 1): S60–S68.
50. Yost TJ, Jensen DR, Haugen BR, et al. Effect of dietary macronutrient composition on tissue-specific lipoprotein lipase activity and insulin action in normal-weight subjects. *Am J Clin Nutr.* 1998; 68: 296–302.
51. Howard BV. Diet, insulin resistance, and atherosclerosis.In: Baba S, Kaneko T, eds. *Proceedings of the 15th International Diabetes Federation Congress, Kobe, 6–11 November 1994.* New York, NY: Elsevier; 1995: 446–450.International Congress Series 1100, Diabetes 1994.
52. Skov AR, Toubro S, Ronn B, et al. Randomized trial on protein vs carbohydrate in ad libitum fat reduced diet for the treatment of obesity. *Int J Obes Relat Metab Disord.* 1999; 23: 528–536.
53. Alford BB, Blankenship AC, Hagen RD. The effects of variations in carbohydrate, protein and fat content of the diet upon weight loss, blood values and nutrient intake of adult obese women. *J Am Diet Assoc.* 1990; 90: 534–540.
54. Executive summary of the Third Report of the National Cholesterol Education Program (NCEP) Expert Panel on Detection, Evaluation, and Treatment of High Blood Pressure (Adult Treatment Panel III). *JAMA.* 2001; 285: 2486–2497.

# Fats: The Good, the Bad, the Trans

## THE STORY

Fats are a dietary paradox. We need them for the essential fatty acids that keep cells healthy, and to help regulate important metabolic processes and transport certain vitamins throughout our bodies. But, for healthy hearts and arteries, we're encouraged to restrict fat to no more than 30 percent of our total daily calorie intake—or about 65 grams a day in a 2,000-calorie diet.

Scientists classify the fatty acids that make up the fat in food as saturated, monounsaturated or polyunsaturated, depending on the degree to which the molecules are saturated with hydrogen atoms (see box "Fat Facts"). While most of the fat we eat contains all three types, one usually predominates. Because saturated fat—the primary fat in red meat and many dairy products—raises blood levels of total and LDL (bad) cholesterol, we're advised to consume no more than 10 percent of total calories as saturated fat. At the other extreme, monounsaturated fats—found abundantly in canola and olive oil—are considered good fats because they lower LDL cholesterol without decreasing HDL (good) cholesterol. Polyunsaturated fats lower both LDL and HDL, but they are also a source of omega-3 fatty acids, which have purported heart-protective properties such as preventing blood clots.

Then there's a fourth category—trans fatty acids (TFAs)—commonly found in cooking oil, margarine, shortening and processed foods made with these ingredients. TFAs arise when hydrogen atoms are added to oils containing mono- or polyunsaturated fats. This so-called hydrogenation process converts liquid oils into a more solid form. Makers of packaged foods and fast-food restaurants use hydrogenated oils extensively because they enhance taste and texture and are more stable during frying and other high-temperature food processing. But a new study suggests that food high in trans fats is just as likely to raise LDL cholesterol as food high in saturated fat—a finding that corroborates results from several other recent studies on TFAs.

To further clarify the effect of TFAs on cholesterol, 36 adults with higher-than-normal blood-cholesterol levels went on five consecutive diets for 35 days each that differed only in trans-fat content. As a benchmark, participants also ate a sixth diet consisting of butter-rich foods (high in saturated fat but low in trans fat) for 35 days. Near the end of each 35-day diet, the Tufts University researchers measured the participants' blood-cholesterol levels.

In all the diets, the fat calories equaled the recommended 30 percent of total daily caloric consumption. Of the five TFA diets, the two diets with the lowest TFA content used liquid oil and semiliquid margarine and had less than 0.5 g of TFAs per 100 g of fat. The diet with the most TFAs included stick margarine and contained 20 g of trans fat. The TFA content of the two remaining diets—made from soft margarine and shortening—fell in the middle of that range. Except for water and noncaloric beverages, participants did not eat or drink anything but the food provided, and no one knew who was getting which diet.

When all the results were compared, the average total and LDL cholesterol levels were highest after people consumed the butter, stick-margarine and shortening diets. The liquid-oil, semiliquid-margarine and soft-margarine diets yielded the lowest average total and LDL levels. When compared with the butter diet, LDL levels from the soft-margarine diet averaged 9 percent lower, those from the semiliquid-margarine diet were 11 percent lower and those from the liquid-oil diet were 12 percent lower.

These findings, in the June 24 *New England Journal of Medicine,* seem straightforward, but how should you apply them to daily food choices?

*—The Editors*

## THE PHYSICIAN'S PERSPECTIVE

*George Blackburn, M.D.*
*Associate Editor*

This study represents really great science, and for people with cholesterol concerns, it corroborates what other similar studies have found: Foods high in trans fat are just as potentially harmful as foods high in saturated fat. The results are especially believable because researchers care-

**Fat Facts**

| Type of Fatty Acid | Primary Sources | State at Room Temperature | Effect on Cholesterol |
|---|---|---|---|
| MONOUNSATURATED | Canola* and olive oils; foods made from and prepared in them | Liquid | Lowers LDL; no effect on HDL |
| POLYUNSATURATED** | Soybean, safflower, corn, and cottonseed oils; foods made from and prepared in them | Liquid | Lowers both LDL and HDL |
| SATURATED | Animal fat from red meat, whole milk, and butter | Solid | Raises LDL and total cholesterol |
| TRANS | Partially hydrogenated vegetable oil used in cooking oil, margarine, shortening, and baked and fried foods | Semi-Solid | Raises LDL and total cholesterol |

○ = Carbon atom
● = Hydrogen atom

*Many nutritionists consider canola oil the healthiest vegetable oil because it's low in saturated fat, high in monounsaturated fat, and has a moderate level of omega-3 polyunsaturated fat.

**Contain the omega-3 and omega-6 essential fatty acids that the human body can't make on its own.

Chart by Mary Tanner

fully controlled the people's diets. This approach is far more reliable than the use of food questionnaires, a more common method of studying the effects of nutrients on health. In questionnaire-based studies, people try to remember what they ate and scientists estimate nutrient intake from those recollections.

But despite the tight dietary controls of this study, we can't generalize the findings to all people, because the participants already had higher-than-normal levels of total and LDL cholesterol. People with normal or low cholesterol levels might not respond the same way. Also, the study involved relatively few people and tracked their cholesterol for a short time. Thus, we don't know if the lower cholesterol levels associated with the low trans-fat diets will last and eventually translate into healthier hearts. A much larger study of more than 80,000 women two years ago found that those who ate less saturated fat and TFAs and more mono- and polyunsaturated fats substantially reduced their risk of heart disease, but that was a questionnaire-based study.

Even if we assume that trans fats are as unhealthy as saturated fats for most of us, it's not easy to determine how much trans fat we're eating. Food labels don't list trans-fat content. So the best you can do is make ballpark estimates by looking at the ingredient list. Any food that lists partially hydrogenated vegetable oil as one of the first three ingredients is likely to contain a significant amount of trans fat. Unfortunately, "partially" does not tell us how hydrogenated the oil is—and the more hydrogenated the oil, the more TFAs it contains.

Realize, too, that the majority of the TFAs consumed in the U.S. come from baked goods and food purchased in restaurants, the latter of which usually has no labeling whatsoever. So, when dining out, there's no way to assess whether the french fries you are considering with lunch are a less harmful indulgence than an apple-pie dessert.

In the near future, monitoring TFAs in food may become easier. The federal government is currently engaged in an every-five-year review of dietary guidelines and might issue recommendations for trans-fat intake. Of course, new guidelines would be of limited value without more informative labels, and thus the Food and Drug Administration has announced that it will eventually require trans-fat content on food labels.

For now, though, my advice is to place the findings from this new study in the context of generally healthy eating. First, concentrate on making the most of your daily calories that *don't* come from fat by eating a variety of whole foods, including at least five servings of fruit and vegetables a day. **When it comes to fat, stick to the 30 percent/10 percent rule for total and saturated fat, respectively, by cutting back on red meat and dairy products such as butter and whole milk. To control your trans-fat consumption, go easy on food made with hydrogenated vegetable oils and eliminate fried foods altogether. Also, choose soft or semiliquid margarine that lists liquid vegetable oil as the first ingredient and use nonhydrogenated oils for cooking.** With creative use of herbs and spices, it's entirely possible to enjoy satisfying meals that provide the healthy fats while limiting the unhealthy ones.

## FOR MORE INFORMATION:

▼ *International Food Information Council, 202-296-6547, ificinfo.health.org*

# Omega-3 Fatty Acids and Health

For over two decades, accepted dietary guidance has stressed the importance of choosing a diet that is low in fat, saturated fat, and cholesterol. Consumer research has shown that people interpret this advice to mean that they should eliminate all fat from the diet, in effect making "fat" a "four-letter word" and something to be avoided as much as possible.

Science is continually evolving, however. Two decades of research has improved our understanding of the health benefits of many foods and food components, including the essential roles of fats and individual fatty acids in the diet, "With continually emerging research we are unravelling the complex relationship between food and health," says Penny Kris-Etherton, Ph.D., R.D., professor of nutrition at Pennsylvania State University. The guidance on dietary fat today reflects this greater understanding of science and is best summarized by the U.S. Department of Agriculture (USDA) 2000 edition of *Dietary Guidelines for Americans* which recommends that people "choose a diet that is low in saturated fat and cholesterol and *moderate in total fat*."

## There Are Fats, and Then There Are Fats

The three major categories of dietary fats—saturated, monounsaturated, and polyunsaturated—have various effects on low-density-lipoprotein (LDL) cholesterol ("bad" cholesterol) and high-density-lipoprotein (HDL) cholesterol ("good" cholesterol) levels. Saturated fats, in general, are shown to elevate LDL-cholesterol levels, and high levels of LDL cholesterol are considered a major risk factor for heart disease. In contrast, diets higher in monounsaturated and polyunsaturated fats are known to lead to lower LDL-cholesterol levels.

There are two subclasses of fatty acids within the polyunsaturated fat category: omega-6 (n-6) fatty acids and omega-3 (n-3) fatty acids. Vegetable oils such as corn, sunflower, safflower and soybean oils are rich in n-6 fatty acids. Soybean oil is also an excellent source of n-3 fatty acids, as are canola oil and deep-sea fish, or "fatty fish."

## Beyond Basic Nutrition: The Functions of n-3 Fatty Acids

New research is showing that n-3 polyunsaturated fatty acids may have significant health benefits. Alpha-linolenic acid (ALA), a precursor to long chain polyunsaturated fatty acids (LCPUFAs) eicosapentaenoic acid (EPA) and docosahexaenoic acid (DHA), are of particular interest. These n-3 fatty acids are thought to help reduce the risk for cardiovascular disease, to play major roles in promoting eye health, and possibly, to improve immune function.

## Getting to the Heart of the Matter

Researchers suggest that EPA and DHA promote heart health by preventing blood platelets from clotting and sticking to the artery walls—effects that are similar to those observed with aspirin. Decreased clotting helps reduce the chances of blockages in an artery and thereby decreases the risk for heart attack or stroke.

EPA and DHA have been shown to reduce the levels of serum triglycerides, which, like cholesterol, are associated with an increased risk for heart disease.

Several clinical studies support the cardiovascular health benefits associated with n-3 fatty acids. For example, the results of a recent study were presented at the American Heart Association's (AHA's) 41st Annual Conference on Cardiovascular Disease Epidemiology and Prevention in March 2000. Its findings suggest that older Americans who consume fatty fish, a rich source of n-3 fatty acids, one or more times a week had a 44 percent lower risk of experiencing a fatal heart attack. The study also reports that n-3 fatty acids appear to have a positive effect on the rhythm of the heartbeat, an effect that specifically reduces the rate of occurrence of a major cause of fatal heart attacks.

In addition to this evidence, research published in the January 2001 issue of the *Journal of the American Medical Association* concluded that consumption of larger amounts of fish rich in n-3 fatty acids (at least one serving per week) was associated with a significant reduction in the incidence of certain types of stroke caused by blood clots. Furthermore, the consumption of larger amounts of n-3 fatty acids was not related to an increased risk of stroke caused by bleeding.

On the basis of a variety of studies similar to these, the U.S. Food and Drug Administration approved, for dietary supplements only, the use of a qualified health claim about n-3 fatty acids and their role in reducing the risk of heart disease. Although this health claim, approved for use in

October 2000, offers some validation for the role of n-3 fatty acids in the diet and their relationship to heart health, it is important to recognize that science is still evolving in this area.

It is especially important to note that if n-3 fatty acids are only *added* to an individual's current diet without lowering the amounts of saturated fat in the diet, it is likely that LDL-cholesterol levels will not improve, and may actually increase. That is, n-3 fatty acids should be seen as a healthful *substitute* for saturated fat in the diet.

## Eye See!

DHA is naturally concentrated in the retina of the eye and is thought to promote healthy retinal function. Results of a study published in the February 2001 issue of the *American Journal of Clinical Nutrition* (AJCN) indicates that the consumption of larger amounts of fish is associated with a decreased risk of development of age-related macular degeneration (AMD). AMD is an untreatable disease that causes fuzziness, shadows, or other distortions in the center of vision and is the leading cause of blindness in older adults.

Researchers at Bristol University in Bristol, United Kingdom, who also published an article in the February 2001 issue of *AJCN*, found that women who ate fatty fish while pregnant gave birth to children who experienced better visual development. In addition, babies whose mothers had significant levels of DHA in their diet while they were breast-feeding experienced faster-than-normal eyesight development. Longer-term studies have shown that at two and four years of age, these differences seem to have disappeared. In further studies, LCPUFA supplementation resulted in improved cognitive function and enhanced information processing in some infants.

## n-3 Fatty Acids and Immunity

At a conference hosted by the National Institutes of Health in September 2000, investigators made several presentations on studies exploring the role of n-3 fatty acids on immune functions. Some of these studies suggested that the addition of vitamin E to a diet rich in n-3 fatty acids may further enhance the beneficial effects of those n-3 fatty acids in delaying autoimmune diseases such as rheumatoid arthritis.

Researchers have also found that n-3 fatty acid supplementation is associated with a reduced incidence of joint tenderness and morning stiffness in study participants with rheumatoid arthritis. The study participants consumed supplements of EPA and DHA, in addition to traditional anti-inflammatory drugs, and some clinical benefits were seen. The effects were not apparent until the compounds were consumed for 12 weeks or longer. In addition to its reported impact on arthritis, the potential effects of n-3 fatty acids are being studied in individuals with a wide range of immune-compromised conditions including asthma, lupus, kidney disease, and cancer.

Even with these intriguing results, some experts recommend a cautious approach to the use of fish oil supplements, one source of n-3 fatty acids. On the basis of the current scientific evidence, the AHA advises that fish oil capsules be used judiciously. Specifically, AHA recommends that fish oil supplements be used only by individuals with severely high triglyceride levels, individuals who have not responded well to conventional treatment for heart disease, and individuals who are not at risk for pancreatitis (inflammation of the pancreas). As with any healthcare decision, consumers should consult with their health professionals to determine the best individual approach.

## Pass the n-3 Fatty Acids Please

ALA, the most abundant n-3 fatty acid in the U.S. diet is found in a variety of foods including tofu, soybean, flax, and canola oils, flaxseed, nuts, and fish. However, very small amounts of EPA and DHA, which is mostly found in fatty fish such as tuna and salmon, are present in the diet. Much of the current research shows health benefits from n-3 fatty acids found in fatty fish, particularly because of recent speculation on the health benefits of EPA and DHA in heart and eye health and the immune system. Even with this range of plant and animal sources of n-3 fatty acids, however, diets in the United States are considered to be low in n-3 fatty acids.

Current dietary guidance rightly continues to stress the importance of choosing a diet that helps reduce saturated fat intake. Ongoing research on a variety of individual polyunsaturated fatty acids, including n-3 fatty acids, supports the recommendations of USDA and others to choose a diet *moderate in total fat*.

Therefore, moderate. Don't eliminate. Implement the AHA recommendation to eat at least two servings of fish per week. With summer weather coming, have a tuna salad or salmon steak with a marinade consisting of oil-and-herbs and throw it on the grill for a flavorful and healthful entree.

---

# Building Healthy BONES

## Every dietician knows that calcium intake is essential to bone health, but there are other nutrients that affect bone health and aid in osteoporosis prevention

BY CAROL M. COUGHLIN, RD

As dietetics professionals, we are aware that osteoporosis is a skeletal disorder characterized by compromised bone strength which leads to an increased risk of fracture. It is estimated that in the United States 10 million people have osteoporosis and 18 million more have low bone mass, placing them at risk for developing this disease. Every dietitian knows that calcium intake is essential to bone health, but there are also other nutrients that affect bone health and aid in osteoporosis prevention.

Although calcium takes center stage in the fight against osteoporosis, bone health clearly requires adequate overall nutrition. This was illustrated in a recent one-year, double-blind, placebo-controlled study of Gambian children, whose mean dietary calcium intake was 300 milligrams daily. The researchers examined the effects of supplementing 1,000 milligrams of calcium carbonate daily for a year. This supplementation resulted in a substantial increase in bone mineral density, but there was no effect on overall skeletal growth (ie, the calcium increased the amount of minerals present within a given bone volume but did not promote bone growth). This suggests that simply supplementing a diet with calcium is not sufficient if the overall diet is nutritionally inadequate in several nutrients.

Dietetics professionals are aware that vitamin D is needed for calcium absorption. Recently, it has been recognized that vitamin D insufficiency, not just extreme deficiency, contributes to osteoporosis. A study at Massachusetts General Hospital of 290 patients in a general medical ward revealed that 57% were vitamin D-deficient and 22% were severely deficient. It takes about 20 to 30 minutes of sunshine daily on the hands and face to manufacture sufficient levels of vitamin D, but many people get nowhere near that amount of time in the sun. They go from their houses to their cars to their offices and back to their homes. People live, work, and even exercise indoors.

Foods that are natural sources of vitamin D such as eel, liver, and egg yolk, probably aren't most people's favorite foods. One study found vitamin D deficiency in 43% of the patients whose intake of dietary vitamin D reached the recommended daily allowance (RDA). Therefore, it's best to suggest that clients consume fortified foods such as fluid milk or fortified soy and rice milk. Some breakfast cereals are also fortified with vitamin D.

An inadequate amount of vitamin D results in a subtle decrease in the ionized calcium concentration in blood, which triggers parathyroid hormone (PTH) secretion. PTH is a potent bone resorbing agent so even a subtle increase results in measurable bone loss.

Scientific research indicates that moderate protein intake (1 to 1 1/2 grams per kilogram body weight) is associated with normal calcium metabolism and, presumably, bone health. Using this definition, only 40% to 50% of adults in the United States consume diets moderate in protein.

When people don't get enough protein, intestinal calcium absorption is reduced, resulting in a rise in serum PTH and calcitriol that persists at least for two weeks. The long-term implications are not yet proven, but epidemiologic data suggest increased rates of bone loss in people on very low protein diets. In addition, protein undernutrition has been shown to affect sex hormone status in animal studies.

The flip side is that people with high protein intake, particularly from animal sources, have hypercalciuria and negative calcium balance. The epidemiologic evidence shows that diets high in animal protein are associated with an increased rate of fractures. This relationship does not hold true for vegetable protein. The greater concentration of sulfur-containing amino acids in meat creates a high acid load. This acid is buffered by the release of basic ions from the bone, leading to a loss of skeletal mass. Research from the United Kingdom indicates that women with the most acidic diets have the poorest bone density (both in axial and peripheral skeleton) and the highest levels of bone resorption. Acid-base homeostasis disruption in adults has been suggested as a reason behind the progressive decline in bone mass with aging. Bone loss may, therefore, be attributable to the life-long mobilization of skeletal salts to balance the acid generated from foods that produce acid.

This acid/base relationship may also explain why recent population-based studies have suggested a positive association between high intakes of fruits and vegetables in the diet and bone mass and metabolism in premenopausal, perimenopausal, and postmenopausal elderly women and elderly men. The mechanism may be the beneficial effect of the alkaline environment induced by a diet rich in fruits and vegetables and the potassium content of these foods. Supplementation with potassium results in a reduction of urinary calcium, and inadequate potassium stimulates bone resorption. Supplementation of potassium bicarbonate in postmenopausal women improves calcium and phosphorus balance, reduces bone resorption, and increases the rate of bone formation. Researchers are currently calculating the protein-to-potassium ratio in the diet and are finding that it predicts net acid excretion via the urine and that, in turn, net acid excretion predicts calcium excretion.

The positive link between fruit and vegetable consumption and bone health was also shown in the Dietary Approaches to Stopping Hypertension (DASH) trial. Increasing fruit and vegetable intake from 3 3/5 to 9 1/2 daily servings resulted in a reduction of urinary calcium excretion from 157 milligrams to 110 milligrams per day. It is generally accepted that salt increases urinary calcium. The reabsorption of calcium and sodium in the proximal tubule of the kidney and loop of Henle are linked. A reduction in renal sodium reabsorption leads to a reduction in calcium absorption and increased calcium urinary losses.

Interestingly, there are minimal data available on the effect of high sodium intake on bone health over the long term; most studies show little or no association. This may simply be due to the lack of long-term follow-up, but further research in this area clearly is warranted.

In addition to vitamin D, other vitamins play a role in bone health and osteoporosis prevention. Low levels of vitamin K are associated with low bone density and bone fractures. The principal noncollagenous protein of bone, osteocalcin (also known as gamma-carboxglutamic acid or bone Gla), and matrix Gla protein are dependent on vitamin K for synthesis. The Nurses Health Study found that women who had the lowest intake of vitamin K had the highest rate of hip fractures.

Clearly, we all know that if **people** would obtain and maintain an intake of **calcium** meeting the dietary **reference** guidelines, our nation's bone **health** would be greatly **enhanced**.

Dietitians can remind clients that, previously, those on anticoagulant medications such as Coumadin were advised to restrict their intake of vitamin K; now most dietitians recommend keeping intake at a steady level. An adequate supply of this nutrient can be obtained from green leafy vegetables, which are also good sources of readily absorbable calcium. The friendly bacteria that live in the digestive system also produce vitamin K. Clients who are on repeated courses of antibiotics may get less vitamin K since antibiotics kill the good bacteria that live in the intestines in addition to killing bacteria responsible for illness and infections. Therefore, dietitians may suggest to clients taking antibiotics that they also take a probiotic supplement of good bacteria, such as acidophilus, or eat food with active cultures, such as yogurt.

Alternately, they could take a prebiotic supplement. Prebiotics are substances that feed the good bacteria that live in the intestines, just as fertilizers promote plant growth. The most common prebiotic is fructooligosaccharide (FOS), which is a naturally-occurring substance consisting of short chains of fructose. The common suggestion is a dosage of 1 to 4 grams daily. Supplementing with FOS not only helps feed the good bacteria that make vitamin K but also helps the absorption of more calcium by lowering the pH of the intestine.

Appropriate gut flora also aid in bone health because of their effect on dietary phytoestrogens. These compounds produce estrogen-like effects in the body only after being converted to the active form by bacteria in the gut. Women who eat higher-carbohydrate diets tend to have healthier gut flora and are, therefore, able to convert more phytoestrogens into the active form. Phytoestrogens, particularly isoflavones, may aid in prevention of bone loss because they act in a fashion similar to estrogen.

Another fat-soluble vitamin with a link to bone health is vitamin A, but its relationship is an opposing one. A recent study showed that women with higher blood levels of vitamin A had a higher risk for hip fracture. For every milligram increase in daily intake of preformed vitamin A, the risk for hip fracture increased by 68%. Aging reduces the ability to rid the body of extra vitamin A, a problem compounded by the fact that vitamin A is one nutrient that is absorbed more readily with aging. Clients should be advised to get adequate amounts of vitamin A, but supplements of preformed vitamin A are generally discouraged.

At a presentation at the World Congress on Osteoporosis 2000 in Chicago, Ill., J. Beynon from the United Kingdom presented the results of his investigation on the role vitamin $B_{12}$ may play in osteoporosis. A total of 263 osteoporotic patients were studied (244 women; 19 men). Of the 44 subjects with low blood vitamin $B_{12}$ levels, 22 had suffered a fracture. (Beynon J, Murray C, Vasishta S. $B_{12}$ deficiency—its role in the development of osteoporosis. *Osteoporos Int.* 2000;11 (suppl 2):S153.) There is some evidence in the literature to suggest that vitamin $B_{12}$ suppresses osteoblastic activity. Further research in this area is required; since it is now recommended that all people over age 50 consume $B_{12}$-fortified foods or take a supplement, this simply reinforces the importance of vitamin $B_{12}$.

In addition to calcium, phosphorus, and magnesium, boron may enhance bone health. There is evidence that adequate intake of boron can decrease the amount of calcium lost in urine. Boron deficiency results in osteoporosis-like symptoms such as thin, brittle bones. Because fruits and vegetables are the best source of boron, this adds to the recommendation of eating a DASH-type diet for bone health.

Fluoride may also have a role in keeping bones strong. Just as fluoride is incorporated into teeth, it is also added to the structure of bones. One study of women found that a fluoride supplement of 40 to 60 milligrams a day increased the bone density of the spine. However, a three-year study found that fluoride supplements did nothing to reduce the rate of bone fracture in women. There simply is not enough evidence yet to recommend supplementing with fluoride as a strategy to prevent or treat osteoporosis or bone fractures.

Clearly, we all know that if people would obtain and maintain an intake of calcium meeting the dietary reference guidelines, our nation's bone health would be greatly enhanced. In addition, if everyone's intake of the recommended nutrients—each playing a small role in slowing bone loss—was optimized, the overall rate of fractures could be reduced and health-care costs could be lowered substantially.

With surveys indicating that the public is fatigued with conflicting messages about nutrition, dietitians can use this information to offer a consistent nutrition message. We can tell people that an overall diet adequate in protein, vitamins, and minerals and rich in fruits and vegetables is the one eating pattern that seems to be optimal not only for bone health but also for reducing the risk of hypertension, diabetes, heart disease, and cancer.

---

Carol M. Coughlin, RD, is a freelance writer in Maine and the executive director of the Massachusetts Dietetic Association.

# VITAMINS & MINERALS: HOW MUCH IS TOO MUCH?

Pick up any vitamin or mineral supplement. The label tells you roughly how much of each nutrient you need. But it doesn't say how much is too much.

For the first time, the National Academy of Sciences has issued Tolerable Upper Intake Levels, or ULs, to tell people how much is a safe upper limit for nearly two dozen nutrients. The Academy has also updated the Recommended Dietary Allowances (RDAs) and other advice on how much of each vitamin and mineral the average healthy person needs.

The Center for Science in the Public Interest, publisher of *Nutrition Action Healthletter*, wants the Food and Drug Administration to require ULs on at least some supplement labels over the next few years. But you needn't wait that long to find out what they are.

*NAH*'s Bonnie Liebman spoke by phone with researcher and physician Robert Russell, who served on two of the four panels that came up with the new RDAs and ULs.

### *Q: What are ULs?*

**A:** The UL is the highest level of a vitamin or mineral that can be safely taken without any risk of adverse effect. Just going a little bit above the UL is not going to harm most people, but as you get higher and higher, you're increasing your risk of side effects.

### *Q: So a person who consumes the UL is not in danger?*

**A:** No. But to protect the population as much as possible, we don't advise taking more than the UL on a daily basis. We're not talking about the occasional time when you might exceed it. That's not something we worry about. Nor do we worry about people who take more than the UL under a doctor's supervision or as part of a clinical trial.

And for the most part, we're not talking about toxicity from food. With the possible exception of vitamins A and D, almost all of the cases of toxicity are based on taking supplements or fortified foods.

### *Q: How did the panels come up with the ULs?*

**A:** We studied toxicity reports in the literature. We tried to get them as clean as possible. For example, if you're looking at liver toxicity, you want to make sure that the patients did not also have alcohol abuse or hepatitis. You want to rule those things out as much as possible, so you can attribute the adverse effect to the large doses of the nutrient and nothing else.

### *Q: And you set the ULs well below those levels?*

**A:** Yes. Wherever possible, we'd start with a No Observed Adverse Effect Level, or NOAEL. If you know that people took X amount—say, 100 milligrams—and there was no toxicity in any individuals, that would be a NOAEL.

If you had NOAEL, you could use a *Lowest* Observed Adverse Effect Level, or LOAEL. If several people had some sign of toxicity at 100 milligrams, that would be a LOAEL. With a LOAEL, we'd use a greater safety factor to bring the level down further.

### *Q: So there's always a safety margin.*

**A:** Yes. The so-called "uncertainty factor" is built into the UL to protect almost all of the population. We divide the NOAEL or LOAEL by the uncertainty factor. So if a study finds a LOAEL of 100 mg, and you use an uncertainty factor of two, the UL would be 50 mg.

If you have only a few case reports of toxicity instead of a whole series of people, you would use a larger safety factor, because you don't really have a good handle on what the upper level should be.

### *Q: Why are some ULs based on relatively minor side effects, like diarrhea for vitamin C?*

**A:** ULs are based on the earliest side effects to occur—not necessarily the most serious one. But that doesn't mean that there are no serious side effects. For example, flushing is the most sensitive indicator on niacin excess. But if people take a much higher dose—like 3,000 to 5,000 mg of niacin a day—to lower their cholesterol, they can get severe liver disease.

We use the most conservative indicator because the ULs are meant to protect the general population. Then we can feel confident that if you take that level on a daily basis, it's safe.

## Getting Too Much

### *Q: Which nutrients most concern you?*

**A:** The UL for vitamin A from retinol is 10,000 IU. You can find single-nutrient supplements with 25,000 IU of vitamin A in any health-food store. You can put yourself in danger by taking those on a daily basis. And children are better off with a daily multi that has no more than the UL for vitamin A, which is 3,000 IU for 4- to 8-year-olds and 2,000 IU for younger children.

Those ULs assume that all of the vitamin A in the supplement comes from retinyl palmitate or other forms of retinol, not from beta-carotene or other carotenoids, which have no UL because there is insufficient evidence of toxicity.

***Q: What does too much vitamin A do?***

**A:** In women who are capable of becoming pregnant, the risk is birth defects. In the rest of the population, it's irreversible liver disease. We're talking about severe, fibrotic, cirrhotic liver disease, not just elevated liver enzymes.

***Q: Are the elderly at greater risk?***

**A:** We can't say for certain. When the elderly consume vitamin A, they clear it from the blood and store it in the liver less efficiently than younger people. And we have customarily taken those higher blood levels as a sign of overload, so it makes sense that the elderly would be more prone to toxicity. But we don't have evidence that they actually develop liver toxicity more often.

***Q: What other nutrients might we get too much of?***

**A:** Some single-nutrient supplements exceed the UL for zinc. And we're a bit worried about excess folic acid. You wouldn't get it from a single supplement, but if you were also eating a number of fortified foods, you might exceed the UL for folic acid, which is 1,000 micrograms a day. That could cover up or precipitate a vitamin B-12 deficiency.

***Q: Can't a blood test tell people if they're low in B-12?***

**A:** Yes, but from a public health point of view, we don't want to depend on that. There is actually a debate over whether to fortify the food supply with vitamin B-12, which would help prevent deficiencies. There are no reports of B-12 toxicity, so there's no UL. It's safe.

***Q: Can people take unlimited quantities of nutrients that have no ULs?***

**A:** No. It may just mean that the data don't exist. For example, there's no UL for arsenic, which may be a nutrient we need in tiny quantities. We know that some kinds of arsenic are poisonous and that the kind found in drinking water may raise the risk of cancer. But there's no data on toxicity from the kind of arsenic found in food.

## Getting Too Little

***Q: The Academy also updated the Recommended Dietary Allowances. Why is the new RDA for B-12 so low?***

**A:** I used to recommend 25 micrograms a day to play it safe for people with atrophic gastritis, a problem for 10 to 30 percent of people older than 50. They produce too little stomach acid to extract B-12 when it's bound to proteins in food. We now know that most people with atrophic gastritis can absorb enough B-12 by taking 2.4 micrograms a day, the new RDA, as long as it's in an unbound form—that is, in a fortified food or a supplement.

***Q: B-12 is the first supplement the Academy has told people to take?***

**A:** Yes. If you're older than 50, you need at least 2.4 mcg of B-12 from a supplement or a fortified food like breakfast cereal.

***Q: Most multis have less than the RDA for vitamin K. Is that a problem?***

**A:** It's too early to say. The question is how vitamin K affects bone. We know that certain markers in the blood go up in people who are vitamin-K-deficient, but there just wasn't enough evidence to say if that raises their risk of bone fracture. The beauty of these new RDAs is that once a critical mass of evidence comes in, they can be revised. We used to have to wait 10 to 15 years.

The RDA for vitamin D, for example, might be raised fairly soon for people over 70. Even though their RDA is high—600 IU a day—that may not be sufficient.

***Q: Why?***

**A:** The skin of older people is much less able to make vitamin D. People in their 70s make roughly half as much vitamin D as children can make from the same ultraviolet sun exposure. And older people's bodies are less able to convert vitamin D to the active form. Plus the older gut has fewer vitamin-D receptors, so you have a malabsorption problem. All that adds up to a significant increase in an older person's requirement.

***Q: And the RDA assumes that you get no vitamin D from the sun?***

**A:** Yes. Some people may get enough from sunlight. But the RDAs are meant to protect the entire population. And in northern latitudes—say, in Boston—the sun isn't strong enough in the winter for your body to make enough vitamin D. That's true across the northern states and Canada.

In the southern states, older people may go out into the sun more. But many don't, and many use sunscreen, which blocks the UV rays. So they may need to take vitamin D anyway.

***Q: Yet the National Academy of Sciences didn't recommend that older people take a supplement?***

**A:** No, but its report definitely implies that you need one for both vitamin D and calcium. Even when older people eat a healthy diet, they're not likely to meet those requirements. That's particularly true for vitamin D. It would take a quart and a half of milk a day to meet the current RDA for people over 70, which is 600 IU. Nobody's going to drink that much.

---

*You won't see RDAs on food and supplement labels, because the numbers vary for men and women, young and old. Instead, labels list Daily Values (DVs), though supplements can also call them U.S. Recommended Daily Allowances (or USRDAs). For each nutrient, the DV (or USRDA) is a single number that is set high enough to protect almost everyone.*

---

Robert Russell is Associate Director of the Jean Mayer U.S. Department of Agriculture Human Nutrition Research Center on Aging at Tufts University in Boston.

## VITAMINS

| Nutrient (other names) | Recommended Dietary Allowance (RDA) | Daily Value (DV) | Good Sources | Upper Level (UL) | Selected Adverse Effects | *Nutrition Action* Comments |
|---|---|---|---|---|---|---|
| **Vitamin A** (retinol) | Women: 700 mcg Men: 900 mcg | 5,000 IU[1] (1,500 mcg) | Liver, fatty fish, fortified foods (milk, breakfast cereals, etc.) | 10,000 IU (3,000 mcg) | *Liver toxicity, birth defects.* Inconclusive: bone loss | The body turns some carotenoids into vitamin A. |
| **Carotenoids** (alpha-carotene, beta-carotene, beta-cryptoxanthin, lutein, lycopene, zeaxanthin) | None. (NAS advises eating more cartotenoid-rich fruits and vegetables). | None | Orange fruits & vegetables (alpha- and beta-carotene), green leafy vegetables (beta-carotene and lutein), tomatoes (lycopene). | None. Panel said don't take beta-carotene, except to get RDA for vitamin A. | Smokers who took high doses of beta-carotene supplements (33,000-50,000 IU a day) had higher risk of lung cancer. | Lutein may lower risk of cataracts and degeneration of the retina. Lycopene may lower risk of prostate cancer. |
| **Thiamin** (vitamin B-1) | Women: 1.1 mg Men: 1.2 mg | 1.5 mg | Breads, cereals, pasta, & foods made with "enriched" or whole-grain flour; pork. | None | None reported. | |
| **Riboflavin** (vitamin B-2) | Women: 1.1 mg Men: 1.3 mg | 1.7 mg | Milk, yogurt, foods made with "enriched" or whole-grain flour | None | None reported | May lower risk of cataracts. |
| **Niacin** (vitamin B-3) | Women: 14 mg Men: 16 mg | 20 mg | Meat, poultry, seafood, foods made with "enriched" or whole-grain flour. | 35 mg[2] | *Flushing (burning, tingling, itching, redness),* liver damage. | Cholesterol-lowering doses of niacin should only be taken under a doctor's supervision. |
| **Vitamin B-6** (pyridoxine) | Ages 19-50: 1.3 mg Women 50+: 1.5 mg Men 50+: 1.7 mg | 2 mg | Meat, poultry, seafood, fortified foods (cereals, etc.), liver | 100 mg | *Reversible nerve damage (burning, shooting, tingling pains, numbness, etc.)* | May lower risk of heart disease (by lowering homocysteine levels). |
| **Vitamin B-12** (cobalamin) | 2.4 mcg | 6 mcg | Meat, poultry, seafood, dairy foods, fortified foods (cereals, etc.) | None | None reported | People over 50 need a supplement or fortified food |
| **Folate** (folacin, folic acid) | 400 mcg | 400 mcg (0.4 mg) | Orange juice, beans, other fruits & vegetables, fortified cereals, foods made with "enriched" or whole-grain flour. | 1,000 mcg[2] (1 mg) | *Can mask or precipitate a B-12 deficiency,* which can cause irreversible nerve damage. | Reduces risk of birth defects. May lower risk of heart disease, cervical and colon cancer, and depression. |
| **Vitamin C** (ascorbic acid) | Women: 75 mg Men: 90 mg (Smokers: add 35 mg) | 60 mg | Citrus & other fruits, vegetables, fortified foods (cereals, etc.) | 2,000 mg | *Diarrhea.* | High doses (1,000 mg a day) may shorten colds. |
| **Vitamin D** | Ages 19-50: 200 IU[3] Ages 51-70: 400 IU[3] Over 70: 600 IU[3] | 400 IU | Sunlight, fatty fish, fortified foods (milk, breakfast cereals, etc.). | 2,000 IU | *High blood calcium,* which may cause kidney and heart damage. | Deficiency can cause bone loss and may raise risk of osteoporosis. |
| **Vitamin E** (alpha-tocopherol) | 15 mg (33 IU—synthetic) (22 IU—natural) | 30 IU (synthetic) | Oils, whole grains, nuts. | 1,000 mg2 (1,100 IU—synthetic) (1,500 IU—natural) | Hemorrhage. | May lower risk of heart disease, prostate cancer, cataracts; may slow Alzheimer's. |
| **Vitamin K** (phylloquinone) | Women: 90 mcg[3] Men: 120 mcg[3] | 80 mcg | Green leafy vegetables, oils | None | Interferes with coumadin & other anti-clotting drugs. | May lower risk of bone fractures. |

| MINERALS | | | | | | |
|---|---|---|---|---|---|---|
| **Nutrient (other names)** | **Recommended Dietary Allowance (RDA)** | **Daily Value (DV)** | **Good Sources** | **Upper Level (UL)** | **Selected Adverse Effects** | ***Nutrition Action* Comments** |
| **Calcium** | Ages 19-50: 1,000 mg[3] Over 50: 1,200 mg[3] | 1,000 mg | Dairy foods, fortified foods, leafy green vegetables, canned fish (eaten with bones). | 2,500 mg | *High blood calcium*, which may cause kidney damage, kidney stones. | May lower risk of osteoporosis, colon cancer. High doses (2,000 mg a day) may raise risk of prostate cancer. |
| **Chromium** | Women: 20-25 mcg[3] Men: 30-35 mcg[3] | 120 mcg | Whole grains, bran cereals, meat, poultry, seafood. | None | Inconclusive: kidney or muscle damage. | May lower risk of diabetes |
| **Copper** | 900 mcg | 2 mg (2,000 mcg) | Liver, seafood, nuts, seeds, wheat bran, whole grains, chocolate. | 10 mg (10,000 mcg) | *Liver damage.* | |
| **Iron** | Women 19-50: 18 mg Women 50+: 8 mg Men: 8 mg | 18 mg | Red meat, poultry, seafood, foods made with "enriched" or whole-grain flour. | 45 mg | *Gastrointestinal effects (constipation, nausea, diarrhea).* | Gene raises risk of iron overload (hemochromatosis) in some people. |
| **Magnesium** | Women: 310-320 mg<br>MCN: 400-42 mg | 400 mg | Green leafy vegetables; whole-grain breads, cereals, etc.: nuts | 350 mg[2] | *Diarrhea.* | May lower risk of osteoporosis, heart disease, or high blood pressure. |
| **Phosphorus** | 700 mg | 1,000 mg | Dairy foods, meat, poultry, seafood, foods (processed cheese, colas, etc.) made with phosphate additives. | Ages 19-70: 4,000 mg Over 70: 3,000 mg | *High blood phosphorus*, which may damage kidneys and bones. | With phosphate additives on the rise, look for low-not high-phosphorus multivitamins. |
| **Selenium** | 55 mcg | 70 mcg | Seafood, meat, poultry; grains (depends on levels in soil). | 400 mcg | Nail or hair loss or brittleness. | May lower risk of prostate, lung, colon cancer. |
| **Zinc** | Women: 8 mg Men: 11 mg | 15 mg | Red meat, seafood, whole grains, fortified foods (cereals, etc.). | 40 mg | *Lower copper levels,* HDL ("good") cholesterol, and immune response | The average person gets about a quarter of the UL from food. |

**Recommended Dietary Allowance (RDA):** We list RDAs for adults only.

**Daily Value (DV):** These levels, also called U.S. Recommended Daily Allowances or (USRDAs), appear on food and supplement labels. Unlike the RDAs, there is only one Daily Value for everyone over age four.

**Tolerable Upper Intake Level (UL):** These levels are upper safe daily limits. We list ULs for adults only.

**Selected Adverse Effects:** What happens if you take too much. *The UL is based on the adverse effect listed in italics.*"Inconclusive adverse effects are based on inconsistent or sketchy evidence.

**Other Tolerable Upper Intake Levels**

| | |
|---|---|
| Boron: 20 mg | Manganese: 11 mg |
| Choline: 3.5 grams | Molybdenum: 2,000 mcg (2 mg) |
| Fluoride: 10 mg | Nickel: 1 mg |
| Iodine: 1,100 mcg (1.1 mg) | Vanadium: 1.8 mg |

[1]We get vitamin A both from retinol and carotenoids, but this number assumes that all of the vitamin A comes from retinol.

[2]From supplements and fortified foods only.

[3]Adequate Intake (AI). The National Academy of Sciences (NAS) had too little data to set an RDA.

# Can Taking Vitamins Protect Your Brain?

Memory loss and losing the ability to think straight is a common fear. Many take vitamins in hopes of keeping it from happening. No one questions that certain severe vitamin deficiencies cause neurological problems. But there is no solid proof yet of extra vitamins protecting the brain, although suggestive studies and a theoretical basis for hope have made this an active area of research.

There are two principal ways that vitamins, or lack thereof, affect brain cells. Some vitamins are *antioxidants*, which means they react with, and therefore blunt the deleterious effects of, oxygen free radicals. *Oxygen free radicals* are a very chemically reactive form of oxygen. What makes them reactive is that they have unpaired electrons. This reactivity means that when they encounter DNA or cellular membranes, they cause damage. The antioxidant properties of some vitamins may be especially relevant in the brain because brain cells are particularly vulnerable to the effects of oxygen free radicals. Brain cells have low levels of *glutathione*, an important cellular peptide, which functions as a natural antioxidant. (Peptides are shorter versions of proteins.) Also, the membranes of brain cells are loaded with polyunsaturated fatty acids, and polyunsaturated fatty acid molecules are easily damaged by oxygen free radicals. Brain cells are highly dependent on large amounts of oxygen for energy production, so they are bound to be exposed to more than their fair share of oxygen free radicals.

The other way that some vitamins affect brain cells is by playing a role in several brain cell *metabolic pathways*, complex chains of biochemical reactions that produce energy and sustain life. A missing vitamin can derail an important metabolic pathway.

Here is a summary of some of the evidence for vitamins that may be important to protecting brain cells.

## B vitamins

Folate (or folic acid), $B_6$, and $B_{12}$ are three of the B vitamins that play an important role in the brain. Epidemiologic studies have hinted at their importance because people with low concentrations in their blood or diet have scored lower on memory and nonverbal abstract thinking tests. Infants fed a formula in which $B_6$ was inadvertently destroyed through heat processing developed convulsions and had abnormal electroencephalograms, which measure electrical activity in the brain. Adults with low $B_6$ diets have been reported to have some of the same problems.

The B vitamins are not antioxidants. Instead, they figure in several key metabolic pathways. They play a role in the production of S-adenosylmethionine (SAMe), an important brain molecule that is currently being marketed as an all-purpose feel-good pill. Homocysteine also shares a pathway with this trio of B vitamins; if the vitamin concentrations are low (especially folate), then homocysteine levels go up. High homocysteine concentrations in the blood have been implicated as a cause of heart disease and stroke. And several studies have shown an association between high homocysteine levels and Alzheimer's disease and depression. Severe $B_{12}$ deficiencies can lead to breakdown of the protective myelin sheath that surrounds nerves, which causes nerve damage both inside and outside the spinal cord and brain.

Whether it is important or effective to get these B vitamins in amounts above and beyond what a good diet will provide is a big, unanswered question. But there is no question that with a good diet you can get the minimum requirements—and many people aren't meeting even those basic dietary levels. Framingham Heart Study researchers found that of participants in that study aged 67 and older, 30% weren't getting enough folate, 20% weren't getting enough $B_6$, and 20–25% weren't getting enough $B_{12}$. Folate (it is called *folate*, a derivative of *foliage*, because it was first found in spinach) is in leafy greens, organ meats, citrus fruits, and whole grains, although there has been a recent push to increase the amount of folate-fortified food. Vitamin $B_6$ is in meat, poultry, and fish, as well as in grain and dairy products. Vitamin $B_{12}$ is found in appreciable amounts only in animal products, and in greater quantities in meat than in dairy foods. Strict vegetarians, therefore, need to be mindful of $B_{12}$ deficiency. But the more common danger is *atrophic gastritis*, an inflammation of the stomach lining caused by the immune system, which in extreme cases prevents $B_{12}$ absorption. Atrophic gastritis is a common condition among older people. In the Framingham study, 37% of the people over age 80 had it, although those weren't all necessarily extreme cases. A blood test of $B_{12}$ levels can be used to detect whether atrophic gastritis is causing a $B_{12}$ absorption problem.

## Vitamin E

Many people already take vitamin E pills in hopes of staving off memory loss and Alzheimer's. Based on what is known about the way vitamin E works in the body, it's not unreasonable to take it. Not only is it a powerful antioxidant, vitamin E is especially active in cell membranes. And because the membranes of brain cells are loaded with polyunsaturated fatty acids, they are prone to oxygen free radical damage.

The research results on the actual use of vitamin E are a mixed bag. An NIH-funded study published in the April 24, 1997, *New England Journal of Medicine* got a great deal of attention because it showed that large amounts of vitamin E (two doses of 1000 IU per day) slowed the progression of Alzheimer's in people classified as having moderate cases of the disease. And a study published in the July 1999 *American Journal of Epidemiology* based on a large national health survey found that as blood levels of vitamin E per unit of cholesterol decreased, so did people's performance on memory tests. On the other hand, plenty of other studies have shown that neither vitamin E intake nor the amount of the vitamin in the blood correlate with better memory or Alzheimer's prevention.

The main sources of vitamin E in the average diet are the vegetable oils—corn, safflower, soybean oil and so forth—and the increasing number of foods—orange juice and breakfast cereal—to which vitamin E has been added. Even with fortified foods, it is virtually impossible to reach the daily intake levels of 1000 IU or more that some studies have hinted might be good for the brain. You have to take vitamin E pills to get to those kinds of intake levels. But be careful: Large doses of vitamin E can interfere with vitamin K, which is important in blood clotting and might also play a role in the brain. Also, if you take warfarin (Coumadin) then you have to be cautious about taking vitamin E because it interferes with vitamin K metabolism.

## Vitamin K

This vitamin is essential for blood clotting. Babies aren't born with the bacteria and liver function necessary to produce vitamin K, so they are given vitamin K shots in the hospital. But vitamin K is found in so many foods that deficiencies in adults are extremely rare. The tragedy of brain-damaged children being born to women taking warfarin, which blocks the action of vitamin K, has raised the possibility of vitamin K playing a role in brain function. Various lines of research suggest that it may be crucial to *nerve growth factors*, highly specific proteins necessary for neurons. Still, the evidence for vitamin K having an effect on the brain is far from conclusive.

## Vitamin C

Like vitamin E, vitamin C is an antioxidant. It is also essential to some important enzyme functions that the body needs to make collagen and *norepinephrine*, a key neurotransmitter. Several studies have shown a correlation between vitamin C blood levels and memory performance, although it's a mistake to take correlation to mean cause and effect. A Swiss study published in the June 1997 *Journal of the American Geriatrics Society* found that in a group of 442 study subjects aged 65–94, high blood concentrations of vitamin C and beta-carotene (a form of vitamin A)—but interestingly, not vitamin E—were associated with better memory performance. But, as the authors noted, vitamin C and beta-carotene come in fruits and vegetables, so this could be a more complicated fruit-and-vegetable effect, not vitamin C and beta-carotene by themselves. That same point has been made about vitamin C with respect to cancer prevention and other health claims made on its behalf.

# When (and How) to Take Your Vitamin and Mineral Supplements

PERHAPS YOUR DOCTOR has recommended that you take a calcium supplement to help forestall osteoporosis. Or extra folate, either as a hedge against heart disease or to protect against birth defects. Or maybe you're in the habit of taking a daily multivitamin/mineral supplement to bolster a diet that's sometimes not as nutritious as you'd like it to be.

In any case, you may have wondered whether your body is really soaking up whatever nutrients are compressed into that little pill. Should you take it with food or without? Avoid certain beverages, like coffee? And, if you're taking more than one kind of vitamin or mineral, swallow the tablets all at once—or spread them throughout the day?

"There's a lot of mythology out there," says Robert Russell, MD, a gastroenterologist at Tufts. To clear up the confusion, we've spelled out what you need to consider when you're looking to get the most from your vitamin or mineral supplements.

## If you take a multivitamin pill...

The advice here is straightforward: take your daily multivitamin/mineral supplement with a meal. A full stomach takes longer to empty, allowing more time for muscles there to agitate and break down the tablet at the same time that they shred food. That lets the pill dissolve more thoroughly and, in turn, be absorbed more easily into the system later on. Having food in the stomach may also help reduce the gastric irritation that some people experience with vitamin pills.

It's not necessary to spend a lot of money on a daily multivitamin. **Supplements marked "timed released," in particular, aren't** worth the extra expense. GNC's Women's Ultra Mega, for example, costs $21.99 for a 45-day supply of horse-sized pills claiming "Timed release for around-the-clock impact." But, "timed release' on vitamin products does not mean anything at all," says Srini Srinivasan, PhD, director of the Dietary Supplements Division at the United States Pharmacopeia (USP), a scientific body of experts that sets quality standards for drugs as well as supplements.

That's because there's no need to maintain a precise, constant level of vitamins in body fluids as you would for prescription drugs such as antibiotics. Thus, any standard preparation, like Theragran-M, One-A-Day Maximum, or a pharmacy brand, will do.

However, make sure to look for a designation of USP on the label. That assures you that the product has been lab-tested to disintegrate and dissolve (so that its ingredients can be properly absorbed), and that its potency and purity meet established standards.

## If you take single vitamins or minerals...

**Iron** Iron is often a concern for women of childbearing age, who may not get enough of it from food to make up for losses of iron-rich blood during menstruation. Women who take iron supplements (or multivitamin/mineral pills that contain iron), should take them at mealtime, or with a glass of juice. Certain foods, including iron-rich meat, fish, and poultry—and vitamin C-rich juice, fruits, and vegetables—help the body to extract more iron from supplements.

If you're a tea or coffee drinker, however, it's best to avoid those two beverages when taking an iron supplement or eating an iron-rich meal. Substances in coffee called polyphenols can inhibit absorption of iron from plant foods by as much as 40 percent. Tannins, the polyphenols found in tea, can inhibit iron absorption up to 70 percent. Wait about an hour and a half before taking your beverage break.

**Another potential iron blocker is the mineral calcium, which has been shown in some lab studies to inhibit iron absorption.** If you depend on a multivitamin/mineral supplement to round out your iron intake, you may be concerned, since many multi's include both calcium and iron. But, according to the USP's Dr. Srinivasan, there's probably not enough calcium in any daily multivitamin/ mineral preparation to cause a problem. "No single multi will give you large doses of calcium, such as the 1,000 to 1,200 milligrams necessary to meet the RDA," he says. It "would be too big to swallow." Multi's tend to contain only between 100 and 200 milligrams of calcium.

If you are taking an iron-containing multi and a separate calcium supplement, you can avoid potential interactions altogether by taking the pills at different meals. But whether you even need to worry about iron calcium interactions is controversial. According to James Fleet, PhD, a mineral expert at the University of North Carolina at Greensboro, the interaction is a valid one. But, he says, "Even the best research doesn't necessarily reflect what happens in the real world," where people eat different foods—in different amounts—every day. In other words, as he puts it, "the debate about calcium and iron may simply be a tempest in a teapot."

Indeed, clinical studies by Bess Dawson-Hughes, MD, who heads the Calcium and Bone Metabolism Laboratory at Tufts's USDA Human Nutrition Research Center, have shown that iron status was virtually unchanged in premenopausal women who took 1,000 milligrams of calcium a day for three months. Granted, some studies have shown impaired iron absorption in women who ate high-calcium test meals in a research lab, but Dr. Dawson-Hughes comments that "we didn't see the same problem in real diets."

The bottom line: Combining iron and calcium is not an issue for most people. However, those whose iron is on the low side might choose to play it safe by taking calcium supplements separately from their iron pills—or taking calcium tablets at a relatively low-iron meal, like a meatless lunch.

**Calcium** If calcium is your priority, as it is for many women trying to forestall brittle bones in their later years, the focus changes from getting enough iron to getting enough calcium.

Calcium carbonate, the most widely available form of calcium (found in Tums and other popular supplements), "is absorbed more consistently" with meals, says Dr. Dawson-Hughes. But the most important thing to remember, especially for those following a high-dose calcium regimen, is to divide the doses. **"If you're taking 1,000 to 1,200 milligrams of calcium a day, you should divide the doses in half, one in the morning, one in the evening, to get the best absorption,"** says Leon Ellenbogen, PhD, adjunct professor at Cornell University Medical College. The body may not be able to absorb larger doses all at once.

Also, it's a good idea in many cases to choose a calcium supplement that contains vitamin D, without which calcium cannot be efficiently absorbed. People who live in northern latitudes (like Boston or Chicago) or otherwise don't get enough sun are at the greatest risk for not getting the 200 to 600 International Units of vitamin D they need each day (vitamin D is manufactured in the skin upon exposure to the sun's rays). They should look for a supplement that has 200 to 400 units of D per 1,000 milligrams of calcium.

It should be noted that a significant portion of the population (an estimated 20 percent of people over 60 and 40 percent of people over 80) cannot absorb some kinds of calcium supplements *unless* they take them at mealtime. These people have a condition called atrophic gastritis, in which they don't secrete enough stomach acid in between meals to break down calcium carbonate.

Most people don't know whether they have atrophic gastritis—it tends to go undiagnosed—but once you're past 60 it doesn't hurt to play it safe and assume you do. Fortunately, there are two ways around it. The obvious one is to take calcium citrate instead of calcium carbonate. It can be absorbed with or between meals, whether or not the stomach secretes enough acid. The drawback is that it's hard to pack enough into a pill: you'd need to take two or three tablets to get the same 500 to 600 milligrams of calcium found in one calcium carbonate tablet. Calcium citrate also tends to be more expensive.

**Chelated minerals** Available at many health food stores, chelated minerals aren't worth the extra money you'll pay for their promises of superiority. The term "chelated" doesn't mean that a mineral is more absorbable or more available to the body than the unchelated form; it merely describes a type of chemical bond that can occur when a mineral is attached to certain compounds. If a manufacturer claims that a particular chelated formulation has been proven more absorbable in scientific studies, "they're lying," says mineral expert Dr. Fleet. "There are no great studies doing direct comparison" of chelated minerals to other kinds.

**The B vitamins** The B vitamins—thiamin, niacin, riboflavin, folate, and vitamins $B_6$ and $B_{12}$—"are generally very easily absorbed," says Tufts's Dr. Russell. The exception, as with calcium, is for people with atrophic gastritis, who can't absorb enough vitamin $B_{12}$ because they don't have enough acid in their stomach to cleave the vitamin from the protein in food. For that reason, people over 50 should take a supplement with 2.4 micrograms of $B_{12}$ (the RDA) or regularly eat $B_{12}$ fortified cereal—regardless of how much they get from foods such as meat, fish, poultry, or cheese. The $B_{12}$ from supplemental sources is easily absorbed whether or not stomach acid is present.

**Vitamins C and E** Although experts continue to debate whether doses beyond the RDA are truly beneficial, vitamins C and E are currently the two most popular vitamins on the market. Since neither one has any significant absorption or interaction problems, the choice (if you choose to take them at all) is whether to buy them in "special" forms—such as natural vitamin E or vitamin C with rose hips or bioflavonids.

**"The natural form of vitamin E (which is simply a different configuration of the same chemical compound) is in fact more rapidly absorbed and more avidly maintained in tissue,"** explains Jeffrey Blumberg, PhD, an antioxidant expert at Tufts University's Human Nutrition Research Center. For that reason, he says, you need more synthetic vitamin E to have the same effect. How much more? Researchers used to think that 1.36 International Units of synthetic vitamin E were equal to one unit of the natural form. But Dr. Blumberg says that recent research indicates the natural form may be nearly twice as strong.

The dose associated with E's potential benefits (protecting against heart disease and boosting immune function), ranges from 100 to 400 units. Depending on how much different preparations cost, it may require doing a bit of math to figure out whether you're better off getting the more expensive natural vitamin E or just taking more of the less costly synthetic form.

Unlike vitamin E, the natural and synthetic forms of vitamin C are equally potent—it doesn't matter whether you get the vitamin from pills, foods, or rose-hip extracts. Paying a premium for esterified vitamin C preparations or "enhancers" like bioflavonoids, which haven't been shown to have any absorption benefits, doesn't appear to be worth the extra money, either.

# Nutrient-Drug Interactions and Food

*by J. Anderson and H. Hart*[1]

**Quick Facts...**

Medications need to be taken at different times relative to meals.

Drugs and medications can interact with nutrients in food.

Consult a physician when health problems persist.

During pregnancy and nursing always consult a physician or pharmacist before taking any medication. Drugs taken by the mother may affect the infant.

Take all medications only with water, unless otherwise advised.

Check with a doctor or pharmacist for the proper way and time to take medication.

It is a difficult and complex problem to accurately determine the effects of food and nutrients on a particular drug. There are many dramatic results or problems caused by food-drug, drug-drug and alcohol-food-drug interactions. The following table is designed to help the reader become more knowledgeable about drug interactions and their effect on food, a nutrient or another drug that may produce unexpected results or cause additional health problems.

## Generic Drugs

Generic drugs often are substituted for brand-name counterparts. They usually are more economical than brand-name drugs. Possible exceptions might be enteric-coated aspirin.

Patients may have concerns about the quality, efficacy, potency or consistency of generic drugs. Generics are therapeutically equivalent to brands approved and rated by the Food and Drug Administration. Many are made by major brand-name companies.

## Over-the-Counter (OTC) Drugs

Points to remember:

- OTC drugs usually are meant only to relieve symptoms, not cure a disease or illness.
- Improper use can make symptoms worse or conceal a serious condition that should be brought to a doctor's attention. Never take OTC drugs longer than recommended on the label. If symptoms persist or if new symptoms occur, see a doctor.
- Read the label carefully before taking an OTC product and every time an OTC product is bought. There may be important changes in indications, warnings or directions.
- People with allergies or chronic health problems should be especially careful to read the ingredient, warning and caution statements carefully. If there are any questions, consult a doctor or pharmacist.
- Check expiration dates from time to time. Destroy in the safest way possible any drugs that are outdated or that have deteriorated, such as discolored eyedrops or ointment, or vinegar-smelling aspirin.
- Keep all drugs and medications out of the reach of children.
- When pregnant or nursing a baby, check with a health professional before taking any drugs.

## Table 1: Effects of food and nutrients on drugs.

| If You Take: | Be Careful With: | Because: |
|---|---|---|
| **Analgesic and anti-inflammatory agents**: Aspirin, Ibuprofen, Indomethacin, Acetaminophen | Co-administration with food. | Absorption rate may be delayed or reduced due to decreased stomach emptying rate. |
| **Antibiotics:** Penicillin Erythromycin Tetracycline | Acidic foods: caffeine drinks, tomatoes, fruit juice. Same as penicillin. Foods rich in calcium: milk, cheese, ice cream, yogurt. Don't avoid milk products but take them at a different time. | Increase stomach acid may increase destruction of this drug in the stomach. Empty stomach for better absorption. Calcium, iron preparations and some antacids decrease absorption of the drug or render it ineffective, probably due to chelation and an increase in gastric pH. |
| **Anticoagulants:** (Blood Thinners) Dicumarol, Coumadin | Green leafy vegetables, beef liver, broccoli, asparagus, mineral oil, tomato, coffee | These foods contain vitamin K (promotes blood clotting), which interfere with the effect of the blood thinner. Mineral oil decreases the absorption of vitamin K and may increase the effect of the anticoagulant. |
| **Antidepressants:** (MAO-monoamine oxidase inhibitors) | Tyramine-rich foods: aged cheese, avocados, wine, sour cream, chicken livers, yeast products, pickled herring. Excessive caffeine: chocolate, tea, coffee. | Tyramine may cause potentially lethal increases in blood pressure, fever, terrible headache, vomiting, possibly death. |
| **Antihypertensives:** (Drugs for high blood pressure) | Natural licorice. Foods with excessive sodium: cured meats, pickled vegetables, canned soups, processed foods, especially cheese, salted snacks, added salt at table. | Natural licorice contains a substance that causes excessive water retention and thereby increased blood pressure. |
| **Bronchodilators:** Theophylline | Charcoal-broiled foods and high carbohydrate diet. Don't eat large amounts of high protein foods: meat, milk, eggs, cheese. | Too much charcoal and carbohydrates decreases absorption of this drug. Protein increases the metabolism of the drug. |
| **Corticosteroids:** Prednisone, Solu-medrol, Hydrocortisone | Foods high in sodium: cured meats, pickled vegetables, canned soups, processed foods, especially cheese, salted snacks, added salt at table. | This class of drugs causes increased sodium and water retention leading to edema. |
| **Diuretics:** **Potassium Wasting:** Modiuretic, Naqua, Lasix, Oretic | Natural licorice | See antihypertensives. Diuretics may cause excessive losses of potassium and severe electrolyte disturbances; also loss of vitamin B complex, magnesium, calcium. |
| **Laxatives:** Dulcolax | Milk | Laxative becomes ineffective and causes stomach irritation. |
| **Iron supplements**: | Taking with bran, or with calcium, zinc or copper supplements. | These minerals and bran make iron unavailable. |
| **Potassium Sparing:** Dyrenium, Aldactone | Potassium-rich foods: bananas, figs, wheat germ, orange juice (2 or 3 glasses), salt substitutes, Monosodium glutamate (MSG), sodium-rich foods. | May cause excessive retention of potassium and cardiac problems. Salt substitutes may contain potassium rather than sodium. |
| **Theophylline:** Theolair, Somophylline Levodopa (L-Dopa) (for Parkinson's disease) | Co-administration with food. High protein foods: milk, meat, eggs, cheese. Foods rich in vitamin $B_6$: beef/pork liver, wheat germ, yeast products. | Decreased absorption rate. An increase in protein decreases the absorption of this drug. $B_6$ antagonizes the drug. |

## Table 2: Effects of drugs on food or nutrients.

| If You Take: | You May Require Extra | Because |
|---|---|---|
| **Alcohol, particularly excessive use.** | Vitamin $B_{12}$, folate, magnesium. | Turnover of these nutrients increases, and food intake decreases. |
| **Analgesics:** Salicylates (aspirin) | Vitamin C, folate, vitamin K. | Aspirin increases loss of vitamin C and competes with folate and vitamin K. |
| **Antacids** | Thiamin (Vitamin $B_1$), taken at a different time. Depending on type of antacid, possibly magnesium, phosphorus, iron, vitamin A, folate. | Inactivates thiamine. These drugs cause decreased absorption of these nutrients. |
| **Antibiotics** | Nutrients | Appetite suppression and diarrhea are caused by some of these agents. |
| **Anticancer drugs.** | Nutrients | See Antibiotics. |
| **Anticholinergics:** Elavil, Thorazine | Fluids | Saliva thickens and loses its ability to prevent tooth decay. |
| **Anticonvulsants** | Folate, vitamin D. | These drugs cause decreased absorption of folate, possibly leading to megaloblastic anemia. Increases turnover of vitamin D, especially in children. |
| **Antidepressants:** Lithium carbonate, Lithane, Lithobid, Lithonate, Lithotabs, Eskalith | Water (2-3 qts./day) and take with food. | This medication may cause a metallic taste, nausea, vomiting, dry mouth, loss of appetite, weight gain and increased thirst. |
| **Sedatives:** Barbiturates | Folate, vitamin D, vitamin $B_{12}$, thiamin, vitamin C. | Drugs increase the rate these vitamins are used by the body. |
| **Anti-inflammatory agents** | Folate | These medications decrease folate absorption. |
| **Cholesterol-lowering medications:** Questran | Fat-soluble vitamins: A, D, E, K, folate, iron. | May cause decreased absorption of these vitamins and minerals. |
| **Corticosteroids:** Prednisone, Solu-medrol Hydrocortisone | Protein, potassium, calcium, magnesium, zinc, vitamin C, vitamin $B_6$. | These drugs cause an increase in excretion. |
| **Diuretics:** Potassium wasting; Naqua, Lasix, Oretic | Potassium, calcium, magnesium, zinc. | These drugs cause an increase in excretion of these minerals. |
| **Mineral oil** | Fat-soluble vitamins: A, D, E, and K; calcium, phosphorus, potassium. | Mineral oil decreases absorption of these vitamins and minerals. |
| **Oral contraceptives** | Vitamin $B_6$ and folate. | They may cause selective malabsorption or increased metabolism and turnover. |
| **Antacids** | Tagamet, Indomethacin, Naprosyn | Antacids inhibit or delay the absorption of these medications. |

## Aspirin vs. Acetaminophen vs. Ibuprofen

Aspirin, acetaminophen and ibuprofen all have analgesic (pain control) and antipyretic (fever control) properties. Only aspirin and ibuprofen also contain anti-inflammatory properties. Acetaminophen does not produce the stomach or intestinal irritation or allergic reactions that aspirin can. Gastrointestinal side effects observed with aspirin are greatly reduced with ibuprofen, although patients with aspirin hypersensitivity can have similar reactions.

To reduce stomach upset from ibuprofen, take it with food or an antacid. Avoid alcohol or aspirin with ibuprofen.

Naproxen sodium, which has analgesic, antipyretic and anti-inflammatory properties, is indicated for the

## Table 3: Effects of drugs on drugs.

| If You Take: | Be Careful With | Because: |
|---|---|---|
| **Anticonvulsant medication:** Dilantin | Anticoagulants. Digitalis heart medications. Sulfa antibiotics. Antabuse. | Many produce toxic levels of Dilantin and cause hemorrhaging by raising the anticoagulant level. After prolonged anticonvulsant therapy, effectiveness of digitalis medication may decrease. May prevent normal elimination of epilepsy drugs. If taken on top of Dilantin, each drug may independently produce serious side effects. Nervous system toxicity and blood ailments are possibilities. |
| **Antidepressants: Tricyclics:** Sinequan Adapin, Elavil Lithium, Norpramin | Alcohol, barbiturates, Tagamet Blood thinners. Diuretics. Anticonvulsants. MAO inhibitors (used for depression or high blood pressure). Minor tranquilizers: Benzodiazepines. | Sedation and drop in body temperature may occur. Decreased absorption. Antidepressant toxicity can occur. Increased anticoagulant effect. Increases effect of Lithium. Antidepressants can increase seizure susceptibility. May cause excitation, delirium, rapid pulse, elevated body temperature and convulsions. Severe sedation may make concentrating difficult and driving dangerous. |
| **Antidiabetic agents (oral and insulin)** | Calcium channel blockers: Isoptin, Calan. Oral contraceptives. MAO Inhibitors, Tetracycline. | These medications alter carbohydrate metabolism. Impair glucose tolerance. Hypoglycemia can occur. |
| **Antihistamines** | Alcohol. | Sedation can occur. |
| **Arthritis medication (potent anti-inflammatory agents)** | Blood thinners. Aspirin, aspirin-containing pain relievers. Birth control pills. | Increases susceptibility to internal hemorrhaging. May result in ulcers. Aspirin can diminish the effectiveness of the more powerful drug. Could decrease effectiveness. |
| **Aspirin** | Diabetes medicine (oral). Drugs for gout. Vitamin C. | May cause excessive lowering of blood sugar. Aspirin can block the beneficial effects. Never combine them. Large doses of vitamin C can prolong and possibly intensify the action of aspirin. Could produce salicylate side effects (headaches or dizziness) in sensitive people. |
| **Barbiturates** | Alcohol. | Increased central nervous system depression. |
| **Benzodiazepine:** Valium, Librium, Tranxene, Xanax | Tagamet. | Increased sedation can occur. |
| **Blood thinners:** Coumadin, Dicumarol | Analgesic pain relievers: aspirin products and arthritis medication. Alcohol. Antibiotics.<br><br>Cholesterol-lowering medications: Atromid-S.<br>Thyroid gland supplements. Questran, laxatives, mineral oil. | These enhance blood thinning response, irritate stomach, and may lead to ulcer and hemorrhage. Can increase or decrease blood thinning effects. Decrease vitamin K production increasing chance of hemorrhage. Augments blood thinning response to serious hemorrhage. When combined with anti-coagulant medication, patient is vulnerable to hemorrhage unless dosage is decreased.<br><br>These drugs decrease absorption. |
| **Calcium channel blockers** | Calcium supplements. | Decreased response to blockers. |
| **Corticosteroids:** Prednisone, Solu-medrol | Cholesterol-lowering medications. | Inhibits absorption. |
| **Digitalis:** Lanoxin | Antacids. Cholesterol-lowering medications. Valium. Diuretics. | Decreased absorption. Decreased length of effect. Increased effect. Digitalis toxicity due to potassium loss. |
| **Oral contraceptives** | Valium. | Oral contraceptives enhance effect of Valium. |
| **Tetracycline** | Antacids. Zinc, iron supplements. | Cuts down on effectiveness of Tetracycline. Same as antacids. |

same conditions as aspirin, ibuprofen and acetaminophen but should not be taken with them. Anyone who generally has three or more alcoholic drinks per day should consult a physician on when and how to take naproxen sodium and other pain relievers.

## References

*Facts and Comparisons Drug Information.* J.B. Lippincott., 1987.

Hansten, P.D., *Drug Interactions.* fifth edition, Lea & Febiger, 1985.

Lewis, K.T., Here's a brief overview of important drug-nutrient interactions. *Pharmacy Times.* May, 1987.

Hecht, Annabel. "OTC Drug Labels: Must Reading," *FDA Consumer,* October 1985, pp. 33–35.

Rados, Bill. "Generic Drugs: Cutting Cost, Not Corners," *FDA Consumer,* October 1985, pp. 27–29.

*Handbook: Interactions of Selected Drugs With Nutritional Status,* Daphne Roe, American Dietetic Association, 3rd Edition, 1984.

*Food and Drug Interaction Guide,* L.H. Rottmann, NebGuide (HEG85-206), 1985.

*Drug-Nutrient Interactions,* Daphne Roe, Hoffman-La Roche, Inc.

Joe Graddon, *The People's Pharmacy 2.* New York: The Hearst Corporation, 1980.

## Note

1. J. Anderson, Colorado State University Cooperative Extension foods and nutrition specialist and professor; and H. Hart, associate specialist; food science and human nutrition.

---

Issued in furtherance of Cooperative Extension work, Acts of May 8 and June 30, 1914, in cooperation with the U.S. Department of Agriculture, Milan A. Rewerts, Director of Cooperative Extension, Colorado State University, Fort Collins, Colorado. Cooperative Extension programs are available to all without discrimination. No endorsement of products mentioned is intended nor is criticism implied of products not mentioned.

# UNIT 3

# Diet and Disease: Through the Life Span

## Unit Selections



## Key Points to Consider

- What are some of the limitations of diet and disease studies?
- What changes should you make in your lifestyle in order to effectively meet your nutrient needs?

**Links: www.dushkin.com/online/**
These sites are annotated in the World Wide Web pages.

**American Cancer Society**
*http://www.cancer.org*

**American Heart Association**
*http://www.americanheart.org*

**The Food Allergy Network**
*http://www.foodallergy.org*

**Go Ask Alice! from Columbia University Health Services**
*http://www.goaskalice.columbia.edu*

**Heinz Infant & Toddler Nutrition**
*http://www.heinzbaby.com*

**LaLeche League International**
*http://www.lalecheleague.org*

**Nutrition and Kids**
*http://www.nutritionandkids.net/1227*

**Vegetarian Pages**
*http://www.veg.org*

In Ancient Greece, Hippocrates, the father of medicine, stated in his oath to serve humanity that the physician should use diet as part of his "arsenal" to fight disease. In ancient times, the healing arts included diet, exercise, and the power of the mind to cure disease.

Since those times, research that focuses on the connection between diet and disease has unraveled the role of many nutrients in degenerative disease prevention or reversal, but, frequently, results are controversial and need to be interpreted cautiously before a population-wide health message is mandated. We have also come to better understand the role of genetics in the expression of disease and its importance in how we respond to dietary change. With the decoding of the human genome, the dietitian will be able to predict susceptibility to disease and prescribe individualized diets. Additionally, research about diet and disease has enabled us to understand the importance and uniqueness of the individual (age, gender, ethnicity, and genetics) and his or her particular relation to diet.

With the recent advances in research in the area of phytochemicals such as flavonoids, carotenoids, saponins, indoles, and others in foods, especially fruits and vegetables, and their potential to prevent disease, thereby increasing both quality of life and life expectancy, we are at the zenith of a nutrition revolution. Several articles in this unit describe the role of these compounds in health and disease. The most prevalent degenerative diseases in industrial countries, which are quickly spreading in developing countries, are cancer, cardiovascular disease, diabetes, obesity, and osteoporosis. Phytochemicals have been reported to lower the risk of certain types of cancer and to decrease cholesterol in blood and prevent oxidation of the LDL lipoprotein—risk factors for developing cardiovascular disease. Furthermore, phytochemicals may protect against the development of diabetes and help prevent obesity. A diet rich in fruits and vegetables is the best source of phytochemicals.

But how is the consumer to know what to believe? Even though epidemiological and clinical studies have their pitfalls, the problem is not always the experts but many people who do not understand how science works. This includes much of the media, since information is usually reported out of context, with the goal of creating a sensation.

In the first article, David Masci examines the pros and cons of controversial issues such as alcohol and megadoses of vitamin supplements, including antioxidant vitamins on a host of degenerative diseases (cancer, heart disease, etc.) He also reviews current evidence on the link between diet, exercise, and the 20 types of cancer. Since, we cannot pinpoint a clear-cut cause-and-effect relationship, it is prudent to advise that cancer risk decreases if one eats a well-balanced diet, high in whole grains, vegetables, fruits, and beans, and low in fat, saturated fat, and cholesterol.

The decoding of the human genome is one of the most crucial medical projects of the all time, and it has improved our understanding of the genetics behind certain diseases. Eventually, it will help "fingerprint" people, thus identifying the exact gene that makes a person susceptible to a certain disease. This can be used to detect and treat disease at early stages, and it will help nutritionists prescribe "individualized" diets for high-risk persons.

Diabetes is a degenerative disease that decreases both quality and quantity of life. It can lead to heart and kidney disease, blindness, nerve damage, and cognitive decline. It is striking that diabetes incidence has increased by 33 percent in the last 10 years, not only in the United States but worldwide. Maintaining normal levels of blood glucose by watching your weight, exercising, and eating high-fiber, low-glycemic-index foods, as well as decreasing saturated and trans fat, will cut your risk for diabetes.

High levels of homocysteine, an amino acid that is a metabolic intermediate in methionine metabolism, seem to be a new risk factor related to heart disease. Ensuring that our diet is adequate in folic acid and vitamin B6 by means of eating a balanced diet that is rich in fish, grains, legumes, green leafy vegetables, and fortified cereals will help keep our levels of homocysteine normal and will prevent heart disease.

Hypertension is a disease that plagues one out of five Americans. Until recently, health professionals advised reducing body weight and dietary sodium as a non-drug approach to reducing high blood pressure. The Dietary Approach to Stop Hypertension (DASH diet) emphasizes low-fat dairy products rich in calcium for every meal and fruits and vegetables rich in potassium and many minerals and vitamins. It will help you reduce high blood pressure and also decrease your risk for heart attack and osteoporosis.

Americans are spending more than $3 billion a year on soy foods because of the endorsements soy has gotten from the FDA and some health professional groups. Are we premature in rushing to take supplements or add soy foods to our diet? In a review from Harvard University's *Women's' Health Watch* magazine, soy's documented benefits on lowering cholesterol, easing menopausal symptoms, and protecting bone strength are reviewed, but its role in breast cancer is questioned. Potential problems with brain cells, the reproductive tract, the thyroid, and allergies are discussed.

Twenty-two percent of the U.S. population by the year 2030 will be composed of people 65 years of age and older. Health care professionals are responsible for ensuring maintenance of good health and functional independence for the elderly thus "adding life to years not years to life." Of course, the elderly are at higher nutritional risk due to a high prevalence of chronic diseases and nutritionally inadequate diets—diets lacking in many vitamins and minerals as well as calcium. Older people should be encouraged to choose foods that contain a high nutrient density and adequate amounts of protein, calcium, vitamin D, vitamin B12, fiber, and water. They should be physically active, avoid smoking, limit alcohol consumption, and choose nutritional supplements carefully.

A widespread problem among women athletes is the triad of eating disorders, menstrual irregularities, and osteoporosis. Pressure on the athletes to look lean leads to erratic eating behaviors and thus eating disorders. This results in menstrual irregularities that eventually can lead to bone loss, making women in their 20s have fragile bones resembling the bones of women in their 70s. Nutrition education to emphasize prevention and teach good nutrition habits will support high levels of performance and reduce the incidence of this triad.

# Diet and Health

## The Issues

By David Masci

At the Safeway supermarket in Washington's affluent Georgetown neighborhood, the produce department—including a modest assortment of organically grown produce—takes up nearly a fifth of the store.

Just a few blocks away, a Fresh Fields Market gives even more attention to its produce. Specializing in all-natural foods, the upscale store offers a cornucopia of organic fruits and vegetables—including more than 10 varieties of lettuce. Beside each display, a tag attests to the nutritional benefit of each product. On a nearby aisle, bins contain grains, rice, dried fruits and nuts and other "health foods."

The increased attention to produce at traditional supermarkets like Safeway and the emergence of specialty chains like Fresh Fields reflects American consumers' growing awareness of the link between food and health.

"Over the last 10 or 15 years," says Debrah Lambert, Safeway's director of corporate public affairs, "the number of produce items we offer has grown rapidly as people have come to understand how healthy fruits and vegetables are for them."

Indeed, says Manfred Kroger, professor emeritus of food science at Pennsylvania State University, a growing number of Americans realize that what they eat may determine the length and quality of their lives. "People are beginning to understand that food is important, and not just for nutritional purposes," he says.

Kroger and other health experts generally agree that the key to healthy eating is foods high in fiber and vitamins and minerals and low in fat. "When you break it down to its most basic level, you need to get people to eat more fruits and vegetables and less fat," says Bonnie Liebman, director of nutrition at the Center for Science in the Public Interest, a health advocacy group.

"Study after study has shown that a largely plant-based diet, along with lots of whole grains, is the best way to go," agrees Reed Mangels—a nutrition adviser at the Vegetarian Resource group, an advocacy organization in Baltimore, Md.

But around the edges of this nutritional monolith there is much disagreement. For instance, while most experts agree that taking a daily multivitamin is a good idea, they differ on the efficacy of pills or supplements that contain single, targeted doses of certain vitamins.

### Americans are Getting Fatter

*Far more Americans are overweight and obese today than in the 1960s. More than half of all adults—54 percent—were overweight according to 1994 data, the most recent available. A greater percentage of men are overweight, but more women are obese*

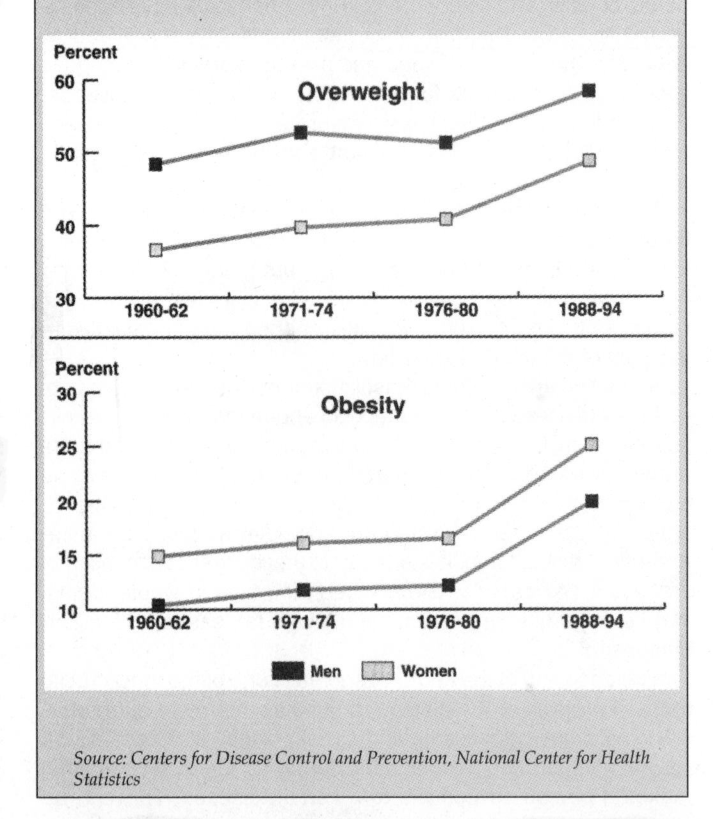


*Source: Centers for Disease Control and Prevention, National Center for Health Statistics*

Jeffrey Blumberg, a professor of nutrition at Tufts University in Boston, says there is "compelling evidence" that taking some vitamins at higher doses helps prevent some diseases. Blumberg and others point, for example, to a host of epidemiological studies indicating that vitamins E, C, and other antioxidants boost immune function and probably help protect against certain forms of cancer, heart disease and other ailments. They also say that folic acid and minerals such as calcium can be beneficial when taken in supplement form.

*As Americans become increasingly aware of the link between food and health, grocery stores have been expanding the size of their produce sections, as well as the variety of fruits and vegetables they offer.*

But Ira Goldberg, chairman of the Preventive Medicine and Nutrition Department at Columbia University's College of Physicians and Surgeons in New York City, argues that vitamins offer no real health benefit. "I tell people not to take vitamins because there's really no evidence that they are useful," he says.

Goldberg and other nutritionists say that clinical trials have produced no conclusive evidence that vitamins prevent disease. Indeed, they say some studies have shown that very high doses of certain nutrients, like beta-carotene, can actually be harmful for certain people.

Experts also differ on the health impact of alcohol. Few would call alcohol a health food, but according to a growing body of research a drink or two a day can actually reduce the risk of heart disease and stroke. Some scientists even argue that doctors should inform their patients about the benefits of moderate drinking.

"The evidence is clear: Drinking boosts good blood cholesterol and reduces clotting in arteries," says Eric Rimm, an associate professor of epidemiology and nutrition at Harvard University's School of Public Health. "People should know that drinking sensibly helps to prolong life."

But many health experts say that the benefits of alcohol are far outweighed by the damage done by immoderate drinking, ranging from liver disease and brain damage to increased risk of auto and other accidents.

Alcohol opponents worry that encouraging "moderate" drinking runs the risk of leading to alcohol abuse. "People may use this as an excuse to drink more, and that can cause great damage," says Richard Levinson, associate executive director of the American Public Health Association (APHA). He contends that doctors can do much more for their patients by encouraging them to eat properly and exercise regularly.

Health professionals also disagree over the benefits of red meat. Some say that moderate amounts of beef, pork or lamb have great health benefits, by providing certain essential nutrients—like vitamin B-12, zinc and iron—that are impossible or difficult to obtain from a plant-based diet.

"Meat has tremendous nutritional value and is very good for you," says Randall Huffman, vice president of scientific affairs for the American Meat Institute. Even the fat in meat is—in some respects—healthy, according to Huffman.

But Mangels at the Vegetarian Resource Group argues that red meat is unnecessary and unhealthy. "You don't really need meat," he says, pointing out that plant-based diets provide almost all necessary nutrients and that vitamin supplements and fortified foods can make up any nutritional shortfalls.

In addition, according to Mangels and other vegetarians, meat contains a high level of saturated fat, which increases the risk of heart disease. Meat has also been linked to diabetes and some cancers, she adds.

As health experts debate the pros and cons of certain dietary choices and their impact on long-term health, here are some of the questions they are asking.

### *Do high doses of certain vitamins help prevent serious illnesses like cancer?*

Almost every day, it seems, contradictory, new studies are announced about the efficacy of vitamin supplements. Vitamin E, for instance, became very popular after a wave of research showed that a single capsule of the antioxidant taken daily could help reduce the incidence of a variety of chronic illnesses, especially heart disease.[1]

But a recent Canadian study involving more than 9,000 people with heart disease found that daily consumption of vitamin E supplements did nothing to lower the risk of a heart attack or stroke. And yet an English study, released at roughly the same time, showed that taking the vitamin each day could lower the rate of non-fatal heart attacks.[2]

"The evidence on vitamin supplements is only partially in, and we shouldn't really be ready to say anything overly definitive about them yet," Levinson says. "We're going to need a lot of long-term studies before we can say for sure what is or isn't worth taking."

Still, many say there is enough evidence, especially with certain vitamins, to justify taking them in supplement form. "We certainly have compelling evidence that some vitamins at higher doses than the recommended intakes can help prevent certain diseases," Tufts University's Blumberg says.

A host of studies demonstrate a connection between regular use of vitamin supplements and disease prevention, according to Blumberg. For instance, he says, there is ample evidence that vitamins C and E and other antioxidants boost immune function and probably help prevent heart disease and certain forms of cancer.

Many researchers support the use of vitamin E supplements. "The safety of vitamin E is now beyond question, and there seems to be the beginnings of good evidence to suggest that it might help prevent cancer, heart disease and stroke," says John Repine, president of the Webb-Waring Institute for Cancer, Aging, and AntiOxidant Research in Denver. Taking the supplement is important Repine says, "because it's clear that most of us don't get enough vitamin E in our regular diets."

*Americans get a third of their calories from eating in restaurants. Eating out can be a healthy experience, but often it isn't. To boost taste, restaurants often load up their dishes with fat and salt, and a single serving can contain more calories than the Agriculture Department recommends for an entire day.*

In addition, Repine argues, the evidence is clear that calcium tablets help women prevent osteoporosis in later life. He also points to research that suggests that selenium might help prevent prostate cancer in men.

### Americans Eating Less Red Meat

*U.S. consumption of chicken has almost doubled since 1970 while beef has fallen by about 20 percent. Medical experts say that's relatively good news, given the link between red meat and heart disease and colon and prostate cancer. However, they remain concerned that the average American still eats more red meat (beef, pork, veal and lamb) than chicken, and that much of the chicken is fried in unhealthy fat.*

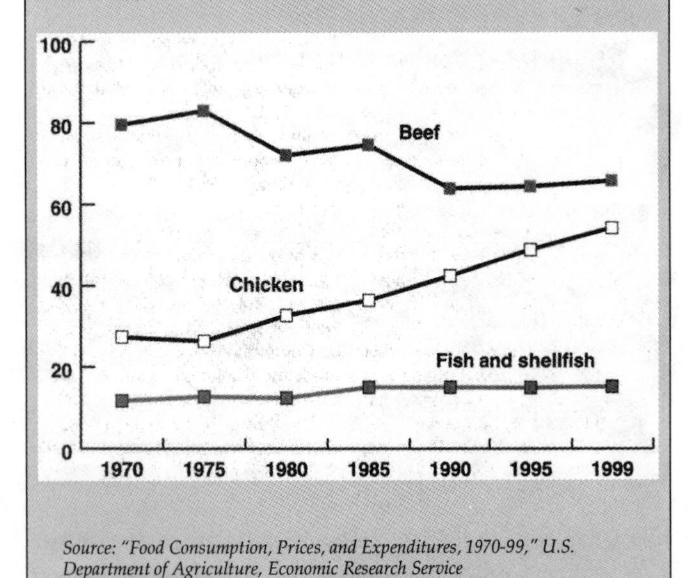


*Source: "Food Consumption, Prices, and Expenditures, 1970-99," U.S. Department of Agriculture, Economic Research Service*

But other researchers argue that high doses of single vitamins probably do little or no good and may even be harmful in certain cases. "It looks to me that when you take a single nutrient like that in a high dose, you produce no appreciable effect," says Robert Russell, a professor of medicine and nutrition at Tufts.

"There's pretty good evidence that taking vitamins doesn't really improve health," agrees Columbia's Goldberg. "Vitamin pills are a big waste of money."

Vitamin opponents argue that there is a huge difference between getting nutrients naturally through the digestion of food and ingesting them in single-dose supplements. "We don't understand it all yet, but there's something in the nutrients in foods that, in combination with each other, are protective," Russell says. "They work in concert, which is something you don't get with a pill."

Russell and Goldberg are among the experts who argue that most of the evidence showing a beneficial effect from taking vitamin supplements is very suspect because it has come from epidemiological studies, which are not the most accurate way of showing a vitamin's ability to prevent disease.

In epidemiological studies, researchers draw conclusions based on past behavior. For instance, scientists might find 500 people who said they've been taking vitamin E and 500 who haven't and then compare how the two groups fare in terms of heart disease or cancer. Such evidence is not useless, Goldberg says, but it is suspect because there is no real way to effectively control for outside influences, like diet or lifestyle choices, which could be the real cause for higher or lower disease rates. "These studies are suggestive, nothing else," he says.

More accurate results come from "clinical trials" or "double-blind studies," in which subjects are chosen by researchers and then given either the vitamin in question or a placebo. This allows scientists more control over the experiment and thus gives them a better chance of removing outside factors that could influence results.

Here, the news doesn't appear to be very good for vitamin takers. "Every time we've had something that looked promising in epidemiological studies, that promise hasn't been born out in clinical trials," says Susan Mayne, an associate professor of epidemiology and public health at Yale University.

Indeed, Mayne and others argue, some double-blind studies of vitamin and mineral supplements actually have been shown to have a negative health impact. A study in Finland with almost 30,000 middle-aged smokers found that taking beta-carotene (a powerful antioxidant) supplements actually increased the chances of getting lung cancer.[3]

Indeed, vitamin opponents say, people who take high-dose supplements may be taking too much of one substance or another. "There's frequently this assumption that if something is good for us, a lot of it is even better," Mayne says. "The truth, though, is that some vitamins in very high doses are clearly toxic and do more harm than good." For instance, she says, a lot of vitamin A can be very harmful because any excess accu-

## Understanding the Need for Fat

Every year, millions of Americans go to great lengths to lose weight. They spend more than $30 billion on everything from draconian diets to surgery in an effort to slim down thighs and bulging waistlines.[1]

But for all the money, time and effort, the nation is getting fatter. More than half of all Americans are overweight, up from 43 percent 40 years ago. And almost a quarter of the population is now obese.

Most people who are overweight try to lose those extra pounds, but few succeed. Dieters often lose weight while they're actively on a diet, but only one in nine actually keeps the fat off for more than a few years. Many overweight people jump from one diet plan to another, hoping that the latest effort will be their last. Not surprisingly, a recent Harris poll found that two-thirds of all adults had gone on an average of 11 diets.[2]

As a result, overweight people are often thought to be undisciplined, unable to control their appetites. But recent research by evolutionary biologists indicates that weight gain may have as much to do with genetics as with uncontrolled eating.

"It's clear that the failure of some people to regulate their body weight is not just a matter of overeating or being lazy," said John Speakman, a professor of zoology at Aberdeen University in Scotland. "One idea is the 'thrifty genotype' hypothesis, which suggests that people who are prone to obesity have been favored by natural selection in the past because they are good at storing fat."[3]

Indeed, fat wasn't always a villain. For almost all of human history, eating foods high in fat was a key to survival. It takes a lot energy to run a human being—especially one constantly on the move in search of sustenance, as our ancestors were—and foods rich in fat are potent energy sources.

Scientists think that before early humans learned how to grow and store food about 11,000 years ago, they often went for days without eating anything substantial.[4] Thus, those who could store fat easily after a successful hunt had a better chance of surviving the inevitable lean times.

The need for fat also explains why hamburgers, cheese and other fatty foods taste so good: Mother Nature made fat tasty to the human palate to encourage us to eat as much of it as we could.

For early man, eating too much fatty food wasn't a problem. After all, few people survived to an age where heart disease and diabetes became risks. In fact, throughout most of human history, average life expectancy has been below age 40.

But everything changed when civilization came along, with its settled agriculture and, eventually, supermarkets and fast-food restaurants. People stopped moving around as much, and their diets became regular. Bodies designed by evolution to crave and store fat had access to unlimited amounts, with predictable results.

Paul Ehrlich, a professor of biological sciences at Stanford University, called the change "a good example of an evolutionary hangover, something that evolved for a very good reason, and then when the environment changes very suddenly, we haven't been able to evolve rapidly enough to keep ourselves protected from that threat."[5]

The result has been "one of the major public health crises in our society," Ehrlich says.[6] Indeed, obesity causes an estimated 300,000 deaths in the United States each year.

Drugmakers are trying to come up with a solution. For example, Millennium Pharmaceuticals, in Cambridge, Mass., has identified a number of genes that seem to predispose humans to eating and storing fat. In partnership with pharmaceutical giant Hoffman-LaRoche, Millennium is developing drugs that aim to, in essence, turn the genes off—ending the hangover.[7]

---

2. Mike Thomas, "Feeling Fat? Blame Your Stone Age Genetics," *Orlando Sentinel*, Sept. 28, 1997.
3. *Ibid.*
4. Quoted in "It's Not My Fault. It's My Genes," *Bristol Evening Post*, March 18, 2000.
5. Jared Diamond, *Guns, Germs, and Steel: The Fates of Human Societies* (1997), p. 86.
6. Quoted from "Talk of the Nation/Science Friday," National Public Radio, Oct. 27, 2000.
7. Quoted in *Ibid.*
8. Geoffrey Carr, "Ingenious Medicine," *The Economist*, July 1, 2000.

mulates in the liver and in fatty tissue, where it can eventually become toxic.

Vitamin opponents believe that the less accurate epidemiological studies show more promise because they study a group self-selected to be healthier. "People who want to take vitamins are probably much more health conscious and so are more likely to be doing the things they need to be doing—in terms of diet and exercise—to stay healthy," Mayne says.

Finally, opponents of supplements argue that they can do great harm by distracting someone from eating a healthy, balanced diet. "It's so much easier for someone with, say, high cholesterol to go to a health-food store and buy an armful of vitamins than it is for them to change their diet and start exercising," Goldberg says.

But vitamin boosters counter that most of the criticism of supplements is wrong or misguided. For one thing, they say, there is ample evidence that the body does absorb vitamins and minerals in supplements. "There are studies showing that when you take folic acid, the levels of foliate in your blood increase," says Harvard's Rimm. "In the case of folic acid, the body actually absorbs more of it from the supplement than from food."

Rimm and others also argue there is real—though not definite—evidence of the efficacy of some vitamins, such as vitamin E, folic acid and selenium. "In addition to the epidemiological evidence, some clinical trials tell us that some vitamins—notably vitamin E—may have benefits," Rimm says. He adds that there also are contradictory studies showing no cardiovascular benefit to taking vitamin E.

Vitamin supporters also claim that single, targeted doses are safe. "There is simply no evidence to suggest that taking single nutrient vitamins on top of a multi is unsafe" Tufts' Blumberg says. "Safety just isn't an issue here."

Finally, supporters contend, vitamins should not be discounted just because someone might use them in place of a balanced diet. "We know that vitamin pills can't replace a healthy diet, which is the reason they're called supplements," Rimm says. "But it's silly to say that they're no good, because someone might use them as an excuse to eat poorly." Indeed, Rimm adds, "it's like telling someone who drives fast not to wear a seatbelt, simply because their driving is already dangerous."

### *Should moderate drinking be encouraged to prevent heart disease?*

In the late 1970s, health researchers began noting a strange health phenomenon. In France—proud home of high-cholesterol foods such as goose-liver pate and rich cheeses—rates of heart disease were significantly lower than in the United States—in fact, fully one-third lower.

Scientists quickly discovered that in France and other countries with lower heart disease rates—including Italy and Spain—wine was consumed by most adults at most meals. The news media soon began hailing the findings as "The French Paradox": wine, which conventional wisdom had long been held to be unhealthy—might actually be good for you.

Since then, more than 60 studies have reported that moderate consumption of alcohol (not just wine) can help protect a person from heart disease. Scientists believe that alcohol helps the heart by boosting the blood levels of high density (HDL) or "good" cholesterol by about 12 percent.[4] A recent study by researchers at Columbia University also linked moderate drinking to reduced risk of stroke.[5]

But many experts question whether moderate drinking (usually defined as one or two glasses per day) should be promoted for health reasons—even if it does help prevent heart disease and stroke.

"The public good is not well served by telling people to drink alcohol," says the APHA's Levinson. "The fact is that you do great harm with immoderate regular drinking."

Many health experts worry that any encouragement of drinking—even the most guarded endorsement—could produce a public overreaction leading to greater alcohol abuse. "People have already used the correlation between alcohol and heart disease to justify drinking more," says Columbia's Goldberg. "Telling someone to start having one drink a night is unrealistic."

The problem, researchers say, is the fine line between the up and down sides of drinking. "Unfortunately, the difference between drinking a small amount and a larger amount is the difference between preventing and causing a premature death," said former Harvard University researcher Charles Hennekens, who conducted some of the first studies on the connection between alcohol and cardiovascular health.[6]

"We have to remember that alcohol is associated with increased risk for hypertension, stroke, liver damage, brain damage and heart damage," Goldberg says, "not to mention death and injury from tens of thousands of motor vehicle accidents each year."

Indeed, the U.S. government estimates that about 100,000 Americans die from alcohol-related causes each year. In addition, about 14 million Americans are problem drinkers, a condition that not only leads to myriad health damage but also causes a host of societal ills, from lost productivity at work to greater incidence of domestic violence.

Finally, opponents of alcohol say, there are safer and healthier paths to good cardiovascular health than alcohol. "People will substitute a glass or two of wine in place of real action like a low-fat diet and exercise," Goldberg says. "In the end, these steps will do you much more good than a drink a day."

But others in the health community argue that the public should be encouraged to use alcohol in a beneficial way. "The benefits of drinking in moderation are clear and should be made known to people," notes Harvard's Rimm, who says he usually has a drink with dinner. "I mean, people who have a few drinks a day tend to live longer, period."

R. Curtis Ellison, a professor of medicine and public health at Boston University's School of Medicine, agrees. "You're doing a disservice to your patients if you do not present the current information on moderate drinking and health outcomes," he says.

Advocates of moderate drinking point to its tremendous benefits for the heart. Not only does alcohol increase good cholesterol, Rimm says, but it also decreases clotting properties in the blood, helping to protect against heart attacks and strokes.

Recent evidence suggests that alcohol may also help protect the brain. Last year, researchers at Boston University announced the results of a study showing that mod-

# Evaluating the Evidence...

*The charts below summarize current evidence on the link among diet, exercise and 20 types of cancer. To use the chart, look across each row to find out about the evidence for a given cancer. Then look up the columns to find out which cancers are influenced by diet, exercise, body size or tobacco use.*

*Factors that are thought to decrease the risk of cancer are [coded A, B, C], those thought to increase the risk are [coded D, E, F]. The information on evidence linking cancer and diet was developed during a four-year study by 17 international cancer experts, who reviewed 4,500 studies on the link between diet and cancer.*

| | Vegetables | Fruits | Carotenoids | Vitamin C in food | Minerals in food | Cereals in food | Starches (grains) | Fiber | Tea | Physical activity | Refrigeration |
|---|---|---|---|---|---|---|---|---|---|---|---|
| Mouth and pharynx | A | A | | C | | | | | | | |
| Nasopharynx | | | | | | | | | | | |
| Larynx | B | B | | | | | | | | | |
| Esophagus | A | A | C | C | | F | | | | | |
| Lung | A | A | B | C | C | | | | | C | |
| Stomach | A | A | C | B | | C | F | | C | | A |
| Pancreas | B | B | | C | A | | | C | | | |
| Gallbladder | | | | | | | | | | | |
| Liver | C | | | | | | | | | | |
| Colon, rectum | A | | C | | | | C | C | | A | |
| Breast | B | B | C | | | | | C | | C | |
| Ovary | C | C | | | | | | | | | |
| Endometrium | C | C | | | | | | | | | |
| Cervix | C | C | C | C | | | | | | | |
| Prostate | C | | | | | | | | | | |
| Thyroid | C | C | | | F | | | | | | |
| Kidney | C | | | | | | | | | | |
| Bladder | B | B | | | | | | | | | |

A: Decreases risk convincing **B**: Decreases risk probable **C**: Decreases risk possible **D**: Increases risk convincing **E**: Increases risk probable **F**: Increases risk possible

*(Box continued on next page)*

# ...Linking Diet and Cancer

*The panel estimates that recommended diets, together with maintenance of physical activity and appropriate body mass, could in time reduce cancer incidence by 30-40 percent. At current rates, on a global basis, this represents 3-4 million cases of cancer per year that could be prevented by dietary and associated means. The American Institute for Cancer Research (AICR) and its international affiliate, the World Cancer Research Fund, sponsored the panel. The nonprofit institute is the only major national cancer charity focusing exclusively on the impact of diet and nutrition on cancer. The AICR is the nation's third-largest cancer charity.*

| | Alcohol | Salt & salting | Meat | Eggs | Cooking | Total & sat'd/animal fats | Cholesterol | Milk & dairy prod. | Sugar | Coffee | Obesity | Other aspects of body size | Smoking tobacco |
|---|---|---|---|---|---|---|---|---|---|---|---|---|---|
| **Mouth and pharynx** | D | | | | | | | | | | | | F |
| **Nasopharynx** | | D *Salted fish* | | | | | | | | | | | F |
| **Larynx** | D | | | | | | | | | | | | F |
| **Esophagus** | D | | | | | | | | | | | | F |
| **Lung** | | | | | | F *Both total & sat'd/animal fat* | F | | | | | | F |
| **Stomach** | | E | | | F *Grilling & bbq* | | | | | | | | |
| **Pancreas** | | | F | | | | F | | | F | | | |
| **Gallbladder** | | | | | | | | | | | | | |
| **Liver** | D | | | | | | | | | | | | |
| **Colon, rectum** | E | | E | F | F *Grilling & bbq* | F *Both total fat & saturated/animal fat* | | | F | | F | F *Greater height in adulthood* | F |
| **Breast** | E | | F | | | F *Both total & sat'd/animal fat* | | | | | E | D *Rapid early growth* | |
| **Ovary** | | | | | | | | | | | | | |
| **Endometrium** | | | | | | F *Saturated/animal fat only* | | | | | D | | |
| **Cervix** | | | | | | | | | | | | | F |
| **Prostate** | | | F | | | F *Both total & sat'd/animal fat* | | | | | | | |
| **Thyroid** | | | | | | | | | | | | | |
| **Kidney** | | | F | | | | | F | | | E | | F |
| **Bladder** | | | | | | | | | | F | | | F |

**A**: Decreases risk convincing **B**: Decreases risk probable **C**: Decreases risk possible **D**: Increases risk convincing **E**: Increases risk probable **F**: Increases risk possible erate drinking may reduce the risk of Alzheimer's disease by as much as 50 percent.[7]

While alcohol advocates say they are not urging doctors to "prescribe" alcohol to patients, they believe that they should suggest a drink every day. Such advice, they say, would not spark a nationwide drinking binge. The risk of such an outcome is "greatly exaggerated," Ellison says. "The American public isn't quite as dumb as we sometimes think."

While others agree, they warn that doctors should be selective about who they urge to drink. "It seems sensible to tailor your message on alcohol based on whom you're talking to," says Michael Thun, head of epidemiological research at the American Cancer Society and a noted expert on alcohol and health.

For instance, Thun says, a doctor shouldn't advise a young patient to begin moderate drinking because the potential benefits are not meaningful to someone who is not at risk for heart disease or stroke. But, "for an older person who is at considerable risk of heart disease, talking to that person about the benefits of alcohol is probably appropriate."

### *Would eliminating meat from the diet significantly lower the chances of getting certain diseases?*

In 1998, the average American ate 195 pounds of meat, poultry and fish—18 pounds more than in 1970. Most of the rise is due to an increase in the popularity of chicken, consumption of which has almost doubled in the last 30 years. Beef, on the other hand has seen a decline in popularity, with consumption falling by 20 percent over the same period.[8] (*See graph, "Americans Eating Less Red Meat"*)

Still, red meat remains immensely popular. Nearly 60 percent of all meat eaten by the average American (115 pounds) is red meat—beef, pork and lamb—and slightly more than half is beef.[9]

For decades, many nutritionists have warned that too much meat, especially red meat, can increase the risk of heart disease, stroke, some forms of cancer and other chronic ailments. The American Heart Association and many other health advocacy groups warn Americans to limit themselves to modest amounts of meat.

Some experts go further, arguing that the healthiest option is removing meat entirely from the diet. "A plant-based diet is by far your best bet," says Mangels of the Vegetarian Resource Group.

But the American Meat Institute's Huffman contends that meat is a healthy and integral part of a good, balanced diet. "There are a wealth of studies and data showing that eating meat in moderation is a key to good health in general," he says. "Meat is nothing like alcohol or tobacco, which really are high-risk foods."

On the contrary, Huffman says, even a little bit of meat provides a host of important nutrients, including vitamins A and B, zinc and iron. "Meat products are nutrient-dense foods, and so they are the easiest and most effective way to get many nutrients into your body," Huffman says.

Moreover, some of the important nutrients found in meat are not found in plants or only can be obtained in limited amounts by people on plant-based diets, according to David Klurfeld, chairman of the Department of Nutrition and Food Science at Wayne State University in Detroit.

"There are several micro-nutrients—vitamin B-12, zinc and iron—that you won't get enough of if you're not eating meat," Klurfeld says. "Meat is a terrific source of all of these."

But vegetarians and others argue that meat is unnecessary because a plant-based diet provides almost everything needed to maintain good health. "If you eat a lot of grains and fruits and vegetables, you're getting all but a few of the nutrients your body needs," Mangels says.

"When you really think about it, you realize that the body has no need for the flesh or even milk of animals," adds Laurelee Blanchard, a spokesman for the Farm Animal Reform Movement (FARM) , an animal rights group in Bethesda, Md.

And, Blanchard and Mangels say, to get the few nutrients not found in plants, vegetarians can turn to an array of non-animal options. "If you make a little effort and choose carefully, you can do just fine," Mangels says. "You can take a supplement, or there are many fortified foods, from soy milk to cereal that will give you B-12, calcium and other things you might not get enough of in a plant-based diet."

*In the 1920s, the first breakfast cereals came on the market in the U.S. In Battle Creek, Mich., the Kellogg brothers brought out Corn Flakes, which along with other similar products helped Americans begin to substitute grains for the traditional breakfast of eggs and meat.*

Making the effort is worth it, Blanchard and Mangels says, because meat contains substances that are generally harmful, including saturated fat, found in abundance in beef and pork. Saturated fat raises the blood level of bad cholesterol, which in turn increases the risk of heart disease. "There's no way around this," Mangels says. "The saturated fat in meat is going to give you a much greater chance of getting heart disease."

In addition, opponents say, meat consumption can put people at greater risk for diabetes. And, says Liebman, the high saturated fat content in meat has been linked to prostate and colon cancer.

"Cancer researchers are telling us to stay away from meat, if for no other reason than it displaces those foods, like fruits and vegetables, that help prevent cancer," Mangels adds.

But Huffman argues that much of the fat found in meat is actually healthy. "Fully one-third of the saturated fat found in meat is steric acid, which actually helps lower blood cholesterol levels," he says.

Huffman also points out that meat is a good source of conjugated linoleic acid (CLA), which, among other things, improves the balance between fat and muscle in the body.[10] "CLA is very useful in preventing heart disease because it helps prevent the buildup of [fatty] plaque in arteries," he says.

When it comes to diet and health, Klurfeld of Wayne State says, the problem is often that Americans tend to have an "all or nothing" attitude. "They hear that too much meat is bad for you, and so they decide they shouldn't eat any," he says.

---

From *CQ Researcher*, February 23, 2001, Vol. 11, No. 7, pp. 131-140. 

# The Human Genome: A Master Code for Better Health

According to the U.S. Centers for Disease Control and Prevention, "The Human Genome Project will be heralded as one of the most astounding medical projects of all time and will provide the foundation for a new era in medicine." Even though the ink is barely dry on the first rough draft of the sequence of the human genome, editorials in the scientific literature and the popular press are peppered with superlatives about its potential to reduce or eliminate many of the diseases that plague humans. This article (the second in a three-part series) will discuss how some of the elegant new techniques being developed to study the human genome are also being used to tackle today's most challenging health problems.

## Predicting Susceptibility to Disease

It has been known for many years that certain diseases have a genetic component. For instance, diseases such as cystic fibrosis and sickle cell anemia are caused by the mutation of a single gene. However, most diseases (e.g., cancer, hypertension and obesity) are linked to multiple genes and may also be subject to environmental influences. Information from the Human Genome Project, in conjunction with powerful new microarray techniques, is making it possible to identify the exact gene (or genes) that influences a person's susceptibility to a disease. These techniques can also be used to screen large numbers of people for the presence of such genes. Once high-risk individuals are identified, measures such as those discussed in this article can be taken to prevent the disease or to detect it early, when treatment methods are most effective.

## Optimal Dietary Counseling for Individuals

When it comes to an optimal diet, one size does not fit all. For example, researchers have discovered that low-density lipoproteins (LDLs; also known as "bad" cholesterol) come in large and small sizes. Most healthy individuals have a predominance of the large LDL, but 20 to 30 percent of the population has more of the small form, which is particularly atherogenic (having the capacity to initiate, increase, or accelerate degenerative changes in arterial walls [atherogenesis]). Some individuals with large LDL respond to a low-fat diet by flipping to the small LDL particle distribution—a genetically predisposed reaction that could actually have *negative* effects. The propensity to flip to the small LDL type appears to be linked to genes that are responsible for the LDL receptor. By using microarray technology, it may be possible to screen individuals for this trait so that they can be given the appropriate dietary advice.

## Functional Foods for Individual Health

There are many additional examples of how individuals respond differently to diet; individuals' vitamin and mineral needs are different; the effects of protective phytochemicals such as isoflavones, flavonoids and resveratrol vary among individuals; sodium increases blood pressure in some but not others; and the ability of dietary fiber to reduce cholesterol is subject to genetic influences. The time is fast approaching when it will be possible to use genetic testing to inexpensively determine an individual's ideal health-promoting diet. Furthermore, great-tasting functional foods can be developed by using biotechnology or conventional agricultural techniques so that such diets will be attractive to consumers. Health care professionals of the future may very well work with individual patients to "prescribe" such foods as a routine component of ongoing health care.

## Cancer Monitoring for High-Risk Individuals

Breast cancer either can be inherited through a mutation in one or more genes, or can occur spontaneously by a noninherited mechanism. Although the inherited form represents only 5 to 10 percent of all tumors, it is particularly important because women with one of the defective genes have a very high chance (40 to 85 percent) of getting the disease. In addition, women who already have the inherited form of breast cancer are at higher risk for the breast cancer to reoccur and for ovarian cancer to develop.

Until recently, it was virtually impossible to tell the difference between spontaneous and inherited breast cancers. However, by examining tumors with microarray technology, scientists have been able to develop a relatively simple way to tell them apart. Use of this technique will enable doctors to identify women with inherited breast cancer so that they can be monitored very closely. In addition, this technology will likely lead to an inexpensive test that will identify disease-free women who have inherited one of the defective genes so that they, too, can be closely monitored. As this technology continues to evolve, it may be possible to predict an individual's susceptibility to virtually any disease linked to defective or mutated genes.

## Developing New Drugs

One of the Human Genome Project's most exciting prospective applications is for the development of new and better drugs. This area is only beginning to be explored, but there are many possible approaches. As noted above, certain diseases (including breast cancer) may be associated with the expression of one or more genes. Another gene-linked process appears to be the metastasis (spreading throughout the body) of cancer cells. Metastasis is the greatest threat to the survival of patients with solid tumors. New research suggests that overexpression of a gene called *rho*C is a critical factor in the spread of melanoma cells in mice. As the factors associated with control of this gene become better understood it might be possible to develop new drugs that modulate this expression—and prevent or reduce the invasiveness of tumors—which would be a major advancement in the treatment and understanding of cancer.

Many genes that perform the same general function have more than one form and are called polymorphisms. Polymorphisms are often due to the difference of a single base in the DNA sequence. The effect of this subtle difference can be dramatic. For example, the difference of a single-base in the *apo*E gene is associated with Alzheimer's disease, and deletion of a single base in a gene called *CCR5* provides resistance to the human immunodeficiency virus. Information from the Human Genome Project is allowing the identification of thousands of different polymorphisms. As biomedical research with DNA arrays and other technology advances, it will be possible to understand whether these mutations are involved in the progression of disease. Once the suspect polymorphisms are known, it may be possible to develop drugs to counteract their harmful effects.

Unfortunately, understanding the genetic cause of a disease does not guarantee that a new drug will be developed. The exact genetic defect that is responsible for sickle cell disease has been known for more than 40 years, but optimal treatment remains elusive. Nevertheless, the potential of this approach has been called revolutionary. An editorial in the *Journal of the American Medical Association* recently said, "The ongoing revolution in biomedical science is of an unprecedented magnitude, is accelerating dramatically, and promises almost unlimited opportunity for the betterment of humankind."

## Gene Therapy for Alzheimer's Disease

Another potential use of information from the Human Genome Project is induction of the function of known genes in the body. Last April the *New York Times* reported on an exciting experiment along these lines. A gene that causes production of a nerve growth factor was inserted into skin cells from a patient with Alzheimer's disease whose brain had lost the ability to produce sufficient amounts of this factor, which is necessary for memory and other cognitive functions. These genetically enhanced cells were injected into the patient's brain where it is hoped that they will produce the missing factor and reverse the disease. Similar experiments in monkeys have been successful. Such research is in its infancy, but the development of new techniques to repair defective genes or to use the function of known genes to correct a metabolic defect is sure to be ongoing.

## Unlocking the Health Secrets of the Genome

The full scope of the Human Genome Project's potential to improve human health is only beginning to be appreciated. The basic strategy of determining the genetic causes of disease, screening individuals (possibly on a population-wide basis) for their level of risk, and providing the appropriate support through individualized dietary counseling, functional foods, new drugs, or medical monitoring is just beginning to be developed. Already, the longevity of roundworms has been increased by 50 percent. With such significant advances for the roundworm, the future applications of genetic research to benefit humans are bounded only by the imagination.

Perhaps the greatest challenge to the appropriate application of this exploding technology will be dealing with the myriad ethical and human rights issues that it raises. That topic will be discussed in the final article of this series in the next issue of *Food Insight.*

# DIABETES

## How to Cut Your Risk

"Diabetes rates rose a striking six percent among adults in 1999," the Centers for Disease Control and Prevention (CDC) declared in January. That jump followed a 33 percent increase from 1990 to 1998.

The news came as no surprise to experts.

"There's been an exponential rise in obesity, and I would expect diabetes to follow right along," says Maureen Harris, an epidemiologist at the National Institute of Diabetes and Digestive and Kidney Diseases (NIDDK) in Bethesda, Maryland.

In fact, the percentage of Americans who have diabetes has been rising for decades. "There's been a three-fold increase in the last 40 years," says Harris. And that doesn't account for the aging of the population, which boosts not just the percentage, but the *number* of people with diabetes.

The first signs of the problem surfaced in 1980, when the National Health and Nutrition Examination Survey first started measuring blood sugar levels in a large sample of Americans.

"Our response was, 'Wow! A lot of people who look totally well are running around with high blood sugar,'" says Harris.

But it wasn't until three years ago that the NIDDK and the CDC launched the National Diabetes Education Program. "We're where we were in the 1970s with high blood pressure," says Harris. "We're trying to alert the public and the medical profession to the fact that there are huge numbers of undiagnosed and untreated diabetics."

The program's first goal is to help keep blood sugar levels stable and sufficiently low in people who have already been diagnosed with diabetes.

"Roughly 55 percent of patients do not have their diabetes under control," says Harris.

Only after that percentage drops, says Harris, "will the National Diabetes Education Program focus on finding undiagnosed patients."

### THE BOTTOM LINE

**To cut your risk of diabetes:**

- Lose weight if you're overweight.
- Walk briskly or engage in some other physical activity for at least 30 minutes a day.
- Eat whole-grain breads and cereals instead of refined breads, cereals, and sugars.
- Eat more fruits and vegetables (other than white potatoes).
- Starting at age 45, get your fasting blood glucose level tested every three years—earlier and more frequently if you have risk factors (see "Who's at Risk?").
- If your fasting blood glucose consistently exceeds 110 mg/dL, use diet and exercise—and, if necessary, drugs—to keep your blood pressure and cholesterol at optimal levels.

That's critical because, left untreated, the disease takes a tremendous toll.

### High Blood Sugar

Heart disease, stroke, blindness, amputations, kidney failure, nerve damage, gum disease, and possibly dementia. Diabetes raises the risk of all these and more (see "The Damage Report").

"Once you have diabetes, there's not much—except cancer—that you're not at higher risk for," says Harris. "It's a multi-system disease because glucose is everywhere in the body."

Type 2 diabetes, which accounts for at least 90 percent of diabetes in the U.S., occurs when the body can't make

## THE DAMAGE REPORT

"As of 1997, the total direct and indirect cost of diabetes was roughly $100 billion a year," says Frank Vinicor of the Centers for Disease Control and Prevention.

"The major direct costs are due to hospitalization for coronary heart disease and kidney disease," he explains. "But blindness and amputations take the greatest toll on the quality of life." Indirect costs pile up when people are disabled and die prematurely.

The cost of diabetes can be cut by preventing its chief complications:

- **Heart Disease and Stroke**. The risk of heart disease and stroke is two to four times higher in people with diabetes than in people without the disease. Heart disease is the leading cause of death for diabetics. And an estimated 60 to 65 percent of people with diabetes have high blood pressure, which raises the risk of both heart attack and stroke.

"We need to aggressively treat high blood pressure and high cholesterol in people with diabetes," says Deborah Wingard of the University of California at San Diego School of Medicine.

- **Kidney Disease**. Diabetes is the leading cause of kidney failure, accounting for about 40 percent of new cases. "ACE-inhibitors—drugs that lower blood pressure—can prevent the progression of kidney disease," says Vinicor. "We could prevent half the cases of kidney failure with early treatment."

- **Blindness**. Diabetes is the leading cause of new cases of blindness in people aged 20 to 74. Each year, 12,000 to 24,000 Americans lose their sight because of diabetes. They needn't.

"If the physician sees changes in the back of the eye indicating progressive damage to the retina, we can use photocoagulation—laser treatment—to stop the bleeding, which stops the loss of vision," says Vinicor. "That and getting blood pressure and blood glucose under control could prevent 90 percent of the cases of blindness due to diabetes."

- **Other Complications**. Periodontal (gum) disease is more common and more severe among people with diabetes, who are also more likely to die of infectious illnesses like the flu or pneumonia. And the risk of birth defects is higher in the children of women who have diabetes.

- **Nerve Damage and Amputations**. About 60 to 70 percent of people with diabetes have mild to severe forms of nerve damage, which can cause slowed digestion, carpal tunnel syndrome, and numbness in the feet or hands.

"Nerve damage can cause people to lose sensation in their feet," explains Vinicor. "If a foot becomes injured, they may not be aware of it. And the resulting foot ulcer can lead to amputation."

Each year, an estimated 67,000 amputations are done in the U.S. on people with diabetes. Early treatment could prevent half of them, says Vinicor.

"We can use a monofilament to detect the loss of sensation in the foot," he explains. "Sometimes all it takes is a pair of running shoes to protect the feet from damage."

- **Cognitive Decline**. Thinking ability appears to deteriorate more quickly with age in people with diabetes, especially if they also have high blood pressure. "This is a relatively new observation," says Vinicor. "We need larger studies to see if it's true and, if so, if the decline is due to accelerated atherosclerosis and stroke or if there's something peculiar about the diminished cognitive function in diabetes."

enough—or can't properly use—insulin. (In *type 1* diabetes, the body makes no insulin at all.)

## Each year, 12,000 to 24,000 Americans lose their sight to diabetes

Insulin is the hormone that allows sugar in the blood to enter cells, where it's stored or burned for fuel. Without enough working insulin, levels of blood sugar, or blood glucose, rise (see "Blood Sugar: Going Up").

It's high blood sugar that causes blindness, kidney disease, and nerve damage. Experts call them "microvascular" complications because they involve small blood vessels.

"There's a clear relationship between eye, kidney, and nerve problems and a fasting blood sugar level of 126 or higher," says Frank Vinicor, director of the CDC's diabetes program. "The higher the blood sugar levels—and the longer they're high—the worse the damage. But damage is very unlikely below 126."

How does high blood sugar cause harm? "The theory with the most credibility is that the glucose attaches permanently to proteins in the retina, kidney, and small blood vessels," explains Vinicor. "These protein-glucose linkages cause the proteins to function abnormally."

In 1997 the American Diabetes Association (ADA) lowered the cutoff for diagnosing diabetes from a fasting blood sugar of 140 to 126. "We realized that even for microvascular complications, a fasting blood sugar of 140 was too high," explains Vinicor.

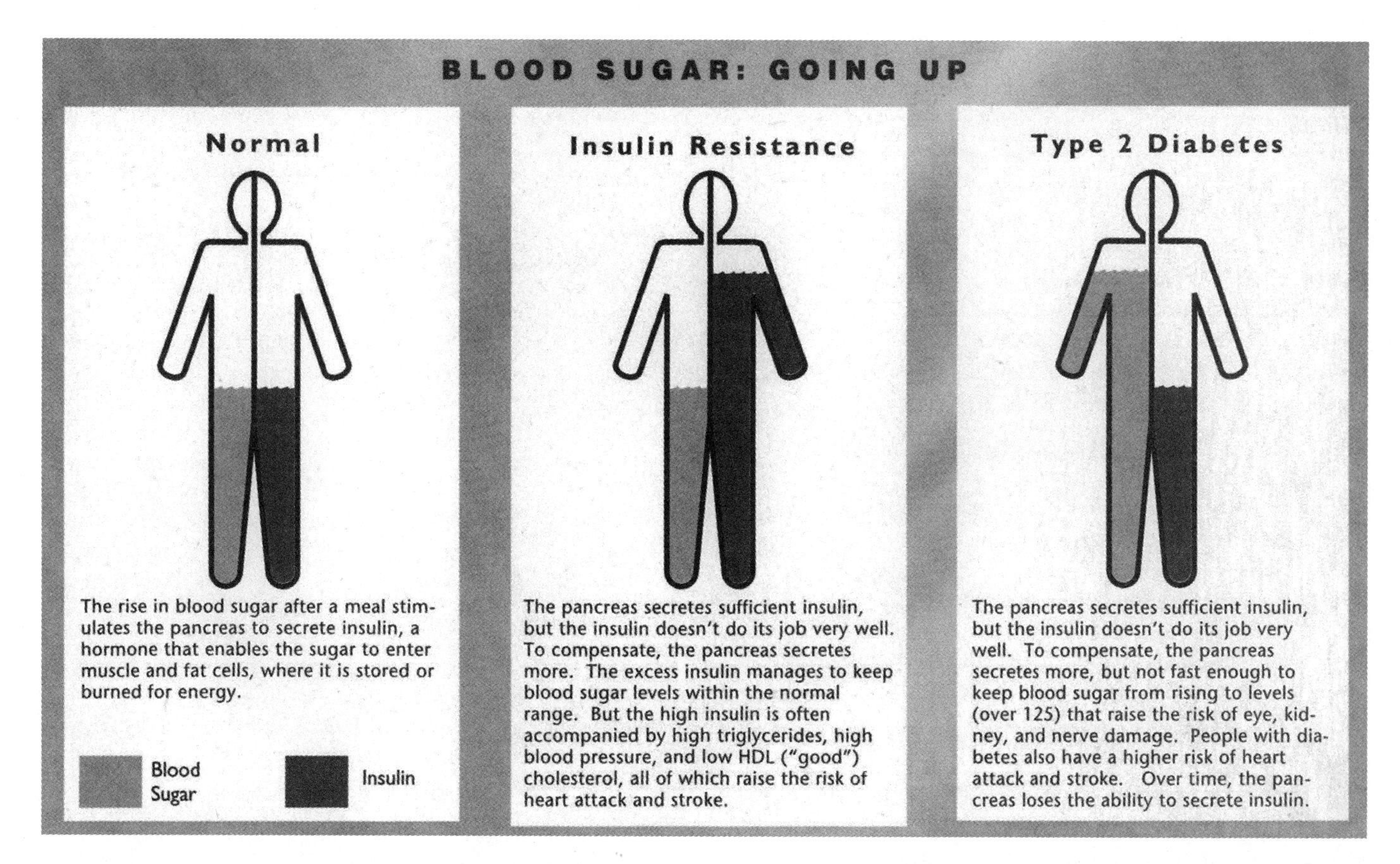


At the same time, the ADA decided that doctors could use *fasting* blood sugar levels to diagnose diabetes. Until then, they were supposed to use a "glucose tolerance test," which meant that patients had to drink a sweetened beverage and then wait two hours to get their blood sugar tested. "The procedure was so cumbersome that doctors just weren't doing it," says Harris.

The ADA now advises anyone aged 45 or older to get a fasting blood sugar test once every three years, and more often if they are at high risk (see "Who's at Risk?"). But a fasting blood sugar under 126 doesn't mean that you're in the clear. New studies suggest that millions of adults have blood sugar levels that are too low to be called diabetes but too high to be called healthy.

## FUTURE TEST: GLYCATED HEMOGLOBIN

When you get a fasting blood sample taken, it tells your doctor how high your blood sugar was that day. But what about other days?

A blood test for glycated hemoglobin, which is also called hemoglobin $A_{1c}$ or *glycosylated hemoglobin*, gives a longer-term read on your blood sugar. (Hemoglobin is the component of red blood cells that carries oxygen.) "Glucose attaches to the hemoglobin in red blood cells and stays there for several months," explains Maureen Harris of the National Institute of Diabetes and Digestive and Kidney Diseases.

Right now, doctors use glycated hemoglobin only to monitor people who already have diabetes. They try to keep levels below 7, which means that seven percent of the patient's hemoglobin $A_{1c}$ has glucose attached to it.

But they don't use glycated hemoglobin to *diagnose* diabetes, because laboratories are not all using the same methods to measure it. That could soon change.

"Right now, one lab may do it differently than others," says Frank Vinicor of the Centers for Disease Control and Prevention. "But probably within a year, the CDC will certify 90 percent of the labs in the U.S. to analyze glycated hemoglobin."

In a recent British study, a glycated hemoglobin under 5 was considered optimal. "Glycated hemoglobin shows great promise in becoming the diagnostic method for diabetes in the U.S.," says Harris. Until then, shoot for a fasting blood glucose of 75 or lower.

## RATE YOUR WEIGHT

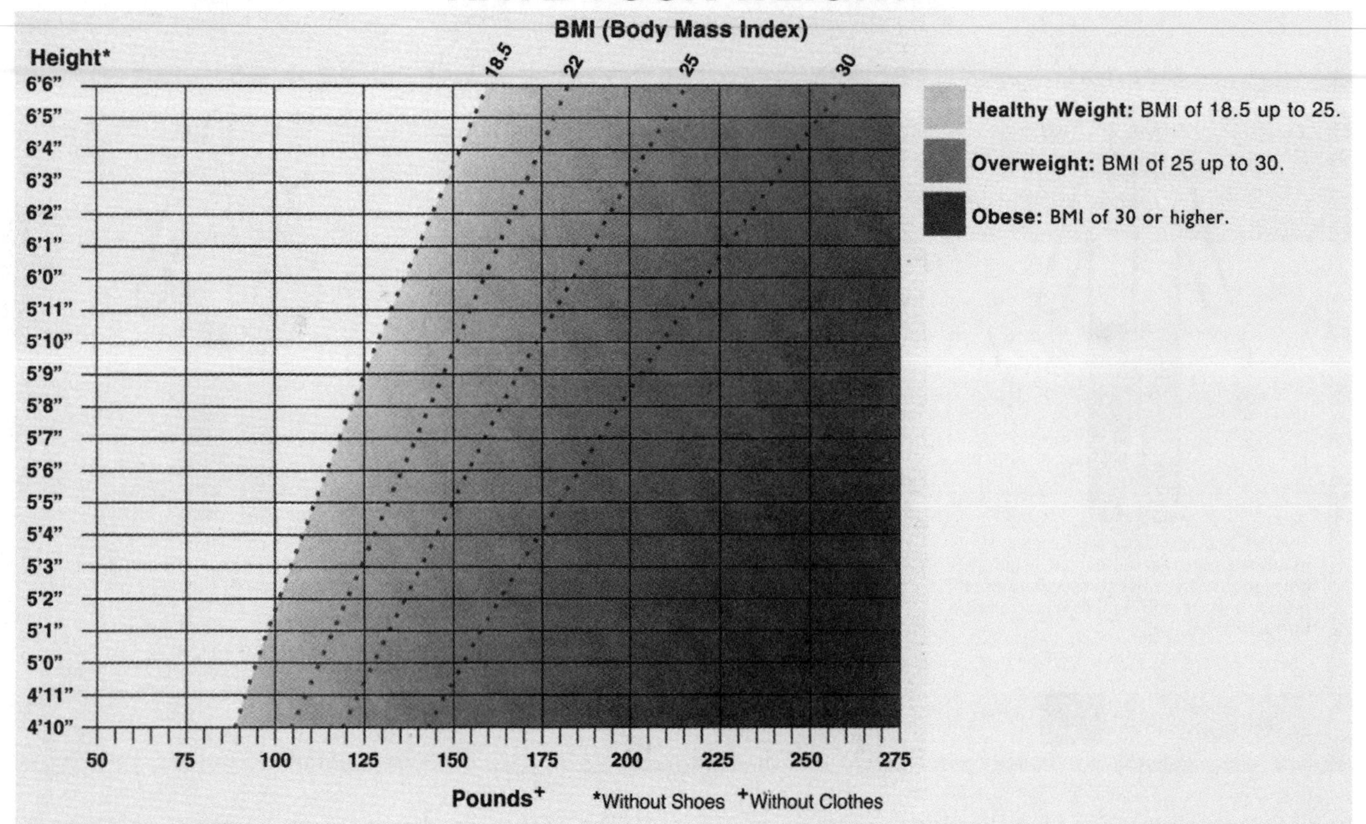


Are you overweight? One way to find out is to check your Body Mass Index (or BMI), which gauges your weight in relation to your height. Find your weight at the bottom of the graph. Go straight up from that point until you come to the line that matches your height. Then check to see which group you fall into.

But this chart doesn't tell the whole story. Although a BMI between 18.5 and 25 is considered "healthy," the risk of diabetes st arts to climb above a BMI of 22, especially for women. One other caveat: BMI shouldn't be used to evaluate the weight of children, the frail elderly, serious bodybuilders, or pregnant or breastfeeding women. If your extra weight comes from muscle, not fat, you may have a high BMI even though you're healthy. Frail or older people may have a low BMI even though they're unhealthy.

Source: adapted from *Dietary Guidelines for Americans, 2000,* U.S. Department of Agriculture and U.S. Department of Health and Human Services.

### Above-Optimal Blood Sugar

Diabetes and its *micro*vascular complications (like blindness) may start when fasting blood sugar levels hit 126, but the *macro*vascular complications—that is, the damage to *large* blood vessels—seem to start at lower levels.

"Until recently, people said you either had diabetes or you didn't, and if you didn't, they weren't too concerned," says Hertzel Gerstein, an endocrinologist at McMaster University in Hamilton, Canada.

"But the blood sugar criteria currently used to differentiate people with and without diabetes is based on the risk of eye and kidney disease. There's no reason to think that it also applies to the risk of cardiovascular events like heart attack and stroke."

In fact, Gerstein found that those risks started to climb when blood sugar levels rose above 75.[1] A new study of more than 4,600 men in Norfolk, England, produced similar results, though it used a long-term measure of blood sugar called glycated hemoglobin (see "Future Test: Glycated Hemoglobin," p. 5).[2]

The shocker: While only five percent of the men in the British study had glycated hemoglobin levels in the diabetic range, 70 percent had levels that raised their risk of heart attack and stroke.

"All but 25 percent of the population we studied had above-optimal levels of blood sugar," says study co-author Kay-Tee Khaw, a professor of clinical gerontology at the University of Cambridge School of Clinical Medicine in England. "It's a population-wide problem, just like high blood pressure and high cholesterol."

Yet most people assume that as long as they don't have diabetes, their blood sugar is normal. "We can't be complacent about elevated blood sugar levels that don't reach the diabetic range," says Gerstein. "It's like blood pressure levels that used to be considered normal, but now we know are high."

"More and more people know how low their blood cholesterol and blood pressure should be," says epidemi-

## NO ONE DIET FOR DIABETES

If you've already been diagnosed with type 2 diabetes, the right diet and exercise can prevent problems.

**1. Lose excess weight.** You don't have to be a fashion model to get your blood sugar under control. In one study, losing more than 15 pounds helped keep blood sugar levels in check.

**2. Move more.** Exercise can help control diabetes, even if you don't lose a pound. The American Diabetes Association recommends 20 to 45 minutes of aerobic exercise at least three days a week (though it cautions patients to use proper footwear, to inspect their feet daily and after exercise, and to avoid exercise in extreme heat or cold and during periods when their blood sugar is poorly controlled).

**3. Eat a DASH diet.** To keep your blood pressure from rising, eat a daily diet that contains eight to ten servings of fruits and vegetables, two to three servings of low-fat dairy products, and less than 2,400 mg of sodium.

**4. Minimize saturated and trans fat.** To lower your LDL ("bad") cholesterol and your risk of heart disease, limit red meats, cheese, ice cream, milk, cakes, pies, and other pastries (unless they're low in fat), as well as fried foods like chicken, fish, and potatoes (unless they're fried in unhydrogenated oil).

**5. Choose between unsaturated fats and carbohydrates.** Once you get enough fruits and vegetables and low-fat protein foods, your remaining calories can come from any combination of unsaturated fats (like vegetables oils, nuts, avocados, and salad dressings) and carbohydrates (breads, cereals, pasta, rice, and sweets).

Just beware: all fats are high in calories. And too many carbs, especially sugars, can boost your triglycerides. Choose whole-grain over refined carbs to get more fiber, magnesium, and phytochemicals.

## WHO'S AT RISK?

The more of these risk factors you have the greater your chances of getting diabetes:

- You're over age 45.
- You have a family history of diabetes (a parent or sibling with the disease).
- Your BMI is 25 or more (see "Rate Your Weight.") (The risk of diabetes starts to climb at a BMI of 22.)
- You don't exercise regularly.
- You are African-American, Latino, Native—American, or a Pacific Islander.
- Your blood pressure is 140 over 90 or higher.
- Your HDL ("good") cholesterol is 35 or lower.
- Your triglycerides are 250 or higher.
- You've been told that you have impaired fasting glucose (fasting glucose between 110 and 125).
- You're a woman who had gestational diabetes or who gave birth to a baby weighing 9 pounds or more.
- You're a woman with polycystic ovary syndrome.

Source: Adapted from American Diabetes Association.

ologist Deborah Wingard of the University of California at San Diego School of Medicine in La Jolla. "They should also know what a good blood sugar is."

"Good" means below 110. "But there's nothing magic about these numbers," explains Wingard. "The higher your blood sugar, the higher your risk."

That's not to say that people should panic about their blood sugar, she adds. "But if you go for a checkup and your blood sugar is slightly elevated, and all you find out is that you don't have diabetes, you might mistakenly wait five years for another test."

Researchers don't know exactly *how* above-optimal blood sugar raises the risk of heart attack and stroke.

"Glycated proteins may make blood vessels more rigid," says Khaw. Too much blood sugar may also alter the protein in low-density lipoproteins, or LDL. "The glucose may turn large, fluffy LDL ['bad'] cholesterol into the more dangerous small, dense LDL," explains Vinicor.

It's also possible that high blood sugar doesn't *cause* heart attacks and strokes at all. "It may just be a marker for insulin resistance," suggests Khaw. That's when cells are resistant to insulin's action, so the hormone doesn't work properly (see "Blood Sugar: Going Up").

People with insulin resistance often have a constellation of risk factors—obesity, high triglycerides, high blood pressure, and low HDL ("good") cholesterol —that are known as "Syndrome X". Insulin resistance, not high blood sugar, may be what raises the risk of heart disease and stroke.

Regardless of *how* high blood sugar harms blood vessels, researchers know what to do about it.

"We know that if we give people statin drugs to lower cholesterol or drugs to lower blood pressure, they will lower the risk of cardiovascular events," says Khaw. That's equally as—if not more—important as lowering their blood sugar. "But it's not feasible to put everyone with elevated blood sugar—75 percent of the adult population—on medication."

Instead, most people need to change their lifestyles. "The vast majority of the population should eat more fruits and vegetables, maintain more-optimal body weight, and increase physical activity," says Khaw. If we could lower average blood sugar levels slightly, "it would lower the risk of cardiovascular disease and diabetes across the population."

## WARNING SIGNS

| Type 1 Diabetes | Type 2 Diabetes |
|---|---|
| Frequent urination | Any of the type 2 symptoms |
| Unusual thirst | Frequent infections |
| Extreme hunger | Blurred vision |
| Unusual weight loss | Cuts or bruises that are slow to heal |
| Extreme fatigue | Tingling or numbness in the hands or feet |
| Irritability | Recurring skin, gum, or bladder infections |

Note: People with type 2 diabetes often have no symptoms

Source: American Diabetes Association.

## Low-Risk Strategy

Here's how to lower your blood sugar level to the optimal range... or how to keep it there:

**1. Watch your weight.** If you're a typical American, your risk of diabetes is already elevated.

"In the U.S., men and women of *average* weight have double the risk of diabetes compared to people with *optimal* weight," says Harvard's JoAnn E. Manson. "Optimal weight is at least ten percent below the average American's weight."

The average American woman is 5'4" tall and weighs 152 pounds. Her optimal weight is 128 pounds, which would give her a BMI of 22 (see "Rate Your Weight"). The average man is 5'9" tall and weighs 180 pounds. Ideally, he should weigh 150 pounds.

But getting the population's average BMI down to an optimal 22 or less isn't realistic, says Manson. "We're not trying to make everyone lean," she explains. "With 97 million Americans overweight or obese, it's tough enough to get the population's average BMI below 25."

What's more, the risk of heart disease, stroke, and most other health problems doesn't climb until your BMI exceeds 25. "Diabetes is the health condition most strongly linked to a BMI between 22 and 25," notes Manson.

**2. Stay off the couch.** No matter how much you weigh, "exercise will go a long way toward reducing the risk of diabetes," says Manson.

And it doesn't have to be strenuous, continuous, time-consuming, or expensive.[3,4] "In several studies, any moderate exercise—even brisk walking—for 30 minutes a day lowered the risk of diabetes by about 30 percent," notes Manson.

Vigorous exercise probably cuts the risk further, she adds, "but it's hard enough to get people off the couch to do moderate exercise."

## Diabetes is the leading cause of kidney failure.

And that same 30 minutes a day can help prevent heart disease, stroke, osteoporosis, and possibly breast and colon cancer, says Manson. "Staying active has a tremendous benefit because it reduces the risk of so many diseases."

**3. Eat wisely.** When it comes to your risk of diabetes, *how much* you eat matters more than *what* you eat. But some foods do appear to lower the risk.[5]

"Whole grains seem to be protective, possibly because they're higher in fiber and magnesium," says Manson. What's more, potatoes and refined grains like white bread increase blood sugar quickly. And that's not good.

"Fruits and vegetables are also great because they're high in magnesium, potassium, and fiber," she adds. And those foods may help protect against obesity because they fill you up without too many calories.

How fats affect the risk of diabetes is still unclear. "Saturated and trans fat may be particularly detrimental," says Manson, "while mono- and polyunsaturated fats may lower the risk."

"But that doesn't mean you can pour on the olive or canola oil," she cautions. "If you're at risk of diabetes, it's best to maintain a low-fat diet because all fats are calorie-dense."

Just don't assume that a low-fat diet means unlimited quantities of low-fat cakes, cookies, and ice cream, or even bread, potatoes, and pasta. The idea is to spend your carbohydrates on vegetables, fruits, and whole grains, which could also cut your risk of cancer, heart disease, and stroke.

Says Manson: "Preventing diabetes really comes down to lifestyle modifications like maintaining a healthy weight, staying physically active, and eating a heart-healthy diet."

## Notes

1. *Diabetes Care 22:* 233, 1999.
2. *British Medical Journal 322*: 1, 5, 2001.
3. *J. Amer. Med. Assoc. 282*: 1433, 1999.
4. *J. Amer. Med. Assoc. 268*: 63, 1992.
5. *Amer. J. Pub. Health 90*: 1409, 2000.

# HOMOCYSTEINE: THE NEW CHOLESTEROL?

A substance in the blood called homocysteine has made headlines repeatedly over the past few years as a possible new risk factor for cardiac disease. But is it? And if so, what should you do about it? *Heart Advisor* asked Killian Robinson, M.D., a Cleveland Clinic cardiologist who has published widely on the topic of homocysteine, for the facts.

## What is homocysteine?

Homocysteine (pronounced HO-mo-SIS-teen) is an amino acid. Several amino acids, including methionine, are essential in human nutrition. Homocysteine is produced when methionine is metabolized. Homocysteine normally stays in the blood only for a short time and is then cleared from the body by the liver.

What makes levels of homocysteine rise? Men have higher levels of homocysteine than women. Medications such as niacin (which is sometimes used for cholesterol lowering) and antifolate drugs (which are used to fight malignant disease) can cause elevated levels. Aging also causes homocysteine to rise.

High levels of homocysteine also occur in a rare inherited disease, homocystinuria, in which a genetic error makes the liver unable to dispose of homocysteine normally. The artery walls of children with this disorder are abnormally thickened and diseased. Patients with homocystinuria may die from blood clots in the brain, heart and kidneys.

## Why is homocysteine suspect?

Despite the appearance of the arteries of young victims of homocystinuria, no one suspected that homocysteine played a role in heart disease until a young medical school graduate, Kilmer S. McCully, M.D., published a research paper in 1969. Based on his observations of homocystinuria, Dr. McCully proposed that homocysteine buildup may in fact also be responsible for atherosclerosis. For the most part, the medical community ignored or scoffed at this theory.

Over the past few years, however, the relationship between atherosclerosis and high levels of homocysteine has become a hot "new" topic. In his book *The Homocysteine Revolution*, Dr. McCully surmises that this may be because, over time, physicians have begun to see that traditional risk factors (such as cholesterol and hypertension) cannot account for a large percentage of heart attacks. In fact, people with no recognized risk factors can have coronary disease.

Researchers from Australia and then Europe published the earliest studies revisiting the homocysteine question. The papers strongly suggested a relationship between homocysteine and cardiovascular disease. In this country, a study by The Cleveland Clinic published 1995 in *Circulation* found that high levels of homocysteine increased the risk of heart disease fivefold. That same year, Tufts University researchers found that subjects who had higher levels of homocysteine were also more likely to have blockage of the carotid (neck) artery, a warning sign of the possibility of a stroke or coronary artery disease. They published their findings in *The New England Journal of Medicine.*

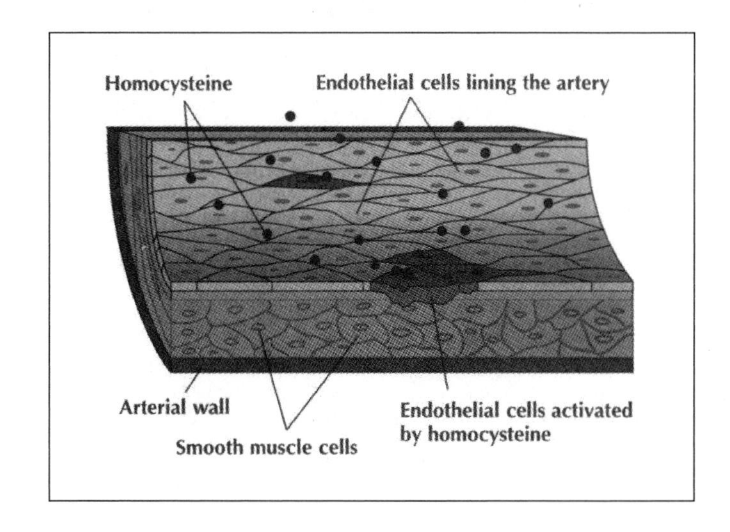


In 1997, the *Journal of the American Medical Association (JAMA)* reported that people with the highest levels of homocysteine in the blood had more than twice the risk of clogged arteries in the heart, brain or elsewhere. A *New England Journal of Medicine* study, also published in 1997, showed that heart patients with high homocysteine levels had higher mortality rates than patients with low homocysteine levels. And a study that year from the Netherlands, published in *Arteriosclerosis, Thrombosis and Vascular Biology*, determined that every 10 percent increase in homocysteine levels meant about a 10 percent increase in the risk of developing coronary disease.

The evidence was mounting, prompting some researchers to wonder out loud whether homocysteine was "the new cholesterol," an artery-clogging substance previously—and erroneously—considered harmless.

## The B vitamin link

Meanwhile, scientists were also looking for a relationship between B vitamins—specifically folate (folic acid), $B_6$ and $B_{12}$—and coronary disease. In homocystinuria patients, doses of B vitamin supplements reduced homocysteine levels. Could B vitamin deficiency be linked to cardiac disease?

### What's a normal homocysteine level?

**Before the dangers of cholesterol were understood, levels as high as 300 milligrams per deciliter (mg/dL) were considered safe. Today, normal is defined as under 200 in otherwise healthy people, and levels over 240 mg/dL call for medical treatment.**

**In a similar vein, the definition of normal levels of homocysteine is the subject of some debate. Different physicians believe "normal" is anywhere from five to 12 micromoles per liter.**

**"Studies show that the risk of cardiovascular disease rises as homocysteine levels go above 10 to 12," Dr. Robinson says. People who are vitamin deficient, taking certain drugs or in renal failure can have levels as high as 100 to 200 .**

**Homocysteine levels are measured by a blood test, best done after fasting. Your physician won't necessarily test you for homocysteine, however, unless you are routinely seen at a teaching hospital where there is an academic interest in the question.**

**If you have been diagnosed with heart disease, or are at risk, you can request a homocysteine test, which may be covered by health insurance.**

It seemed so. A 1996 Canadian study in *JAMA* found that participants who did not have diagnosed heart disease at the start of the study but who had the lowest folate levels were much more likely to die of coronary disease than those in the group with the highest levels of folate (who also began the study free of cardiac disease).

The Nurses' Health Study of more than 80,000 nurses found that the women who consumed the lowest amounts of folic acid and $B_6$ were more likely to develop heart disease, despite the fact that they had no known heart problems at the start of the study. The women who got the most folic acid and $B_6$ over the years cut their risk of heart disease in half.

A case-control study by Dr. Robinson and members of the European Concerted Action group, published in the Feb. 10, 1998, issue of *Circulation*, determined that lower levels of folate and $B_6$ conferred an increased risk of atherosclerosis. The study examined 1,550 patients under age 60 in 19 countries.

Results of a double-blinded, placebo-controlled study reported at the 1998 International Joint Conference on Stroke and Cerebral Circulation showed that a combination of folic acid, $B_6$ and $B_{12}$ could lower homocysteine levels in patients who had had a stroke.

At the August 1998 Congress of the European Society of Cardiology in Vienna, it was reported that heart disease patients who are folate deficient are 1.7 times more likely to have a heart attack than those who have normal levels.

But findings from other, "prospective" studies (in which the research question is posed before the data are collected) have been less consistent. Some have shown a definite relationship between coronary artery disease and elevated homocysteine levels as well as an inverse correlation with B vitamins. Yet other large, well-designed studies—for example, The Atherosclerosis Risk in Communities (ARIC)—have not. In the July 21, 1998, issue of *Circulation*, ARIC authors stated that they could find no consistent relationship between homocysteine and the risk of disease.

The differences could be because of design problems or methodological limitations of the different studies, or even differences in tests used to measure homocysteine and sample size.

"It is perturbing that the prospective studies do not always bear out the findings of earlier case-control studies," Dr. Robinson says. "We need to determine whether there is a true cause-and-effect connection between heart disease and homocysteine.

"Of course, an association does not always prove causality. It's possible that what we are seeing when homocysteine levels are high is an 'epiphenomenon,' or a fellow traveler of vascular disease rather than a cause of it.

"The true question at this point in time," Dr. Robinson continues, "is if you treat the problem—high homocysteine—does the risk of cardiac disease disappear? This is what current trials are designed to find out."

## What you can do

In general, doctors are loath to recommend any kind of treatment when a theory is still unproven. However, the intervention needed to keep homocysteine levels low—increasing your B vitamin intake—is so benign that many doctors are recommending it as a safe course of action until the study results become available in the next four to five years.

Dr. Robinson recommends starting with a heart-healthy diet that includes good sources of B vitamins. It's fairly easy to get enough $B_6$ and $B_{12}$—good sources include fish, poultry, lean meat, bananas, prunes, dried beans and whole grains.

It's a bit harder to reach the recommended dietary allowance (RDA) for folic acid, which was recently raised to 400 micrograms (mcg). Green leafy vegetables such as spinach and brussels sprouts, dried peas, beans, lentils and nuts are your best bets, in addition to some fortified cereals.

The government recently began fortifying breads and grains with folic acid, primarily to prevent birth defects that have been associated with folate deficiency. Check the nutrition label on foods you buy made with grain—there may be added folic acid.

Many doctors are advising their cardiac patients to take a multivitamin tablet daily to ensure adequate folic acid. "There's probably very little risk to taking a multivitamin supplement," Dr. Robinson says.

## Warning

If you choose to supplement your diet with folic acid, it may be wise to also take 500 mcg of vitamin $B_{12}$. "Too much folic acid can mask a deficiency of $B_{12}$ that is more common as we age," Dr. Robinson explains. "The deficiency may lead to nerve damage that could persist or worsen if undiscovered."

Alternatively, you could have your levels of $B_{12}$ checked by your physician every six months. If they're normal, you would not need to add $B_{12}$.

Note: Even multivitamin pills should be taken under medical supervision if you have had a heart attack.

---

From the *Cleveland Clinic Heart Advisor,* Vol. 2, No. 2, February 1999, pp. 4-5. 

# DASH Diet May Prevent Heart Attacks

The DASH (Dietary Approaches to Stop Hypertension) diet that includes three servings of low-fat dairy foods and eight to 10 servings of fruits and vegetables, which was shown to help lower blood pressure, may have another lifesaving benefit—protection against heart disease, the country's leading cause of death. According to David A. McCarron, professor of medicine, Oregon Health Sciences University, Portland, a study placed 118 participants on one of three randomly assigned diets used in the original DASH hypertension trial: a control regimen (the typical American diet), one that emphasized fruits and vegetables, and the DASH combination diet. After following the assigned regimens for eight weeks, those on the DASH combination diet saw the greatest reduction in artery-damaging homocysteine compared to the other subjects.

Homocysteine is an amino acid that is a by-product of protein metabolism. High levels of it have been associated with an increased risk of heart attack and stroke. Several studies have pointed to homocysteine as an independent risk factor for heart disease along with elevated cholesterol levels, high blood pressure, diabetes, obesity, and physical inactivity.

"This study stresses the importance of choosing even more low-fat dairy foods, fruits, and vegetables in your diet," McCarron points out. "If people make the choice to switch to this kind of diet, they could lower their risk of heart disease by seven to nine percent, and that's in addition to the benefits of reduced blood pressure, which the DASH authors have previously estimated lower heart attack risk by 15% and stroke risk by 27%."

The study's authors suggest that the increased folate, vitamin B6, and vitamin B12 in the DASH diet may play a role because they work together to reduce the amount of homocysteine in the blood. They note that, while B6 and B12 likely contribute to the DASH diet's homocysteine-lowering effect, it was only the folate content of the diet that actually predicted the decrease in the amount of homocysteine in the blood.

"Interestingly, while fruits and vegetables are often associated with folate and lowering homocysteine levels, only when low-fat dairy foods were added to the fruits and vegetables did the homocysteine levels decline," McCarron indicates. "Low-fat dairy foods provide a powerful nutrient package and, when eaten with fruits and vegetables throughout the day, can have dramatic results for your heart."

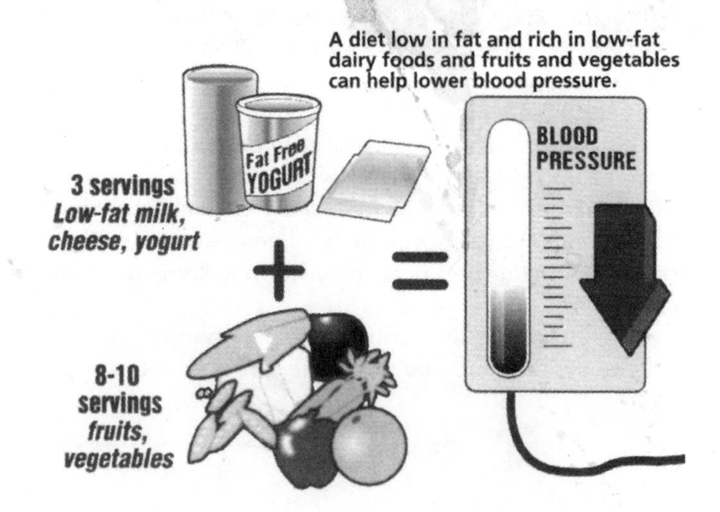


Jean Ragalie, vice president of nutrition communications for the National Dairy Council, maintains that "Taking the right steps can be as easy as making a few lifestyle changes, including incorporating low-fat dairy foods into every meal and taking advantage of seasonal fruits and vegetables." She offers the following mealtime tips to help people get on the right track:

**Get naturally sweet**. Calm your morning sugar cravings by enjoying a bowl of cereal with low-fat milk topped with your favorite seasonal berries.

**Eat a mid-morning snack**. Cut up pieces of fresh fruit and vegetables with plain yogurt for dipping.

**Avoid lunchtime laziness**. Get in the habit of preparing a healthful lunch you can bring to work. A pita with grated carrots, cucumbers, bell peppers, and sprouts topped with low-fat cheese is the perfect portable lunch.

**Prepare mixed meals**. Serve up a variety with at least two different types of fruits and vegetables. Dessert is the ideal time to experiment with fresh fruit. Low-fat vanilla yogurt topped with sauteed apple slices is a pleasing DASH dessert.

# What We Still Don't Know About Soy

In Asia, soy foods have been a dietary staple for centuries. In the United States, health guru and breakfast food entrepreneur John Harvey Kellogg introduced soybean products in the 1920s as healthful substitutes for milk and meat. Yet for decades most Americans thought of soy primarily as an unappealing health food store staple or as a mystery meat extender served in cafeterias and mess halls.

Over the last several years, however, American attitudes toward soy have shifted from dubious to near-devotional. Now supermarket shelves are graced by thousands of soy products—everything from snack foods and breakfast cereals to cheese and coffee substitutes. It's estimated that we will spend more than $3 billion this year on soy foods, not counting supplements made from concentrated soy compounds.

What happened? To a large extent, we became convinced that soy equals healthy. Soybeans are unique among plant foods in supplying all the essential amino acids that the human body needs, making soy protein similar in quality to meat protein—but with largely unsaturated instead of saturated fat. In addition, soy contains the isoflavones *genistein* and *daidzein*, plant hormones that seem able to either mimic or counter the effects of estrogen. They have been proposed as helpful in preventing several hormone-related diseases.

Soy's biggest official boost came with endorsements from the Food and Drug Administration (FDA), in 1999, and the American Heart Association (AHA), last year, for its ability to lower cholesterol. That spurred the recent boom in soy marketing. But it also worries some experts who believe that our rush to consume large amounts of soy—and, in particular, to take supplements with large amounts of soy isoflavones—is premature, given the current evidence on soy's health benefits and possible risks.

## EVIDENCE ON BENEFITS

• ***Lowering cholesterol.*** Soy's impact on the risk for heart attack and stroke has not been directly evaluated. However, last November, the AHA recommended that people include soy protein foods as part of a low-fat, low-cholesterol diet in order to promote heart health. The AHA's Nutrition Committee acted after reviewing evidence from a 1995 meta-analysis of 38 controlled clinical trials, along with several newer studies assessing soy's impact on lipid levels. It concluded that consuming 25–50 grams of soy protein daily could reduce LDL cholesterol by 4%–8%. People with normal cholesterol levels show slight improvement, and benefits are proportionately greater with moderately high cholesterol levels. But the impact of dietary soy is decidedly modest—roughly equivalent to the effect of adding soluble fiber (for example, from oat bran or pectin) to your diet.

In the human studies reviewed by the AHA, soy protein that contained isoflavones lowered cholesterol significantly more than soy protein without isoflavones. And isoflavones separated from soy protein did not lower cholesterol. It may be that the cholesterol-lowering effect of soy products is due to a synergy among soy protein, isoflavones, and other components of soy.

• ***Easing menopausal symptoms.*** Because soy isoflavones have certain estrogenic effects, women and researchers have looked to soy as a possible alternative to standard hormone replacement therapy. Greater intake of dietary soy has been proposed to explain why Japanese women report fewer hot flashes than American women. Within Japan, researchers found that women with the highest consumption of soy products and the highest intake of isoflavones had fewer hot flashes than those who ate little soy.

But when soy is given to Western women in controlled studies to prevent hot flashes, the benefits have been slight. For example, in a trial of postmenopausal women in Italy, those taking soy protein reported 45% fewer moderate or severe hot flashes after 12 weeks of treatment, but women taking a non-soy protein powder also improved, by 30%. In comparison, hormone replacement therapy has been shown to reduce hot flashes by at least 70%.

• ***Protecting bone.*** Two prospective studies have found some evidence that soy consumption might help prevent the bone loss associated with menopause. In one, perimenopausal women still having regular periods but experiencing 10 or more hot flashes a week were assigned to groups receiving supplements, variously, of isoflavone-rich soy, isoflavone-poor soy, or a whey protein control. After six months, women receiving whey had significant losses in bone mass and density. Those receiving isoflavone-poor soy had non-significant bone loss, while those receiving isoflavone-rich soy showed a small improvement. In another six-month study, postmenopausal women showed an increase in bone mineral content and density in their lumbar spine (but not in the thigh) after taking an isoflavone-rich soy preparation. Milk protein and soy protein with a low concentration of isoflavones gave no protection.

If the level of protection documented in these studies continued for many years, women taking isoflavone-containing soy products might be at lower risk for osteoporosis. However, the researchers caution that six months is a relatively short period of time in terms of bone turnover. Longer-term trials are underway.

## SOY AND BREAST CANCER: PROMISE OR PERIL?

Asian nations with high soy consumption have lower rates of breast cancer, which suggests that components in soy may somehow protect breast tissue. But population-based differences are far from proof of a cause-and-effect relationship. Many other features of a particular culture, including other dietary components, could account for such patterns. Studies undertaken in China and Japan have not identified any consistent relationship between soy intake and breast cancer risk. For now, it's unclear whether adding soy to the diet might reduce a woman's risk of developing breast cancer, and there's no evidence that soy is of any particular benefit for women who already have breast cancer.

Still, there are reasons for the research interest in this connection. Soy isoflavones resemble tamoxifen and raloxifene, selective estrogen receptor modulators already used for breast cancer prevention. Like these medications, isoflavones attach to estrogen receptors but act differently from estrogen in some tissues. In addition to hormonal influences, isoflavones also have anti-tumor activity and block the formation of blood vessels in chemically induced breast tumors in animals. Researchers are investigating the possibility that they may act against non-hormonal cancers as well as the hormonally influenced cancers of the breast and prostate.

Soy's effects on breast tissue are not well understood. Its impact on breast cancer may depend on when in a woman's life she consumes it. There is the possibility, bolstered by some animal studies, that soy must be consumed early in life to exert a protective effect on breast tissue. Animal studies also suggest that prepubertal exposure to the soy component genistein is protective. And when premenopausal women drink isoflavone-containing soymilk, it significantly lowers their circulating levels of both estrogen and progesterone, potentially protecting them from estrogen's cell-stimulating effects. On the other hand, one small, randomized study found that soy consumption (in the form of textured vegetable protein) was associated with increased breast tissue proliferation in a group of premenopausal women with benign or malignant breast disease. In postmenopausal women with little estrogen production, isoflavones with even a weak estrogen-like effect may potentially stimulate the growth of estrogen-dependent breast tumors.

Women receiving tamoxifen as treatment for breast cancer often wonder whether it would be valuable or safe to add soy foods or supplements to their daily regimen. Unfortunately, no definitive studies are available,

### *How Things Stand*

At this time, research does not suggest that soy, or any of its components, is a magic bullet, or that consumers receive special health benefits from soy in the absence of a generally healthy lifestyle. Also, it's clear that we don't fully understand soy's action in breast tissue or in the brain. For now, soy foods are best viewed as a good protein source to include in a healthy, balanced diet that is low in saturated fats and includes a mix of proteins, vegetables, fruits, and whole grains. Soy is not a substitute for strategies that are known to lower cholesterol and reduce the risk for osteoporosis, such as diet, exercise, and medications. Soy supplements, in particular, have not undergone rigorous testing and are best avoided.

- In light of how little we know about soy's effects on breast tissue and memory, Walter C. Willett, M.D., Ph.D., Chairman, Department of Nutrition, Harvard School of Public Health, suggests eating soy in moderation. In his recently published book *Eat, Drink, and Be Healthy: The Harvard Medical School Guide to Health Eating*, he recommends about two to four servings per week of soy-based foods such as tofu or soymilk. But if your customary diet contains more than this, there is not enough evidence to suggest that you should change.
- George L. Blackburn, M.D., Ph.D., the S. Daniel Abraham Associate Professor of Nutrition at Harvard Medical School, advises that the health benefits of soy come as part of a "soy lifestyle." This involves an Asian-style diet—including lean meat, fish, poultry, and plentiful vegetables—portion and weight control, and lots of exercise such as walking and biking. In this context, it's reasonable to substitute soy for some servings of meat or milk.
- *Harvard Women's Health Watch* editorial board member Helen K. Delichatsios, M.D., S.M., notes that in some positive studies, soy may simply be a marker for a healthy lifestyle. She warns against just adding soy and giving up other good things you are doing or should be doing.

according to researchers at Harvard Medical School. Some experts caution that anything with desirable estrogenic effects can also have unwanted estrogenic effects, e.g., increased cell reproduction. This may be especially true of concentrated soy supplements. Others researchers believe that breast cancer patients are probably fine if they follow an Asian diet and lifestyle in which soy foods are substituted for *some* meat protein, and lots of vegetables and exercise are included. Certainly before starting isoflavone supplements or changing your diet to incorporate large amounts of soy, you should discuss it with your oncologist.

## POTENTIAL PROBLEMS

• ***Brain cells***. In the 1960s, researchers took dietary information from about 8,000 men of Japanese descent participating in the Honolulu Heart Study. In tests administered three decades later, when the men were ages 71–93, those who had eaten the most tofu (more than two servings a week) performed less well on cognitive tests. The researchers also tested their wives and found a similar decline in cognitive function among those women who ate the most tofu. Among men for whom the researchers had brain imaging or autopsy results, greater tofu consumption was associated with more brain atrophy. The brains of men who ate a lot of tofu generally resembled those of men about five years older who had eaten little tofu.

• ***Reproductive tract***. Because of the hormonal effects of soy isoflavones (which have been found in human amniotic fluid), some scientists worry that large amounts of soy may cause deleterious changes in the reproductive tract, particularly during early life. Indeed, animal studies suggest that exposure to genistein before and just after birth may affect ovarian follicle development.

In May, the National Toxicology Program called for further study of the health effects of genistein because of credible evidence that hormone-like chemicals can produce changes in the female reproductive tract and the prostate gland. The National Institutes of Health is also sponsoring an infancy-to-adulthood study to detect possible adverse effects of consuming soy-based formulas in infancy.

• ***Thyroid***. Some physicians have reported cases in which women developed goiter or symptoms of hypothyroidism while consuming large amounts of soy. In the laboratory, genistein interferes with a key enzyme in the thyroid gland, thyroxine peroxidase, making some scientists concerned about the impact of soy on thyroid function. But researchers tracking hormone levels in premenopausal and postmenopausal women taking soy isoflavones have found no clinically significant changes in thyroid function.

As a precaution, if you are being evaluated for a thyroid problem or are receiving thyroid medication, tell your endocrinologist about your use of soy foods and supplements. If you are taking thyroid hormone to correct hypothyroidism, soy may interfere with the absorption of the medication in your intestines. To minimize this impact (thereby allowing you to take the lowest possible dose), your endocrinologist may advise you not to take your thyroid medication within 2–3 hours of a meal that contains soy. In infants who require thyroid hormone because of congenital hypothyroidism, soy formula can cause a significant absorption problem and should not be consumed.

• ***Allergies***. Soy is one of the eight food groups most often responsible for allergic reactions. It's difficult to avoid soy entirely, since it turns up in small amounts in many products, such as water-packed tuna, that are not themselves soy foods. In May, a group of major food manufacturers agreed to label products containing even tiny amounts of soy and other common allergens.

---

# AGING WELL WITH GOOD NUTRITION

**ABSTRACT** *As we enter the 21st century, the life expectancy of older Americans continues to increase and by the year 2030, nearly one-fourth of the total population will be comprised of the elderly. To maintain an optimal quality of life, extended longevity in the elderly should be accompanied by good health, free from disease and disability. However, many of these individuals in our society are at risk for malnutrition due to various physiological, socioeconomic, and psychological factors. The Nutrition Screening Initiative founded in 1989 developed simple screening tools that increase public awareness about the risk factors that affect the nutritional status of the aged. Family and Consumer Sciences professionals have a vital role to play in helping our senior citizens age well with health and functional independence.*

**PADMINI SHANKAR, Ph.D., RD**
*Assistant Professor*
*Department of Family & Consumer Sciences,*
*Georgia Southern University*

**By the year 2030, nearly 22% of the total population will be comprised of elderly persons (65 years old and over), compared to 4% at the beginning of the 20th century.**

America is in the midst of a demographic revolution as the life expectancy of older persons continues to increase. By the year 2030, nearly 22% of the total population will be comprised of elderly persons (65 years old and over), compared to 4% at the beginning of the 20th century (U.S. Census Bureau, 1990). The fastest growing segment of the elderly population are the oldest-old (85 years and over), which grew by 40% between 1980 and 1990, while the population of all other ages grew by 10% (Smith, 1997). As the baby boomers continue to age, it is the responsibility of health care professionals to ensure that they maintain good health and functional independence, thereby enhancing their quality of life. This view is illustrated in the motto of the Gerontological Society of America (1998), "adding life to years, not just more years to life." Adequate nutrition directly impacts the quality of life of the elderly, by promoting health and preventing disease and disability.

## FACTORS INFLUENCING THE NUTRITIONAL STATUS OF OLDER AMERICANS

Nutritional status plays a vital role in the overall health of the elderly. Many of these individuals are at high risk for malnutrition (Wellman et al., 1996). Ponza et al. (1996) conducted a comprehensive evaluation of the Elderly Nutrition Program (ENP), which is the largest U.S. community nutrition program, providing an average of one million meals per day to older Americans with the greatest economic or social need. The study reported that more than two-thirds of the ENP participants are at risk for malnutrition. This concern is also reflected by Greeley (1990): "Without proper supervision, many millions of older Americans exist in a nutritional twilight zone, grappling with the daily challenge of eating—and often not eating well-balanced meals or any meals at all." Malnutrition increases morbidity and mortality among the elderly and results in lengthy hospitalizations. Nutritional imbalances are not entirely due to the process of aging and can be caused by other significant risk factors that include chronic diseases, inadequate nutritional consumption, poverty, and social isolation.

One important factor that can place the elderly people at nutritional risk is the prevalence of chronic diseases. Almost 80% of older adults suffer from at least one chronic degenerative condition such as heart disease, cancer, stroke, osteoporosis, osteoarthritis, diabetes, visual and sensory impairments, dementia, and depression (Barrow, 1996; Petrella, 1999; Reker, 1997). Mortality rates from circulatory disease increase with age more rapidly than cancer mortality rates. In 1990, cancer was the cause of nearly 40% of deaths in persons aged 50–69 compared to 4% of deaths among centenarians (Smith, 1997). These chronic conditions can precipitate malnutrition due to loss of appetite, diminished smell and taste perceptions of food, and altered nutrient digestion, metabolism, and utilization. Confusion or memory loss associated with dementia affects at least one out of five elderly people (Wellman et al., 1996) . Disease and disability increases the dependency of the over 80 population, with 33 % of them needing assistance with at least one basic activity of daily living compared to the 5–8% of those 65 years and older (Guralnik and Simonsick, 1993). Over 20% of the oldest-old have increased dependency due to their frailty and need longterm care (Silverstone, 1996).

**Nutritional imbalances are not entirely due to the process of aging and can be caused by other significant risk factors that include chronic diseases, inadequate nutritional consumption, poverty, and social isolation.**

Second, poor nutritional status is a cause for concern in the elderly. Nutritionally inadequate diets can put them at risk for malnutrition, worsen chronic health problems associated with aging, and delay recovery from illnesses. The diets of many older Americans do not provide the required amounts of nutrients needed to maintain health and vitality. Calories, protein, calcium, vitamins D, B-12, B-6, and magnesium and zinc are most frequently below the recommendations for the elderly, whereas the intake of total fat, saturated fat, cholesterol, and sodium is excessive (Weimer, 1997). Another trend seen among older people is the use of supplements to meet nutrient requirements rather than eating a balanced diet. In the U.S., nearly 50% of the 65 and over population take vitamin or mineral supplements (Mulley, 1995). Due to the possibilities of nutrient toxicities and drug-nutrient interactions, elderly people should be careful about using supplements. Moreover, excessive alcohol consumption can adversely affect the nutritional status in the elderly. Not only does alcohol displace essential nutrients from the diet, but [it] may cause liver disorders. In addition, older people are often at risk for urinary tract infections and dehydration because of inadequate fluid intake. Two major reasons that account for inadequate fluid intake are decreased response to thirst and self-restriction of fluids due to fear of urinary incontinence (Kendrick and Nelson-Steen, 1994).

Among the socioeconomic factors, poverty can adversely affect dietary intake in the elderly. Lack of financial resources prevents some elderly from buying nutritionally adequate foods and also hinders them from accessing appropriate medical help to treat chronic conditions that arise as a result of malnutrition. The U.S. Bureau of Census (1999) reported that 36 % of the 65+ aged population reported an income of less than $10,000 for 1998, and the net worth was below $10,000 for 16 % of older households (including those of 75+ years). One of every six (17%) older persons was poor or near poor (income between the poverty level and 125% of this level) in 1998. Moreover, 1 % of the chronically ill elderly spent at least 25% of the household income on prescription drugs, and the financial burden is three times as high for the 75–84 year-old population compared to those aged 66–69 years (Rogowski et al., 1997).

A social factor that influences the nutritional status of older people is social isolation. In a study of 516 adults aged 70–105 years, Horgas et al. (1998) reported that most (about 10.5 hours) of the day was spent alone and at home. Elderly, living alone, often lose interest in food; they may not feel the necessity to cook for themselves and this can lead to a diet inadequate in quality as well as quantity (Arcury et al., 1998).

## NUTRITION SCREENING INITIATIVE

The Nutrition Screening Initiative (NSI) was founded in 1989 in an effort to maintain the health and vitality of the nation's elderly and to reduce health care costs associated with the treatment of chronic disease conditions. The NSI is a collaborative effort led by The American Academy of Family Physicians, The American Dietetic Association, and The National Council on the Aging. The primary goal of the NSI is to encourage the incorporation of nutrition screening and intervention as an integral part of the health care for the elderly. The activities of the NSI are designed to increase public awareness about the factors that affect the nutritional status of the aged. The complications associated with malnutrition result in increased expenditure of health care dollars for the treatment of elderly people. Routine nutrition screening and intervention are cost-effective because they help health care professionals identify potential nutritional risk factors at an early stage.

As the first step toward identifying those elderly people at nutritional risk, the NSI developed a simple self-assessment tool, the Determine Your Nutritional Health checklist. The word DETERMINE is an acronym that stands for the nine warning signs: Disease, Eating poorly, Tooth loss/mouth pain, Economic hardship, Reduced social contact, Multiple medicines, Involuntary weight loss/ gain, and Needs assistance in self-care, and Elder years above age 80. The self-assessment checklist contains simple statements that address the nine issues mentioned above, with a numerical score for each issue. A total score of six or more identifies the elderly person to be at high nutritional risk. Those at risk are then followed up with more elaborate screening procedures: Level I and Level II screens. The Level I screen, administered by social workers and health care professionals, includes assessment of anthropometric (height, weight, body mass index) measurements, adequacy of dietary intake, socioeconomic (availability of food, social isolation) factors, and functional status of the elderly. The Level II screen, performed by physicians and other health care professionals, helps identify serious nutritional problems. In addition to the Level I assessment criteria, Level II screening includes evaluation of lab data, cognitive status, and chronic medication use. Health professionals are encouraged to obtain the Nutrition Screening Initiative assessment materials and use it as an integral component of routine health care for the elderly.

## RECOMMENDATIONS FOR AGING WELL

### *Consume a Nutritionally Adequate Diet*

As one ages, calorie needs decrease, whereas vitamin and mineral requirements remain constant. Older people should be encouraged to choose nutrient dense foods (for example, choosing fruit instead of soft drinks, fat-free cheese and whole-wheat crackers instead of cookies and ice cream). Other nutrients that should be consumed in adequate quantities to achieve optimal health are proteins (from fish, poultry, soy protein foods like tofu, legumes, low-fat dairy products), calcium (from low-fat milk and milk products, tofu, calcium-fortified orange juice, kale, broccoli, fish with bones), vitamin $B_{12}$ (from low-fat meat, poultry, fish, low-fat cheese, fortified cereals), vitamin D (from fortified milk and milk products, fortified cereals, and fatty fish), fiber (from vegetables, fruits, legumes, and whole-grain cereals), and at least 6–8 cups of water every day.

### *Exercise Regularly*

A sedentary lifestyle is an independent risk factor for cardiovascular disease, which is the leading cause of death in older people. Some of the significant health benefits of exercise in the elderly are prevention of osteoporosis, control of Type 2 diabetes and hypertension, and decreased incidence of coronary artery disease. Physical activity can increase muscle strength even in the frail elderly (Mulley, 1995). Light exercise like brisk walking for at least 30 minutes a day, 4–5 times a week is a good way to incorporate physical activity for a healthy lifestyle.

### *Choose Nutritional Supplements Carefully*

Older people should be advised to eat a balanced diet instead of relying on supplements for their nutrient requirements. There is a lack of evidence to support the claims of many of the supplement manufacturers and false advertising often misleads the elderly people. It is important to be aware of nutrient toxicities arising from supplement usage. However, the use of vitamin E supplements in the elderly has proven to beneficial due to their immunostimulatory properties (Meydani, 1995).

### *Limit Alcohol Consumption*

Excessive alcohol consumption is associated with many liver, cardiovascular, gastrointestinal, and neurological disorders (Patterson and Chambers, 1995). There is some evidence that low-to-moderate alcohol (especially red wine) consumption is associated with cardio-protective properties.

**The focus of health care delivery should be more on the promotion of a healthy lifestyle rather than the treatment of chronic conditions.**

### *Avoid Smoking*

Smoking is a major risk factor for circulatory, respiratory, and malignant diseases. Elderly people should be encouraged to avoid smoking and using tobacco products.

## FUTURE DIRECTIONS

As we enter the new millennium, the greatest triumph of science and technology is the extended longevity of human beings. It is, however, essential that longer life be accompanied by good health, free from disease and disability. Rowe and Kahn (1997) have defined "successful aging" as multidimensional, encompassing three components, namely, "the avoidance of disease and disability, the maintenance of high physical and cognitive function, and sustained engagement in social and productive activities." Optimal nutritional status is vital to maintain good health and functional independence in the elderly. Periodic screening to identify nutritional risk factors and early nutrition intervention in the elderly are essential to delay the onset of disabling conditions and to prevent costly hospitalizations. A recent report by the National Academy of Sciences, entitled *The role of nutrition in maintaining health in the nations elderly: Evaluating coverage of nutrition services for the Medicare population* reiterated that nutrition services are an integral component of the comprehensive approach to the treatment of many chronic conditions affecting the nation's elderly. The proposed Medicare portion of charges for coverage of nutrition therapy during the 2000–2004 period is estimated to be $1.43 billion.

Family and Consumer Sciences professionals have a pivotal role to play in helping our senior citizens successfully grow old. Many of the chronic diseases in older people are preventable by adopting good nutritional habits throughout life. The focus of health care delivery should be more on the promotion of a healthy lifestyle rather than the treatment of chronic conditions. The Nutrition Screening Initiative's assessment tools have made it easy to identify potential risk factors in the aging population. We should treat every encounter with the elderly as an opportunity to educate and provide resources that will help them age well with good health and vitality.

## References

Arcury, T. A., Quandt, S. A., Bell, R. A., McDonald, J., and Vitolins, M. Z. (1998). Barriers to nutritional well being for rural elders: Community experts' perceptions. *The Gerontologist, 38(4)*, 490–498.

Barrow, G. M. (1996). Aging, the Individual and Society (6th ed.). St. Paul, MN: West Publishing Company.

Gerontological Society of America. (1998). A brief history [Online]. Available: http://www.geron.org/history.html.

Greeley, A. (1990). Nutrition and the elderly. *FDA Consumer, 24(8)*, 24–28.

Guralnik, J. M., and Simonsick, E. M. (1993). Physical disability in older Americans. *Journal of Gerontology, 48*, 3–10. Horgas, A. L., Wilms, H., and Baltes, M. M. (1998). Daily life in very old age: Everyday activities as expression of successful living. *The Gerontologist, 38(5)*, 556–568.

Kendrick, Z. V., and Nelson-Steers, S. (1994). Exercise, aging, and nutrition. *Southern MedicalJournal, 87(5)*, S50–60.

Meydani, M. (1995). Vitamin E. *Lancet, 345*, 170–175.

Mulley, G. P. (1995). Preparing for the late years. *Lancet*, 345, 1409–1413.

Patterson, C., and Chambers, L. W. (1995). Preventive health care. *Lancet, 345*, 1611–1615.

Petrella, R. J. (1999). Exercise for older patients with chronic disease. *Physician and Sportsmedicine, 27(11)*, 79.

Ponza, M., Ohls, J. C., and Millen, B. E. (1996). Serving elders at risk: The Older Americans Act Nutrition Programs, National evaluation of the elderly nutrition program, 1993–1995. Washington, DC: Mathematica Policy Research, Inc.

Reker, G. T. ( 1997). Personal meaning, optimism, and choice: Existential predictors of depression in community and institutional elderly. *The Gerontologist, 37(6)*, 709–716.

Rogowski, J., Lillard, L. A., and Kington, R. (1997). The financial burden of prescription drug use among elderly persons. *The Gerontologist, 37(4)*, 475–482.

Rowe, J. W., and Kahn, R. L. (1997). Successful aging. *The Gerontologist, 37(4)*, 433–440.

Silverstone, B. (1996). Older people of tomorrow: A psychosocial Profile. *The Gerontologist, 36(1)*, 27–32.

Smith, D. (1997). Centenarians: Human longevity outliers. *The Gerontologist, 37(2)*, 200–207.

U.S. Census Bureau. (1999). Current population reports, "Consumer Income" [Online]. Available: http://www.aoa.gov/aoa/stats/profile/

U.S. Census Bureau. (1990). Current population reports, Series P-25. Washington, DC: U.S. Government Printing Office.

Weimer, J. P. (1997). Many elderly at nutritional risk. *Food Review, 20(1)*, 42–48.

Wellman, N. S., Weddle, D. 0., Kranz, S., and Brain, C. T. (1996).*ADA Hungerline. Spring (6)*,1–3 [Online]. Available: http://www.fiu.edu/nutreldr/Elder_Insecurities.htm

From *Journal of Family and Consumer Sciences,* 2000, Vol. 92, No. 2, pp. 37-39. 

# The Female Athlete Triad: Nutrition, Menstrual Disturbances, and Low Bone Mass

The female athlete triad represents the combination of disordered eating, amenorrhea, and osteopenia or osteoporosis. Women who otherwise consider themselves to be in exceptional condition may be most vulnerable to these complications. This manuscript provides a review of literature pertaining to the female athlete triad and examines the related nutritional risks.

LEE E. THRASH, BS, AND JOHN J.B. ANDERSON, PhD

## INTRODUCTION

The female athlete triad—disordered eating behaviors, oligomenorrhea/amenorrhea, and osteopenia/osteoporosis (Fig. 1)—is an area of immense concern for women who otherwise consider themselves to be in superior physical condition. Highly competitive women in sports or other activities that emphasize endurance (long-distance running, rowing, etc.) or physical conformation and appearance (gymnastics, ballet dancing, figure skating, diving, etc.) may be at greatest risk of succumbing to the triad.[1] One study, for example, performed on a group of lean, college female gymnasts revealed that the majority were not satisfied with their current body weight and appearance.[2] These results suggest the presence of underlying issues, such as psychological factors and societal pressures, that may negatively affect the women's perspective of themselves.

The triad of disordered eating, menstrual irregularity, and osteopenia afflicts too many female athletes.

The first manifestation of the triad is usually erratic eating behaviors to control body weight, including poor food choices and meal skipping, which are typically combined with high-intensity exercise.[2] In order to enhance performance or to comply with society's view of the ideal for thinness, many females further reduce their caloric consumption to lose pounds or to maintain a low body weight. This decreased caloric intake by athletes may lead to deficiencies in numerous micronutrients, including calcium, and the rates of peak performance may decline because of reduced intakes of both energy and nutrients. Amenorrhea or oligomenorrhea in female athletes may result from the subsequent exercise stress and low energy availability.[3] Consequently, lower circulating plasma estrogen levels may reduce calcium retention by bone and lead to osteopenia (low bone mass) and premature osteoporosis.[2] The lack of menstruation for extended periods of time (more than six months) may cause a decrease in bone density that is potentially irreversible. Low bone mineral density (BMD) heightens the risk of stress fractures, especially of the spine and hip.[2] The combined strain of these factors may also lead to future complications. Singly, or in combination, the components of the female athlete triad may contribute to decreased physical performance, morbidity, and the deterioration of health. The aim of this manuscript is to provide a review of current information relating to these aspects of the female athlete triad.

## EATING DISORDERS

Some female athletes, especially gymnasts and dancers, begin training as young as the age of three. By the time they reach adolescence, an ideal "body image" for their sport pressures them to look lean and perfectly fit. In addition, some females want to obtain an optimally thin

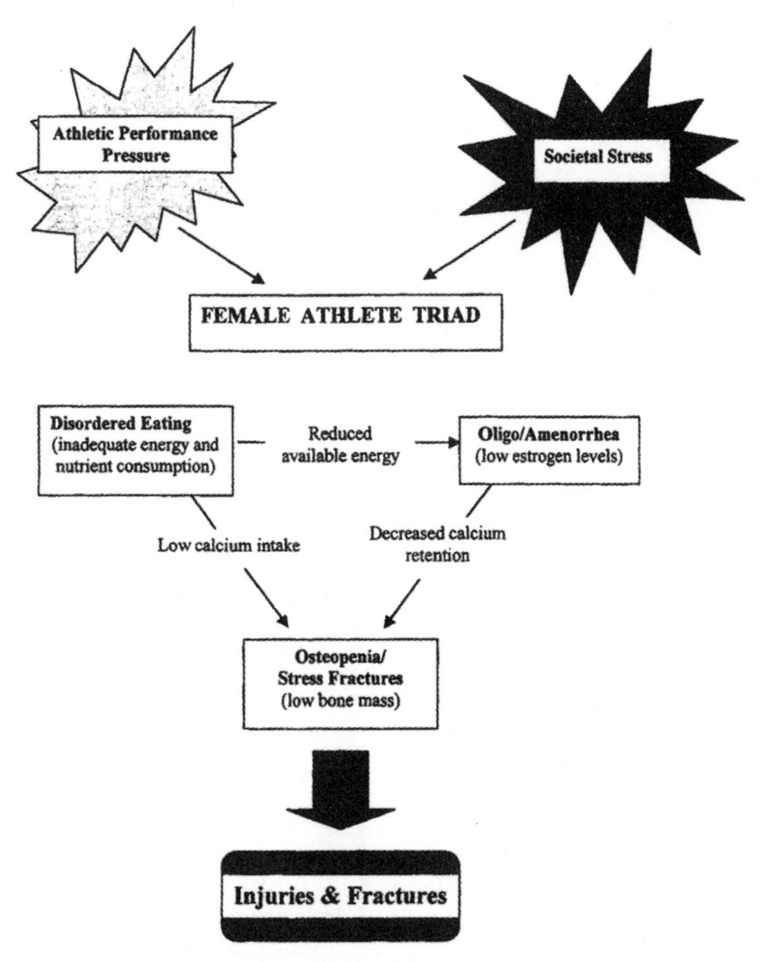


**FIGURE 1.** The female athlete triad.

body weight to enhance athletic performance. These pressures on many female athletes to be thin may lead to disordered eating behaviors, including, but not limited to, anorexia nervosa (a psychiatric disorder consisting of an unwillingness or inability to consume enough calories to maintain a healthy weight), bulimia nervosa (binge eating followed by purging, vomiting, or excessive laxative use), anorexia or bulimia with excessive exercise, and/or normal food intake with excessive exercise patterns. Any of these behaviors creating low energy availability may be associated with the cessation of menstruation. In turn, amenorrhea leads to inadequate production of estrogen, especially during the critical adolescent period. These problems are most commonly observed in activities that are judged in part on appearance (such as gymnastics, ballet, diving, and figure skating), and a fear of losing one's level of athletic performance may contribute to one of the above practices. However, in actuality, the women are depriving their own bodies of essential nutrients and ultimately harming their performance and encouraging potential injuries.

Further ramifications of disordered eating by female athletes, other than poor performance and deficient nutrient intakes, include fatigue, decreased immunity, cognitive losses, decreased concentration, and risk of depression, suicide, and other psychological problems related to low self-esteem.[4] If a severe eating disorder such as anorexia nervosa ensues, an athletic woman may experience seizures, cardiac arrhythmia, myocardial infarction, or other critical complications—possibly leading to morbidity and chronic disease.

Osteopenia is a known complication of anorexia nervosa. In a retrospective investigation measuring BMD of the hip and lumbar spine in 18 recovered anorexic women, an unexpectedly high incidence of osteopenia was found, with 14 of the 18 women affected. The previous duration of amenorrhea and the duration of anorexia nervosa of the subjects were both highly correlated with reduced BMD.[5]

Female athletes too frequently make poor food choices that do not adequately meet the energy needs of their active lifestyles because of peer and societal pressures to be thin. For example, some vegetarian choices may deprive these women of energy and selected micronutrients, such as vitamin B12 and iron. In a vegetarian (vegan) athlete, this potential deprivation may be detrimental to her general health in addition to her performance. A vegetarian diet may, however, be beneficial because of nutrients pro-

**Table 1.** POSSIBLE EXPLANATIONS FOR THE PREVALENCE OF EATING DISORDERS AMONG FEMALE ATHLETES

| | |
|---|---|
| • Competitive athletic atmosphere | • Ability to block pain and hunger |
| • Constant pressure to succeed | • Willingness to take unnecessary risks to win |
| • Heightened body awareness | • Importance of aesthetics in sport or dance |
| • Compulsiveness and perfectionism | • Belief that body leanness optimizes performance |
| • Fluctuation of self-esteem with fluctuation of performance | • Lack of identity beyond the sport or dance |

Adapted from Anderson et al.[14]

vided by increased fruit and vegetable consumption and decreased intake of foods high in fat, salt, and sugar. Physicians and nutritionists recommend, nonetheless, that strict vegetarians, ie, those following a vegan diet, may need to be screened for potential disordered eating behaviors.[6]

Risk factors for the development of eating disorders in female collegiate athletes were examined in a correlational study[7] that suggests that symptoms of eating disorders are significantly influenced by the interaction of the sociocultural pressure for thinness, athletic performance anxiety, and negative self-appraisal of athletic achievement. If having these risk factors leads to excessive concern with body size and shape, then the emergence of an eating disorder is more probable.[7] Related critical trigger factors associated with the onset of disordered eating among female athletes include prolonged or erratic periods of dieting, skipping of meals, frequent weight fluctuations, a sudden increase in training volume, and traumatic personal injuries. Table 1 summarizes possible explanations for the prevalence of eating disorders among female athletes.

Athletes with the female athlete triad are strongly advised to obtain nutrition counseling for the wise selection of foods that provide adequate nutrients, especially calcium-containing dairy foods. The goal is to prevent the relapse of eating disorders, a common occurrence,[8] as well as to delay osteoporosis and to prevent other consequences of the triad.

Eating disorders prove to be a continuing concern for female athletes. Body image is drastically emphasized in many sports; some events even incorporate this image into judging and performance. The pressure placed upon young athletes sometimes proves too intense, resulting in abnormal eating behaviors or binge/purge cycles. Society and performance demands greatly contribute to this incredible pressure to be thin, and, for some athletes, eating disorders may become permanent.

## MENSTRUAL IRREGULARITIES

Amenorrhea is defined as the absence or suppression of the menstrual period to fewer than four per year, *ie*, 0 to 3. Primary amenorrhea consists of no menses prior to age 16, while the secondary form is classified as one or more episodes of menstrual bleeding prior to cessation. Oligomenorrhea is classified as a sporadic menstrual cycle (3–9 menses per year). Amenorrhea and especially oligomenorrhea are more common in athletes than in nonathletes, and particularly in endurance performers. Altered menstrual cyclicity approached 70% in strenuously exercising women, according to one study.[9]

### CASE STUDY OF A DISTANCE RUNNER

A case study of an 18-year-old cross-country distance runner illustrates the female athlete triad and its applicable treatment.[14] This young athlete experienced aggravated pain in her left thigh and right tibia and she was diagnosed with the following: multiple stress fractures, iron deficiency anemia, exercise-associated oligomenorrhea, and a possible eating disorder. Her eating practices, *ie*, too little food consumption, were typical of those experiencing the female athlete triad. Consequently, the young woman noted a general decline in energy and complained of feeling lightheaded during intense interval training and a slowing of her usual race times. At her one-month follow-up, the athlete displayed good compliance with iron replacement as manifested by the reappearance of menses and the return of red blood cell indices toward normal. Furthermore, at 10 weeks, she showed satisfactory clinical healing of the stress fractures. This case highlights the great need for, and efficacy of, education among highly competitive athletes concerning diet and osteoporosis.[14]

Blood concentrations of estrogen and progesterone depend on a balance between production, metabolism, and clearance rates. Intensive physical exercise may affect this balance via different mechanisms, such as stress and dieting.[10] Amenorrhea or oligomenorrhea may occur as a result of abnormalities of the female reproductive tract,

**Table 2.** RECOMMENDED INTAKES OF NUTRIENTS FOR ADULT FEMALE ATHLETES (18 AND OLDER) IN RELATION TO BONE HEALTH

| Nutrient Variable | Recommended: RDA or AI | Additional Amounts Needed According to ↑ Energy Expenditure |
|---|---|---|
| Energy, kcal | 2200 (RDA) | + |
| Protein, g | 50 (RDA) | + |
| Calcium, mg | 1000 (AI) | + |
| Magnesium, mg | 280 (RDA) | + |
| Vitamin D, IU | 400 (AI)* | |
| Vitamin K, mg | 70 (RDA) | + |

*Note:* RDA = Recommended Dietary Allowance; AI = adequate intake.

*400 IU = μg

Adapted from Anderson et al.[14]

hypothalamus, or pituitary gland; ovarian failure; chromosomal anomalies; steroid use; insufficient body fat stores; or a genetic disorder.[11] Amenorrhea may also be associated with emotional or physical stress; severe dieting, including eating disorders; or increased levels of exercise. Other potential factors that contribute to irregularities are depression, malnutrition, drugs, chronic illness,[12] strict vegetarianism, low caloric intakes, and specific training behaviors.[13]

Although the precise mechanism is unknown, exercise-associated amenorrhea is considered most likely to be a form of hypothalamic amenorrhea.[14] Specifically, amenorrhea is caused by a reduction in the frequency of gonadotrophic releasing hormone (GnRH) secreted from the hypothalamus.[3] Both exercise stress and energy availability are being investigated as potential causes of this disruption.[3] Exercise, in particular, has been shown to activate the hypothalamic-pituitary-adrenal axis acutely.[15] For instance, cortisol levels of amenorrheic athletes remain elevated throughout the day and evening, unlike the normal, ie, eumenorrheic (having regular menses), pattern of cortisol elevation solely in the early morning.[16]

Menstrual disturbances and bone density problems are related.

Optimal treatment for exercise-associated amenorrhea remains controversial, but the following figures from a recent survey reflect physician practices regarding preferred management of female athletes: 92%—sex steroid replacement, 87%—calcium supplementation, 64%—increased caloric intake, 57%—decreased exercise intensity, 43%—weight gain, and 26%—vitamin supplementation.[17] These findings suggest that increasing circulating levels of estrogens and progestins and incorporating elevated calcium intakes may prove to be the most effective methods of treatment. Usually these will promote the resumption of menses. However, the inconsistent treatment practices evident in this survey show the need for further research as well as education of physicians in treatment options.

## OSTEOPENIA/OSTEOPOROSIS

The nutritional needs of female athletes are principally determined by their size (weight and height), training load (frequency and duration), and lean body mass. Table 2 lists general dietary recommendations for the optimal bone health of athletes, as well as necessary increases in particular nutrients when energy expenditure is high. Peak bone mass, which is defined as the greatest amount of bone at any time of life, is typically attained by the age of 30 years or even earlier. Before this age, bone modeling, or the development of this dynamic tissue, predominates; skeletal growth (height) of girls is normally completed by 16 to 18 years, depending on the age of menarche. Bone remodeling is the process through which bone is lost and reformed; this occurs throughout life. Osteopenia is defined as low BMD, while the accepted definition of osteoporosis is BMD greater than 2.5 standard deviations below the mean values for healthy young adults.[18]

Stress fractures occur in a small percentage of athletes, especially runners, but they may account for as much as 10% of all sports-related injuries. A stress fracture (minimal or traumatic) is a partial or complete fracture of bone resulting in the inability of the athlete to withstand rhythmic, nonviolent stress applied repeatedly in a submaximal manner.[19] Stress fractures are a major concern for athletes, not only because of the physical consequences but also because of the temporary (or permanent) cessation from training. Female athletes, especially those women with decreased BMD and menstrual disturbances, experience these fractures much more often than

**Table 3.** CROSS-SECTIONAL STUDIES OF BMD IN FEMALE ATHLETES

| Study | Subjects | Bone Mineral Density |
|---|---|---|
| Alfredson et al.[32] | Volleyball players | Total body, lumbar spine, femoral neck, Ward's triangle, trochanter, nondominant femur, humerus are all significantly higher in athletes than in controls. |
| Kirchner et al.[33] | Gymnasts | Athletes maintained higher BMD than controls. |
| Robinson et al.[22] | Runners and gymnasts | Eumenorrheics maintained slightly higher BMDs than amenorrheics. Runner's whole body BMD lower than gymnasts or controls. |
| Young et al.[34] | Dancers | BMD was elevated at weight-bearing sites. BMD deficits similar to those found in anorexics in non-weight-bearing sites. |
| Haenggi et al.[35] | Nonathletes | BMD is lower in amenorrheic women than in eumenorrheic controls. Hormone-replacement therapy resulted in increased BMD. |
| Rutherford[36] | Triathletes and runners | Lumbar spine, arm, trunk, total spine—Amenorrheics less than eumenorrheics. Lumbar and total spine—Amenorrheics less than controls. |
| Myerson et al.[37] | Runners | Amenorrheics less than eumenorrheics, but not significantly different from controls. |
| Wolman et al.[38] | Elite athletes | Amenorrheics less than eumenorrheics and OCA users. |
| Snead et al.[39] | Runners | Lumbar spine--oligomenorrheics and amenorrheics less than eumenorrheics. |

BMD = Bone Mineral Density

men.[20,21] As a result, low BMDs in athletic women may serve as a signal of potential risk for future bone injury.

Female military populations have been shown to be at risk of stress fracture 1.2 to 10 times that of men. This increased rate persists even when training loads are gradually increased to moderate levels. Possible reasons for these findings include lower BMD, differences in gait, slender bones, unfavorable biomechanical conditions, greater percentage of body fat, endocrine factors, and/or lower initial physical fitness.[20]

Low concentrations of ovarian hormones in amenorrhea and oligomenorrhea are associated with reduced bone mass and increased rates of bone loss.[3] Many studies have been performed on female athletes to examine the beneficial and adverse effects of menstruation status and certain activities on their BMD. Eumenorrheic women and those participating in weight-bearing exercises seem to maintain higher BMDs. Table 3 provides a summary of important cross-sectional research findings concerning the BMDs of female athletes in relation to specific sports and menstruation.

In one investigation of forty-four 20-year-old female gymnasts and runners, approximately one third of each group exhibited amenorrhea and oligomenorrhea; all control subjects were eumenorrheic.[22] Percent change of BMD was measured over an eight-month period, and it was shown that menstrual cycle status had a significant effect on percent change, which varied depending on skeletal site and type of sport. The decrease in BMD was greater in those athletes with irregular menstrual cycles. Initially higher BMD measurements in gymnasts, and continued improvement over time while active, suggest that the skeletal benefit results from both higher impact loads on the skeleton during training and greater calcium consumption.[22] A second study on gymnasts and runners confirmed the results of the previous study.[23]

Unfortunately, the effects on vertebral bone loss in oligomenorrheic/amenorrheic athletes seem to be irreversible and, therefore, intervention is necessary to prevent further bone loss. Keen et al.[24] suggested that in spite of several years of normal menses and/or the use of contraceptives, former oligomenorrheic/amenorrheic athletes continued to have a significantly lower BMD of the lumbar spine in comparison with athletes who had always had regular cycles. Their lumbar vertebral BMD was approximately 85% of that of the eumenorrheic athletes. Although resumption of regular menses for several months between episodes of amenorrhea or oligomenorrhea may exert a protective effect on bone, this study suggests that complete normalization of the vertebral BMD in former amenorrheic athletes is not likely.[24]

In other studies of female gymnasts, Lewis et al.[25,26] found that some athletes may be at risk for osteoporosis because of the combination of restrictive eating, intense exercise, and irregular menstruation. They compared the lumbar spine, hip bone, and whole body BMD of 26 female college gymnasts to a group of nonathletes of similar size, age, and weight. They also studied 18 former college gymnasts, aged 29–45 years, and compared them to another control group of women who had never competed in sports. Despite the gymnasts' restricted diets (especially inadequate dietary calcium) and high prevalence of menstrual irregularities, the younger gymnasts consistently had higher BMDs than their nonathlete counterparts.[25] Even the former gymnasts, whose lifestyles had since been altered to a more normal diet and exercise regimen, maintained elevated BMDs compared to other women their own age.[26] The critical skeletal sites that retained greater BMDs in both groups of gymnasts included the vertebrae, hip, and whole body. The main conclusion from these studies is that participation in gymnastics, and possibly other weight-bearing sports, actually helps to maintain BMD of vertebrae, hips, and whole body and might even protect these athletes from developing osteopenia and osteoporosis,[27] despite abnormal menstrual status during participation.

The prevention of osteoporosis and the subsequent reduction in fracture risk rests on the identification of those modifiable lifestyle factors that increase peak bone mass and, then, the optimization of behaviors that promote health. A threshold level of weight bearing (from exercise and body weight) is necessary to stimulate bone growth (osteogenesis), according to one study.[28] An understanding of the relationship between weight-bearing exercise and BMD is important in devising strategies to maximize the skeletal strength of females. Other research has revealed that women who participate regularly in high-impact physical activity during the premenopausal years have higher BMDs at most skeletal sites than nonathletic control subjects.[29]

## The triad of problems is best dealt with by prevention

Cyclic hormone therapy with conjugated estrogens (essential for maintaining normal bone density) and progesterone, or oral contraceptives, may also be beneficial, as may daily supplements of 1.5 grams of elemental calcium. Decreased intensity of training until menstruation resumes may be necessary as well.[19] Many young female athletes have low concentrations of circulating estrogens, which may lead to decreases in BMD, and these athletes would appear to benefit from hormone and diet therapy.

### SUMMARY

Data on the prevalence of the triad do not exist. The prevalence of eating disorders in female athletes, however, has been determined to range from approximately 15% to 62%, while the prevalence of amenorrhea has been estimated to be 3.4% to 66%.[30] The broad ranges of values seem to overlap. The two mechanisms always present in amenorrheic women are psychologic stress and recent weight loss,[31] which also correlate highly with the female athlete triad. In addition, approximately 25–30% of women who are vegetarian athletes have menstrual irregularities, compared to 3–5% of women in the omnivorous population.[31] Many of these "health-conscious" females, and numerous others with atypical eating habits, are athletes. Irregular eating habits, combined with intense physical activity, may lead to weight loss. Peer and societal pressures to be thin and to accommodate a particular physique may cause some athletes to go to extreme measures. These adverse relationships advance the cycle of the female athlete triad and may contribute to its prevalence.

The duration of amenorrhea has also been found to be a powerful predictor of BMD.[4] It has been estimated that 40–60% of normal BMD develops during adolescence when sex hormones become active.[7] When a young athlete does not menstruate for an extended period of time, her bones may not accumulate sufficient mineral calcium to develop optimal strength and hardness and to achieve peak bone mass. Young amenorrheic female athletes in their early 20s who have consumed poor diets and produced inadequate amounts of estrogen, may have thin, fragile bones resembling women in their 70s.[7]

The female athlete triad represents the combination of disordered eating, amenorrhea, and osteopenia or osteoporosis. Although the typical group at risk tends to be high school and intercollegiate athletes and others in highly competitive settings, a large number of physically active girls and women are also at risk for developing the health problems associated with the triad. Good nutritional habits, in particular, are important for maintaining a high level of performance for all athletes. Low food intake of energy and inadequate consumption of many critical nutrients are of concern. Therefore, nutrition education of female athletes needs to receive greater emphasis in preventing the rising occurrence of sports-related injuries and other consequences of the female athlete triad. Alone, or in combination, these disorders may impair normal health and stamina and ultimately lead to fatigue, injury, future complications (including difficulties with childbearing), and fractures. All three components are integrally related and they should be treated as such.

## REFERENCES


1. Wallace C. Female athletes at risk for the female athlete triad. Children's Hospital Medical Center of Akron News Source, 1996;12;1.
2. Nickols-Richardson SM, Lewis RD, O'Connor PJ, Boyd AM. Body composition, energy intake and expenditure, and body weight dissatisfaction in female child gymnasts and controls. J Am Diet Assoc 1997;9:A-14.
3. American College of Sports Medicine. The female athlete triad position stand. Med Sci Sport Exerc 1997;29:i.
4. Krucoff C. Female athletes at risk. Washington Post Health News Source 1997;8:16.
5. Ward A, Brown N, Treasure J. Persistent osteopenia after recovery from anorexia nervosa. Int J Eat Disord 1997;22:73.
6. Neumark-Sztainer D, Story M, Resnick MD, Blum RW. Adolescent vegetarians. A behavioral profile of a school-based population in Minnesota. Arch Pediatr Adolesc Med 1997;151:823.
7. Williamson DA, Netemeyer RG, Jackman LP, Anderson DA, Funsch CL, Rabalais JY. Structural equation modeling of risk factors for the development of eating disorder symptoms in female athletes. Int J Eat Disord 1995;17:387.
8. Strober M, Freeman R, Morrell W. The long-term course of severe anorexia nervosa in adolescents: survival analysis of recovery, relapse, and outcome predictors over 10–15 years in a prospective study. Int J Eat Disord 1997;22:339.
9. Broso R, Subrizi R. Gynecologic problems in female athletes. Minerva Ginecologica 1996;48:99.
10. Arena B, Maffulli F, Morleo MA. Reproductive hormones and menstrual changes with exercise in female athletes. Sports Med 1995;19:278.
11. Stone J, Milord N, Durkin C. Coaches, female athletes, and menstrual irregularities. Olympic Coach Magazine, 1994;2.
12. Barber-Murphy L. Missed "period" (amenorrhea). Healthy Devil Online-Duke University Women's Health 1994;1.
13. Benson JE, Engelbert-Fenton KA, Eisenman PA. Nutritional aspects of amenorrhea in the female athlete triad. Int J Sport Nutr 1996;6:134.
14. Anderson JJB, Stender M, Rondano P, Bishop L, Duckett A. Nutrition and bone in physical activity and sport. Nutrition in Exercise and Sports 3rd ed. Boca Raton, FL: CRC Press; 1998, p. 219.
15. Farrell PA, Gustafson AB, Gaarthwaite TL, Kalthoff RK, Cowley AW, Morgan WP. Influence of endogenous opioids on the response of selected hormones to exercise in humans. J Appl Physiol 1986;61:1051.
16. Loucks AB, Mortola JF, Girton L, Yen SSC. Alterations in the hypothalamic-pituitary-ovarian and hypothalamic-pituitary-adrenal axes in athletic women. J Endocrinol Metab 1989;68:402.
17. Haberland CA, Seddick D, Marcus R, Bachrach LK. A physician survey of therapy for exercise-associated amenorrhea: a brief report. Clin J Sport Med 1995;5:246.
18. Anderson JJB. Introduction. In: Nutritional concerns of women. Boca Raton, FL: CRC Press; 1996, p. 36.
19. Sallis RE, Jones K. Stress fractures in athletes. Postgraduate Medicine, 1997; 1:89.
20. Brukner P, Bennell K. Stress fractures in female athletes. Sports Med 1997;24:419.
21. Bennell KA, Malcolm SA, Thomas SA, Reid SJ, Brukner PD, Ebeling PR, Wark JD. Risk factors for stress fractures in track and field athletes. A twelve-month prospective study. Am J Sport Med 1996;24:810.
22. Robinson TL. Bone mineral and menstrual cycle status in competitive female athletes: a longitudinal study. International Institution for Sports & Human Professionals 1996;1:230.
23. Robinson TL, Snow-Harter C, Taaffe DR, Gillis D, Shaw J, Marcus R. Gymnasts exhibit higher bone mass than runners despite similar prevalence of amenorrhea and oligomenorrhea. J Bone Miner Res 1995;10:26.
24. Keen AD, Drinkwater BL. Irreversible bone loss in former amenorrheic athletes. Osteoporosis International 1997;7:311.
25. Kirchner EM, Lewis RD, O'Connor PJ. Bone mineral density and dietary intake of female college gymnasts. Med Sci Sport Exerc 1995;27:543.
26. Kirchner EM, Lewis RD, O'Connor, PJ. Effect of past gymnasts participation on adult bone mass. J Appl Physiol 1996;80:226.
27. Fosgate H. Women athletes build body and bone. Resource Communication at the University of Georgia, 1998.
28. Ogawa A, Andrews AFB, Armstrong DW, Drake AJ. Weight bearing exercise predicts total bone mineral content in female midshipmen. J Am Diet Assoc 1997;9:A-19.
29. Dook JE, Henderson NK, James C, Price RI. Exercise and bone mineral density in mature female athletes. Med Sci Sports Exerc 1997;29:291.
30. Resch M. The female athletes' triad: eating disorders, amenorrhea, osteoporosis. Orvosi Hetilap 1997;138:1393.
31. Talbott S. The female triad. Strength and Conditioning, 1996;4:128.
32. Alfredson H, Nordstrom P, Lorentzon R. Bone mass in female volleyball players: a comparison of total and regional bone mass in female volleyball players and non-active females. Calcif Tissue Int 1997;60(4):338–342.
33. Kirchner EM, Lewis RD, O'Connor PJ. Bone mineral density and dietary intake of female college gymnasts. Med Sci Sport Exerc 1995;27(4):543–549.
34. Young N, Formica C, Szmukler G, Seeman E. Bone density at weight-bearing and nonweight-bearing sites in ballet dancers: the effects of exercise, hypogonadism and body weight. J Clin Endocrinol Metab 1994;78:449.
35. Haenggi W, Casez JP, Birkhaeuser MH, Lippuner K, Jaeger P. Bone and mineral density in young women with long-standing amenorrhea: limited effect of hormone re-

placement therapy with ethinylestradiol and desogrestrel. Osteoporos Int 1994;4:99.
36. Rutherford OM. Spine and total body bone mineral density in amenorrheic endurance athletes. J Appl Physiol 1993;74:2904.
37. Myerson M, Gutin B, Warren MP, Wang J, Lichtman S, Pierson RN. Total bone density in amenorrheic runners. Obstetrica Gynecologica 1992;79:973.
38. Wolman RL, Clark P, McNally E, Harries MG, Reeve J. Dietary calcium as a statistical determinant of spinal trabecular bone density in amenorrheic and estrogen-replete athletes. Bone and Mineral 1992;17:415.
39. Snead DB, Stubbs CC, Weltman JY, Evans WS, Vwldhuis JD, Rogol AD, Teates CD, Weltman A. Dietary patterns, eating behaviors, and bone mineral density in women runners. Am J Clin Nutr 1992;56:705.

Lee E. Thrash, a BS graduate in public health nutrition from the University of North Carolina at Chapel Hill, is currently a dual-degree graduate student in nutrition and public health at the University of Tennessee-Knoxville.

John J.B. Anderson, PhD, is Professor of Nutrition in the Schools of Public Health and Medicine at the University of North Carolina at Chapel Hill and President of the American College of Nutrition. His research focuses on calcium an bone metabolism as they are influenced by dietary intake.

*The authors thank Sanford C. Garner, PhD, for critiquing the manuscript. The critical reading of the manuscript by Agna Boass, PhD, is also appreciated.*

# UNIT 4

# Obesity and Weight Control

## Unit Selections

25. **Healthy People 2010: Overweight and Obesity**, *Healthy Weight Journal*
26. **Why We Get Fat**, Shawna Vogel
27. **Size Acceptance, Alternative to Fat Phobia**, Ellen S. Parham
28. **Diet vs. Diet: Battle of the Bulge Doctors**, Bonnie Liebman
29. **Weight Loss Diets and Books**, J. Anderson and K. Wilken
30. **A Guide to Rating the Weight-Loss Websites**, *Tufts University Health & Nutrition Letter*
31. **Nondiet Approach to Treatment of Binge Eating Disorder**, Jaime Ruud and Anna Calhoun

## Key Points to Consider

- As the incidence of obesity increases, how can it best be prevented?
- What sort of health risks can be affected by some of the more popular weight-loss methods?
- What are some of the causes behind a person's becoming obese?

**Links: www.dushkin.com/online/**
These sites are annotated in the World Wide Web pages.

**American Anorexia Bulimia Association/National Eating Disorders Association**
*http://www.edap.org*

**American Society of Exercise Physiologists (ASEP)**
*http://www.css.edu/users/tboone2/asep/toc.htm*

**Calorie Control Council**
*http://www.caloriecontrol.org*

**Eating Disorders: Body Image Betrayal**
*http://www.geocities.com/HotSprings/5704/edlist.htm*

**Shape Up America!**
*http://www.shapeup.org*

Overweight and obesity have become epidemic in the United States during the last century and are rising at a dangerous rate worldwide. Approximately 5 million adults are overweight or obese, according to the new standards set by the U.S. government using a body mass index (BMI) of 30 to 39.9. Reports suggest that by the year 2050, half of the U.S. population would be considered obese. This problem is prevalent in both genders and all ages, races, and ethnic groups. Twenty-five percent of U.S. children and adolescents are overweight or at risk, which emphasizes the need for prevention, as obese children become obese adults. The catastrophic health consequences of obesity are heart disease, diabetes, gallbladder disease, osteoarthritis, and some cancers. The cost for treating these degenerative diseases in the United States is approximately $100 billion per year.

Even though professionals have tried hard to prevent and combat obesity with behavior modification, a healthy diet, and exercise, it seems that these traditional ways have not proven effective. In a society where fast-food eateries are the mainstay of meals, where "big," including food servings, is better, where there is a universal reliance on automobiles, and where the food industry is more interested in profit than in the health of the population, we should not be surprised that obesity has become an epidemic.

Thus, there is a great need for a multifaceted public health approach that would include health officials, researchers, educators, legislators, transportation experts, urban planners, and businesses, which would cooperate in formulating ways to combat obesity. A sound public health policy would require that weight-loss therapies have long-term maintenance and relapse-prevention measures built into them. Healthy People 2010 is the U.S. government's prevention agenda, designed to ensure high quality of life and reduce health risks. One of the 28 areas of focus is overweight and obesity. Its main objectives are to reduce the proportion of overweight and obese children, teens, and adults to 15 percent and increase the proportion of adults who are at a healthy weight. Twice as many teens from poor households are overweight in comparison to those from middle to high income. Women with less education and lower incomes have higher rates of obesity, and the rates of obesity are higher among African American women than Caucasian. Gender differences in the incidence of obesity have been observed in Hispanics and African Americans revealing an 80 percent greater incidence in women than men.

One of the many factors that predispose a person to weight gain is genetics. Professionals are considering how genes interact with a person's environment. At least 130 genes that cause obesity have been discovered. Some determine how quickly the stomach informs the brain that it is full; others decide how efficiently the body converts extra calories to body fat. This discovery also explains the genetic variability among individuals and emphasizes the importance of individualized treatment rather than one-size-fits-all remedies. It also alerts us to the fact that each person's weight and body shape is a mark of his or her individuality.

Ellen Parham presents a "new model" for weight loss based on accepting your "size" and creating happier and healthier lives at any size. What is size acceptance? Who needs it? How does one achieve it? The model is an ongoing journey that focuses on health and happiness rather than weight, and it focuses on internal cues rather than guilt as to determine how much to eat. Parham also believes talking to like-minded people frees us from social pressures and helps us accept our body and change our eating habits.

Even though there is plenty of evidence that suggests healthy ways to eat and lose or maintain weight, many nonnutrition "experts" publish diet books, which are followed by a plethora of Americans that used the books and had no long-term success. Most of these diets are dangerous to your health, and there is no scientific research to support the "experts" claims. Bonnie Liebman discusses the pros and cons of different "in fashion" diets.

There is a myriad of weight loss programs, "quick and easy" diets, and fad diet books that promise quick weight loss and perpetuate the obsession of the population with losing weight. Most people want a quick fix for the present and are deceiving themselves into thinking that weight will not be regained when they get off the fad diets. Ways to get around the quick-fix mentality are described in some of the articles, and the strengths and weaknesses of the most popular weight-loss diets and books are included.

For people who are frustrated trying to lose weight but are too busy or too embarrassed to be with a group of people, help is on the way. Virtual weight loss centers are here. People find the structure and moral support that is needed to achieve their goals. Nutritionists from Tufts University have thoroughly researched some Web weight-loss sites to help consumers in their search.

In a country where obesity has become an epidemic it is ironic that eating disorders, especially *anorexia nervosa,* are reaching also epidemic proportions. Approximately 5 million Americans, especially young women, battle eating disorders and the deleterious effects on health that these disorders bring. Many symptoms that we surmised to be unique to anorexia and *bulimia nervosa* have been found to be the result of starvation. The focus on slimness and dieting all over the world, the use of "skinny" fashion models by the fashion industry, and the preoccupation of a culture with outward appearance, other sociocultural influences, and family dynamics are some of the causes of the above syndromes. A newcomer to the realm of eating disorders, but prevalent in the overweight population is the Binge Eating Disorder. It is frequently associated with personality disturbances, depression, low self-esteem, a distorted body image, and preoccupation with food. These individuals eat large amounts of foods without purging afterward. A non-diet approach to treatment seems to work best with these individuals. Emphasizing healthy bodies and fitness, making a commitment to lifelong healthy eating, preparing children for the changes of puberty, and praising them for goals that they accomplish should be the focus of our society rather than thinness.

# Healthy People 2010: Overweight and Obesity

Healthy People 2010 is the US prevention agenda for the next decade, designed to reduce health risks and increase the quality and years of healthy life. Ten Leading Health Indicators are selected as priority areas from the 28 sections. One of these is overweight and obesity, which is major part of the nutrition section.

## What Is Healthy People 2010?

Healthy People 2010 is the document that sets the prevention agenda for the United States for the next 10 years. It is designed to identify the most significant preventable threats to health and establish national goals to reduce these threats.

The two overarching goals of Healthy People 2010 are (1) to increase the quality and years of healthy life for everyone—to add years to our lives and life to our years—and (2) to eliminate health disparities so that all people have access to better health care and opportunities.

The report includes 28 focus areas with 467 objectives in a large two-volume format. To make this more manageable, 10 Leading Health Indicators are selected as priority areas. These will provide a quick measure of progress—a snapshot of the health of the nation.

Healthy People 2010 was developed by leading federal agencies with input from more than 350 national membership organizations and 250 state health, mental health, substance abuse, and environmental agencies. Additionally, through a series of regional and national meetings and an interactive website, more than 11,000 public comments on the draft objectives were received.

Many of the objectives focus on interventions designed to reduce or eliminate illness, disability, and premature death among individuals and communities. Other focus on broader issues, such as improving access to quality health care, strengthening public health services, and improving the ability and dissemination of health-related information. Each objective has a target for specific improvements to be achieved by the year 2010. These targets will be the measure for assessing the progress of a wise array of federal and local programs.

Healthy People 2010 offers a simple but powerful idea: profile the objectives in a format that enables diverse groups to combine their efforts and work as a team. It is to be a road map to better health for all, used by many different people, communities, professional organizations, businesses, and state and federal programs who are encouraged to integrate it into current programs, special events, publications, and meetings to improve health for all. Most states are now working with community coalitions, developing their own versions tailored to their specific needs.

Healthy People 2010 is coordinated by and available from the Office of Disease Prevention and Health Promotion, US Department of Health and Human Services, Room 738G, 200 Independence Avenue SW, Washington, DC 20201 (202-205-8583). For more information, visit www.health.gov/healthpeople or call 1-800-336-4797.

The two main objectives for tracking progress in this priority area are

- Reduce the proportion of children and adolescents who are overweight or obese.
- Reduce the proportion of adults who are obese.

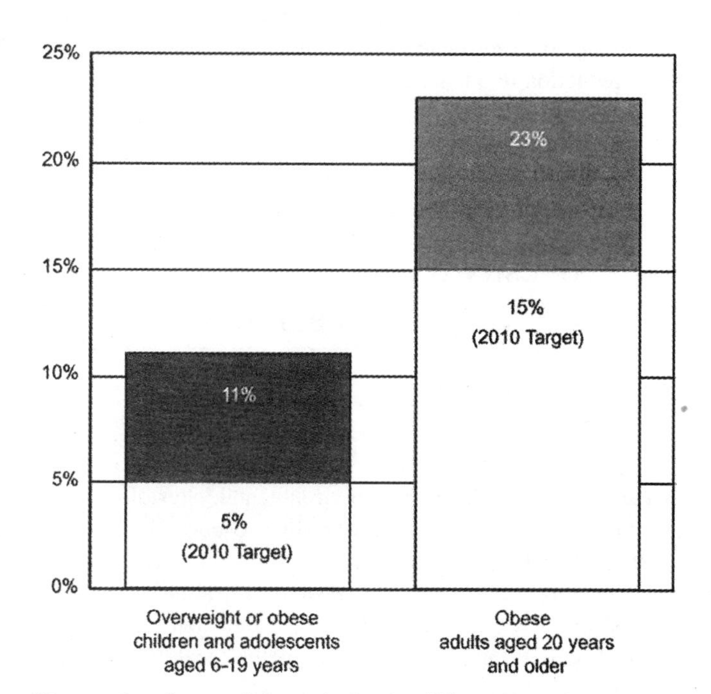


**Figure 1** Overweight and obesity, US, 1988–1994.

Baseline data (Figure 1) show that 11 percent of youth age 6 to 19 are overweight or obese using the definition of measuring at or above 95th percentile (US Growth Charts, 2000). The target is to reduce this to 5 percent. Baseline data for adults age 20 and over show that 23 percent are obese using the definition of a body mass index (BMI) of 30 or more, including 20 percent of males and 25 percent of females. The target is 15 percent.

A third objective aims to

- Increase the proportion of adults who are at a healthy weight.

Only 42 percent of adults are considered at the healthy weight, defined as a BMI of 18.5 to less than 2.5 (Table 1). This includes 38 percent of males and 45 percent of females. The target is 60 percent.

Overweight (BMI of 25–29.9) and obesity (BMI of 30 or more) affect a large percent of the US population: 55 percent of adults. In two decades, obesity has increased from 14.5 to 22.5 percent of adults (Table 2). There is much concern about the increasing prevalence of obesity in children, that it may persist into adulthood and increase the risk of some chronic diseases later in life. Almost twice as many adolescents from poor households are overweight as from middle- and high-income households.

An estimated 107 million adults in the United States are overweight or obese, and rates are especially high among women with lower incomes and less education, according to this report. Obesity is more common among African-American and Hispanic women than among Caucasian women. Among African Americans, the number of women who are obese is 80 percent higher than for men. This gender difference is also seen among Hispanic women and men, but the percentage of Caucasian women and men who are obese is about the same.

**Table 1.** Healthy weight. Adults age 20 years and older, 1988–1994. Age adjusted to the year 2000 standard population. Categories without data are omitted from this chart. Objective 19–1.

| | Healthy Weight, % | | |
|---|---|---|---|
| | *Total* | *Female* | *Male* |
| Total | 42 | 45 | 38 |
| Race and ethnicity | | | |
| Black or African American | 34 | 29 | 40 |
| Caucasian | 42 | 47 | 37 |
| Hispanic or Latino | | | |
| Mexican American | 30 | 31 | 30 |
| Not Hispanic or Latino | | | |
| Black or African American | 34 | 29 | 40 |
| Caucasian | 43 | 49 | 38 |
| Age | | | |
| 20–39 years | 51 | 55 | 48 |
| 40–59 years | 36 | 40 | 31 |
| 60 years and older | 36 | 37 | 33 |
| Family income level | | | |
| Lower income (≤130 percent of poverty threshold) | 38 | 33 | 44 |
| Higher income (> 130 percent of poverty threshold) | 43 | 48 | 37 |
| Disability status | | | |
| Persons with disabilities | 32 | 34 | 30 |
| Persons without disabilities | 41 | 45 | 36 |
| Select populations | | | |
| Persons with arthritis | 36 | 37 | 34 |
| Persons without arthritis | 43 | 47 | 40 |

Although BMI alone is used to screen for overweight and obesity, it is not entirely satisfactory, the report acknowledges. A truly health-oriented definition would be based on the amount of excess body fat at which health risks begin to increase; however, no such definitions currently exist.

**Table 2.** Prevalence of obesity. Adults age 20 years and older, 1988–1994. Age adjusted to the year 2000 standard population. Categories without data are omitted from this chart. Objective 19–2.

| | Obesity, % | | |
|---|---|---|---|
| | *Total* | *Female* | *Male* |
| Total | 23 | 25 | 20 |
| Race and ethnicity | | | |
| Black or African American | 30 | 38 | 21 |
| Caucasian | 22 | 24 | 20 |
| Hispanic or Latino | | | |
| Mexican American | 29 | 35 | 24 |
| Not Hispanic or Latino | | | |
| Black or African American | 30 | 38 | 21 |
| Caucasian | 21 | 23 | 20 |
| Age (not age adjusted) | | | |
| 20–39 years | 18 | 21 | 15 |
| 40–59 years | 28 | 30 | 25 |
| 60 years and older | 24 | 26 | 21 |
| Family income level | | | |
| Lower income (≤130 percent of poverty threshold) | 29 | 35 | 21 |
| Higher income (> 130 percent of poverty threshold) | 21 | 23 | 20 |
| Disability status | | | |
| Persons with disabilities | 30 | 38 | 21 |
| Persons without disabilities | 23 | 25 | 22 |
| Select populations | | | |
| Persons with arthritis | 30 | 33 | 27 |
| Persons without arthritis | 21 | 23 | 19 |

Overweight and obesity are associated with increased risk of illness from high blood pressure, high cholesterol, type 2 diabetes, heart disease, stroke, gallbladder disease, arthritis, sleep disturbances and problems breathing, and endometrial, breast, prostate, and colon cancers. Obese individuals may also suffer from social stigmatization, discrimination, and lowered self-esteem. Thus, maintenance of a health weight is a major goal in the effort to reduce the burden of illness and its consequent reduction in quality of life and life expectancy.

In two decades, obesity has increased from 14.5 to 22.5 percent of adults.

The development of obesity is a complex result of a variety of social, behavioral, cultural, environmental, physiologic, and genetic factors. For many overweight and obese individuals, substantial change in eating, shopping, exercising, and even social behaviors may be needed to develop a healthier lifestyle. It is noted that any reduction in BMI in youth should emphasize physical activity and balanced diet so that healthy growth is maintained.

## Note

Tables and figures in this article taken from Healthy People 2010 (Conference Edition). Washington, DC: January 2000, *www.health.gov/healthypeople*.

From *Healthy Weight Journal,* January/February 2001, Vol. 15, No. 1, pp. 4-5. 

# WHY WE GET FAT

## The good news is recent research indicates fat might not be your fault. The bad news is you might not be able to do much about it

**By Shawna Vogel**

John Rossi was a model employee at Kragen Auto Parts in Berkeley, California. In his ten years there, first as a clerk and then as a manager, he had missed only three days of work and had regularly put in 50- to 60-hour weeks. So it was something of a surprise when Rossi's manager told him one day in 1991 not to come to work anymore.

A spokesman for the store later said that Rossi was fired for poor job performance. But the only reason Rossi could see for his dismissal was his weight. A high school football star, Rossi had struggled with obesity throughout his adult life. By the age of 21, when he started working at Kragen, he weighed 275 pounds. Over the next decade he tried everything from fasting to hypnosis, and at one point had his jaws wired shut. On the day he was fired, Rossi weighed about 400 pounds.

## Genes predispose some toward toe tapping, hair twirling, and other calorie-burning fidgeting

Still, laudatory letters from customers and the company's own evaluations were clear: weight had never affected Rossi's job performance. So he decided to sue. In 1995, jurors awarded him $1,035,652 for lost compensation and emotional distress. They concluded that Rossi couldn't legally be dismissed for a condition beyond his control. What convinced them, says Rossi's lawyer, Barbara Lawless, was testimony from a medical witness that each person's weight is controlled primarily by genetics—the witness attributed 80 percent to genes and only 20 percent to environment.

The jury's decision reflects a profound shift in the way our culture views people who are excessively overweight. No longer can we equate significant weight with lack of willpower. With every passing month, scientists announce the discovery of new genes and gene neighborhoods that can be associated with obesity. The count is up to 130 and climbing. In each of us, these genes combine to produce different results. Richard Atkinson, an obesity researcher at the University of Wisconsin in Madison, says, "If you think about all the combinations and permutations of those 130 genes, there are going to be dozens, hundreds, thousands of different kinds of obesity." But knowledge is power, too. An understanding of the genetics of weight control is helping researchers develop a new generation of drugs for weight control.

What does it mean for a gene to be associated with obesity? Although all human beings share the same basic genetic blueprint, genes that make up that blueprint, or genome, vary from individual to individual. For example, imagine two people, each dressed in the same garments: underwear, pants, socks, shoes, shirt, and so on. If one wears a cashmere sweater and the other a cotton sweater, the one in cashmere will probably be warmer. But not necessarily. What if the cashmere-clad person is caught in an Arctic snowstorm while the cotton wearer visits a Florida beach? In that case, the one in cashmere will feel considerably chillier despite the warm sweater because of the different environment. Similarly, someone who inherits the version of a particular gene that's associated with obesity will be more likely to wind up fat than someone who inherits a normal version, but that tendency can be affected by environmental factors such as how much fattening food is available. So once researchers have identified the genes of obesity, they must find out how the genes interact with a person's environment.

The revolution in obesity research began less than five years ago with the landmark discovery of a gene for lep-

## WHEN IT'S NOT YOUR FAULT

With John Wayne bluntness, David West, a geneticist and obesity physician at Parke-Davis in Alameda, California, says, "Some people have the good genes, some people don't. Some patients, especially the very morbidly obese, are pretty much a biological problem. They have a real nasty set of genes. As long as they have enough calories to eat, they're going to be fat no matter what environment they're in and despite their best efforts."

Nevertheless, West says most people don't get fat unless they follow a certain style of life. To gain weight they have to work at it: sit behind a desk all day, wolf down a big lunch, collapse at home with a few beers, then wake up the next day and repeat the process. Genes may make them susceptible to weight gain, but a fattening environment makes the gain happen.

In a way, most of us are a lot like a group of mice West has been studying for the past six years. The mice get fat only when they are fed a delectable brand of rat chow that resembles cookie dough—sugar, condensed milk, minerals, and powdered rodent food. As in a typical North American diet, 40 percent of the calories come from fat. And one group of rats in related experiments become obese only when they are offered many different, tasty items at once. Researchers call that a "supermarket" or "cafeteria" diet, and its similarity to the food available to most Americans needs no elaboration.

When West's mice become fat, they show all the associated biological changes that people do. Their blood sugar goes up, they get more gallbladder and cardiovascular diseases, and they develop problems with insulin similar to human type II diabetes. Geneticists have shown that this reaction to a rich environment stems from not just one gene but a multitude of genes that contribute to the animals' susceptibility, and they believe people have a similar genetic profile.

But just as genes can make us susceptible to obesity, they can also make us resistant. Intriguingly, some strains of mice never become obese despite efforts to fatten them up. Studying these animals may help us understand why some people can eat more than others and never gain weight. The same idea of genetic resistance and susceptibility applies not only to obesity but also to obesity-related illnesses. West says that "there are a fair number of people walking around out there who are 60, 80 pounds overweight but have normal blood sugar and normal blood pressure. Their joints are fine. They don't have gallbladder disease. There doesn't seem to be a greater risk for cancer.

"Why? I think it's because they have another set of genes that protects them from these adverse effects of being fat."

—S.V.

tin, the weight-regulating hormone found in both mice and people. Fat mice and skinny mice flashed across TV screens around the world when scientists could finally say that the only difference between them was a single gene. Since then geneticists have uncovered many more weight genes. One, a gene mutation that is also associated with red hair, causes severe obesity. In its normal form, the gene produces a hormone that inhibits eating and also influences hair pigmentation. A mutation in the gene produces a damaged version of the hormone, or no hormone at all. In one case, researchers noticed that both a five-year-old boy and a three-year-old girl who had each inherited two copies of the faulty gene were obese by the age of five months.

Another newly discovered family of genes makes compounds called uncoupling proteins, which allow people to convert excess fat into heat instead of storing it. Researchers have shown that animals with high levels of these proteins do not gain weight as easily as those with lower levels.

Obesity-related genes affect different aspects of weight control. For example, some genes might determine how quickly the gut lets the brain know that it is full. Others might dictate how effectively the body turns extra calories into body fat. There's a genetic component to how much fuel muscles need just to get through a sedentary day. And genes also lie behind a tendency that some people have toward spontaneous physical activity—fidgeting, toe tapping, hair twirling—which burns up a substantial number of calories.

It is now widely accepted among weight researchers that a person's particular complement of genes determines what activities make him or her susceptible to weight gain as well as how strong that susceptibility is. The bottom line is that genes alone don't make people fat. All of us simply have a greater or lesser genetic tendency to gain weight. Those with the strongest tendency—the worst combination of genes—are almost guaranteed to join the minority of people who weigh 300 pounds and up. The rest lie somewhere on a continuum that extends all the way down to those lucky people who can eat all the doughnuts they want and never need to punch a new hole in their belts.

## WHY DIETS DON'T WORK

Despite the role genes play in making people fat against their will, diet and exercise remain significant factors. As any dieter knows, losing pounds is never easy. That's because the body uses a remarkably efficient set of tricks to keep fat at a stable level. Researchers refer to this level as the set point. When people successfully lose weight, their bodies undergo a change in metabolic rate that may seem counterintuitive. For example, participants in one study who held their weight at 10 percent below their set point showed a 15 percent drop in daily energy expenditure.

Their bodies slowed down energy use to counteract the pounds they had lost. Researchers find this shift in metabolism to be just as marked after a weight gain too. In the same study, subjects who increased their weight showed 10 to 15 percent increases in metabolism.

So if our bodies are so good at maintaining a set point, why do people get fat at all? William Ira Bennett, a doctor at Cambridge Hospital in Massachusetts, wrote in the *New England Journal of Medicine* that although our bodies continue to defend their set points, external factors, such as habitual levels of physical activity and the composition and tastiness of diets, can reset them. Bennett believes that over time a sedentary life and the mere availability of rich, palatable food will slowly increase the weight the body is geared to defend. Because of genes, some people are more susceptible to a change in set point than others. They will always have more trouble keeping off any weight they lose through dieting.

—S.V.

What's more, even if two people seem to have roughly the same tendency to gain weight, they may do so for different reasons, simply because of genetic variety. In 14 years of work at the National Institute of Diabetes and Digestive and Kidney Diseases in Phoenix, obesity researcher Eric Ravussin (now at Eli Lilly in Indianapolis) recently uncovered some fascinating examples. He looked at the differences in how people burn energy and how those differences contribute to weight gain. The work made him appreciate how widely metabolic rates can vary.

## People with the same weight and height may burn vastly different amounts of energy

In a study of more than 500 volunteers, Ravussin and his colleague Pietro Tataranni analyzed resting metabolic rates—how much energy the body uses when it's just trying to maintain the status quo. The researchers gathered this information using a clear plastic ventilated hood that looks like something out of a viral-scare movie. It fits snugly around a subject's neck, continuously drawing in and siphoning off air. The wearer must lie awake for 40 minutes without moving. By measuring how much oxygen he consumes and how much carbon dioxide he breathes out, researchers can determine how much energy the subject spends on such basic functions as temperature control and involuntary muscle activity. Ravussin and Tataranni found that some of their volunteers burned as few as 1,067 calories a day, while others burned as many as 3,015.

## CAN A VIRUS MAKE YOU FAT?

Although the idea sounds more like the premise of a B movie than scientific theory, two scientists at the University of Wisconsin in Madison believe they've found a virus that causes some people to get fat. Nikhil Dhurandhar and Richard Atkinson reported recently that when they injected a virus known as AD36 into mice and chickens, the animals' body fat increased. Because humans were unlikely to volunteer for such experimentation, the scientists decided to test for the presence of antibodies to the virus. Of 154 people tested, about 15 percent of those who were obese had the antibodies. None of the lean people did.

However, the findings don't necessarily prove that the virus caused obesity in the test group. As several virologists have pointed out, obese people may simply be more susceptible to such a virus. Still, in recent years researchers have been surprised to find that viruses can be linked to so many diseases that had been thought to have other origins. For example, viruses are now implicated in several types of cancer, hardening of the arteries, and even mental disorders such as depression. In addition, five viruses besides AD36 have already been shown to cause obesity in animals. The good news is that the same methods that produce flu shots each year could ultimately be used to create an antiobesity injection.

—S.V.

Contrary to what many people think, a slow metabolism doesn't necessarily go hand in hand with weight gain, Ravussin says: "Most obese patients will tell you, 'I have something wrong with my metabolism.' And I believe that something is wrong. But it may not be their metabolic rate." When Ravussin has measured rates, he has found that people with the same physical characteristics—same weight, same height, same basic shape—may nevertheless burn dramatically different amounts of energy each day.

Other researchers have shown that exercise has remarkably different effects on different people. When people exercise regularly for three to four months, their bodies can change dramatically: their hearts and muscles get stronger, and they can exercise harder for longer periods. But that is not true for everyone. When exercise physiologist Claude Bouchard of Laval University in Sainte-Foy, Quebec, put a group of 47 young men on a training program for 15 to 20 weeks, he found that some showed 100 percent improvement in their maximal oxygen uptake—a measure of how efficiently lungs, heart, and circulation can dispense oxygen to tissues crying out for it. Other men, however, showed almost no change. Bouchard has seen the same lack of effect on other measurements of how people adapt to exercise, such as heart size, muscle fiber size, and how much work people can perform in 90 minutes. "We believe that it is quite remarkable," he says, "that for all the determinants that have been considered in a series of investigations performed in our laboratory, one can find nonresponders—even after 20 weeks of regular exercise at a frequency of five times a week over the last several weeks of the program."

When it comes to weight, it has long been our habit to group heavy people together as if they all suffer from the same condition and should respond to the same cure. Every diet-and-exercise program is pitched as a one-size-fits-all remedy. As scientists begin to understand how different bodies control weight, they are learning to characterize various types of obesity and treat people accordingly. To many researchers and pharmaceutical companies, that treatment means drugs. By one recent count, 62 new compounds for treating obesity are in various stages of testing and development. "I expect we'll see something like one or two new drugs being submitted to us every year for the next five to ten years," says Leo Lutwak, a medical officer with the FDA's Center for Drug Evaluation and Research.

These include the family of so-called exercise pills, drugs designed to boost the rate at which bodies burn fat and dissipate the energy as heat—an effect that would provide many of the benefits of regular mild exercise. Other pharmaceutical approaches use leptin and related molecules to tell the body that its fat stores are already ample, or to target brain chemicals that control appetite. Other pills prevent our bodies from absorbing some of the fat that we eat.

But even without new drugs, knowledge of the differences between bodies can lead to more thoughtful ways of dealing with weight. For example, some people tend to burn less fat than others. As a result, when they're exposed to a high-fat diet, they gain weight more readily. For them, cutting down on fatty foods might be a far easier and more effective way to maintain weight than, say, embarking on a vigorous exercise program. Ultimately we will be forced to accept that each person's weight is as much a mark of his individuality as his face. And that could make weight really interesting.

# Size Acceptance, Alternative to Fat Phobia[1]

**Ellen S. Parham, PhD, RD, LCPC**
Northern Illinois University, DeKalb, Illinois

"Dying to be thin!" screams the cover of a popular magazine. Inside hair-raising features tell the stories of people who put their lives at risk in desperate efforts to be thin. Each of these people died as a result of their pursuit of thinness. They are indeed casualties in the struggle with fat phobia. Their stories are unique only because of the extreme price they paid. Being fat is everyone's worse nightmare.

In spite of all these efforts, we Americans are not thin. Every passing year shows higher statistics for the prevalence of both overweight and eating disorders.[1] For most of us there is quite a discrepancy between the realities of our body sizes and shapes and the ideal urged upon us on every side. This discrepancy takes a major toll in self-esteem and life satisfaction. Most American women and many men are so discontent with their body size that their weight is never far from mind and they repeatedly turn to ineffective dieting and other weight loss efforts.

This article explores a new response to the discrepancy between the reality and ideal: body size acceptance. We will consider the origins of fat phobia, the effectiveness of weight loss strategies, and the nature of the size acceptance movement.

## Fat Phobia—Where Does It Come From?

We get some of our strong feelings about weight from interpretations or models that are passed along in our culture. Our earliest ancestors probably interpreted being fat as a good sign, indication that they had been usually successful in their hunting and gathering. This interpretation is long gone from our contemporary scene where our attitudes are daily shaped by two competing models, a moral interpretation and a medical model.[2] The moral model considers that fatness is evidence of weakness, laziness, and gluttony, the outcome of willful behavior of eating too much. The remedy is to exert will power to eat less. The medical model views fatness as a disease and emphasizes reliance on external control exerted by diet plans, exercise prescriptions, and other authoritative guidance. Both models explain fatness as bad, unhealthy, and a threat to quality of life. The huge weight loss industry profits from the perpetuation of these explanations.

These moral and medical interpretations of weight tie into some other characteristics of our western culture. Our belief in self-improvement makes us especially receptive to notions that we can change our body size and shape at will. We value feeling in control of ourselves and of our lives. How better can we express this control than to control our weights? Furthermore, the size of our population and the pace of our lives mean that we have very little time to get to know other people. Without time to explore people's values, personalities, and character in depth, we rely on appearance to form opinions about each other.[3]

So we have all the ingredients to produce nationwide obsessions about weight—extremely negative interpretations of fatness and an appearance-focused culture that believes in the power of self-improvement and the strength of control. Add to this situation fortunes to be made from making people feel discontented about their bodies and media to carry the message of discontent into every second and every corner. Is it any wonder that we are experiencing a magnitude of fat phobia as never before?

## Why Not Just Lose Weight?

Is there is a single adult American who has not dieted and dropped a few pounds? Most of us have demonstrated to ourselves that if we eat less and/or exercise more, we will lose weight... at least in the short run. In the long term, it is a far different situation. The body implements strategies to modify our metabolic processes and the mechanisms for control of food intake so that we return to our original weight. Accounts in professional journals of weight loss attempts typically show a sharp and rapid initial weight loss that slows down and frequently plateaus even while the treatment is continued. When individuals discontinue their diets, there is a gradual regain of most, if not all, of the lost weight.

In 1998 the National Institutes of Health (NIH) convened a group of experts to make recommendations about weight management[1]. They started by examining the evidence about the effectiveness of weight loss interventions. They pored over all the well-designed and thoroughly documented reports available in the professional literature. They concluded that, although some people didn't lose any weight at all, on the average a combination of a low calorie diet and exercise could be expected in six months to produce losses of 8–10% of a dieter's original body weight. Losses of this magnitude may produce some significant health improvements (lower blood pressure, better glucose tolerance, or normalized levels of lipids in the blood), but they are usually insufficient to meet the cultural expectation of extreme thinness. And the hard part is just beginning.

The NIH group went on to note that regardless of the method used to lose weight, weight losses didn't usually continue beyond six months and that as soon as people left the active phase of weight loss effort, the regains started. So they recommended that people continue to use the active weight loss interventions indefinitely. If people can sustain their weight-loss efforts forever, they can be successful in keeping off small weight losses. This is a big *if*. For a variety of reasons, most people are not able to keep up the efforts required. The amount of effort required varies from person to person and is probably influenced by one's heredity and previous weight. For most people it involves a lot of vigorous exercise, usually a[n] hour or more every single day, and constant dietary restriction. Concern about weight has to become one's highest priority.

Of course, we have a distressing number of people who need no urging to make weight their highest priority. These people, often but not exclusively young and female, find the will-power to implement extreme weight loss efforts. The outcome is eating disorders.

## Enter a New Model, Health at Any Size

As researchers and practitioners worked with obesity, many became disillusioned with the fit of the traditional interpretations of weight to the realities they encountered. They saw that heavy people were not lazy gluttons but were ordinary people who tried really hard to be slender. They saw that our medical interventions did not produce lasting slenderness. They grew tired of urging people to distort their lives to give weight control the highest priority. They were confused by the fact that, although they saw many heavy people who had serious health problems, they saw as many or more who did not. They felt uncomfortable that even as they strived to accept diversity of skin color, abilities, and such, they were continuing to assume that all people should conform to a narrow range of weight.

These questions led to some new approaches in dealing with weight.[4] Health professionals of all kinds began to ask not "how can we get our clients slender and keep them that way?" but rather "how can we help our clients to have healthier, happier lives at any size?"

These pioneers began to talk about nondieting, turning away from diets and focusing more on using the body's own signals to control food intake. Most especially they spoke of size acceptance, accepting one's body size and shape as it is. First called the New Weight Paradigm, this approach has more recently evolved into the Health at Any Size model.[5]

## What is Size Acceptance?

We Americans are not particularly good at acceptance. It is a concept that appears to contradict our goals of self-improvement. Self-acceptance is an active process of self-affirmation rather than passive resignation to an unhappy fate. It involves changing one's interpretation of the importance and meaning of body size. Even more importantly it means expanding one's body experience to include aspects other than size. Body acceptance is a matter of recognizing the strengths, beauty, and abilities of one's body even while dispassionately recognizing the weaknesses, unattractive features, and awkwardnesses.

For most of us size acceptance feels rather risky. There are some good questions that need to be addressed in order to assess whether size acceptance is a good idea.[6] Size acceptance may be viewed by some as turning away from the goals of slenderness and health. The paragraphs below describe some of the typical doubts and suggest facts and perspectives that may be useful to challenge them.

**How can we deny the health risks of obesity?** Size acceptance does not involve denying the health risks of obesity. The risks of certain chronic health problems including hypertension and diabetes are clearly high in heavy people. What is less clear is whether these risks are the direct result of fatness and whether losing weight will produce long-term reductions in risk.[7] Using generalized health concerns to justify body dissatisfaction is problematic for several reasons: not all fat people are at risk, weight loss interventions have a poor success rate, and awareness of the risks does not consistently lead to improved behaviors. Fear is a tricky motivator, often producing irrational and/or erratic behaviors or a sense of being overwhelmed.

Lacking widely effective and lasting means of weight loss intervention, it may be more appropriate to find other ways to cope with the risks, either by reducing the risks through means other than achieving slenderness or by accepting the risks. Loss of relatively small amounts of weight may produce significant improvements in risk factors.

**If you relieve the pressure, won't people get fatter?** For the most part, the idea that body dissatisfaction provides the momentum necessary for lasting weight loss is an untested hypothesis. Anecdotal evidence suggests just the opposite—pick the heaviest persons you know and ask them if they have ever felt bad about their weights and whether these negative feelings helped make them more slender. Size acceptance programs that help people increase self-esteem and feel better about their bodies do not show weight gains.[8]

Pressure to be slender seems to be effective in increasing the prevalence of dieting, although not necessarily among those are most overweight and evidently without a lot of lasting effect on the prevalence of obesity. The author has monitored weight changes and self-reported efforts to lose weight among one hundred women over five years. In none of the years was the correlation between reported dieting and long-term weight changes significant.

**Isn't losing weight the best way to improve body image?** Weight loss is viewed as the universal cure-all in this culture—isn't it the best way to improve body image? That is what people with eating disorders tell themselves and many of them are very effective in losing weight, but they continue to have very negative body images. There are some reports that heavy people have better feelings about their bodies after losing weight, but that the effect lasts only as long as the weight loss maintenance, not very long.

**How can you accept something that isn't positive?** Although size acceptance is more than just re-labeling the meaning of size, it does involve accepting that one is heavier than the cultural ideal and that being heavy is not catastrophic. Life presents everyone with some degree of unavoidable pain and hardship. In face of the severe limitations of weight loss interventions, is it appropriate to urge heavy people to continue to loathe their bodies? It may be helpful here to consider an analogy to aging. Only the most optimistic would characterize growing old as a positive process. Yet people do find it appropriate to accept the aging process and to find ways to grow old gracefully, maintaining good physical, social, and emotional health as much as possible.

**Aren't you asking people to give up?** Shifting attention from useless fretting about body size to more productive goals hardly can be characterized as giving up. Pursuing health and happiness directly rather than relying on evasive slenderness to provide them gives one plenty to do. Achieving new health goals will require of most people significant and sustained effort. Size acceptance involves recognition of one's value as a person, a good foundation for making any number of changes.

## Who Needs Size Acceptance?

Anyone, whether large or small, is a candidate for size acceptance. If one is troubled about the size and shape of one's body, working to feel more comfortable about it is appropriate. Working for size acceptance does not require that one abandon all weight management efforts. Some people will choose to continue to attempt to lose weight. This is especially appropriate if they have a health problem that weight loss will relieve. Given that achievement of slenderness is rare even among those who are successful in losing weight and keeping it off, size acceptance can increase satisfaction with the modest losses. Furthermore, most of us have rather unrealistic expectations of the attractiveness that will be ours if we are thinner. Again, size acceptance is in order.

## How Does One Achieve Size Acceptance?

Many people start their journey to size acceptance by questioning the conventional wisdom that if they are not slender, it is because they have not tried hard enough. Everything in their experience says otherwise and all it takes to start the doubting is a little confirmation from an article, a speaker, a friend, or a group. The transition from this questioning and doubting to pursuit of more accepting attitudes and behaviors is not easy, however. Doing so involves defying the messages, pressures, and downright sabotage of all kinds of people important in one's life. Most people need some support from others to continue on the road to size acceptance.

As they focus on their health and happiness rather than their weight, most people find they want to change their food habits to rely more on internal cues and less on guilt for guidance as to how much to eat. Finding enjoyable sources of exercise is a critical step for most.

Size acceptance is an on-going journey. Most of those who start it find that there are times when their confidence and courage ebb. At those times, checking the reality of one's own experiences and talking with like-minded friends are helpful.

Many persons are not ready to accept their bodies; for them, progress may consist of reaching a point where they can begin to consider the *possibility* of size acceptance. For individuals with mental disorders or deep-seated body image disturbances, size acceptance may be achievable only after intensive examination and working through of early experiences and past and current relationships.

## Note

1. Based on presentations given at the Women's Retreat, Celebrate Health at Every Size, Richardton, ND, Sept. 2000 and at the workshop Gotta to be Thin: Addressing Weight Obsession and Eating Disorders in Young People. DeKalb, Marion, and Champaign, IL, May 2000.

## References


1. National Institutes of Health, National Heart, Lung, and Blood Institute. Clinical guidelines on the identification, evaluation, and treatment of overweight and obesity in adults—the evidence report. *Obesity Research* 1998; 6 supplement 2:51S–210S.
2. Sobal J. The medicalization and demedicalization of obesity. In: Mauer D, Sobal J, eds. *Eating Agendas: Food and Nutrition as Social Problems.* NY: Aldine de Gruyter; 1995; 67–90.
3. Pipher M. *Reviving Ophelia: Saving the Selves of Adolescent Girls.* NY: Ballatine Books; 1994.
4. Parham, ES. Is there a new weight paradigm? *Nutr Today.* 1996:31:155–161.
5. Berg FM. *Women Afraid to Eat: Breaking Free in Today's Weight-Obsessed World.* Hettinger ND: Healthy Weight Network; 2000; 214–225.
6. Parham E S. Promoting body size acceptance in weight management counseling. *J Am Diet Assoc.* 1999;99:920–925.
7. Ernsberger P, Koletsky RJ. Biomedical rationale for a wellness approach to obesity: An alternative to a focus on weight loss. *J Social Issues.* 1999; 55:221–260.
8. McFarlane T, Polivy J, McCabe RE. Help, not harm: Psychological foundation for a nondieting approach toward health. *J Social Issues.* 1999; 55:261–276.

# DIET VS DIET

## BATTLE OF THE BULGE DOCTORS

BY BONNIE LIEBMAN

It's almost bathing-suit season, the time of year when diet-book sales typically take off. But these days, with one out of two Americans overweight, diet books have taken up permanent residence on the bestseller list. The pursuit of weight loss has become a way of life.

Last February, the U.S. Department of Agriculture held a "Great Nutrition Debate" (it should have been called a "Great Dieting Debate," given that most of the speakers were diet-book authors, not nutrition experts). Sparks flew between Dr. Robert Atkins, *The Zone* author Barry Sears, Dean Ornish, John McDougall, *Sugar Busters!* co-author Morrison Bethea, and other panelists. What didn't fly was good research.

Ornish was the only speaker who has published studies comparing people randomly assigned to his eating plan versus a "control" group. The catch is that his Life Choice Program isn't just a diet. It also gets people to exercise, stop smoking, and participate in stress-reduction. So, chances are, diet alone—which Ornish hasn't studied—didn't account for his patients' entire weight loss (25 pounds after one year, which shrank to 13 pounds after five years).[1]

Ornish aside, the research cupboard is largely bare. A handful of studies (mostly on normal-weight people) has found that when people eat less fat—without trying to cut calories—they lose about five pounds.[2] But it could be the lower density of low-fat diets that the difference, not fat *per se*. Either way, that's not much evidence for a nation of dieters to go on... especially for people who want to keep weight off over the long haul.

The popular diets "all produce weight loss and they all do it the same way—they cut calories," said Keith-Thomas Ayoob of Albert Einstein College of Medicine in New York. "The problem isn't weight loss, but long-term weight management."

The panelists agreed that there's a dearth of good data. When Dr. Atkins claimed lack of funding to explain his lack of evidence, Ayoob retorted, "Ten million books in print and you can't fund a study?"

It's not just Atkins who's to blame. One might ask a similar question of the USDA or the Department of Health and Human Services: Americans spend $50 billion a year on weight-loss regimens and you can't fund a study to compare how good—and how safe—those diets are?

### The Million-Dollar Question

Safety aside, good diet studies ask one of two questions:

**1. Is a calorie a calorie?** Researchers randomly assign people to eat either the test diet or a control diet, and make sure that each has the same number of calories.

*Dr. Atkins, The Zone*, and *Protein Power* all claim that calorie for calorie, low-carbohydrate diets lead to more weight loss than high-carb diets. Though researchers haven't tested their specific diets, dozens of studies have found that if you cut *any* calories—from fat, protein, or carbs—you'll lose the same amount of weight.

"Any differences in how well calories are used by the body are trivial," says Susan Roberts, head of the Energy Metabolism Laboratory at the Jean Mayer U.S. Department of Agriculture Human Nutrition Research Center on Aging at Tufts University in Boston.

**2. Do some diets help people eat fewer calories?** Little long-term research has tackled this question. But a few studies suggest that what you eat may affect *how much* you eat. For example, in the first decent study to compare how much food people eat on a high-protein versus a high-carbohydrate diet, more protein led to more pounds shed.

Arne Astrup and colleagues at the Royal Veterinary and Agricultural University in Copenhagen randomly assigned 60 overweight men and women to either a control group (whose members were told not to change their eating habits) or to one of two diets: high-protein (25 percent protein, 45 percent carbs) or high-carb (12 percent protein, 58 percent carbs).[3] Both diets got 30 percent of their calories from fat.

After six months, the high-carb group lost an average of 11 pounds, while the high-protein group lost nearly 20 pounds. On average, the high-protein-eaters consumed about 450 fewer calories a day than the high-carb-eaters. (The control group didn't lose weight.)

"The main difference in the foods available to the two groups was that people on the high-protein diet were allowed to select fat-reduced dairy products and lean cuts of beef, pork, poultry, lamb, and fish," says Astrup, "whereas the high-carbohydrate group ate a mainly vegetarian diet with more vegetables, fruits, breads, rice, and pasta, and were also allowed to cheer themselves up with chocolate and sweets."

Less opportunity to eat sweets may have helped the high-protein group. "High-protein diets restrict variety

## Rules for Healthy Weight-Loss

Get used to it. Diet books will continue to captivate and confuse the public. With Americans moving less and eating more, obesity rates—and interest in the latest diets—can't go anywhere but up. Until better diet studies are done, our advice is to exercise and make sure your diet is healthy. It should be:

• **Low in saturated and *trans* fat to cut your risk of heart disease and possibly colon and prostate cancers.** That means eating low-fat versions of meats, cheese, ice cream, and milk, and cutting way back on fried foods (french fries, fried chicken, doughnuts) and fatty sweets (pies, frosted cakes, pastries, cookies, chocolate). It also means substituting oil or tub margarine for butter or stick margarine.

**Why?** LDL ("bad") cholesterol may rise, or it may drop slightly, when you cut calories or lose weight, even if you're eating foods that are high in saturated fat[1] But LDL will drop far more on a diet that's low in sat and *trans* fat.

And even if your LDL drops on a diet high in saturated fat, your risk of colon and possibly prostate cancer won't. Missing from much of the debate over diets is the evidence that either red meats or saturated fat—studies can't tell which—are linked to a higher risk of two out of the four cancers that claim the most American lives (lung and breast are the other two).

• **Rich in vegetables and fruit to cut your risk of cancer, heart disease, and stroke.** Go for eight to ten servings of vegetables and fruit a day. French fries, chips, and ketchup don't count. Sorry.

**Why?** In numerous studies, people who eat more fruits and vegetables have a lower risk of cancers of the lung, colon, stomach, esophagus, throat, and mouth. Other studies show that diets rich in fruits and vegetables lower blood pressure and are linked to a lower risk of stroke and heart disease.

• **Low in (largely) empty-calorie foods.** As most dieters know, if you're trying to lose weight, you start by cutting back on high-calorie foods that don't add many vitamins, minerals, fiber, or phytochemicals to your diet. That means fewer sweets like regular soft drinks and desserts. If you still need to cut, limit (skinless white) potatoes and bread, pasta, rice, cereals, and crackers made of refined flour.

**Why?** Short-term studies show that people eat fewer calories when they eat foods with lower calorie density.

### Take Your Pick

The above rules apply to everyone. The rest of your diet should depend on which foods help *you* curb calories:

**1. If you're able to resist unhealthy carbs** and you want the fiber in bran and whole grains to stay regular, lean more heavily towards *healthy carbs* (like whole-wheat cereals and breads and beans), not sweets, white bread, and refined pasta.

**2. If you have a sweet tooth** and you find bread and pasta irresistible, lean towards more *healthy protein* (larger servings of seafood or low-fat dairy or poultry), not beef and cheese.

**3. If you have high triglycerides and low HDL ("good") cholesterol**—both signs of Syndrome X (see *NAH*, March 2000), lean towards more *unsaturated fats* (like olive or canola oil, salad dressings, nuts, and avocados). But don't go overboard. Their high calorie density means you can only eat small quantities.

1. *Amer. J. Clin. Nutr. 71*: 706. 2000

enormously," says Roberts. The fewer the choices, the less people eat.

Another explanation: "High-protein foods have a much higher satiety value than high-carbohydrate foods," says Astrup. In other words, they're more likely to make people feel full.

And some studies suggest that when people cut carbs from their diets, they don't compensate by eating an equal amount of protein, even if they're allowed to.[4]

### Calories Per Pound

Other research suggests that what matters isn't protein vs. carbohydrates, but high vs. low calorie density—that is, calories per pound (or gram or any weight) of food. Books like *Volumetrics* and *The Pritikin Principle* argue that the key to losing weight and keeping it off is eating foods with few calories and lots of bulk. Translation: lots of vegetables, fruits, and only low-fat dairy, poultry, meat, salad dressing, and mayo... but not low-fat, high-calorie foods like fat-free cakes and ice cream.

"These books are low-fat, high-fiber diets packaged with a few bells and whistles like adding water or air to foods," says Roberts. "Studies show that lower-fat diets lead to modest weight loss—four or five pounds on average. Whether the additional effects of adding water or air are real is something we need to study further."

### Diet Safety

Which diets are safe?

When it comes to high-sat-fat, very-low-carb diets, the most obvious problem is LDL ("bad") cholesterol, which rose an average of 18 percent in a 1980 study of 24 people on the Atkins diet.[4] Other studies suggest that a diet rich in saturated fat may not raise LDL, as long as you're cutting calories or losing weight.[5] But dieters eventually stop doing both. What's more, a recent study found that a diet that's low in saturated fat cuts LDL about 20 percent more than one that's high in sat fat.[5]

And it's not just LDL, but the risk of colon and prostate cancers, that could climb when people switch to a diet loaded with sat fat, or, more precisely, red meat.

"I'm not aware of a single, trustworthy piece of evidence that suggests that high-protein diets like Atkins's are a healthy way to eat," says Roberts. "The epidemiological studies point to fruits, vegetables, and whole grains as healthy foods."

Earlier reports cautioned that excess protein might burden the kidneys.[6] But if you look at the *grams* of protein eaten on an Atkins-type diet,

## RATING THE DIET BOOKS

Just about every diet book is jam-packed with what Dr. Atkins calls a "rationale" (along with the testimonials, the "you'll never be hungry again" promises, and the obligatory "why this diet works when all others failed" chapter).

Many rationales are irrelevant because they don't do the obvious: test the author's diet against a "control" diet to see if one enables people to lose more weight... and keep it off.

Without a control group, studies are worthless. "I can make anyone lose 20 pounds just by bringing them into our research center for a few weeks," says Tufts University researcher Susan Roberts.

On these pages we ignore the "rationales" and instead size up the diets. Because the "unacceptable" diets often give no serving sizes, our numbers may grossly underestimate their fat and sat fat levels (see Note).

### UNACCEPTABLE

#### *Dr. Atkins' New Diet Revolution*

*by Robert Atkins, M.D.*

**Claim**: Only carbs make you fat. Strict limits on carbs enable the body to burn fat.

**What you eat**: Meats, poultry, seafood, eggs, cheese, butter, cream, oil, nuts, some (non-starchy) vegetables, artificial sweeteners.

Calories: 1,800
Fat: 110 g (55%)
Sat Fat: 36 g (18%)
Protein: 135 g (30%)
Carbs 60 g* (15%)
Fiber: 10 g*

**Comments**:
- Too high in saturated fat.
- Low in fruits and whole grains.
- Low in calcium and fiber.
- May cause bad breath and constipation.
- Our numbers average the induction, weight-loss, and maintenance diets.

#### *Protein Power*

*by Michael R. Eades, M.D., and Mary Dan Eades, M.D.*

**Claim**: Limiting carbs lowers insulin, and insulin causes obesity.

**What you eat**: Same as Atkins (meats, poultry, seafood, eggs, cheese, butter, cream, oil, nuts, artificial sweeteners), but with more fruits and vegetables.

Calories: 1,700
Fat: 105 g* (60%)
Sat Fat: 34 g* (18%)
Protein: 110 g (25%)
Carbs: 70 g (15%)
Fiber: 20 g

**Comments**:
- Too high in saturated fat.
- Restricts some healthy foods (like whole grains and beans).
- Low in calcium.

#### *Sugar Busters!*

*by H.L. Steward, M.C. Bethea, S.S. Andrews, and L.A. Balart*

**Claim**: Refined carbs cause obesity by raising blood sugar.

**What you eat**: No sugars, white flour, carrots, corn, or beets.

Calories: 1,600
Fat: 70 g* (40%)
Sat Fat: 20 g* (10%)
Protein: 100 g (25%)
Carbs: 140 g (35%)
Fiber: 20 g

**Comments**:
- Advice is inconsistent. The book recommends limiting sat fat, but its list of "acceptable" foods includes cream, butter, cheese, milk, lamb, pork, and "lean" beef (which is often fatty).
- Daily menus range from 7 to 44 grams of saturated fat.
- Restricts or excludes some healthy foods like carrots and bananas.
- Low in calcium.

#### *The Carbohydrate Addict's Diet*

*by Dr. Rachael F. Heller and Dr. Richard F. Heller*

**Claim**: If you're a carbohydrate addict, carbs boost insulin, which causes weight gain.

**What you eat**: Meat, poultry, seafood, oils, butter, margarine, eggs, cheese, cream, selected vegetables. Calories, etc., can't be calculated because one daily "reward meal" can contain *any* foods.

**Comments**:
- Advice is inconsistent. Recipes are too high in sat fat... unless you use optional ingredients, some of which ("lean bacon") don't exist. (Which readers are the *fatty* ingredients for?)
- Another inconsistency: The book recommends two cups of vegetables in every non-reward meal, but most sample meals and recipes have less or none.

*(continued)*

depending on the serving sizes you choose, you may eat no more protein than you would on some higher-carb diets. Other side effects (if the carbs are low enough) are bad breath (from the ketones in your blood) and constipation (from lack of fiber).[7]

Atkins's diet—like many other weight-loss diets—also runs short on some nutrients. To play it safe, dieters should take a multivitamin-and-mineral supplement as well as calcium (see *NAH*, April 2000).

What about diets—like Astrup's—that limit sat fat and don't restrict carbs as much as Atkins's? They should be reasonably healthy as long as you get enough fruits and vegetables—which should help reduce the risk of cancer, high blood pressure, and possibly heart disease.

In separate studies, Astrup found no adverse effect on kidney function or bone loss in people on his higher-protein diet.[8] "I think this diet is safe, but our findings should be confirmed by other studies before we allow them to influence dietary guidelines," he says.

### Notes


1. *J. Amer. Med. Assoc. 280*: 2001, 1998.
2. *Nutrition Reviews 56*: S29, 1998.
3. *Int. J. Obesity 23*: 528, 1999.
4. *J. Amer. Diet. Assoc. 77*: 264, 1980.
5. *Amer. J. Clin. Nutr. 71*: 706, 2000.
6. *J. Amer. Med. Assoc. 224*: 1415, 1973.
7. Eric Westman, Durham VA Medical Center, unpublished data.
8. *Int. J. Obesity Relat. Metab. Disord. 23*: 1170, 1999, and personal communication.

## RATING THE DIET BOOKS *(continued)*

### ACCEPTABLE

### *The Zone*
*by Barry Sears, Ph.D.*

**Claim**: The correct ration of carbs to protein to fat (40:30:30) promotes weight loss (and health) because it keeps insulin levels in "The Zone."

**What you eat**: Low-fat protein (like chicken breast, fish or cottage cheese) the size of your palm, and fruits and vegetables on the rest of the plate, with a small amount of olive or canola oil.

| | |
|---|---|
| Calories: 1,000 | Protein: 70 g (30%) |
| Fat: 30 g (60%) | Carbs: 115 g (45%) |
| Sat Fat: 8 g (8%) | Fiber: 20 g |

**Comments**:
- Low calorie density and reasonably healthy (low in sat fat, with ample fruits and vegetables).
- Low in whole grains and calcium.

### *Dieting with the Duchess*
*by Sarah, Duchess of York, and Weight Watchers*

**Claim**: Dieters choose foods within their "point" budget. (Points are based on a food's calorie, fat, and fiber content.)

**What you eat**: Low-fat dairy, poultry, meat, seafood; fruits, vegetables, bread, pasta, cereals.

| | |
|---|---|
| Calories: 1,400 | Protein: 90 g (25%) |
| Fat: 30 g (20%) | Carbs: 190 g (55%) |
| Sat Fat: 10 g (6%) | Fiber: 25 g |

**Comments**:
- Low calorie density and healthy (low in sat fat, ample fruits and vegetables).
- If your triglycerides are high (above 200), cut back on carbs and add more unsaturated fats.

### *Volumetrics*
*by Barbara Rolls, Ph.D., and Robert A. Barnett*

**Claim**: Cutting calorie density is the key to weight loss.

**What you eat**: Fruits, vegetables, pasta, oatmeal, soups, salads; low-fat poultry, seafood, meats, dairy. Few fatty foods. Limited dry foods (crackers, popcorn, pretzels, etc.).

| | |
|---|---|
| Calories: 1,700 | Protein: 95 g (20%) |
| Fat: 40 g (20%) | Carbs: 260 g (60%) |
| Sat Fat: 62 g (6%) | Fiber: 35 g |

**Comments**:
- Low calorie density and healthy (low in sat fat, ample fruits and vegetables).

### *The Pritikin Principle*
*by Robert Pritikin*

**Claim**: Cutting calorie density is the key to weight loss.

**What you eat**: Fruits, vegetables, pasta, oatmeal, soups, salads, low-fat dairy; limited amounts of low-fat poultry, seafood, meat. Few fatty foods. Limited dry foods (crackers, popcorn, pretzels, etc.)

| | |
|---|---|
| Calories: 1,500 | Protein: 95 g (25%) |
| Fat: 15 g (9%) | Carbs: 265 g (70%) |
| Sat Fat: 3 g (1%) | Fiber: 20 g |

**Comments**:
- Low calorie density and healthy (low in sat fat, ample fruits and vegetables).
- Restricts some healthy foods like seafood and low-fat poultry.
- Low in calcium.
- If your triglycerides are high (above 200), cut back on carbs and add more unsaturated fats.

### *Choose to Lose*
*by Dr. Ron Goor and Nancy Goor*

**Claim**: Cutting fat is key to weight loss. You choose how to spend your fat budget.

**What you eat**: Low-fat dairy, poultry, meat, seafood; fruits, vegetables, bread, pasta, cereals.

| | |
|---|---|
| Calories: 2,200 | Protein: 115 g (20%) |
| Fat: 20 g (8%) | Carbs: 410 g (75%) |
| Sat Fat: 5 g (2%) | Fiber: 50 g |

**Comments**:
- Low calorie density and healthy (low in sat fat, ample fruits and vegetables).
- If your triglycerides are high (above 200), cut back on carbs and add more unsaturated fats.

### *Eat More, Weigh Less*
*by Dean Ornish, M.D.*

**Claim**: If you eat fat-free, healthy foods, you can feel full and still lose weight.

**What you eat**: Vegetables, fruits, whole grains, beans, limited non-fat dairy (yogurt, cottage cheese), egg whites.

| | |
|---|---|
| Calories: 1,500 | Protein: 60 g (15%) |
| Fat: 10 g (6%) | Carbs: 290 g (80%) |
| Sat Fat: 2 g (1%) | Fiber: 40 g |

**Comments**:
- Low calorie density and healthy (low in sat fat, ample fruits and vegetables).
- Restricts healthy foods like seafood and low-fat poultry and dairy.
- Low in calcium.
- If your triglycerides are high (above 200), cut back on carbs and add more unsaturated fats.

*Note about our numbers: We calculated (rounded) numbers by averaging three to five days' worth of menus from each book. (If a number is marked with an *, you could get 50 percent more or less than the average on any given day.) When a book gave no serving sizes, we used its recipes to estimate portions or used (very modest) portions recommended by the U.S. Department of Agriculture. We also omitted ingredients (like butter) if they were optional. The percentages of calories from fat, carbs, and protein may not add up to 100 due to rounding. If you want to compare the books' numbers to official recommendations, the government's Daily Values are 65 grams of fat, 20 grams of saturated fat, and 25 grams of fiber. There are no DVs for carbohydrates or protein.*

*Numbers calculated by Ingrid Van Tuinen and Jackie Adriano.*

# Weight Loss Diets and Books

*by J. Anderson and K. Wilken*[1]

Approximately 30 percent of Americans are overweight. Carrying too much weight increases risk of health problems such as hypertension, heart disease, gall bladder disease and diabetes. Losing weight—and keeping it off—can be challenging. Controlling fat intake, exercising and changing behavior are the keys to weight management.

## Quick Facts...

- The most effective way to lose and maintain weight is to limit fat intake, follow a healthy balanced diet and exercise regularly.
- Weight loss strategies should encourage setting realistic goals and making permanent changes in eating habits.

## Fat Intake

At 9 calories per gram, fat contains more than twice the calories of protein and carbohydrates (4 calories/ gram each). Limiting your total daily fat intake to 30 percent or fewer calories from fat not only reduces fat and calories, but also reduces a risk factor for cardiovascular disease.

You can estimate your desirable fat intake with the following rules of thumb: To maintain your weight, divide your current weight in pounds by two. If you want to lose weight, divide your current weight in pounds by three. This is your daily fat gram goal.

Watching your fat intake doesn't mean you must give up your favorite foods. Choose lean meats and dairy products. Use oils and spreads sparingly. Be aware of hidden fats in foods such as bakery products, crackers, nuts and salad dressings. Learn to modify recipes and use substitutions to lower the fat content.

## Weight Loss Diets

Fad diet books often promise quick weight loss. The diets usually are difficult to continue for a long period and are not nutritious. Although people may lose weight initially, they easily regain it. At two-year follow-ups, fad diets have a very low success rate.

Safe and more effective weight loss plans have the following characteristics:

- Recommend no more than 1 to 2 pounds weight loss per week.
- Do not go below 1,200 calories per day.
- Refer to the Food Guide Pyramid and Dietary Guidelines.
- Focus on limiting fat intake rather than calories.
- Encourage exercise.
- Include a variety of nutritionally balanced foods from all food groups.
- Do not have a list of forbidden foods.
- Minimize hunger.
- Do not require special foods or vitamin supplements.
- Encourage setting realistic weight loss goals and making slow, moderate changes.
- Establish lifelong habits.
- Fit into your lifestyle.

## Sample Weight Loss Diets and Books

***Dr. Atkins' New Diet Revolution***

1992—Robert C. Atkins, M.D. Another book: *Health Revolution*

- **Characteristics**: High protein, high fat, low carbohydrate. Claims diet may help people with food intolerances or allergies, heart disease, diabetes, yeast infections. Megavitamin and mineral supplements daily.
- **Weaknesses**: Nutritionally unbalanced. Recommends as little as 15 grams carbohydrate

a day. No bread, pasta or cereal. Low fruits and vegetables. Ketoacidosis is encouraged.

- **Comments**: Does not teach good eating habits. Can be dangerous. Claims are not nutritionally sound. May initially lose water weight.

## Breaking the Behavior Chain

Behavior modification techniques can help alter poor eating habits. Begin by recording your eating habits to identify places, emotions or activities that lead to inappropriate eating.

To change those habits, use simple modification techniques. For example, make a rule to not eat when watching television. When you feel stressed, go for a walk or call a friend instead of eating cookies.

Taking personal responsibility for losing weight, believing you can succeed and having support from family and friends also are important factors in losing weight.

***Eat More, Weigh Less***

1993—Dean Ornish, M.D.

- **Characteristics**: Life Choice vegetarian diet. Low in fat, high in complex carbohydrates and fiber. Believes large changes are easier to make than moderate ones. Includes over 250 appetizing recipes. 10 percent of calories from fat.
- **Strengths:** Heart healthy diet. Does not limit amounts of food (no counting calories). Encourages moderate exercise.
- **Weaknesses:** Advocates giving up all meat, poultry, fish, oils, margarine, sugar, dairy (except nonfat) and products exceeding 2 grams of fat per serving.
- **Comments**: May be difficult to follow long-term, especially for non-vegetarians.

***Fasting***

- **Characteristics:** Often claimed to detoxify the body and lead to quick weight loss. Often followed by very low-calorie diets.
- **Weaknesses:** May feel weak, light-headed and shaky. Can lead to ketosis, kidney stones, nausea, fatigue and elevated uric acid levels. Life-threatening (especially thin people and over 75).
- **Comments**: Weight loss from water and muscle loss, then fat loss. When eating resumes, weight gain is primarily fat. Exercise accentuates the problems.

***Fit for Life***

1985—Harvey and Marilyn Diamond.

- **Characteristics**: Based on the erroneous theory of "detoxification." Toxic wastes build up and lead to obesity. Certain foods or food combinations detoxify the body.
- **Weaknesses:** Contains misinformation; nutritionally unbalanced; no dairy; deficient in calcium, zinc, vitamin D and B-12; low protein.
- **Comments:** Probably not dangerous but potentially unhealthy. Unsafe for children, adolescents, pregnant and lactating women. Will lead to weight loss as food intake is restricted.

***The Fit-or-Fat Woman***

1989—Covert Bailey. Other books: *The New Fit or Fat, The Fit-or-Fat Target Diet*

- **Characteristics:** Recommends aerobic exercise, balanced diet and weightlifting/body building. Focuses on body fat percentage, not weight loss. Covers stress, eating disorders, PMS, gaining weight.
- **Strengths:** Emphasis on exercise and balanced diet with more fiber and less fat and sugar. Warns against vitamin and mineral megadoses.
- **Weaknesses:** Recommends only 10 to 15 grams fat per day for obese women with 36 percent or more body fat.
- **Comments**: Straightforward, sound approach to reducing body fat.

***The G-Index Diet***

21-day diet. 1993—Richard N. Podell, M.D.

- **Characteristics:** Classifies foods based on how they affect blood sugar response (glycemic index). Claims eating high G-Index (GI) foods at one meal causes overeating at the next meal. Claims low GI foods lower insulin levels and rev up metabolism so you burn an extra 200 calories.
- **Strengths**: Emphasizes whole grains, low sugar, low fat. Recommends regular exercise.
- **Weaknesses:** Restricts nutrition-rich foods like baked potatoes, pineapple, raisins and carrots. True glycemic index of many foods is unknown.
- **Comments:** Eating a combination of high and low glycemic foods should avoid big blood sugar swings.

*The McDougall Program*

12-day program. 1990—John McDougall.

- **Characteristics**: High complex carbohydrates and fiber, low fat. Unlimited amounts of "the right food" such as rice, potatoes and pasta. Restricts animal-derived foods and refined plant foods (white flour). High fat or sugar foods (honey, maple syrup, soybeans, nuts) for special occasions.
- **Strengths**: Reduction in sugar, salt and fat.
- **Weaknesses**: No meat, dairy, mayonnaise or oils, sugar, salt, coffee, cola, chocolate.
- **Comments:** Extremely low fat intake (5 to 6 percent of calories). If followed for a long time, potential for nutrient deficiencies in protein, calcium, zinc, vitamins D and B-12, and riboflavin. Unbalanced.

## Exercise

People are more successful in losing weight when they alter eating habits and exercise regularly. Physical activity burns calories, raises metabolism, and helps you lose body fat (increasing the percentage of lean body mass). Exercise also promotes a sense of well-being and has beneficial effects on HDL cholesterol.

Contrary to popular belief, moderate activity does not increase your appetite. Find an activity that you enjoy. If you are very overweight or have other health problems, consult with your doctor before beginning an exercise program. Start slowly, then work up to at least 15 minutes a session, three to five times a week.

*Outsmarting the Female Fat Cell*

1993—Debra Waterhouse, M.P.H., R.D.

- **Characteristics**: OFF Plan focuses on exercise, changing eating habits—eat only when hungry, stop dieting, don't overeat, control night snacks, eat small frequent meals, choose low-fat foods (20 percent of calories from fat).
- **Strengths**: Emphasizes slow and permanent body fat loss. Uses behavior modification techniques. No restriction of foods.
- **Weaknesses**: Encourages eating only the first 12 hours of the day.
- Comments: Realistic plan for weight control. Allows individual tailoring of plan. Deals with emotional eating.

*The New Pritikin Program*

1990—Robert Pritikin

- **Characteristics**: Designed for lifelong nutrition, weight loss, and prevention of diseases such as heart disease, high blood pressure, cancer and diabetes. High in fiber and complex carbohydrates, low in fat. Low in cholesterol, sugars, salt, alcohol, coffee, tea. Foods categorized as "Go," "Caution," or "Stop." Includes stress management.
- **Strengths:** Exercise is encouraged. Variety of foods daily. Adequate carbohydrates, emphasizing complex carbohydrates. May be beneficial for some disease states.
- **Weaknesses**: Only 10 percent of calories from fat. Recommends limiting low-fat dairy and avoiding whole dairy, animal fats, tropical oils, caffeine, salt products, etc. For fast weight loss, recommends 1,000 calories/day for women and 1,200 calories/day for men.
- **Comments**: May be difficult to follow long-term due to low fat intake.

*The T-Factor Diet*

21-days of menus. 1989—Martin Katahn.

- **Characteristics**: Initially count daily fat grams. Add fat-free foods to avoid feeling hungry. For faster weight loss, follow Quick Melt program (count calories and fat grams). Recommends physical activity to avoid regaining weight.
- **Strengths**: Focuses on low-fat, high-fiber foods. De-emphasizes calorie counting. No elimination of foods.
- **Weaknesses**: Claims people are overweight because they eat too much fat. Quick Melt meets RDAs but is low in calories (1,100–1,300/day for women, 1,600–1,800/day for men).
- **Comments:** Lower ranges of recommended fat gram intake are quite low. Lose weight too quickly on Quick Melt.

*The Zone Diet*

Barry Sears, Ph.D. 1995.

- **Characteristics**: "Enter the Zone" maintains that carbohydrates are bad because they raise your blood sugar level and cause the release of the hormone insulin—supposed monster hormone. Claims insulin makes it hard to become thin. Supposedly takes the high-carbohydrate food and stores it as fat rather than using it for energy.

- **Strengths**: Promotes eating regular meals low in calories. Restricts fat to no more than 30 percent of total calories.
- Weaknesses: Promotes diet higher in protein, lower in carbohydrates than recommended. Carbohydrates, not proteins, are the preferred source of energy. If protein is used for energy, nitrogen must be removed. This can overtax the kidneys. Metabolic pathways supposedly connecting diet, insulin-glucogen and eicosanoids sound impressive but do not exist. Carbohydrates and insulin don't make you fat. Eicosanoids don't cause disease.
- **Comments**: The Zone is based on half-truths, mixed messages and theories, not grounded in peer-reviewed research. There is nothing magical about The Zone Diet, it's just a very low-calorie diet.

*Sugar Busters*

Edited by Stewart Leighton, 1998. By three physicians and a businessman.

- **Characteristics**: Sugars and foods high in sugar are claimed to be "toxic" and the root of all health problems, including obesity, diabetes and heart disease. These are attributed to insulin that regulates sugar. To "bust" sugar out of the diet, the book recommends avoiding foods with high glycemic index (fruits and vegetables) and compensating with protein (meat) and fat.
- **Strengths**: None.
- **Weaknesses**: Promotes foods high in cholesterol, saturated fat. Eliminates many foods that provide essential vitamins and minerals. Recommends not drinking "excessive" fluids (water) with meals. No basis to claim fluids "bypass proper chewing," "dilute digestive juices."
- **Comments**: Insulin plays essential role in energy balance. Carbohydrates are important in diet. No scientific evidence for claims made. Claims are false. Not recommended.

## Note

1. J. Anderson, Cooperative Extension food and nutrition specialist and professor; and K.Wilken, Cooperative Extension food and nutrition specialist food science and human nutrition.

Issued in furtherance of Cooperative Extension work, Acts of May 8 and June 30, 1914, in cooperation with the U.S. Department of Agriculture, Milan A. Rewerts, Director of Cooperative Extension, Colorado State University, Fort Collins, Colorado. Cooperative Extension programs are available to all without discrimination. No endorsement of products mentioned is intended nor is criticism implied of products not mentioned.

# A Guide to Rating the Weight-Loss Websites

MANY PEOPLE who are successful at weight loss go it alone. But research suggests that at least half use formal programs such as Weight Watchers or Jenny Craig. The structure and moral support offered by such programs help many reach their goals.

But what if you're caught in the middle? What if you're someone who's frustrated trying to lose weight solo but too embarrassed to attend meetings—or too busy for yet another activity? Enter virtual weight-loss centers.

That's right. An increasing number of ambitious weight losers are going online for help, signing on with one of a burgeoning number of websites created to bring dieters together with health professionals—and other dieters—who can guide and cheer them on. It's convenient and social, yet with privacy built in.

Does it work? Can virtual assistance lead to actual weight loss? Some preliminary research from Brown University suggests that joining a weight-loss website *can* be a practical alternative to in-person diet counseling. But how do you sort through the sites to find the right match?

By using the eight questions we've established to rate them. That's what we asked a Web-savvy dietitian from the Tufts community to do in assessing eight of the most popular weight-loss sites now operating.

None of the ones she looked at are all good or all bad. But different sites have different "personalities" that will appeal to some consumers and not others. For instance, a few, like **Cyberdiet** and **DietWatch**, provide strong online "communities" that offer a "we're in this together" camaraderie. Others, like **eFit**, are more straightforward clearinghouses of information with less social interaction.

Some sites, like **eDiets** and **Shape Up and Drop 10**, charge a fee. It is not essential to pay for online weight-loss information—there are several good sites that provide free access to their dieting and fitness features. But a few of the sites that do charge money offer some pretty good personalized services that you can't get for free.

We do have some favorites among the sites we visited. Of the free sites, we'd choose the easy-to-use **Shape Up America** (the no-cost counterpart to Shape Up and Drop 10—both are operated by former Surgeon General C. Everett Koop, MD). For a fee, we'd opt for the great customer service offered by eDiets. But the sites profiled here are only a sampling of everything that's available online to potential dieters.

As you surf the choices out there, keep in mind that even an authoritative-looking home page doesn't guarantee that the author of a dieting site knows anything about dieting, healthful or otherwise. That's why it's particularly important to apply our set of questions—not just to see which site is the right "fit" for you but also to weed out those that aren't the right fit for *anybody*.

### 1. Who provides the diet plans and advice to members?

All the sites we visited except one, **Asimba**, provide diet plans that have been formulated by registered dietitians—health professionals trained in nutrition. Meal plans on Asimba are generated by a computer program that uses guidelines set by an exercise physiologist, and the lack of a dietitian's professional touch shows. One of the meal plans e-mailed to our dietitian reviewer included a lunch of cinnamon oatmeal, a peach, 1/2 cup of grapes, and 3/4 cup of green beans—an odd combination of foods.

### 2. What claims are made by the site as to how much or how fast weight can be shed on its diet plan?

A reasonable rate of weight loss is about 1 to 2 pounds a week. Responsible websites should use a person's height, weight, age, and activity level (usually gathered at the outset) to suggest a calorie level that will allow for this moderate rate of weight loss. Ediets pushes the goal somewhat, promising new clients that they will lose 10 pounds within a month of joining.

Adults should not attempt to follow a diet that provides fewer than 1,200 calories daily. That's too little food to meet essential nutrient needs. None of the sites we reviewed, including eDiets, offered meal plans that were too low in calories.

### 3. What kind of meal plan does the site offer?

Some sites are able to customize meal plans more than others. Does the entry questionnaire ask about dietary restrictions, food preferences, and food allergies? Are vegetarian and/or vegan meal plans available? Ediets, for example, can adapt menus to accommodate low-sodium or low-cholesterol plans. The eDiets questionnaire also asks potential members to what extent they want convenience foods, like Healthy Choice frozen dinners, incorporated into their menus.

Several sites give dieters some do-it-yourself meal-planning options. Cyberdiet members, for example, can go one of three ways. Those whose dieting philosophy is "just tell me what to eat" can download 30 days' worth of menus. But those who want to make their own food choices can use one of two inventive meal planners.

| | 1. Who designs the diet plan? | 2. Does the diet make reasonable weight-loss claims? | 3. Does the meal plan consider dietary restrictions, food preferences? | 4. Do members have access to staff professionals? | 5. Is member-to-member support available? | 6. Does the site include an exercise plan? | 7. Cost/length of contract? | 8. Does the site offer a weight maintenance plan? |
|---|---|---|---|---|---|---|---|---|
| **Asimba (www. asimba.com)** | Exercise physiologist | Yes | Vegetarian, non-dairy meal plans available | Option to sign up with a personal coach for a fee | Bulletin boards | Yes | Members pay for personal coach, other features free | No |
| **Cyberdiet (www. cyberdiet. com)** | Registered dietitian | Yes | No, but meal-planning options include meat-free, dairy-free food choices | Dietitian, chef, others host chats | Chat rooms, bulletin boards, e-newsletter | Yes | Free | Weight-maintenance bulletin board |
| **Dietwatch (www. dietwatch. com)** | No diet plan available | — | — | Dietitian hosts some chats | Chat rooms, bulletin boards, e-newsletter | Yes | Free | No |
| **eDiets (www. ediets.com)** | Registered dietitian | Yes, but pushes the limit, saying you'll lose 10 pounds in the first month | Menus available for vegetarian, milk- or egg-free, low-sodium, low-cholesterol diets | Yes, by talking with a dietitian via e-mail or during moderated chat | Chat rooms, bulletin boards, e-newsletter | Yes | $10/month | Members can receive weight-maintenance meal plans |
| **eFit (www. efit.com)** | Registered dietitian | Yes | Vegetarian, low-sodium menus available; meal plans can exlude fish, nuts, milk | No | E-newsletter | Yes | Free | Members can receive weight-maintenance meal plans |
| **nutrio.com (www. nutrio.com)** | Registered dietitian | Yes | Low-fat, low-cholesterol, low-sodium, vegetarian meal plans available | No | Bulletin boards, e-newsletter | Yes | Free | No |
| **Shape Up America (www. shapeup.org)** | Registered dietitian | Yes | No, but meal-planning options include meat-free, dairy-free food choices | No | Bulletin boards | Yes | Free | No |
| **Shape Up and Drop 10 (www. shapeup.org)** | Registered dietitian | Yes | Choose from regular, non-dairy, lacto-ovo, vegan meal plans | Members contact the dietitian through customer service | Bulletin boards | Yes | $10/week | Members can receive weight-maintenance meal plans. |

One, the Express Menus feature, lets readers design their own meal plans from lists of food choices. Meals planned using this option really are express—dieters select items from lists that include fast foods like McDonald's hamburgers, Taco Bell burritos, and frozen entrees from Stouffer's Lean Cuisine and Healthy Choice. The other, Cyberdiet's 1-2-3-Step program, provides even more flexibility—members can design meals around their own recipes. For instance, if you plug in your favorite meatloaf recipe, the program will tell you how big a slice you can have and still fit within your calorie level.

Dieters accessing Shape Up America enter the site's Cyberkitchen to plan their meals. Cyberkitchen is easy to use and includes lots of calorie-controlled meals to choose from. To come up with a meal, dieters click on a "breakfast," "lunch," or "dinner" icon to bring up a list of food choices. The available selection of items varies in calorie value, allowing dieters to make a higher-calorie choice for one meal and a lower one at the next. Try to go over the allotted calorie allowance for the day and the computer program says, "Oops, try again."

Shape Up and Drop 10 customers, who pay a fee, don't engage in their own menu planning. After filling out an assessment questionnaire they receive a meal plan with recipes. The recipes are nicely designed and also sized to serve a family rather than just one person—a practical consideration for dieters who cook for a crowd.

**Nutrio.com** and eFit provide calorie-controlled menus as well—a week's worth. They are standard meal plans that will look familiar to veteran dieters, but the menus are nutritionally balanced and include enough calories to allow for a reasonable rate of weight loss. Both sites also have features that let members make changes in their meal plans from a list of acceptable food substitutions. (EFit visitors should note, however, that an interactive feature that is supposed to make it easier for members to make substitutions was not working at the time of review.)

Asimba's meal-planning pages, as we said earlier, could use some retooling. The meal plans allow for a reasonable rate of weight loss but include some odd food combinations. Computer-generated menus make sense only if the computer is programmed to recognize acceptable food combinations that people consider "normal."

#### *4. Do members have access to staff professionals?*

When Brown University researchers looked into the effectiveness of computer-based weight-loss counseling, they found that people who had regular online interaction with a dietitian lost more weight than those who simply downloaded a weight-loss plan from their computers and followed it themselves.

But only the weight-loss sites that charge a fee really duplicate this personal touch. Ediets, in particular, tries hard to promote communication between staff and clients. Ediets clients can e-mail the site's support dietitian if they have any questions about their diet plan or some other aspect of the program. The questions we posed were answered the next business day. For general questions such as how to access the chat rooms, eDiets's customer service desk is reachable by e-mail or phone (toll-free) 7 days a week.

Shape Up and Drop 10 clients don't have direct access to a staff professional—questions are sent to the site manager to be forwarded to a registered dietitian—but our questions were still answered promptly the next business day.

While free sites do not usually give members one-on-one access to their professional staffs, some, like Cyberdiet and DietWatch, host dietitian-moderated chat sessions in which all members can receive nutrition advice—a nice touch for a site that does not charge a fee.

Free professional advice from Asimba is limited to a not very helpful "Ask the Expert" feature. Several questions that we posed went unanswered.

Those who want more personalized guidance from Asimba can hire an online diet or fitness coach for a fee. Clients choose their coaches from a list that includes registered dietitians and personal trainers and then contact them by e-mail. Fees for this service vary, as they are set by the coaches, not the site.

#### *5. Can members share ideas and support?*

DietWatch and eDiets members can sign up for a "diet buddy" to help them over the rough spots as they begin their weight-loss efforts. Communication is conducted via e-mail. But most of the member-to-member contact on diet sites is not one-on-one. Rather, it is conducted through chat rooms and bulletin boards.

A chat, if you're new to the cyberworld, is just what it sounds like: Members log on to a site at a preappointed time and communicate "live" with other members, and all chatters can read the conversation as it appears on the screen. Chat schedules are posted on the site so that members know when to log on. Some chat sessions on Cyberdiet, eDiets, and DietWatch are moderated by a health professional such as a dietitian, chef, or personal trainer and thereby give members a chance to ask questions on particular aspects of cooking, exercise, or weight control.

People new to chats might be confused by the relative chaos of online conversations. **Not everyone logs on to talk about dieting. During a recent DietWatch dietitian-moderated chat, we "listened" to a woman complain about a damaged planter in front of her house**. And a crowd participating in a dietitian-moderated chat on eDiets seemed to be more interested in chatting with each other than in speaking to the dietitian. In spite of the confusion, though, chats are a popular stop on most of the weight-loss sites we visited.

Bulletin boards are also just what they sound like—a place to post and receive messages. Members use them to pass on dieting tips, recipes, gripes, and encouragement. Cyberdiet, eDiets, and nutrio.com have very active bulletin boards. Both Shape Up America and Shape Up and Drop 10 have bulletin boards that let members exchange dieting tips and encouragement, but they do not appear to attract much traffic.

A word on chats and bulletin boards. They constitute the motivational backbone of most weight-loss sites, providing the much needed virtual contact that is missing from an otherwise impersonal experience. Viewers should keep in mind, however, that while these interactive features are monitored for offensive material, there is no guarantee that the opinions posted are scientifically sound. A message we saw on one of the DietWatch bulletin boards, for instance, came from a member concerned about sudden hair loss. Of the seven readers who responded, only one suggested that the person seek medical help. The lesson here: While chat rooms and bulletin boards offer great opportunities for social dieting, they are not the best places to get health advice. Use them cautiously in that regard.

*Note*: eFit has no chat rooms or bulletin boards, only an e-mail newsletter. But its motivational ace is its "morphover" feature, which lets members submit a digitalized photo and receive a computer-altered image of themselves 15 pounds lighter.

#### *6. Does the site focus only on diet, or are members encouraged to increase their physical activity?*

Successful weight loss requires both diet *and* exercise, so consumers should look for a site that offers advice on how to work physical activity into their daily routines. Just like with choosing a diet plan, there is no one right exercise regimen that will fit everyone's needs, so potential members should visit several sites to find one that works for them.

EFit and Asimba are sports-oriented sites, with pages of advice on how to start and maintain a program of running, water sports, cycling, yoga, or walking. Both also provide members with individual activity plans. A nice feature on Asimba is its "very easy" walking program, a good place to start for novice exercisers. Members on this program start with a daily half-mile walk and work up to 2 miles a day within a month. EFit provides aerobic exercise routines that are explained in print as well as video clips (this feature requires users to download Real Media or Microsoft Media plug-in).

All of the exercise routines in the eDiets program are illustrated with animated graphics, using a virtual instructor who demonstrates how to do each activity. It's a really clever feature, kind of like the online version of an exercise video.

The "Health Club" pages of Cyberdiet are less high-tech, but they do provide easy-to-follow routines, explained via text and pictures, that focus either on strength training, aerobics, or increased flexibility. Nutrio.com features a similar type of exercise program, although its exercise pages do not include any pictures at all.

Shape Up America's fitness pages come with a big plus. They place a significant emphasis on "thinking around" barriers—like fatigue or a hectic work schedule—that can prevent some people from starting and maintaining a diet and exercise program. Too hot or too cold to exercise? Walk at the mall. Too busy? Break up a half-hour exercise routine into three 10-minute sessions. The site's authors encourage dieters to keep a daily activity log in order to identify times of the day when a sedentary activity (like watching television or sitting at the computer) could be replaced with a more vigorous activity, like walking.

### 7. Does the site charge a fee? How long is the contract?

Sites that charge an access fee may offer a reduced rate to clients willing to sign up for several weeks or months at a time. Be wary, though, of getting locked into a long-term contract. While it may take several months to get comfortable with a particular weight-loss site, you might regret buying into a program that requests payment for 6 months or more up front. Neither of the two fee-for-use sites reviewed here requires a long-term commitment. Shape Up and Drop 10 clients pay by the week, and eDiets clients pay in 3-month installments.

### *8. Does the site offer a weight-maintenance plan?*

Unfortunately, there isn't much focus on weight maintenance on any of the sites we visited, although eFit, eDiets, and Shape Up America and Shape Up and Drop 10 offer weight-maintenance meal plans for interested members. Cyberdiet also acknowledges that the battle isn't over once the weight is lost and hosts a "weight maintenance" bulletin board to support those who have reached goal weight. Given how hard it is to hold onto hard-won weight goals, support for "maintainers" deserves more attention on all of these sites.

---

# NONDIET APPROACH TO TREATMENT OF BINGE EATING DISORDER

BY JAIME RUUD, MS, RD, LMNT; ANNA CALHOUN, RD, LMNT

Binge eating disorder is a serious and prevalent problem among the overweight population. According to national statistics, binge eating disorder affects about 2% of all adults and is more common in women than in men.

Binges eating disorder is characterized by recurrent overeating episodes in which an individual consumes a large amount of food while feeling a loss of control over eating behaviors.[2] This disorder differs from bulimia nervosa in that compensatory behaviors, such as purging (self-induced vomiting, laxatives, diuretics), fasting and compulsive exercise are not present. To meet criteria for the diagnosis, a person must engage in binge eating at least 2 days per week for 6 months and report marked distress about their symptoms.[2]

Current treatment approaches to binge eating disorder include cognitive behavior therapy (CBT), interpersonal psychotherapy (IPT), antidepressant medication, and self-help groups.[3,4] Practitioners have not yet determined which methods or combinations of methods are most effective in treating binge eating disorder. Outcome studies suggest that traditional weight-loss programs have not been successful because of the psychiatric comorbidity associated with binge eating disorder.[1] Binge eating disorder is frequently associated with a history of depression, low self-esteem, and personality disturbances. A distorted body image and preoccupation with food are also prevalent.

The goal in treating clients with binge eating disorder is to provide them with individualized plans to meet their specific needs and goals.[1] Nutrition counseling is directed at normalizing eating and separating actual hunger from emotional hunger.[5] The following case studies describe a nondiet approach to treatment of BED in 2 female clients at Nutrition Link, a private nutrition consulting company in Lincoln, Neb.

## CASE STUDY: **MARY**

Mary, a 42-year-old female, came to Nutrition Link in 1997 for weight loss. At the initial session, she was 5′6" and weighed 165 lb (BMI 26.6). She reported a history of dieting, having "tried every diet imaginable," including diet pills in 1996, which allowed her to lose 30 lb only to regain the lost weight and more. Mary wanted a diet plan that would help her lose weight and keep it off. Together, we discussed diet and exercise goals and planned to meet weekly. She was especially interested in a personalized menu plan.

During the fifth counseling session, Mary's mood seemed unusually low. She stated that she was frustrated because her clothes didn't fit and the "menu thing just wasn't working." She shared for the first time her struggles with food and feelings of shame and low self-esteem. She reported being overweight as a child and using food to cope with her emotions. She talked about her mother's preoccupation with food and how her mother influenced her thoughts and feelings about her weight and appearance.

Mary's signs and symptoms were classic of binge eating disorder: bingeing at least 3 times a week, usually late in the afternoon or evening; feeling a loss of control over food; "feeling fat"; and being highly dissatisfied with her body.

Mary was interested in the nondiet approach to weight management and how it could help build a healthy relationship with food and body image and enhance her self-esteem. Although Mary's primary goal was to lose the weight, she was willing to try this "new" concept and was truly relieved not to be on another diet.

During the next several sessions we focused on nondiet strategies: 1) eating in response to physical hunger, 2) normalizing feelings about food, and 3) size acceptance. Mary identified specific cues and consequences associated with her binge eating episodes. Psychological cues included boredom, stress, and mental images of being "fat." She also reported that comments from her mother about her weight and eating habits were especially difficult and often "triggered" a binge. We worked on coping mechanisms (eg, goals setting, planning ahead) to help reduce stress and avoid relapse.

One of the most difficult sessions occurred when Mary weighed herself (something she hadn't done in months). She had gained 10 lb. She cried, "I can't do this without a diet," and I feared she would give up on everything she had worded on. Mary began to question the nondiet approach. She said that old thoughts had come back. We talked about measures of success, such as her decrease in compulsive feelings about food and bingeing, but she continued to have a great deal of body dissatisfaction and felt disgusted with how she looked.

One marker of successful treatment for BED is improvement of self-concept and body image.[6] Mary often compared herself to many of her thin friends who were dieting. Social pressure to be attractive and acceptance from others were major factors associated with Mary's low self-esteem and poor body image. "I don't really get support from what I'm doing (except from my nutrition counselor and therapist), and I don't have anyone to talk about it with. The nondiet concept is probably the hardest thing that I've ever done It's such a radical concept for me. This is truly a lifestyle change and an extremely slow, up and down process. There is no quick fix."

Throughout the year, Mary continued to work on normalizing her feelings about food and exercise. She reported a few relapses; returning to old eating patterns—bingeing, although for a very short time and to a much lesser degree. A binge was precipitated by "feeling fat" (premenstrual bloating and "tiny friends who ask if they are fat"). Mary was able to get back on track by reading *Intuitive Eating* by Evelyn Tribole and Elyse Resch (1996) and talking to herself—"everyone is entitled to one mistake."

In December 1999, I received an e-mail from Mary. "I am doing absolutely great! I just get more and more convinced as time passes that this nondieting approach is the way to go. I don't think about food most of the time anymore. It's been wonderful not to classify foods as good or bad and not to binge because I had a bad food and blew it. I still can hardly believe it and never would have guessed 2 years ago that I would be here today! I've been able to really enjoy food and not feel guilty."

## CASE STUDY: **CHRISTY**

Christy, a 32-year-old female, contacted Nutrition Link in 1998 for a nutrition check-up, which included a personal profile of nutrition needs and exercise recommendations. She returned a year later wanting help with weight loss. She was 5'3" and weighed 230 lb (BMI 40.7). Christy expressed concern about her eating behaviors. She reported thinking about food all the time, never being hungry but eating anyway, eating large amounts of food in an uncontrollable way, and feeling guilty and depressed. "I was ready to get to the bottom of the 'why' of my eating problems. I already know the 'shoulds,' and I was tired of beating myself up over them."

Christy shared some of the events in her life that contributed to her problems with weight. For example, she remembered gaining a significant amount of weight in the 5th grade and bingeing and purging in college. She stated that she felt sad and scared about moving forward and losing the weight.

Together, we worked on internal vs external hunger cues and body dissatisfaction. Christy quickly adapted to using the hunger scale, a tool that presents hunger on a continuum from 1 (starving) to 10 (absolutely stuffed). She also began to journal her thoughts and feelings. Journaling helped Christy identify external cues: eating when she was bored, angry, tired, or stressed out.

> Although our understanding of binge eating disorder is still in its infancy, experience shows that the nondiet approach to treatment is a successful option for clients who are ready to give up dieting.

Although Christy was learning to distinguish between emotional and physical hunger, she became frustrated by the lack of visible results. Christy, like others who suffer from BED, was very critical of her body. She worried about the number on the scale. "I made the mistake of weighing myself and almost giving up. Instead, I looked deeper and found I needed help with some unresolved issues from my past." With the help of a therapist, she was able to identify specific events in her life that led to her binge eating disorder.

At Nutrition Link, we use several activities (eg, photographs of women in popular fashion magazines; reading material from journals, book, and newsletters; and videos such as Green Roth's *Breaking Free From Compulsive Eating* to help clients explore their thoughts and feelings about weight and body size. Working through these types of activities, Christy felt better about herself and her body.

Where is Christy today in the counseling process? "At this point, I sometimes feel as I'm in the middle of a raging storm. What's changed, though, is the way I treat myself through the really hard periods. I give myself much more care, and I am learning to reach out to the people I love for support. I believe 'normal' eating is something I will achieve. Even more important, I'm learning to give up the pursuit of perfection and unrealistic expectations of what others perceive as ideal."

Using the nondiet approach, Christy has learned to deal with emotional triggers without overeating. She is also more aware of how food makes her feel. She continues to work on planning regular meals and staying active. Christy has excelled in her job, and her superiors have commented on her positive attitude and initiative at the office.

Although our understanding of binge eating disorder is still in its infancy, experience shows that the nondiet approach to treatment is a successful option for clients who are ready to give up dieting. The nondiet approach can help decrease compulsive feelings about food, decrease bingeing, decrease negative thoughts about body size, and increase self-esteem.

—Jaime Rued and Anna Claxon are coowners of the Nutrition Link, a private consulting company in Lincoln, Neb., that offers personalized nutrition counseling and contract services.

## REFERENCES

1. Bruce B, Wilfley D. Binge eating disorder among the overweight population: a serious and prevalent problem. *J. Am Diet Assoc.* 1996;96:58–61.
2. American Psychiatric Association. *Diagnostic and Statistical Manual-Fourth Edition (DSM-IV)*. 4th ed. Washington DC: American Psychiatric Association; 1994.
3. Peterson CB, Mitchell JE. Treatment of binge-eating disorder in group cognitive-behavioral therapy. In: Joellen W, ed. *Treating Eating Disorders.* San Francisco: Jossey-Bass, Inc.;1996.
4. Wilfley DE, Cohen LR. Psychological treatment of bulimia nervosa and binge eating disorder. *Psychopharmacology-Bulletin.* 1997;33:437–454.
5. Popkess-Vawter S, Brandau C, Straub J. Triggers of overeating and related intervention strategies for women who weight cycle. *Appl Nurs Res.* 1998;11:69–76.
6. Goodrick GK, Pendleton VR, Kimball KT, Carlos Poston WS, Reeves RS. Foreyt JP. Binge eating severity, self-concept, dieting self-efficacy and social support during treatment of binge eating disorder. *Int J. Eat Disord.* 1999;26:295–300.

# UNIT 5

# Health Claims

## Unit Selections



## Key Points to Consider

- How can consumers protect themselves from misinformation in the nutrition field?
- How do you interpret the different types of research studies so that you can get at the truth of health claims?
- What are some of the positive and negative aspects of the information available on the Internet?
- What are some of the truths about the effect of herbs in a person's diet?

**Links: www.dushkin.com/online/**
These sites are annotated in the World Wide Web pages.

**Consumer Information Center--Fraudulent Health Claims**
*http://www.pueblo.gsa.gov/cic_text/health/fraudulent-health/frdheal.htm*

**Federal Trade Commission (FTC): Diet, Health & Fitness**
*http://www.ftc.gov/bcp/menu-health.htm*

**Food and Drug Administration**
*http://www.fda.gov/default.htm*

**Healthcare Reality Check**
*http://www.hcrc.org*

**National Council Against Health Fraud**
*http://www.ncahf.org*

**QuackWatch**
*http://www.quackwatch.com*

Americans spend approximately $25 billion a year on alternative treatments. According to an American Dietetic Association (ADA) survey, 90 percent of consumers polled get their nutrition information from television, magazines, and newspapers.

Americans are confused and overwhelmed about the controversies surrounding food and health, and they have stopped paying attention to the contradictory claims reported by news media. In addition, the Internet is a source of information that allows distribution and promotion of just about anything. About 29 percent of Americans turn to the Internet for information. We need to be vigilant as to the type of information we get from different Web sites. How to judge the validity of information and guidelines for recognizing and avoiding unreliable sites is described in the article entitled "The Mouse That Roared."

Herbs and nutrition supplements are the subjects of one of the articles in this unit. Herbs have been used for medicinal purposes in the East for thousands of years. The World Health Organization reports that 70 percent of the world uses herbal medicines for some aspect of health care. In the United States, herbal supplement sales exceed $3 billion per year. Since the FDA classifies herbs as dietary supplements, they are not tested for safety or efficacy. Only when it is proven that an herbal product has produced ill effects or death can the FDA take regular action. Even though many herbs have documented health benefits, many more are toxic. Herbs have not had the rigorous testing that pharmaceuticals have. Their active ingredients are not standardized, and their safety and long-term effects have not been studied in well-controlled trials. Presently the herbal industry is attempting to resolve the issue of standardization. The recently formed consumer lab (CL) assays products for purity, identity, activity, and consistency.

Functional foods are foods that may provide a health benefit beyond basic nutrition, and they are becoming one of the fastest growing segments of the food industry especially among affluent baby boomers. The U.S. government has no regulatory category of functional foods. Despite their popularity, their efficacy and safety is questionable due to lack of scientific evidence. So we are far from declaring them "magic bullets" to improve health and prevent disease. The consumer should be advised to eat a variety of foods in moderation and view functional foods as part of an overall healthful diet.

There is also no regulation for supplements by the government. The consumer cannot trust what the label claims the supplement contains. Laboratory tests reveal that labels often overstate the amount of the active ingredient in a pill. Lists of supplements that meet their claims are offered along with possible interactions with medications in the article "Does the Supplement You Buy Contain What its Label Says?"

Nutrition is a field that is vulnerable to quackery. The Food and Drug Administration (FDA) defines quackery as misinformation about health. Quacks abound in our culture, from health food store salespeople to popular talk show hosts to self-proclaimed "nutritionists" with no background in nutrition or credentials from accredited schools. Quacks also pretend to be able to cure a health problem or a disease. Nutritionists and dietitians have worked hard through the years to set the record straight and distribute reliable and valid information.

Among the population groups that are most vulnerable to using megadoses of herbs, vitamin/mineral supplements, and ergogenic aids are athletes. Selective ergogenic aids and dietary supplements, including the health risks involved, are presented in the article, "Nutrition Supplements: Science vs. Hype."

This unit concludes with an article on the very popular energy bars. Sales of energy bars targeting just about every section of the population are on the rise. The misconceptions about the bars being an "energy food" imply that they are well-balanced in carbohydrate, protein, and fat. High protein bars, high carbohydrate bars, and others are explained, and the myths about their nutritional benefits are dispelled.

# The Mouse that Roared: *Health Scares on the Internet*

The World Wide Web is a tremendous resource for consumers and others who want an additional outlet to help them take control of their health. "The Internet is full of important, even lifesaving, medical information," stated Randolph Wykoff, M.D., M.P.H., of the U.S. Food and Drug Administration (FDA). But, not all Internet information passes the test of the Hippocratic oath. Enter: Doctor Deception who now makes house calls.

On occasion, some not-so-sound information spoils a wealth of excellent information on the Internet. With a click of the mouse, a word-of-mouth phenomenon can be multiplied exponentially via the World Wide Web or electronic mail and result in questionable nutrition, food safety and health stories being sent directly to your computer. In the age of the Internet and instantaneous global communication—in tandem with an increasing interest in nutrition's relation to health—it is not surprising that anyone with a modem can send consumers and others into a food and health panic.

Most of us have heard at least a few of the following myths that have been started and perpetuated on the Web: the great kidney harvest caper; the antibacterial sponge made with agent orange; the fluorescent lights that leach vitamins from your body; the cancer-causing shampoo, and dozens, maybe hundreds more.

These would all be simply entertaining if everyone recognized them as practical jokes, the mantras of unhappy people, or simply misunderstandings given life on the Internet. But not everyone can recognize these tall tales as fiction.

## The Bias Belt

Some of the most egregious myths come from legitimate sounding individuals who have fallen in love with their theories. They believe they are serving the public by warning them of dire health consequences as the result of touching, smelling, eating or drinking a perfectly safe product. Many consumers are confused and unwittingly oblige in the scam by forwarding the frightening electronic mail or referencing the site to family, friends and associates believing they are doing them a service. And, receiving one of these reports from a family member or friend adds to its alleged authenticity.

A recent *TIME Magazine* article (April 26, 1999) sums it up well: "The Web is praised as a wondrous educational tool, and in some respects it is. Mostly though, it appears to be a stunning advance in the shoring up of biases, both benign (one's own views) and noxious (other views)."

In most cases, there is no harm intended by those who position their opinions as facts. In other instances, the sly intent of the author may be relatively easy for health professionals, who have a strong science background, to detect. But, for some consumers with little frame of reference to tell fact from fiction, it can be misleading.

For example, an innocent Web surfer looking for information about dietary fats may stumble across one of several Web sites spreading fear and confusion about a frequently used cooking oil. With a masthead featuring a skull and crossbones, or the headline: "Canola Oil: Deadly for the Human Body!," such sites may cause baseless consumer concern. If the consumer does not seek unbiased information, he or she will miss the real story: canola oil, a safe, monounsaturated oil, can help lower blood cholesterol levels when substituted for saturated fats in the diet.

## Where Did You Hear That?

"At one time, doctors were the primary source of health information for consumers, but in the late 1990s the paradigm for securing this type of information changed," remarked Fergus Clydesdale, Ph.D., University of Massachusetts. Now, for both consumers and health professionals, the primary source of information is the news media. This information

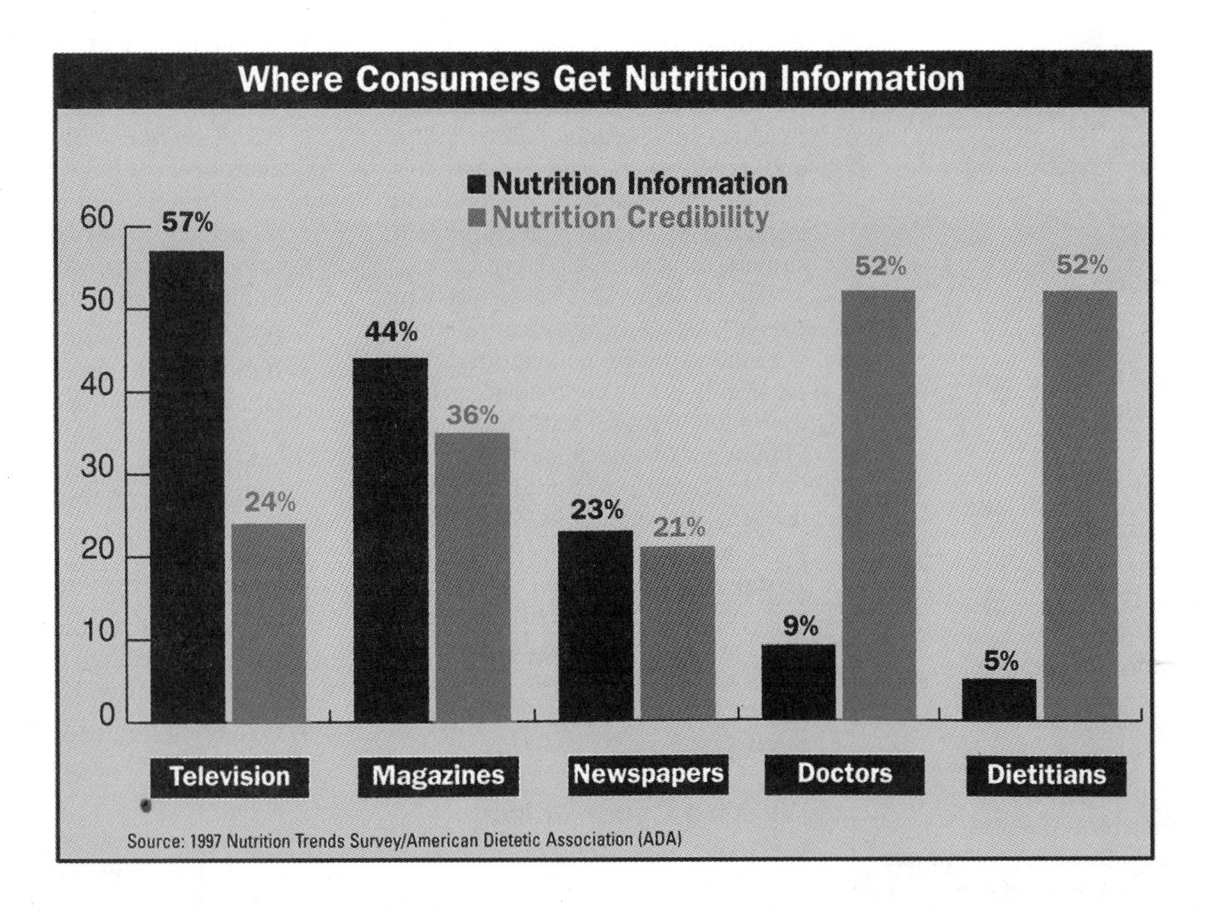


source replaces the traditional physician-patient relationship for consumers. For health professionals, media accounts now precede the medical journals and attendance at academic meetings. Often, a consumer first raises an issue with his or her health professional by asking about a story that ran in an on-line story, the local paper or on the evening TV news before health professionals have even received their journals.

A recent telephone survey conducted by Schwarz Pharma, Inc., and reported in the *American Journal of Public Health*, noted that approximately 29 percent of Americans have turned to the Internet for medical information—a number that, although not high compared to other media outlets, is likely to grow.

According to the *1997 Nutrition Trends Survey* conducted by The American Dietetic Association (ADA), 57 percent of consumers named television as their main source of nutrition information, followed by magazines at 44 percent and newspapers at 23 percent. Doctors and dietitians were at just 9 and 5 percent, respectively (see graph).

The same ADA survey, however, found that the tables were turned in terms of credibility. Information from doctors and dietitians/nutritionists was found to be "more valuable" (52%) than that from television news and newspaper articles (24% and 21%, respectively). The Internet may follow this same pattern of delivery versus credibility—the Internet or World Wide Web was found to be the least believable source of medical and health news according to respondents in the 1997 report, *Americans Talk About Science and Medical News* from the National Health Council. While the Internet can be a valuable source for scientifically accurate health information, it can also be a frontier town with no sheriff for assuring the truth of the information presented.

John Renner, M.D., of the National Council for Reliable Health Information remarked, "There is a health information shock factor on the Internet because there is so much information, both good and bad, marvelous and terrible. We've moved from a small library of information with a friendly librarian, to a huge warehouse with lots of people offering information," he continued. Consumers have not faced this situation before. The problem is the public can be deceived—believing that because they have seen something on the Web, it must be true.

A perfect example of how the public can be misled is a recent Internet article by a Nancy Markle that has taken on a "cyberlife" of its own. The article alleges that aspartame (a sweetener found in food and beverages) causes lupus, multiple sclerosis (MS) and other diseases and conditions, none of which has any scientific validity. Highly respected health professional organizations were fraudulently associated with the story, and numerous vulnerable people were needlessly frightened by this scientifically false allegation.

One of the marvels of the Internet is that as easily as you can receive

### Internet sources for sound nutrition and health information

- Tufts University Nutrition Navigator **http://navigator.tufts.edu**
- The American Dietetic Association **http://www.eatright.org**
- The International Food Information Council Foundation **http://ificinfo.health.org**
- Medline **http://www.nlm.nih.gov/databases/freemedl.html**
- National Institutes of Health **http://www.nih.gov**
- The U.S. Food and Drug Administration **http://vm.cfsan.fda.gov**
- Mayo Health Oasis (of the Mayo Clinic) **http://www.mayohealth.org**
- Johns Hopkins Health Information **http://www.intelihealth.com/IH/ihtIH**
- World Health Organization **http://www.who.int**
- Food & Agriculture Organization **http://www.fao.org**
- Government healthfinder **http://www.healthfinder.gov**

*inaccurate* information, you can search for and find *accurate* information. If consumers were concerned about the alleged aspartame connection with MS, they could check the Multiple Sclerosis Foundation's Internet site for accurate information. David Squillacote, M.D., senior medical advisor of the MS Foundation wrote in his response to the Internet scare, "This series of allegations by Ms. Markle are almost totally without foundation. They are rabidly inaccurate and scandalously misinformative." Fortunately, numerous reliable organizations, Internet sites and publications have refuted this particular epidemic of hysteria and provided additional context for consumers.

The FDA's website is an excellent source for accurate information. Consumers wishing to counteract or confirm the aspartame story can find the following information from the FDA which could allay their fears: "After reviewing scientific studies, the FDA determined in 1981 that aspartame was safe for use in foods.... To date, the FDA has not determined any consistent pattern of symptoms that can be attributed to the use of aspartame, nor is the agency aware of any recent studies that clearly show safety problems."

## What's a Cyber-Citizen to Do?

How can consumers judge the validity of information received via electronic mail or popping up in a Web search? The foremost guideline for sorting the "trash" from the "treasure" is—just because something is printed on the Internet does not mean that it is true or credible.

Unfortunately for most of us, the best defense against nutrition misinformation and quackery on the Internet is in-depth scientific knowledge. Since not everyone has the level of scientific awareness or advanced degrees necessary to judge the validity of every story, the following tactics may be useful:

- Ask questions. Anecdotes and one individual's personal story are not scientific evidence.
- Look at the source of the information. A professional medical organization or government agency such as the American Academy of Family Physicians or the U.S. Department of Agriculture is more likely to have reliable information than an unknown person or group of people.
- If the story mentions a specific health condition, such as diabetes or breast cancer, search the Internet for reputable health professional organizations and foundations devoted to that disease. An example would be the American Diabetes Association or the American Cancer Society.
- Watch out for use of buzzwords like "conspiracy" and "poison."
- Don't take assertions at face value—give the other side of the issue the benefit of the doubt. Do your homework and call or e-mail appropriate health professional organizations to get a balanced picture.
- Consult with your doctor, a registered dietitian or other health professional.

The Internet has been a boon to consumers who want research and information on voluminous issues and topics at the tip of their fingers. It has also empowered many people to find health information to help them improve their well-being. Nevertheless, the ease of Web publishing has also given an unregulated forum to unreliable sources. Careful scrutiny and a healthy dose of skepticism are still necessary to determine what applies to you and what may need a second opinion.

From *Food Insight*, May/June 1999, pp. 1, 4-5. Reprinted with permission from the International Food Information Council Foundation.

# Herbals for Health?

*by E. Serrano and J. Anderson*[1]

Using herbs and plants for medicinal purposes has a long tradition. In India and China, these traditions date back thousands of years.

Once thought of as "traditional medicine" used by native or ancient cultures, herbal medicine has emerged as a popular alternative or supplement to modern medicine. According to the World Health Organization, 4 billion people, almost 70 percent of the world population, use herbal medicine for some aspect of primary health care.[1]

## Quick Facts...

People take herbs for many reasons and many conditions.

Natural does not mean safe.

The Food and Drug Administration does not test herbs for safety or efficacy.

The best prescription for disease prevention is a healthy lifestyle.

It is estimated that in the United States alone, botanical dietary supplements exceed $3 billion per year.[2] Herbal products can be found in grocery stores and on the Web, as well as natural food markets, their traditional source. Forty percent of Americans take dietary supplements. About half of these people take vitamin and mineral supplements, a third take some type of herbal product, and the rest take other ergogenic aids, such as amino acids or protein powders.[3] The herbal market is growing steadily at about 20 percent each year.[2] With this increase, however, come many questions.

The term herbs in this fact sheet refers to plants used for oral medicinal purposes, not herbs for cooking. It includes botanicals, herbs, herbals, herbal products, herbal medicines, herbal remedies and herbal supplements.

## Why Take Herbs?

People take herbs for many reasons and many conditions. One of the biggest reasons is that herbs are considered natural and therefore healthier and gentler than conventional drugs. (Ironically, many prescription drugs are of herbal origin.) They are used for everything from upset stomachs to headaches. Some people take them for overall health and well-being, not for any specific condition. For others, herbal use is grounded in traditions passed down from generation to generation or recommended by folk healers.

## Are Herbs Effective?

Many herbs have health benefits. Research has shown that echinacea cuts the length of colds and that powdered ginger is effective against motion sickness and nausea. Overall, however, research is lacking, especially well-controlled studies. There are many unanswered questions. At this point, our understanding is largely anecdotal. We don't know all of the short-term and long-term benefits and risks of many herbs, let alone all of their active or beneficial ingredients.

To address this uncertainty, federal law states that herbs cannot claim to *prevent, diagnose, treat,* or *cure* a condition or disease. Herbs may carry health-related claims about effects on the "structure or function of the body" or "general well-being" that may result from the product. This definition is very loose and gives rise to misleading health claims. Ultimately, the consumer is responsible for checking their validity and avoiding products with fraudulent claims. See fact sheet 9.350, *Nutrition Quackery*.

The best prescription for disease prevention is a healthy lifestyle. This includes a diet high in whole grains, fruits and vegetables, and low in fat. Physical activity also plays an important role. Finally, there is no data to suggest that herbs are more beneficial than conventional drugs for treating illnesses.

## Are Herbs Safe?

Because herbs are natural, many people believe they are safe. Unfortunately, this is not always the case. While many herbs may be considered safe, some have hazardous side effects. In fact, in the past few years there have been several deaths related to herbal products. In some cases, small amounts of herbs, even those found in teas, have had devastating effects. To date, the following herbs are considered toxic and, given their side effects, should be avoided:[4,5]

- Chapparal—liver damage.
- Comfrey—liver damage.
- Ephedra/ma huang—rapid heart beat, heart attack.
- Germander—liver damage.
- Lobelia—breathing problems, rapid heartbeat, coma, death.
- Magnolia/stephania—kidney damage.
- Kombucha—linked to a possible death.
- Willow bark—Reye's syndrome in children.
- Wormwood—nerve damage, arm/leg numbness, delirium, paralysis.

- Yohimbe—anxiety, paralysis, gastro-intestinal problems, psychosis.

Herbs also may interact with prescription medications, over-the-counter drugs, vitamins and minerals. For example, ginkgo taken with aspirin may lead to spontaneous and/or excessive bleeding.[6] High doses of garlic may enhance the blood-thinning activities of anti-inflammatory medications and vitamin E.[6] Proceed cautiously. Herbs are not tightly regulated like drugs and other medications, even though they often are used for similar purposes. Advise your doctor, pharmacist and other health professionals of all herbs you are taking.

*If you do take herbs:*

- *Follow the instructions on the label.*
- *If any unusual side effects arise, discontinue immediately.*

Medical professionals suggest taking herbs for only short periods. It is unclear if short-term benefits continue over a longer time or if long-term herb use could actually be detrimental to health. Follow the instructions on the label. If any unusual side effects arise, discontinue immediately. In addition, herbs are not recommended in place of medical treatment or conventional medicine for chronic conditions or diseases, such as severe depression, diabetes, hypertension and heart disease. Herbs also are not recommended for people who may be immuno-compromised, such as the elderly or those with HIV; people with kidney damage or liver disease; anyone who may be undergoing surgery or other invasive procedures; and pregnant or lactating women. Herbal products also are not recommended for children under 6.

## How Are Herbs Regulated?

If herbs can be unsafe, why are they so readily available? This is because herbal products—like vitamin and mineral supplements—are classified by the U.S. Food and Drug Administration (FDA) as dietary supplements, not drugs. As a result, they are not tested for safety or efficacy. Thus herbal products can be marketed at any time, without scientific research and without approval from the FDA. Drug companies, on the other hand, must conduct clinical studies to determine the effectiveness of the drugs, safety, possible interactions with other substances, and appropriate dosages. The FDA must review the data and authorize the drug's use before the product may be marketed. The FDA can take regulatory action on an herbal product only after it has received a sufficient number of reports of ill effects and can show the product is unsafe. At this point, the FDA can recommend the product be withdrawn from the market and/or labeled to reflect potential side effects. This system of regulation is always after the fact, not before.

*Medical professionals suggest taking herbs for only short periods. Do not take them in place of medical treatment or conventional medicine for chronic conditions or diseases. They are not recommended for people with certain medical conditions nor for children under 6.*

Moreover, herbs—unlike drugs—are not standardized. When you buy a drug, even an over-the-counter one, you know that each capsule contains the same amount of active ingredient. Drug companies have to follow strict quality-control measures. Herb companies do not. Doses differ between herb capsules and from product to product. The active ingredients also vary depending on the plant part (flower, root, seeds, nuts, bark, branch), plant form (dried, extract, tincture, tea) and plant species. An independent test by *Consumer Lab* in early 2000 found that nearly a quarter of the 30 brands of ginkgo biloba they tested did not have the expected levels of active ingredients. Furthermore, every single product that failed their test claimed it was standardized.

The herbal industry is taking steps to address standardization. Much work is still needed. Currently, if manufacturers follow certain protocols for extracting or drying herbs, they can include USP (for the United States Pharmaceopia) or NF (for Natural Formulary) on their label. It does not ensure that doses are the same from one bottle to another, or that the product is safe. It does attempt to eliminate huge differences. The most rigorous stamp of approval is from the newly formed *Consumer Lab* (CL). CL conducts independent tests of products for identity and potency (proper labeling), purity (any contaminants), and consistency (the same identity, potency and purity from one batch to the next). Products that pass their tests are listed on CL's Web site.

## Summary

The herb industry is growing. More herbs are available than ever before, and Americans are embracing their use. To date, however, herbs have not been well studied and are not well understood. Until we have a clearer picture, consumers must become informed in order to protect themselves from questionable health products and services. Here are some tips to do so:

- Determine whether you really need an herbal supplement.
- Be an informed consumer. Research the product to determine: safety, validity of claims, dosage, most effective form, plant part, species, how long to use it, side effects, any counter-indications with other supplements or medications, and reasonable price.
- Inform your doctor, pharmacist and other health care professionals of any herbs you are considering or that you routinely use. Consult them with any questions.
- Pick brands that have been tested for consistency in dosage by looking for the USP or NF symbols.
- Read the product label and follow the instructions.
- Use herbal products only for minor conditions and only for

## Table 1: Top ten most commonly used herbs.

| Common name, source | Main uses | Apparent efficacy | Possible side effects | Comments |
|---|---|---|---|---|
| Echinacea *(Echinacea angustifolia)* | • Reduce duration of colds.<br>• Boost immune system.<br>• Heal wounds | +<br>+<br>+ | • Minor GI symptoms, chills, short-term fever reaction, nausea and vomiting (uncommon and mild).<br>• Allergic reactions (especially people allergic to the daisy/aster family) | |
| Evening primrose oil *(Oenothera biennis)* | • Reduce menopausal symptoms, sore breasts.<br>• Treat allergic skin rash.<br>• Prevent heart disease.<br>• Treat rheumatoid arthritis, Raynaud's | +/-<br>+/-<br>+<br>+/- | • Headaches, GI distress at high doses. | • Clinical evidence of its safety is inconclusive.<br>• Good source of cis-gamma-linolenic acid (GLA).<br>• Anticoagulant, so may enhance effect of blood thinners. |
| Feverfew *(Tanacetum parthenium)* | • Reduce migraines, headaches.<br>• Treat arthritis | +<br>+/- | • Mouth ulcers, inflamed mouth tissues from chewing leaf.<br>• GI discomfort and dry mouth. | • Do not take with blood thinners—may inhibit platelet activity. |
| Garlic *(Allium sativum)* | • Prevent heart disease.<br>• Lower high blood cholesterol.<br>• Lower high blood pressure.<br>• Improve blood clotting disorders.<br>• Prevent cancer.<br>• Used as antibiotic, antibacterial, antiviral | +<br>+<br>+<br>+<br>+/-<br>+/- | • Breath and skin odor.<br>• Possible nausea, heartburn, dizziness.<br>• Topical garlic can cause skin irritation, blistering and burns. | • Fresh garlic is the best form.<br>• Garlic contains allin and allicin.<br>• If consuming high doses of garlic, do not take blood-thinning drugs, ginkgo or high-dose Vitamin E. |
| Ginger *(Zingiber officinale)* | • Improve motion sickness.<br>• Reduce nausea.<br>• Used as digestive aid. | +<br>+<br>+ | • No side effects observed at recommended dosages. | • People with gallstones should not take ginger without consulting a doctor. |
| Ginkgo biloba *(Ginkgo biloba)* | • Improve memory in Alzheimer's patients.<br>• Improve blood flow.<br>• Used as antioxidant. | +/-<br>+/-<br>+ | • Allergic skin reaction.<br>• Headaches.<br>• Seed ingestion dangerous.<br>• GI upset (rare). | • Do not take with other blood-thinning drugs or high doses of garlic or Vitamin E. |
| Ginseng *(Panax ginseng)* | • Improve fatigue.<br>• Enhance physical performance.<br>• Reduce stress | +<br>-<br>+/- | • Side effects rare.<br>• Menstrual abnormalities, breast tenderness.<br>• Insomnia. | • Not recommended for people with high blood pressure, hypoglycemia.<br>• Do not take with stimulants, including excessive caffeine. |
| Kava kava *(piper methysticum)* | • Lower anxiety, tension, restlessness.<br>• Enhance sleep. | +<br>+ | • Mild GI disturbances.<br>• Red eyes, puffy face, muscle weakness.<br>• Extended continuous intake can result in temporary yellow discoloration of skin, hair, nails.<br>• Enlarged pupils.<br>• Rare allergic skin reactions. | • Not recommended for depressed people.<br>• Do not drive or operate machinery when taking kava kava.<br>• Do not take with alcohol, other barbituates. |
| St. John's wort *(Hypericum perforatum)* | Internally:<br>• Treat depression.<br>• Improve premenstrual depression.<br>• Treat seasonal affective disorder (SAD).<br>Externally:<br>• Used for wounds (inflammation), muscle aches, first-degree burns. | +<br>-<br>+/-<br>+ | • Photosensitivity, especially in fair-skinned people.<br>• May cause allergic reaction. | • Not recommended for severe or chronic depression.<br>• May enhance effects of MAO inhibitors.<br>• Do not take with anti-depressants or alcohol. |
| Saw palmetto *(Serenoa repens)* | • Treat benign prostatic hyperplasia.<br>• Improve overall prostate health.<br>• Enhance sexual vigor, enhance breast size. | +<br>+/-<br>- | • GI disturbances, headaches (rare).<br>+/• Large amounts may cause diarrhea. | |

+ Research supports efficacy/safety of this product when used appropriately. See disclaimer below.
+/- Clinical evidence is inconclusive.
- Research finds that it is ineffective/unsafe.
Except where noted in comments, research indicates these 10 herbs appear to be safe when used appropriately.
Disclaimer: What we know about herbs is constantly changing, so take any herb with caution. Herbs generally are not recommended for people suffering from autoimmune disorders or liver disease, people undergoing surgery or other invasive medical procedure, pregnant or lactating women, or infants and small children. Use herbs only for minor conditions and only for the short-term. Discontinue if you experience any adverse side effects.

the short-term. If a condition is serious or chronic, consult your doctor.

- Discontinue herbs if you experience *any* adverse side effects.
- Avoid herbal therapies if you suffer from certain conditions or under certain circumstances. (See Are Herbs Safe?)
- Do not take herbal products known to be toxic. The list in this fact sheet may not include all potentially toxic herbs, so regularly check the resources listed in this fact sheet for additional toxic herbs.

## Resources

*The following are reliable resources for information on herbs and other dietary supplements*:

*Foster S., Tyler V.*: Honest Herbal *(4th edition), Binghamton, N.Y., The Haworth Press, Inc. 1999*

*Stephen Barrett*, Quackwatch: *www.quackwatch.com.*

*Healthcare Reality Check: www.hcrc.org/index.html.*

*Consumer Lab: www.consumerlab.com.*

## References

1. *Abramov, V. Traditional Medicine. N 134, 1–3. 1996. World Health Organization.*
2. *The U.S. Food and Drug Administration, Center for Food Safety and Applied Nutrition. Economic Characterization of the Dietary Supplement Industry Final Report. 1999.*
3. *Industry Overview*. Nutrition Business Journal. *1999, 4:1–5.*
4. *Foster S., Tyler V.*: Honest Herbal *(4th edition), Binghamton, N.Y., The Haworth Press, Inc. 1999.*
5. *SupplementWatch: www.supplementwatch. com. 2000.*
6. Herbal Medicine: Expanded Commission E Monographs. *Blumenthal, M., Goldberg, A., Brinckmann, J., eds. American Botanical Council. 2000.*

[1]*E. Serrano, Colorado State University Cooperative Extension food and nutrition specialist, and J. Anderson, Cooperative Extension food and nutrition specialist and professor; food science and human nutrition.*

Issued in furtherance of Cooperative Extension work, Acts of May 8 and June 30, 1914, in cooperation with the U.S. Department of Agriculture, Milan A. Rewerts, Director of Cooperative Extension, Colorado State University, Fort Collins, Colorado. Cooperative Extension programs are available to all without discrimination. No endorsement of products mentioned is intended nor is criticism implied of products not mentioned.

# FUNCTIONAL FOODS: AN OVERVIEW


## SUMMARY

Health-conscious consumers are seeking out functional foods (designer foods and sometimes considered as nutraceuticals) to control their own health and well-being. There is no legal definition specific for functional foods. However, these foods are considered to elicit benefits to health and well-being or to have disease-preventing properties beyond their inherent nutritional value.

Recent growth in the functional foods market stems from a variety of factors. These include identification of physiologically active components in foods (e.g., phytochemicals, omega-3-fatty acids, conjugated linoleic acid, probiotic bacteria cultures), as well as an aging population and rising health care costs which are leading consumers to take more responsibility for their own health. Some functional foods are targeted to specific health problems such as osteoporosis, cancer, heart disease, a compromised immune system, and lack of mental acuity.

*Dairy foods can be included in the functional food category because of their content of calcium, specific health-enhancing proteins, conjugated linoleic acid, sphingolipids, butyric acid, and probiotic cultures.*

Dairy foods can be included in the functional food category because of their calcium content which can help to reduce the risk of osteoporosis, hypertension, and possibly colon cancer, among other disease. Health-promoting effects have been described from other dairy food components including protein (e.g., bioactive peptides) and milk fat (e.g., conjugated linoleic acid, sphingolipids, butyric acid). Dairy foods are also excellent carriers for probiotic cultures.

Probiotic dairy foods containing health-promoting bacteria are an important segment of the functional foods market. A variety of health benefits has been attributed to specific strains of lactic acid bacteria (e.g., *Lactobacillus, Bifidobacterium*) or foods containing these probiotic cultures. Potential benefits include alleviation of symptoms of lactose maldigestion, shortened duration of antibiotic associated diarrhea, maintenance of a healthy intestinal flora, decreased risk of some cancers and heart disease, and stimulation of host immune systems. For many of these conditions, well-controlled human intervention studies are needed to substantiate the alleged benefits. Additionally, individual strains of the same bacterial species often differ in their physiological properties and effects. In recent years, considerable interest has also focused on the health benefits of prebiotics (i.e., non-digestible food ingredients that benefit the host by selectively stimulating the growth and/or activity of probiotic bacteria residing in the gastrointestinal tract) and synbiotics (i.e., combination of prebiotics and probiotic cultures).

Although the future for functional foods appears promising, it ultimately depends on scientific evidence of their efficacy, safety, and organoleptic quality. Biomarkers are needed to adequately access the physiological impact of functional foods. Importantly, consumers must become aware of the beneficial health effects of functional foods. Because our knowledge of functional foods is in its infancy, it is especially important that these foods be considered in the context of an overall healthful diet and lifestyle and not as a "magic bullet" to improve health and prevent disease.


## INTRODUCTION

Consumer interest in foods containing components that may enhance health beyond their nutritional value is at an all-time high (1–4a, 5). Many new so-called functional foods (designer foods and sometimes considered as nutraceuticals) are being developed and marketed to consumers to deliver specific health benefits such as reducing risk of coronary heart disease or boosting the immune system. Functional components (e.g., calcium, conjugated linoleic acid, sphingolipids, probiotic cultures) found in many traditional dairy foods continue to be identified, and new food products are being designed to enhance or include these beneficial components.

This *Digest* reviews the definition, growth, and potential health benefits of functional foods, as well as challenges related to marketing these foods. One of the most promising areas for the development of functional foods, particularly dairy foods, is the use of probiotic cultures. The health benefits of probiotics and the future of functional foods are also discussed.

## FUNCTIONAL FOODS

***Definition.*** There is no accepted international definition of functional foods. The terms functional foods and nutraceuticals are often used interchangeably and are variably defined (1). Functional foods are generally characterized as foods similar in appearance to conventional foods, consumed as part of a usual diet, and providing health-related benefits beyond meeting basic nutritional needs (2, 6a, 7). A food can be considered naturally "functional" if it contains a food component that affects one or more targeted functions in a beneficial way. For example, dairy foods can be said to be functional because of their content of calcium. Foods can also be made functional by either adding certain functional components (e.g., antioxidants, probiotics) or replacing components with more desirable ones (8). While functional foods are generally presented as "food," nutraceuticals are often considered to be the products produced from foods but sold in other forms (e.g., pills, powders) and demonstrated to have physiological benefits (6a).

According to a 1998 survey by the International Food Information Council, consumers prefer the term functional foods over nutraceuticals to describe the types of foods and food components believed to convey health benefits (9). Of interest, Japan is the only country worldwide where a legal definition and regulatory approval process for functional foods exist (2). As of June 1999, 149 products have been licensed in Japan as *Foods for Specified Health Use* (FOSHU) and are certified with a seal of approval from the Japanese Ministry of Health and Welfare.

***What is driving the demand for functional foods?*** Several factors help explain why functional foods is one of the fastest growing categories of foods. These include the following:

- Advances in nutritional science, agricultural technologies, and processing techniques (e.g., biotechnology, genetic engineering) (4a, 5, 6b, 10).
- Ready access to nutrition and medical information through widespread media coverage, the internet, and other avenues.
- Escalating health care costs which are placing more emphasis on disease prevention (3, 4a).
- Recent legislative events such as government regulations which have changed how foods are marketed and labeled. The more flexible the regulatory environment, the easier it is to market functional foods (3).
- The rise in the aging population which is increasing the demand for healthier foods or food ingredients to improve health (2, 3, 11). By 2030, an estimated one-third of the U.S. population will be over 65 years of age and this population is particularly interested in functional foods to improve health.
- The growing self-care movement (9, 12, 13). Consumers are becoming more responsible for their own health and are taking an active role in improving their health through foods. According to a 1999 Food Marketing Institute survey, about 60% of consumers are moderately or highly involved in their own health, compared to 50% in 1998 (13).

***Types and Promising Benefits of Functional Foods.*** A wide variety of functional foods and food components of plant and animal origin is available (2, 3, 6b, 10, 14, 15). Phytochemicals (i.e., lycopene, flavoniods, indoles, phenols) in plant-based foods are linked to reduced cancer risk; oats are documented to lower blood cholesterol levels; and several anticarcinogens (e.g., protease inhibitors, saponins, isoflavones) have been identified in soybeans (2).

*In the U.S., there is no separate regulatory category for functional foods. A functional food may be labeled as a conventional food or as a dietary supplement depending on its intended use, among other factors.*

Functional foods from animal sources include fish because of the presence of omega-3 fatty acids, meat because of its content of conjugated linoleic acid (CLA), and dairy foods (2, 6b, 14). Dairy foods contain many functional or health-promoting components (2, 6b). Calcium, an essential nutrient in milk and other dairy foods, has been demonstrated to help reduce the risk of osteoporosis, hypertension, and possibly colon cancer, among other diseases. Milk proteins such as casein-based bioactive peptides and whey proteins (e.g., lactoferrin, lactoperoxidase, lysozyme, and immunoglobulins) have several unique properties including anticarcinogenic and antimicrobial functions (16). Lipid-based bioactive compounds in milk and other dairy foods such as CLA, sphingolipids, and butyric acid may inhibit chronic disease such as cancer and heart disease as well as enhance immune function (6b, 17). As discussed below, cultured and culture-containing dairy foods such as yogurt are considered functional foods because of the presence of probiotic cultures such as *Lactobacilli* and *Bifidobacterium* which may improve microbial balance in the intestine (6b, 14). Not only can traditional dairy foods be considered functional foods, but the functional attributes of these foods could be further enhanced by technology such as bioprocessing or genetic engineering (6b).

***Regulatory, Bioavailability, and Safety Issues.*** How should functional foods be regulated and labeled? At present, there is no separate regulatory category for functional foods in the U.S. (1, 5, 6a, 18, 19). The 1990 Nutrition Labeling and Education Act (NLEA) regulates how nutrition information is provided in food labeling, while the Dietary Supplement Health and Education Act (DSHEA) of 1994 specifies labeling regulations for dietary supplements (18). Functional foods may be regulated as conventional foods under the NLEA or as dietary supplements under the DSHEA, depending on their intended use and the nature of claims made on the food package.

Both foods and dietary supplements may carry structure/function claims (e.g., "calcium building strong bones") (18). However, the Food and Drug Administration has approved only certain health claims. To bear a health claim, there must be substantial scientific evidence of a clear relationship between the food or food component and the specific health benefit (1). At present, the scientific evidence related to the health benefits of most functional foods is still evolving (15). Interactions among components in functional foods, the bioavailability of nutrients, and the effect of processing on the health-enhancing potential of functional foods all must be considered in labeling functional foods (2, 3, 4a, 20). The key to adequately assessing the health-related benefits and safety of functional foods is the availability of accepted sensitive and reliable biological markers (4a, 19).

*Dairy foods are a preferred medium for probiotics or health-promoting bacteria. Specific strains of lactic acid bacteria appear to alleviate symptoms of lactose maldigestion and reduce the duration of diarrhea, as well as possibly protect against several other diseases/conditions.*

**PROBIOTICS, PREBIOTICS, AND SYNBIOTICS**

***Definitions.*** The use of probiotics, prebiotics, and synbiotics is a promising area for the development of functional foods (6b, 21, 22, 23a). Dairy foods appear to be the preferred medium for introducing probiotic bacteria such as human-derived species of lactic acid bacteria (e.g., *L. acidophilus, L. casei, L. gasseri, L. rhamnosus, L. reuteri, Bifidobacterium bifidum, B. breve, B. infantis, and B. longum*) (6b). *Lactobacillus spp.* (naturally found in the human small intestine) and various *Bifidobacterium spp.* (a major organism in the human large intestine) are the most commonly used probiotic cultures (8).

Probiotic (derived from the Greek word meaning "for life") generally refers to live bacteria that beneficially affect the host by improving its intestinal microbial balance (21, 22). A prebiotic is a nondigestible food ingredient that benefits the host by selectively stimulating the growth and/or activity of health-promoting bacteria, such as *Bifidobacterium* in the colon, over undesirable or pathogenic microorganisms (2, 22, 23b, 24-26). Starches, dietary fibers, other nonabsorbable sugars, sugar alcohols, and oligosaccharides are examples of prebiotics (25). The potential health benefits on non-digestible oligosaccharides such as inulin and oligofructose have received recent attention (4b, c, d, e, 22, 25).

A synbiotic is a product in which both a probiotic and a prebiotic are combined to have an additive or synergistically beneficial effect on the host by improving the survival and/or implantation of the probiotic in the intestinal tract (2, 4f, 21, 24–26). In laboratory rats treated with a carcinogen, the combination of bifidobacteria (i.e., a probiotic) and oligofrustose (i.e., a prebiotic) has been demonstrated to reduce colon cancer risk (4f). Most functional foods containing synbiotics are currently yogurt products found primarily in Europe (2, 14).

***Potential and Established Health Benefits.*** Few well-designed, well-conducted human clinical trials of probiotics have been conducted over the past 30 years (21). Only in recent years has the importance of choosing probiotic strains of demonstrated efficacy been recognized (21, 22). Only in recent years has the importance of choosing probiotic strains of demonstrated efficacy been recognized (21, 22). With respect to health benefits of probiotics, research studies indicate the following:

- **Improved intestinal health.** Certain probiotic strains have been demonstrated to shorten the duration of diarrhea (i.e., antibiotic-associated diarrhea, acute infantile diarrhea, traveler's diarrhea), suppress harmful intestinal microbes, and increase resistance to infectious diseases, particularly of the intestine (6b, 21, 22, 23a, 26–29). An investigation in Finland demonstrated that the duration of acute diarrhea in children between 4 and 45 months of age was shortened following intake of a specific strain of *Lactobacillus (Lactobacillus rhamnosus GG)* in a fermented drink or in a freeze-dried form (28). Dairy foods such as milk and yogurt with specific strains of probiotic cultures can favorably influence the intestinal microflora in experimental animals and humans (30–312). It has been reported that specific strains of probiotics may also help to alleviate constipation (23a).

- **Modulation of the immune response**. In both experimental animals and humans, probiotic cultures have been observed to influence local and systemic immune responses (4c, 6b, 21, 22, 23c, 33, 34). Various *Lactobacillus* and *Bifidobacteria* strains per se or in foods such as yogurt have been demonstrated to enhance nonspecific immunity by increasing macrophage activation and natural killer cell activity (22, 33). In humans consuming a fermented milk product with either *L. acidophilus LA1* or *B. bifidum Bb12*, there was no change in lymphocyte population, although macrophage phagocytosis of *E. coli* increased (34). Other studies report contradictory findings regarding the role of probiotics in immune function (4g, 35). Nevertheless, researches suspect that probiotics have a possible beneficial role in immune response (4g).
- **Reduced risk of cancer**. Studies indicate that probiotics may reduce the risk of colon cancer (36–42) and possibly breast (43, 44) and intestinal (45) cancers. For the most part, studies have been conducted in experimental animals and in vitro. Additionally, studies demonstrate that probiotic strains differ in their ability to reduce cancer risk (36, 44). Probiotics may reduce the risk of cancer by several mechanisms. These include reducing fecal enzymes (e.g., β-glucuronidas, azoreductase, nitroreductase) associated with the conversion of procarcinogens to carcinogens, stimulating the host's immunological defenses, and altering the acidity (pH) of the colon rendering the environment less conducive to the development of cancer (2, 6b, 22, 23a, 36, 37, 41, 42).
- **Reduced risk of heart disease**. Probiotics may potentially reduce risk of heart disease by lowering blood cholesterol levels, increasing resistance of low density lipoprotein (LDL) cholesterol to oxidation, and reducing blood pressure (2, 22). In experimental animals, intake of yogurt or cultured milk has been demonstrated to reduce blood cholesterol levels (46–48). However, data from studies of the effects of milk and other dairy foods with probiotic cultures of blood cholesterol levels are contradictory (2, 4g, 49–51).
- **Improved tolerance to milk**. Probiotics may improve tolerance to lactose and reduce milk allergy (6b, 21, 22). Alleviation of lactose maldigestion symptoms is well established for some probiotics and dairy foods containing probiotics (21, 52–57). Intake of yogurt made from milk fermented with *Lactobacillus bulgaricus* and *Streptococcus thermophilus* has been demonstrated to enhance lactose digestion in individuals with lactase nonpersisence (52, 53). This beneficial effect of yogurt with probiotic strains is due primarily to the presence of the enzyme, [[eq]]-galactosidase, which digests the lactose in yogurt (52, 53). Whether or not other dairy foods with probiotics aid digestion of lactose depends on the strain of the probiotics used and the concentration of the culture, among other factors (54–57). Bifidobacteria may improve lactose digestion because these probiotics have a relatively high level of β-galactosidase activity and are stable under normal storage conditions (57). Probiotics, such as dairy foods with *Lactobacillus spp.*, may also reduce food allergies including sensitivity to milk proteins, although additional investigations are necessary to establish this health benefit (58–62).
- **Other**. Limited scientific findings indicate that probiotic bacteria may help to protect against vaginal/urinary tract infections (27, 63). However, many of the studies to date are uncontrolled and involve a small number of subjects (27, 63). Probiotics may also reduce ulcers by decreasing the growth of ulcer-inducing bacteria (i.e., *Helicobacter pylori*) (64, 65).

***What lies ahead for probiotics?*** Although several studies indicate that specific strains of probiotic cultures alleviate lactose maldigestion symptoms and reduce the duration of diarrhea, additional research is needed to scientifically substantiate many other alleged beneficial health effects of probiotic bacteria, as well as the mechanisms underlying these effects (21). To better understand the potential beneficial properties of probiotics such as *Lactobacillus* and *Bifidobacterium*, researchers are identifying the genetic characteristics of these probiotics (22, 66). Genetic analysis and modification of probiotics can lead to the development of new probiotics with beneficial health effects, improved effectiveness of existing properties of probiotic strains in vitro and in vivo, and development of probiotic products for specific functional characteristics (22).

*The future of functional foods depends on their effectiveness in reducing the risk of disease, their safety, their organoleptic quality, and consumers' confidence in the health benefits of these foods.*

Before probiotics and in particular probiotic-enhanced dairy foods can become mainstream in the U.S., the quality and viability of these cultures in dairy foods must be ensured. Information is needed on what strain or combination of strains and what levels of specific strains of probiotics are required to achieve an intended health benefit. Also, the shelf life limitations of probiotics in foods such as dairy foods must be determined. Although most strains of lactic acid probiotics have a good record, the safety of new prebiotics and probiotics, including genetically modified bacteria, must be confirmed (21). Rigorous clinical trails in humans are necessary before probiotic therapy will be truly accepted.

## WHAT IS THE FUTURE OF FUNCTIONAL FOODS?

Whether or not functional foods will be successful long-term depends on several factors including their effectiveness, safety, and quality, as well as how the benefits of these foods are communicated to consumers (2, 3, 5, 6b, 8, 13, 18, 67–70). Our understanding of functional foods and their market potential is in its infancy and little is known about their long-term health benefits. It therefore is important for consumers to select a variety of foods from all food groups in moderation (2). Functional foods should be viewed as part of an overall healthful diet and not as "magic bullets" to improve health and reduce risk of disease (3, 69, 70).

## REFERENCES


1. The American Dietetic Association. J. Am. Diet.Assoc. *95*:493, 1995.
2. Hasler, C.M. Food Technol. *52*:63, 1998.
3. Milner, J.A. Food Technol. *52*:24, 1998.
4. Milner, J.A., and M. Roverfroid (Eds). J. Nutr. *129(suppl 7)*, 1999, a) Milner-p. 1395s; b) Roberfroid-p. 1398s; c) Jenkins et.at.-p. 1431s; d) Taper and Roberfroid-p. 1488s; e) Reddy et.al-p. 1478s; f) Gallaher and Khil-p. 1483s; g) Van de Water et.al.-p 1492.
5. Witwer, R.S. Food Technol, *53*:50, 1999.
6. Mazza, G. (Ed). *Functional Foods. Biochemical & Processing Aspects.* Lancaster, PA: Technomic Publ. Co., Inc., 1998, a) Stephen-p. 403; b) Jelen & Lutz-p. 347
7. Salminen, K. Nutr. Rev. *31(suppl)*: 1s, 1996.
8. Hilliam, M. Nutr. Rev. *54(suppl)*: 189s, 1996.
9. International Food Information Council. *Food Insight*, May/June 1998.
10. Bidlack, W.R. and W. Wang. In: *Modern Nutrition in Health and Disease.* Ninth Edition. Philadelphia: Williams & Wilkins, 1999, p. 1823.
11. Hollingsworth, P. Food Technol, *53*:38, 1999.
12. Sloan, E. Nutraceuticals World *2*:58, 1999.
13. Food Marketing Institute and PREVENTION Magazine. *Shopping for Health 1999. The Growing Self-Care Movement.* Washington, DC: Food Marketing Institute and Emmaus, PA: PREVENTION Magazine, 1999.
14. Pszczola, D.E. Food Technol. *52*:30, 1998.
15. Hasler, C.M., and J.B. Blumberg. J. Nutr. *129*:756, 1999.
16. Parodi, P.W. Aust. J. Dairy Technol. *53*:37, 1998.
17. Parodi, P.W. J. Nutr. *127*:1055, 1997.
18. Storlie, J., M.J. O'Flaherty, and K. Hare. Food Technol.*52*:62, 1998.
19. Clydesdale, F.M. Nutr. Rev. *55*:413, 1997.
20. Pszczola, D.E. Food Technol. *52*:38, 1998.
21. Salminen, S., C.Bouley, M.-C. Boutron-Ruault, et.al. Br. J. Nutr. *80(suppl)*:147s, 1998.
22. Tannock, G.W. (Ed). *Probiotics. A Critical Review.* Norfolk, England: Horizon Scientific Press, 1999.
23. Salminen, S., and A. Von Wright. *Lactic Acid Bacteria. Microbiology and Functional Aspects.* 2nd ed. New York: Marcel Dekker, Inc., 1998, a) Salminen et.al.-p. 211; b) Salminen et.al.-p. 343; c) Isoauri et.al.-p. 255.
24. Gibson, G.R., and M.B. Roverfroid. J Nutr. *125*:1401, 1995.
25. Roberfroid, M.B. Br. J. Nutr. *80(suppl)*:197s, 1998.
26. Collins, M.D., and G.R. Gibson. Amer. J. Clin. Nutr. *69(suppl)*:1052s, 1999.
27. Elmer, G.W., C.N. Surawicz, and L.V. McFarland. JAMA 275:870, 1996.
28. Isolauri, E., M. Juntunen, T. Rautanen, et.al. Pediatrics *88*:90, 1991.
29. Kaila, M., and E. Isolauri, Nutr. Today *31(suppl)*:16s, 1996.
30. Djouzi, Z., C. Andrieux, M. -C. Degivry, et.al. J. Nutr. *127*:2260, 1997.
31. Guerin-Danan, C., C. Chabanet, C. Pedone, et.al. Am. J. Clin. Nutr. *67*:111, 1998.
32. Benno, Y., F. he, M. Hosoda, et.al. Nutr. Today *31(suppl)*:9s, 1996.
33. De Simone, C., R. Vesely, B. Salvadori, et.al. Int. J. Immunother, *9*:23, 1993.
34. Schiffrin, E.J., F. Rochat, H. L. Link-Amster, et.al. J. Dairy Sci. *78*:491, 1995.
35. Wheller, J.G., M.L. Bogle, S.J.Shema, et.al. Am. J. Med. Sci. *313*:120, 1997.
36. Wollowski, I., S.-T. Ji, A.T. Bakalinsky, et.al. J. Nutr. *129*:77, 1999.
37. Singh, J., A. Rivenson, M. Tomita, et.al. Carcinogenesis *18*:833, 1997.
38. Gallaher, D.D., W. H. Stallings, L. L. Blessing, et.al J. Nutr, *126*:1362, 1996.
39. Pool-Zobel, B.L., C. Neudecker, I. Domizlaff, et.al Nutr. Cancer *26*:365, 1996.
40. Abdelali, H., P.Cassand, V. Soussotte, et.al. Nutr. Cancer *24*:121, 1995.
41. Ling. W.H., R. Korpela, H. Mykkanen, et.al. J. Nutr. *124*:18, 1994.
42. Perdigon, G., J.C. Valdez, and M. Rachid. J. Dairy Res. *65*:129, 1998.
43. Rice, L.J., Y.-J. Chai, C.J. Conti, et.al. Nutr. Cancer *24*:99, 1995.
44. Biffi, A., D. Coradini, R. Larsen, et.al. Nutr. Cancer *28*:93, 1997.
45. Goldin, B.R., L.J. Gualtieri, and R.P. Moore. Nutr. Cancer *25*:197, 1996.
46. Zommara, M.N. Tachibana, M. Sakono, et.al. Nutr. Res. *16*:293, 1996.
47. Benna, A., and V. Prasad. J. Dairy Res. *64*:453, 1997.
48. Akalin, A.S., S. Gonc, and S. Duzel. J. Dairy Sci. *80*:2721, 1997.
49. Pearce, J. Int. Dairy J. *6*:661, 1996.
50. Taylor, G.R.J., and C.M. Williams. Br. J. Nutr. *80(suppl.2)*:225s, 1998.
51. Anderson, J.W., and S.E. Gilliland. J. Am. Coll. Nutr. *18*:43, 1999.
52. Kolars, J.C., M.D. Levitt, M. Aouji, et.al. N. Engl. J. Med. *310*:1, 1984.
53. Vesa, T.H., P. Marteau, S. Zidi, et.al. Eur.J. Clin. Nutr. *50*:730, 1996.
54. Sanders, M.E., D.C. Walker, K.M. Walker, et.al. J. Dairy Sci. *79*:943, 1996.
55. Montes, R.G., T.M. Bayless, J.M. Saavedra, et.al. J. Dairy Sci. *78*:1675, 1995.
56. Mustapha, A., T. Jiang, and D.A. Savaiano. J. Dairy Sci. *80*:1537, 1997.
57. Jiang, T., A. Mustapha, and D.A. Savaiano. J. Dairy Sci. *79*:750, 1996.
58. Majamaa, H., and E. Isolauri, J. Allergy Clin. Immunol. *99*:179, 1997.

59. Pessi, T., Y. Sutas, A. Marttinen, et.al. J. Nutr. *128*:2313, 1998.
60. Salminen, S. Nutr. Rev. *54(suppl)*:99s, 1996.
61. Isolauri, E. Nutr. Today *31(suppl)*:28s, 1996.
62. Pelto, L., S.J. Salminen, and E. Isolauri. Nutr. Today *31(suppl)*:45s, 1996.
63. Shalev, E., S. Battino, E. Weiner, et.al. Arch. Farm. Med. *5*:593, 1996.
64. Aiba, Y., N. Suzuki, A.M. Kabir, et.al. Am. J. Gastroenterol. *93*:2091, 1998.
65. Michetti, P., G. Dorta, P.H. Wiesel, et.al. Digestion *60*:203, 1999.
66. Klaenhammer, T.R. Int. Diary J. *5*:1019, 1995.
67. Dwyer, J. Nutr. Today *34*:155, 1999.
68. Glinsmann, W.H. Nutr. Today *34*:158, 1999.
69. Milner, J.A. Nutr. Today *34*:146, 1999.
70. Pariza, N.W. Nutr. Today *34*:150, 1999.

## ACKNOWLEDGEMENTS

National Dairy Council® assumes the responsibility for this publication. However, we would like to acknowledge the help and suggestions of the following reviewers in its preparation:

- Clare M. Hasler, Ph.D.
  Executive Director
  Functional Foods for Health Program
  University of Illinois at Urbana-Champaign
  Department of Food Science and Human Nutrition
  Urbana, Illinois
- Todd R. Klaenhammer, Ph.D.
  Director, Southeast Dairy Foods Research Center
  William Neal Reynolds Professor
  Food Science & Microbiology
  North Carolina Sate University
  Raleigh, North Carolina

The *Dairy Council Digest*® is written and edited by Lois D. McBean, M.S., R.D.

# Nutrition Supplements: Science vs Hype

**In Brief:** Aggressive marketing has led millions of recreational and elite athletes to use nutrition supplements in hopes of improving performance. Unfortunately, these aids can be costly and potentially harmful, and the advertised ergogenic gains are often based on little or no scientific evidence. No benefits have been convincingly demonstrated for amino acids, L-carnitine, L-tryptophan, or chromium picolinate. Creatine, beta-hydroxy-beta-methylbutyrate, and dehydroepiandrosterone (DHEA) may confer ergogenic or anabolic effects. Chromium picolinate and DHEA have adverse side effects, and the safety of the other products remains in question.

**Thomas D. Armsey Jr, MD; Gary A. Green, MD**

Nutrition supplements are a lucrative business in the United States. According to the Council for Responsible Nutrition,[1] the retail sale of dietary supplements generated $3.3 billion in 1990, and revenues increase each year. This enormous expenditure is largely the result of aggressive advertising aimed at high school, college, and recreational athletes, all eager for anabolic-steroid-like gains through dietary aids. Riding the crest of the fitness wave, nutrition supplements appeal to millions of consumers willing to pay billions of dollars for alleged benefits that are too good to be true.

Unfortunately, these supplements are subject to little regulation by the US Food and Drug Administration (FDA). Advertised claims to the contrary, many supplements have not been subjected to the scientific scrutiny required of prescription drugs. Furthermore, given the size and continued growth of the supplement industry, the FDA will probably never be able to monitor its products effectively. The resulting lack of regulation can lead to unscrupulous advertising, impurities in manufacturing, and potentially dangerous reactions among supplement users.

Such potential outcomes obligate physicians to learn about current nutrition supplements so they can educate patients about the effects and risks of supplement use. Team physicians in particular can advise athletes, coaches, and administrators in these matters. Competing with slick advertisements and exaggerated claims can be difficult, but by using recent scientific research on commonly used supplements, their mechanisms of action, and possible adverse reactions, physicians can offer sound recommendations to patients who are either users or interested in trying these aids.

## Creatine Monohydrate

Creatine, or methylguanidine-acetic acid, is an amino acid that was first identified in 1835 by Chevreul. It is synthesized from arginine and glycine in the liver, pancreas, and kidneys and is also available in meats and fish.[2] Creatine was first introduced as a potential ergogenic aid in 1993 as creatine monohydrate and is currently being used extensively by athletes throughout the United States. A National Collegiate Athletic Association (NCAA) study, publication pending, revealed that 13% of intercollegiate athletes have used creatine monohydrate in the past 12 months (Frank Uryasz, personal communication, February 1997).

According to current theory, creatine supplementation increases the bioavailability of phosphocreatine (PCr) in skeletal muscle cells. This increase is thought to enhance muscle performance in two ways. First, more available PCr allows faster resynthesis of adenosine triphosphate (ATP) to provide energy for brief, high-intensity exercise, like sprinting, jumping, or weight lifting. Second, PCr buffers the intracellular hydrogen ions associated with lactate production and muscle fatigue during exercise. Therefore, creatine supplementation may provide an ergogenic effect by increasing the force of muscular contraction and prolonging anaerobic exercise.[3]

Numerous well-designed studies have demonstrated that creatine supplementation has an ergogenic potential. Greenhaff et al[4] showed that 5-day oral dosages of 20 g/day increased muscle creatine availability by 20% and significantly accelerated PCr regeneration after intense muscle contraction. Birch et al[5] and Harris et al,[6] in laboratory and field studies, demonstrated significant performance enhancement in male athletes, in both brief, high-intensity work and total time to exhaustion, using creatine supplementation of 20 to 30 g/day.

Recent data reveal that the mean creatine concentration in human skeletal muscle is 125 mmole/kg-dm (dry muscle), with a normal range between 90 and 160 mmole/kg-dm.[7] This wide spectrum of creatine concentration may explain why some of the published studies have not demonstrated significant ergogenic effects. In a study by Greenhaff,[7] approximately half of the tested athletic subjects exhibited concentrations lower than 125 mmole/kg-dm, with strict vegetarians substantially lower. These individuals exhibited the most significant increases in muscle creatine concentration, PCr regeneration, and performance enhancement with the use of creatine. On the other hand, athletes with elevated baseline levels of creatine showed little or no ergogenic effect when tested after ingesting creatine.

While creatine use has skyrocketed, no serious side effects have been scientifically verified in subjects using relatively brief (less than 4 weeks) creatine regimens. However, there are anecdotal reports of a dramatic increase in muscle cramping associated with the use of creatine monohydrate (J. Kinderknecht, MD, personal communication, June 1996). Future research will, we hope, clarify whether these adverse reactions are caused by creatine supplementation.

## Chromium Picolinate

Chromium is an essential trace mineral present in various foods, such as mushrooms, prunes, nuts, whole grain breads, and cereals.[8] A normal American diet contains 50% to 60% of the recommended daily allowance (RDA) of chromium. It has an extremely low gastrointestinal absorption rate, so supplement manufacturers have bound chromium with picolinate (CrPic) to increase the absorption and bioavailability.

Chromium supplementation became popular after it was found that exercise increases chromium loss, raising the concern that chromium deficiency may be common among athletes[9]. Chromium seems to function as a co-factor that enhances the action of insulin, especially in carbohydrate, fat, and protein metabolism. Promoters of CrPic claim it increases glycogen synthesis, improves glucose tolerance and lipid profiles, and increases amino acid incorporation in muscle.

CrPic supplementation gained scientific credence in the early 1980s when researchers demonstrated anabolic-steroid-like effects with dosages of 200 micrograms/day. Evans[10,11] and Hasten et al[12] demonstrated a decreased percentage of body fat and increased lean mass among college athletes and students who took CrPic supplements and performed resistance exercise training. However, critical analysis of these studies reveals that imprecise measurement techniques, rather than CrPic supplementation, may account for these "ergogenic" results. More recent studies by Clancy et al[13] and Hallmark et al[14]), using more precise measurement techniques, failed to demonstrate any significant improvement in percent body fat, lean body mass, or strength.

Most studies of CrPic supplementation reveal no side effects except gastrointestinal intolerance with dosages of 50 to 200 micrograms/day for less than 1 month. However, anecdotal reports of serious adverse effects, including anemia,[15] cognitive impairment,[16] chromosome damage,[17]) and interstitial nephritis[18] have been reported with CrPic ingestion in increased dosages and/or durations. Therefore, the use of chromium picolinate supplementation as an ergogenic aid should be strongly discouraged and considered potentially dangerous.

## Amino Acids

Amino acids are the basic structural units of proteins, and one might expect that the more amino acids ingested, the greater the potential for building skeletal muscle. According to the 1989 RDA, an average adult must ingest 0.8 g/kg lean body mass/day of protein in order to fulfill the body's protein requirements. Athletes, however, have traditionally been assumed to need significantly more protein than the average individual, so they commonly use various protein supplements.

Theories suggest that increasing the bioavailability of amino acids promotes protein synthesis and attenuates the muscle loss that occurs during both strength and endurance exercise. These theories have gained support through scientific experimentation in protein metabolism. Fern et al[19] and Lemon et al[20] demonstrated that strength trainers increased protein synthesis with substantially increased protein ingestion during 4 weeks of resistance training. By tracking the nitrogen balance of these athletes, a new daily protein requirement (1.4 to 1.8 g/kg lean mass/day) was developed for strength athletes.

Amino acid supplementation also plays a role in endurance athletes. Lemon[21] and Gontzen et al[22] demonstrated that endurance athletes who train at moderate intensity (55% to 65% of $VO^2$ max) and high intensity (80% of $VO^2$ max) for more than 100 minutes significantly increase protein breakdown unless their protein intake equals 1.2 to 1.4 g/kg lean mass/day.

Several factors make the amount of amino acids that athletes need less clear. Although all of the cited studies demonstrate the advisability of protein intakes higher than the current RDA, no well-designed study has yet shown that amino acid supplementation enhances performance. In addition, no scientific evidence supports protein supplementation in dosages greater than 2 g/kg lean mass/day. Finally, the improved conditioning that occurs over a 4- to 8-week training period may decrease protein breakdown, which may result in a maintenance protein requirement much closer to the current RDA.

**Table 1. Daily Dose Costs of Various Nutrition Supplements Used by Athletes.**

**Creatine**

- 20-30 g/day (loading dose): $7.20/day for one week
- 10-15 g/day (maintenance dose): $3.60/day

**Chromium**

200 mg/day: $.043/day

**L-Carnitine**

2.0 g/day: $2.67/day

**Beta-Hydroxy-Beta-Methylbutrate**

- 13 g/day: $3.48/day
- 11.5 g/day: $1.74/day

**Dehydroepiandrosterone**

- 150 mg/day: $0.67/day
- 1100 mg/day: $1.34/day

**L-Tryptophan**

Currently unavailable in pure form due to federal regulation

Sources: National Supplement Association and General Nutrition Centers

## L-Carnitine

Carnitine is a quaternary amine whose physiologically active form is beta-hydroxy-gamma-trimethylam-monium butyrate. This is found in meats and dairy products and is synthesized in the human liver and kidneys from two essential amino acids, lysine and methionine. L-carnitine is thought to be ergogenic in two ways. First, by increasing free fatty acid transport across mitochondrial membranes, carnitine may increase fatty acid oxidation and utilization for energy, thus sparing muscle glycogen. Second, by buffering pyruvate, and thus reducing muscle lactate accumulation associated with fatigue, carnitine may prolong exercise.

Early studies by Gorostiaga et al,[23] Wyss et al[24]), and Natalie et al[25] indirectly demonstrated an ergogenic effect of this compound. These studies showed a decreased respiratory exchange ratio (RER) with L-carnitine supplementation (2 to 6 g/day) during exercise, suggesting that fatty acids rather than carbohydrates were used for energy. However, these studies had several problems in methodology, including the use of the RER as the sole measure of enhanced fatty acid oxidation. The RER is an indirect measure of lipid utilization that is influenced by many factors, such as preexercise diet, fitness level, and exercise intensity and duration.[26] These confounders were not controlled and may have influenced the results.

A more controlled study by Vuchovich et al[27] avoided these problems by directly measuring muscle glycogen and lactate levels through biopsy and serum analysis. This study failed to demonstrate any glycogen-sparing effect or reductions in lactate levels while supplementing with 6 g/day of L-carnitine. Furthermore, no study to date has confirmed performance enhancement with carnitine supplementation. Finally, many currently available supplements actually contain D-carnitine, which is physiologically inactive in humans but may cause significant muscle weakness through mechanisms that deplete L-carnitine in tissues. Therefore, carnitine should not be advocated as an ergogenic supplement.

## L-Tryptophan

L-tryptophan, an essential amino acid, is not commercially available in its pure form but is found in many combination supplement products and reportedly remedies insomnia, depression, anxiety, and premenstrual tension.[28] Athletes in the past decade have taken L-tryptophan because of its advertised ergogenic effects. The theoretical mechanism for these effects is an increase in serotonin levels in the brain; these increases produce analgesia and reduce the discomfort of prolonged muscular effort, thereby delaying fatigue. This theoretical model gained scientific credence in 1988 when Segura and Ventura[29] demonstrated a 49% increase in total exercise time to exhaustion when subjects ingested a total of 1.2 g of L-tryptophan (four 300-mg doses within 24 hours of exercise) vs placebo. Such a profound improvement in performance is difficult to imagine, and these results have never been replicated. Two larger, well-designed studies by Seltzer et al[30] and Stensrud et al[31] failed to demonstrate any improvement in subjective or objective outcome measures when supplementing with 1.2 g of L-tryptophan vs placebo. The results of these two studies are more consistent with current research data on exercise.

Physicians should be aware of two other developments that argue against supplementing with L-tryptophan. Its use has declined among elite athletes, possibly suggesting that they are recognizing its minimal ergogenic effects. More important, L-tryptophan ingestion was linked to multiple cases of eosinophilia myalgia syndrome and 32 deaths.[28] Though these cases were probably due to contamination of L-tryptophan produced by one Japanese manufacturer, and not to the amino acid itself, they illustrate the quality and purity questions regarding unregulated supplements.

## Beta-Hydroxy-Beta Methylbutyrate

One of the most recent additions to the nutrition supplement market is beta-hydroxy-beta-methylbutyrate (HMB). It is a metabolite of the essential branched-chain amino acid leucine and is produced in small amounts endogenously. HMB is also found in catfish, citrus fruits, and breast milk. In the early 1980s, researchers at Iowa State University hypothesized that HMB was the bioactive component in leucine metabolism that regulates protein metabolism. The exact mechanism of this process is unknown, but promoters hypothesize that HMB regulates the enzymes responsible for protein breakdown. They propose that high HMB levels decrease protein catabolism, thereby creating a net anabolic effect.

Research in livestock[32-36] and humans seems to suggest that supplementation with HMB may increase muscle mass and strength. Nissen conducted two randomized, double-blind, placebo-controlled studies[37,38] to evaluate the ergogenic potential of HMB in exercising men. In the first study, 41 untrained subjects participated in a 4-week resistance training program. The subjects, whose diets were controlled, were given either HMB supplements of 1.5 or 3 g/day or a placebo. Those receiving HMB supplements showed significant improvements in muscle mass and strength as well as significant decreases in muscle breakdown products (3-methylhistidine and creatine phosphokinase) when compared with placebo subjects. The second study evaluated trained and untrained male subjects in a similarly designed weight training program. Relative to a placebo group, the subjects supplementing with 3 g/day demonstrated significant increases in muscle mass and one-repetition maximum bench press as well as decreases in percent body fat.

Further studies of HMB may continue to support the supplement's anabolic effects and elucidate its role in protein metabolism. No side effects of HMB supplementation have been reported, but the safety of this agent is still unknown. Therefore, it is premature to recommend its use as a safe and effective ergogenic aid.

## Dehydroepiandrosterone

Attention focused on dehydroepiandrosterone (DHEA) in 1996 when the FDA banned its sale and distribution for therapeutic uses until its safety and value could be reviewed. The ensuing media attention popularized this supplement, and manufacturers began selling it as a nutritional aid rather than a therapeutic drug.

DHEA was identified in 1934 as an androgen produced in the adrenal glands. It is a precursor to the endogenous production of both androgens and estrogens in primates.[39] It is also available in wild yams, which are sold in many health food stores as a source of DHEA. As a precursor to androgenic steroids, DHEA may increase the production of testosterone and provide an anabolic steroid effect. Promoters claim that this compound slows the aging process and accordingly advertise it as the "fountain of youth."

**Table 2. Protein Supplements Cost Comparison: Daily Cost of 2 g Protein/kg for a 70-kg Individual**

Brand name of protein powder: $9.80/day ($0.07/g protein)

Generic Protein Powder: $2.80/day ($0.02/g protein)

Tuna: $2.80/day ($0.02/g protein)

Source: National Supplement Association

Only a few randomized, double-blind, placebo-controlled studies on the effects of DHEA supplementation have been published. Two have demonstrated significant increases in androgenic steroid plasma levels, along with subjective improvements in physical and psychological well-being, while supplementing with 50 mg/day for 6 months[40] or 100 mg/day for up to 12 months.[41] Whether DHEA has any effect on body composition or fat distribution is still unclear. Its effect on healthy individuals younger than 40 years old is also virtually unstudied.

DHEA users have reported few adverse effects from the supplement, but one is irreversible virilization in women, including hair loss, hirsutism, and voice deepening.[42] In addition, men have reported irreversible gynecomastia, which may result from an elevation in estrogen levels. Because this supplement is so new, long-term adverse effects are unknown. Unlike most other nutrition supplements, DHEA may substantially increase the risk of uterine and prostate cancer that accompanies prolonged elevation in the levels of unopposed estrogen and testosterone. Therefore, the safety of this supplement must be questioned.

Of particular interest to competitive athletes is the effect that DHEA supplementation may have on the test used by the International Olympic Committee and NCAA in their screening for exogenous testosterone use. Using DHEA could alter the testosterone-epitestosterone ratio so it exceeds the 6:1 limit set by both groups (personal communication, Don Catlin, MD, 1997); thus DHEA users could risk disqualification from international competition.

Given the lack of evidence that DHEA enhances athletic performance and its potentially devastating adverse effects, DHEA supplementation is not recommended.

## Purity, Cost, and Final Thoughts

Although some of the supplements discussed here may have benefits, physicians should remain skeptical about the use of any supplement. The purity of agents available to consumers is in doubt, as we have seen with L-tryptophan. *The Medical Letter*, for example, analyzed several commercial preparations of melatonin and found unidentifiable impurities in four of six samples.[43] The supplements used for the research reported in this review were pure, but consumers in the largely unregulated marketplace cannot be assured of that same purity in the products they buy.

There is also the issue of cost (tables 1 and 2). At current rates, doses of the supplements discussed range as high as $7.20/day, the cost of a loading dose of creatine (20 to 30 g/day). It makes little sense to invest in supplements that offer minimal or no benefit, especially for athletic departments in this era of shrinking budgets.

The key word in nutrition supplements is nutrition. NCAA guidelines state that "there are no shortcuts to sound nutrition, and the use of suspected or advertised ergogenic aids may be detrimental and will, in most instances, provide no competitive advantage."[44] Physicians need to educate athletes, parents, coaches, trainers, and athletic administrators in sound dietary practices or see to it that a nutrition professional does so. Then nutrition supplements can be put in proper perspective, and decisions regarding their use can be based on proper scientific study and proven benefit to the individual.

## References


1. Cowart VS: Dietary supplements: alternatives to anabolic steroids? Phys Sportsmed 1992;20(3):189–198
2. Walker JB: Creatine: biosynthesis, regulation and function. Adv Enzymol Relat Areas Mol Med 1979;50:177–242
3. Maughan RJ: Creatine supplementation and exercise performance. Int J Sport Nutr 1995;5(2):94–101
4. Greenhaff PL, Bodin K, Soderlund K, et al: The effect of oral creatine supplementation on skeletal muscle phosphocreatine resynthesis. Am J Physiol 1994;266(5 pt 1):E725–E730
5. Birch R, Noble D, Greenhaff GL: The influence of dietary creatine supplementation on performance during repeated bouts of maximal isokinetic cycling in man. Eur J Appl Phys 1994;69(3):268–276
6. Harris RC, Soderlund K, Hultman E: Elevation of creatine in resting and exercised muscle of normal subjects by creatine supplementation. Clin Sci 1992;83(3):367–374
7. Greenhaff PL: Creatine and its application as an ergogenic aid. Int J Sport Nutr 1995;5(suppl):S100–S110
8. Clarkson PM: Do athletes require mineral supplements? Sports Med Digest 1994; 16(4):1–3
9. Campbell WW, Anderson RA: Effects of aerobic exercise and training on trace minerals chromium, zinc, and copper. Sports Med 1987;4(1):9–18
10. Evans GW: The role of picolinic acid in metal metabolism. Life Chem Reports 1982;1:57–67
11. Evans GW: The effect of chromium picolinate on insulin controlled parameters in humans. Int J Biosocial Med 1989;11:163–180
12. Hasten DL, Rome EP, Franks ED, et al: Effects of chromium picolinate on beginning weight training students. Int J Sport Nutr
13. Clancy SP, Clarkson PM, DeCheke ME, et al: Effects of chromium picolinate supplementation on body composition, strength, and urinary chromium loss in football players. Int J Sport Nutr 1994;4(2):142–153
14. Hallmark MA, Reynolds TH, DeSouza CA, et al: Effects of chromium and resistive training on muscle strength and body composition. Med Sci Sports Exerc 1996; 28(1):139–144
15. Lefavi RG: Sizing up a few supplements. Phys Sportsmed 1992;20(3):190–191
16. Huszonek J: Over-the-counter chromium picolinate. [Letter] Am J Psychiatry 1993;150 (10):1560–1561
17. Stearns DM, Wise JP, Patierno SR, et al: Chromium picolinate produces chromosome damage in Chinese hamster ovary cells. FASEB 1995;9(15):1643–1648
18. Wasser WG, Feldman NS: Chronic renal failure after ingestion of over-the-counter chromium picolinate. [Letter] Ann Int Med 1997;126(5):410
19. Fern EB, Bielinski RN, Schultz Y: Effects of exaggerated amino acid and protein supply in man. Experimentia 1991;47(2): 168–172
20. Lemon PW, Tarnopolsky MA, MacDougall JD, et al: Protein requirements, muscle mass/strength changes during intensive training in novice bodybuilders. J Appl Physiol 1992;73(2):767–775
21. Lemon PW: Effect of exercise on protein requirements. J Sports Sci 1991;9 (special): 53–70
22. Gontzen I, Sutzecu P, Dumitrache S: The influence of muscular activity on the nitrogen balance and on the need of man for proteins. Nutr Rep Int 1974;10:35–43
23. Gorostiaga EM, Maurer CA, Eclache JP: Decrease in respiratory quotient during exercise following L-carnitine supplementation. Int J Sports Med 1989;10(3):169–174
24. Wyss V, Ganzit GP, Rienzi A: Effects of L-carnitine administration on $VO^2$ max and the aerobic-anaerobic threshold in normoxia and acute hypoxia. Eur J Appl Physiol 1990;60(1):1–6
25. Natalie A, Santoro D, Brandi LS, et al: Effects of acute hypercarnitinemia during increased fatty substrate oxidation in man. Metabolism 1993;42(5):594–600
26. Krogh A, Lindhard J: The relative value of fat and carbohydrate as sources of muscular energy. Biochem J 1920;14(July):290–363
27. Vuchovich MD, Costill DL, Fink WJ: Carnitine supplementation: effect on muscle carnitine and glycogen content during exercise. Med Sci Sports Exerc 1994; 26(9):1122–1129
28. Teman AJ, Hainline B: Eosinophilia-myalgia syndrome. Phys Sportsmed 1991; 19(2):81–86
29. Segura R, Ventura JL: Effect of L-tryptophan supplementation on exercise performance. Int J Sports Med 1988; 9(5):301–305
30. Seltzer S, Stoch R, Marcus R, et al: Alterations of human pain thresholds by nutritional manipulation of L-tryptophan supplementation. Pain 1982;13(4):385–393
31. Stensrud T, Ingjer F, Holm H, et al: L-tryptophan supplementation does not improve running performance. Int J Sports Med 1992;13(6):481–485
32. Gatnau R, Zimmerman DR, Nissen SL, et al: Effect of excess dietary leucine and leucine catabolites on growth and immune response in weanling pigs. J Animal Sci 1995;73(1):159–165
33. Nissen SL, Fuller JC, Sell J, et al: The effect of b-hydroxy b-methylbutyrate on growth, mortality, and carcass qualities of broiler chickens. Poultry Sci 1994; 73(1): 137–155
34. Nissen SL, Morrical D, Fuller JC: The effects of the leucine catabolite β-hydroxy β-methylbutyrate on the growth and health of growing lambs. J Animal Sci 1992; 77(suppl 1):243
35. Ostaszewski P, Kostiuk S, Balasinska B, et al: The effect of the leucine metabolite β-hydroxy β-methylbutyrate (HMB) on muscle protein synthesis and protein breakdown in chick and rat muscle. J Animal Sci 1996;74(suppl):138

36. Van Koevering MT, Dolezal HG, Gill DR, et al: Effects of β-hydroxy β-methylbutyrate on performance and carcass quality of feedlot steers. J Anim Sci 1994;72(8): 1927–1935
37. Nissen SL, Sharp R, Ray M, et al: The effect of the leucine metabolite beta-hydroxy beta-methylbutyrate on muscle metabolism during resistance-exercise training. J Appl Physiol 1996;81(5):2095–2104
38. Nissen SL, Panton J, Wilhelm R, et al: The effect of beta-hydroxy beta-methylbutyrate (HMB) supplementation on strength and body composition of trained and untrained males undergoing intense resistance training. FASEB J 1996;10(3): A287
39. Hardman JG, Limdird LE (eds): Goodman and Gillman's The Pharmacologic Basis of Therapeutics, ed 9. New York City, McGraw-Hill, 1996, p 1413
40. Morales AJ, Nolan JJ, Nelson JC, et al: Effects of replacement dose dehydroepiandrosterone in men and women of advancing age. J Clin Endocrinol Metab 1994; 78(6):1360–1367
41. Yen SS, Morales AJ, Khorram O: Replacement of DHEA in aging men and women: potential remedial effects. Ann NY Acad Sci 1995;774(Dec 29):128–142
42. Abramowicz M (ed): Dehydroepiandrosterone (DHEA). The Medical Letter On Drugs and Therapeutics 1996;38(985):91–92
43. Abramowicz M (ed): Melatonin. The Medical Letter On Drugs and Therapeutics 1995;37(962):111–112
44. Benson MT (ed): NCAA Sports Medicine Handbook 1994–95, ed 7. Overland Park, Kansas, National Collegiate Athletic Association, 1994, p 30

---

Dr. Armsey is a clinical instructor and sports medicine fellow, and Dr. Green is a clinical associate professor in the Department of Family Medicine at the University of California, Los Angeles, Medical Center. Address correspondence to Gary A. Green, MD, University of California, Los Angeles, Medical Center, Box 951683, Los Angeles, CA 90095-1683; e-mail to *ggreen@fammed.medsch.ucla. edu.*

---

# Does the Supplement You Buy Contain What Its Label Says?

*Lab analyses show that labels often overstate the amount of active ingredient in a pill*

IMAGINE PURCHASING a bottle of *Ginkgo biloba* pills that claims to be able to help forestall memory loss but doesn't contain the amount of the active ingredient stated on the label. Or buying a glucosamine or chondroitin supplement to mitigate the pain of osteoarthritis, the degenerative joint disease suffered by millions of Americans, that also doesn't have what its label promises? Or coming across a similar gap between label claims and actual ingredients for SAMe, purported to combat depression.

It happens far more often than consumers realize, according to findings by a new company called ConsumerLab.com, which has embarked on a mission to find out whether the supplements you buy contain what their labels say they do. Some of the independent company's findings are dismaying, to say the least.

For instance, **ConsumerLab.com purchased some 30 leading brands of supplements containing ginkgo and, upon laboratory analysis, found that nearly one in four did not not have expected levels of the chemicals believed to be responsible for the herb's salutory effects.**

It was an even worse scenario for supplements of glucosamine and chondroitin. The company bought 25 brands of glucosamine, chondroitin, and combined glucosamine/chondroitin products and found that among the combination pills, nearly half did not contain stated amounts. Nearly a third failed overall. When it came to SAMe, six out of 13 products sent for laboratory analysis did not have the amount of SAMe stated on the label.

Deciding whether to take a particular supplement can be tricky enough in itself. The difficulty in making a decision becomes particularly heightened when the supplement contains herbs or other substances for which the evidence of benefit looks intriguing but remains inconclusive. For example, while some research suggests that ginkgo helps stave off memory loss, the evidence is quite preliminary; researchers are divided on the herb's efficacy. And even if it does help, it's not appropriate for all people. Ditto for glucosamine, chondroitin, and SAMe. Add in the uncertainty of whether the supplement even contains what it claims to contain, and making a decision becomes stickier still. How do you decide whether to plunk down $15 to $30 on a bottle of ginkgo pills that may be better spent on dinner out, or a movie, or simply not spent at all?

Chalk up the gap between label claims and actual contents to the fact that the supplement industry goes largely unregulated. Even though a number of supplements are taken like drugs, they are not required to submit to the rigorous testing that a drug must go through before the Food and Drug Administration allows it on the market. It's all too easy for a company to put some pills in a bottle, label the pills however it wants, and charge a premium for them.

Not that the regulatory laxness appears to be giving people much pause. Americans now spend an estimated $14 billion a year on dietary supplements, nearly twice the amount they were spending just 6 years ago.

But ConsumerLab.com hopes to help people become more informed consumers by listing on its website (www.consumerlab.com) those supplements it has tested which "pass," meaning the contents in the product match the amount stated on the label. We list the company's passes for ginkgo, glucosamine, chondroitin, and SAMe on the following pages.

Note, however, that **even if a product contains the amount of active ingredient it claims to, that doesn't mean there are no contaminants in the pills.** For example, herbs, which are plant extracts, have many chemicals besides the active ingredient, and they may or may not be harmful.

Having a specified amount of the active ingredient also doesn't mean that the pills dissolve, which is necessary for the ingredient to be absorbed into the bloodstream rather than simply sink like a stone through the GI tract and pass from the body intact. That's a whole other area that remains to be tested.

Furthermore, as stated above, it's not at all clear that any of these supplements actually do what they are purported to do. None are proven remedies (we will explain just how far along the research is for each). But in spite of the uncertainties, at least the "passes" in terms of supple-

## Ginkgo Products that Meet Their Content Claims*

| | Manufacturer and/or Distributor |
|---|---|
| Acuity Plus (40 milligrams per caplet) | Shaklee |
| Centrum Herbals, Standardized Ginkgo Biloba Natural Dietary Supplement (60 milligrams per capsule) | Whitehall-Robins Healthcare |
| Country Life, Herbal Formula, Ginkgo Biloba Extract (60 milligrams per capsule) | Country Life |
| CVS, Premium Quality Herbs, Ginkgo Biloba Standardized Extract (120 milligrams per caplet) | Distributed by CVS |
| Ginkai, Ginkgo Biloba (50 milligrams per tablet) | Lichtwer Pharma |
| Ginkgo Biloba Plus with Aged Garlic Extract (40 milligrams per capsule) | Wakunaga of America |
| Ginkgo Biloba and DHA (53.3 milligrams per softgel) | Nutrilite (Amway) |
| Ginkgo-go, Triple Strength Formula (120 milligrams per caplet) | Wakunaga Consumer Products |
| Ginkgold (60 milligrams per tablet) | Nature's Way |
| Gingolidin, Ginkgo Biloba Standardized Extract (40 milligrams per capsule) | PhytoPharmica |
| Ginkoba, Mental Performance Dietary Supplement (40 milligrams per tablet) | Pharmaton Natural Health Products |
| Enzymatic Therapy, Ginkgo Biloba 24% (40 milligrams per capsule) | Enzymatic Therapy |
| GNC, Natural Brand (50 milligrams per tablet) | GNC |
| MotherNature.com, Standardized Ginkgo Biloba Extract (60 milligrams per capsule) | Manufactured for MotherNature.com |
| Natrol (60 milligrams per capsule) | Natrol |
| Nature Made Herbs (40 milligrams per softgel) | Nature Made Nutritional Products |
| Nature's Bounty, Herbal Harvest (30 milligrams per tablet) | Nature's Bounty |
| Nature's Resource, Premium Herb, Extra Strength (60 milligrams per capsule) | Distributed by N.R. Products |
| One-A-Day, Memory and Concentration (60 milligrams per tablet) | Bayer |
| Puritan's Pride, Inspired by Nature, Ginkgo Biloba Standardized Extract (60 milligrams per tablet) | NBTY |
| Quanterra, Mental Sharpness (60 milligrams per tablet) | Warner-Lambert |
| Spring Valley, Ginkgo Biloba Dietary Supplement, Standardized Extract (40 milligrams per tablet) | Leiner Health Products/Distributed by Wal-Mart |
| Sundown Herbals, For Mental Alertness (20 milligrams per capsule) | Distributed by Sundown Vitamins |
| Thompson (60 milligrams per capsule) | Thompson Nutritional Products |
| Walgreens, Ginkgo Biloba Standardized Extract (60 milligrams per tablet) | Distributed by Walgreens |
| Your Life, Ginkgo Biloba Standardized Herbal Extract (60 milligrams per caplet) | Leiner Health Products |

*The ginkgo products that "passed" also met ConsumerLab.com's standards for quality and proportions of ingredients.

ment contents give consumers who choose to take these pills a place to start.

## *Ginkgo biloba* supplements

*Caveats to keep in mind*

Packages of ginkgo tablets claim that the herb "improves memory and concentration and enhances mental health." Such claims are a stretch, to say the least. Everyone experiences memory loss from time to time, or has difficulty focusing, but ginkgo is not going to help most people avoid such lapses. So who might benefit by taking it?

The group for which studies have shown that ginkgo improves short-term memory and concentration consists of people with impaired blood flow to the brain. As people age, it becomes more common for arteries leading to the brain to become clogged, or narrowed. That results in decreased blood flow to the brain cells. The potential upshot: short-term memory loss and difficulty concentrating. Ginkgo appears to mitigate the problem by acting as a blood thinner, which in turn improves circulation.

How do you know if you have decreased blood flow to the brain? You don't, unless you've seen a physician who has diagnosed you with blocked or narrowed arteries. On the other hand, scientists such as Varro Tyler, PhD, renowned researcher of botanical products and professor emeritus at the Purdue University School of Pharmacy, believe ginkgo at least won't cause you any harm if you want to give it a try. The usual recommended dose is 120 milligrams a day, given either in three 40-milligram tablets or two 60-milligram ones.

If you take the recommended dose for a month or so and don't see any improvement, you're probably not going to and should stop taking the herb. Furthermore, if you are experiencing a truly significant loss in recall or ability to concentrate, you should make an appointment to see a doctor. You may have a disorder such as a vitamin $B_{12}$ deficiency, which, if not treated early enough, can cause essentially irreversible damage to nerves that affect your brain functioning.

Following are the ginkgo supplements that, upon laboratory analysis, passed muster with ConsumerLab.com for having the amount of active ingredient stated on the label. The ginkgo extract used in most clinical trials contained specific types (and proportions) of naturally occurring chemicals called flavonal glycosides and terpene lactones, and that's what the company was looking for.

Note that there are certain people who should not take *any* ginkgo. This group consists of anyone taking blood thinning agents such as aspirin, vitamin E, garlic, ginger, the prescription drug warfarin (Coumadin), or any other drug that lists thinning of the blood as a possible side effect. Since ginkgo itself is a blood thinner, taking it with another one could put you at risk for excessive bleeding in the case of, say, an accident or hemorrhagic stroke—uncontrolled bleeding in the brain.

## Glucosamine and Chondroitin Supplements

*Worth getting all out of joint for?*

Some 21 million Americans suffer from the stiff knees, aching hips, and other swollen joints of osteoarthritis, the most common form of joint disease. And the majority of them either are using or have used glucosamine, according to the medical director of the Arthritis Foundation. Many use chondroitin as well. Should they?

The evidence is certainly intriguing. A study of Navy SEALs published last year showed that 8 weeks of therapy with a supplement that contained both glucosamine and chondroitin relieved symptoms of knee arthritis in half of a small group of men who were experiencing chronic pain. And in a look back at 13 research projects that examined the effects of the two substances, researchers at Boston University found that they appeared to provide substantial benefits.

It makes intuitive sense. Both glucosamine and chondroitin are found in cartilage, the protective coating that covers the ends of the two bones in a joint. When the cartilage wears down, the pain begins. But glucosamine is believed to stimulate cartilage "building blocks" called glycosaminoglycans and proteoglycans, and chondroitin is part of a protein that lends cartilage its "springy" quality.

The problem is that while taking the two substances seems to make sense for blocking joint wear and tear, the evidence, even though there's a fair amount of it at this point, is just too sketchy. All the studies conducted thus far are either quite small or of uneven quality. Methodological problems range from a failure to define a "case" of arthritis to lack of an objective way to judge relief from pain.

Thus, the medical community as a whole doesn't recommend it. But arthritis doctors are not discouraging patients who want to try it on their own. Some pointers for people who want to give either or both of the substances a go and are willing to spend the requisite $30 to $45 a month—or more:

- The two substances, if they help at all, probably help relieve only mild to moderate cases of osteoarthritis.
- Shoot for 1,500 milligrams a day of glucosamine; 1,200 milligrams of chondroitin. Those are the doses that most research studies have used.
- Try the supplement(s) for 2 to 4 months. If you don't get relief in that time, you're probably not going to.
- Anyone with diabetes who's taking glucosamine should have his or her blood sugar checked regularly. There's some suspicion from animal studies that it could raise insulin resistance and thereby obstruct the uptake of sugar from the bloodstream.
- People on anticoagulants, including aspirin, should have blood clotting times checked when taking chondroitin. It may alter blood clotting activity.

Following are ConsumerLab.com's glucosamine and chondroitin "passes."

## SAMe Supplements

*An alternative to Prozac?*
*An alternative to nonsteroidal anti-inflammatory drugs?*

In Italy, SAMe (pronounced "Sammy") reportedly outsells Prozac for the treatment of depression. It also appears to reduce pain in people with osteoarthritis. Italian scientists made that discovery somewhat serendipitously more than 20 years ago. When they were testing SAMe in humans who were suffering from depression, they happened to discover that those subjects with osteoarthritis were able to walk with more ease.

How does SAMe, which is short for the chemical compound S-adenosyl-methionine, work? Well, researchers aren't sure. It is known that SAMe is produced biochem-

## Glucosamine and Chondroitin Products that Meet Their Content Claims

| | Manufacturer and/or Distributor |
|---|---|
| CosaminDS Double Strength (500 milligrams glucosamine, 400 milligrams chondroitin per capsule) | Nutramax Laboratories |
| Glucosamine/Chondroitin Double Strength (500 milligrams glucosamine, 400 milligrams chondroitin per capsule) | Walgreens |
| Maximum Strength Glucosamine/Chondroitin (500 milligrams glucosamine, 400 milligrams chondroitin per tablet) | CVS |
| Nature's Bounty Chondroitin Complex with Glucosamine (250 milligrams glucosamine, 200 milligrams chondroitin per capsule) | Nature's Bounty |
| Osteo-Bi-Flex Glucosamine/Chondroitin (250 milligrams glucosamine, 200 milligrams chondroitin per tablet) | Sundown |
| Pain Free (also sold as Move Free) Joint Support Formula (500 milligrams glucosamine, 400 milligrams chondroitin per caplet) | Schiff |
| Spring Valley Glucosamine/Chondroitin Maximum Strength (500 milligrams glucosamine, 400 milligrams chondroitin per tablet) | Wal-Mart (manufactured by Park-Taft Laboratories) |
| **Glucosamine Only** | |
| Aflexa Glucosamine (340 milligrams free glucosamine per tablet equiv. to approx. 500 milligrams glucosamine sulfate) | McNeil Consumer Healthcare |
| Enzymatic Therapy GS (500 milligrams per capsule) | Enzymatic Therapy |
| Fields of Nature Natural Joint Nutrient (500 milligrams per capsule) | Fields of Nature |
| GNC Glucosamine (600 milligrams per capsule) | GNC |
| Natrol Glucosamine Complex (500 milligrams per capsule) | Natrol |
| Nature Made Glucosamine (500 milligrams per tablet) | Nature Made |
| Now Glucosamine Sulfate Complex (750 milligrams glucosamine per tablet) | Nature Made |
| Nutrilite Glucosamine with Boswellia (375 milligrams per caplet) | Amway |
| One-A-Day Joint Health (with vitamins C & E—500 milligrams glucosamine per tablet) | Bayer |
| OsteoJoint Triple Formula for Healthy Joints (500 milligrams per caplet) | Your Life |
| Osteokinetics (467 milligrams glucosamine per capsule) | Shaklee (Formulas) |
| PhytoPharmica (500 milligrams per capsule) | Phytopharmica |
| Puritan's Pride (1,000 milligrams per capsule) | Puritan's Pride |
| Spring Valley Glucosamine Complex (500 milligrams per tablet) | Wal-Mart (Manufactured by Leiner Health Products) |
| **Chondroitin Only** | |
| *None passed product review. ConsumerLab.com says one possible explanation is "economic-chondroitin costs manufacturers approximately four times as such glucosamine."* | |

ically in all humans to help perform more than 100 functions in the body—everything from preservation of bone strength to proper DNA replication.

In the case of depression, it's speculated that the substance somehow affects brain levels of the neurotransmitters noradrenaline, serotonin, and possibly dopamine. An imbalance of those substances is believed to be involved in depression's origins.

When it comes to osteoarthritis, studies suggest that SAMe not only has pain-relieving and anti-inflammatory properties but may also actually help rebuild eroded cartilage lining the joints. It's thought to accomplish that task by stimulating production of the cartilage materials called proteoglycans.

Making SAMe seem more attractive still is the fact that it appears to come with few, if any, side effects. For instance, unlike traditional drugs to treat depression, such as Prozac or Paxil, it isn't believed to cause sexual dysfunction, weight gain, or sleep disturbances. And unlike nonsteroidal anti-inflammatory drugs, or NSAIDs, that are often used to dull osteoarthritis pain, it apparently doesn't contribute to gastric bleeding or ulcers.

But the final verdict is far from in. For instance, while there have been quite a few studies on SAMe, many in-

**Companies that pass ConsumerLab.com's test for content may purchase from the firm the right to place this seal on their product. Keep in mind, however, that the seal does not guarantee that the supplement is free from contaminants or that it dissolves in your GI tract, which is necessary for proper absorption.**

cluded only small numbers of people, lasted only for a short time, or were not double-blinded, meaning that either the subjects or the researchers knew who was getting SAMe and who was getting the placebo, or dummy pill. And that can impact results. In addition, because of the short-term nature of the research, nobody knows whether SAMe could become toxic to the body over time.

Furthermore, SAMe is thought to be dangerous for those with severe or bipolar depression (commonly referred to as manic-depression). It's suspected to make things worse for people with obsessive-compulsive or addictive tendencies, too. And SAMe could be a problem for people with a family history of heart disease, as it can potentially trigger coronary problems.

Even if you're not in one of the at-risk groups, there's the question of just how much SAMe to take. Some research has suggested that 400 milligrams a day is the right amount for treating mild to moderate depression, while up to 1,600 milligrams might be necessary to quell osteoarthritis pain.

However much you take, make sure the supplement is enterically coated. That ensures that it will remain intact in the stomach and not dissolve until it reaches the small intestine, the organ from which SAMe can be absorbed by the bloodstream. To improve absorption even more, some researchers recommend taking SAMe on an empty stomach.

ConsumerLab.com points out that the recommendation for people who are starting a SAMe regimen is to begin with a dose of 200 to 400 milligrams the first day and increase it thereafter. Daily amounts should not be taken all at once but in divided doses, such as 200 milligrams twice a day for a total of 400 milligrams, or 200 milligrams four times a day for a total of 800. Noticeable improvements can take from a few days to 4 or 5 weeks.

Whatever you do, don't take SAMe without a doctor's supervision. While it's a supplement in the U.S., it's considered a drug in several other countries and should be treated as such.

### SAMe Products that Meet Their Content Claims

| | Manufacturer and/or Distributor |
|---|---|
| GNC SAMe (100 milligrams) | Distributed by GNC |
| Natrol SAMe (200 milligrams) | Distributed by Natrol |
| Nature Made SAMe (200 milligrams) | Nature Made |
| NutraLife SAMe (200 milligrams) | NutraLife Health Products |
| Puritan's Pride Inspired by Nature SAMe (200 milligrams) | Manufactured for Puritan's Pride |
| Source Naturals SAMe (200 milligrams) | Source Naturals |
| The Vitamin Shoppe SAMe (200 milligrams) | The Vitamin Shoppe |
| TwinLab SAMe (200 milligrams) | Twin Laboratories |

Finally, be very skeptical when choosing a SAMe supplement not on the list. Roughly half of the 13 brands tested by ConsumerLab.com failed to contain the amount of the substance stated on the label. Among the failures, the amount of SAMe was, on average, less than half of the stated amount. In one product, the SAMe present was below detectable levels (less than 5 percent of the labeled amount).

# Bar Exam

## Energy Bars Flunk

By Bonnie Liebman & David Schardt

"For $50,000 or $100,000 you can be in the bar business," Brian Maxwell, president and CEO of PowerBar Inc, told *Food Processing* magazine last year.

That's one reason that supermarket, health food store, and drug store shelves carry a burgeoning selection of bars. (You can often find them at the front counter, with the other "impulse" items.) Sales of energy bars rose more than 50 percent last year, to $114 million, according to the trade publication *Supermarket News*. And energy is just the beginning.

To create a niche for a new bar in a dog-eat-dog marketplace, each manufacturer needs a new twist. Names like Ironman and Steel sell, but they're no longer enough. Viactiv and Luna bars are targeted at women. Protein Revolution, Pure Protein, and Perfect Solid Protein push the nutrient that muscles are made of. GeniSoy and Soy Sensations stake a claim on soy. Clif and Boulder go the natural route. And Think! promises to boost your brain power with herbs and vitamins.

This is one hot market. Why else would Nestlé have bought PowerBar, Kraft have bought Balance Bar, and Rexall Sundown have bought Met-Rx? So when it comes to advertising, chances are we ain't seen nothin' yet.

Do you need any of this stuff?. This month we take a look at some of the biggest and boldest bars around. But first, a short course on the "energy" scam.

### Energy for Sale

Luckily for food companies out to make a buck, "energy" has a double meaning. To most people, a food that supplies "energy" makes you feel energetic. But to scientists and the literal-minded regulators at the Food and Drug Administration, "energy" means calories.

**To the folks who are in charge of keeping food labels honest, any food with calories is an "energy" food.**

That's right. To the folks who are in charge of keeping food labels honest, any food with calories is an "energy" food.

Never mind that no more than one in a million consumers would ever guess that, especially when ads for energy bars show people running, leaping, and otherwise looking energetic. Never mind that a simple disclosure on labels could explain to consumers that an "energy food" means simply that it "contains calories." Years after the Center for Science in the Public Interest (publisher of *Nutrition Action*) petitioned the FDA to require that kind of disclosure, the agency still hasn't lifted a finger to let consumers in on the energy secret.

Taking advantage of this irresistible loophole, companies have hit on a clever marketing scheme. While few people compete in long-distance athletic events, millions slog through a demanding day with no time for lunch. Marketing "energy" to the average office worker, stay-at-home mom, or just about anyone was a stroke of genius that's paying off big-time... but not necessarily for you.

"I caution people not to replace wholesome food with energy bars," says Elizabeth Applegate, a nutritionist and exercise expert at the University of California at Davis. "Manufacturers don't put everything you need from food into them. We don't even know everything in food that *should* be put in them."

Applegate, who consults for the food industry, does advise some people to eat energy bars, but not because they make the eater more energetic. "If you're going to grab a candy bar or a box of cookies or two bags of M&Ms from a vending machine for lunch, it's better to have an energy bar," she says.

Why? "Most bars are low in saturated and hydrogenated [*trans*] fat. And they can have as much as five grams of fiber and a handful of vitamins and minerals, just like a bowl of breakfast cereal.

"But if the wrappers are starting to accumulate on the floor of your car, back off," she adds. "You're better off with real food, like a sandwich on whole-grain bread, fresh fruit, and some baby carrots."

## High-Carb Bars

"Don't bonk," say ads for PowerBars.

The original PowerBar, launched in 1987, was designed to keep athletes from bonking—that is, running out of gas in the middle of a marathon or other long-distance event. The high-carbohydrate, low-fat bars consist largely of high-fructose corn syrup and grape and pear juice concentrate, with added vitamins and minerals. They have a taffy-like texture that seems more functional than flavorful.

### THE BOTTOM LINE

- The word "energy" on any label simply means that the food supplies calories, not that eating it will make you more energetic.
- Eating healthy, whole foods like fruits and vegetables beats eating energy bars because foods contain phytochemicals and other constituents that aren't added to bars.

It didn't take long for competitors (and PowerBar itself) to come up with energy bars that taste more like food than fuel. Clif, Boulder, PowerBar Harvest, and others started adding real food—like oats, nuts, and fruit—to their recipes. The final products taste like something between cookies and granola bars. But judging by the little research that's been done, there's nothing special—other than convenience—about getting your carbs in a compact wrapper.

David Pearson and colleagues at Ball State University in Muncie, Indiana, conducted one of the few studies on high-carb bars, though so far only a summary has been published.[1] First, nine trained cyclists rode for an hour to lower the levels of stored carbohydrate (glycogen) in their muscles. The next day, they rode for another half-hour and then sprinted.

After a one-hour rest, the cyclists were randomly assigned to eat 1,000 calories' worth of PowerBars, Tiger's Milk bars, or cinnamon-raisin bagels over a four-hour period. An hour later, they rode for another hour while the researchers measured their energy output and blood sugar levels.

"The bagels resulted in the same aerobic performance as the energy bars," says Pearson, whose study was funded by Nabisco. "There's no magic to the bars. As long as you're getting the same number of calories and carbs in each food, there's no advantage to eating energy bars, and they're much more expensive."

Of course, most people don't even need carbs when they exercise. "High-calorie, carbohydrate-dense bars are really only for athletes doing long-term exercise," Pearson explains. "People think, 'if top-grade athletes eat these bars, I need them for my workout." That's a misconception."

Pearson's hard-pedaling cyclists performed better with bars (or food) than with just water because they needed carbs. But unless you're running, cycling, cross-country skiing, or doing some other aerobic activity continuously for more than an hour at a stretch, you don't need a quick carb fix.

"The bar wouldn't empty out of your stomach before the event is over," says Pearson. What's more, he adds, "most people burn off fewer calories in the workout than they get from the bar."

So the next time you run a marathon, you may find it easier to pack some high-carb bars instead of bagels. (Some experts recommend taking one bite every ten minutes until the bar is gone.) But if you're just looking for a snack or pick-me-up after a game of tennis, save your money.

## 40-30-30 Bars

With the high-carb field sewn up, competitors like Balance, Ironman, and ProZone entered the market with bars that have a 40-30-30 ratio of carbohydrates to protein to fat, as touted by the best-selling diet book *The Zone*.

"The companies that market these bars have done a fabulous job of getting people to think that one bar makes their whole diet 40-30-30," notes Applegate.

Reaching 40-30-30 in a bar isn't difficult. It simply means replacing some of the high-fructose corn syrup with protein (from whey or soy protein isolate or casein) and with fat (often palm kernel oil).

Palm kernel oil is popular because it's saturated enough to stay solid at room temperature, so the coating doesn't smear all over your hands. Whether it smears all over the walls of your arteries is another question. Palm kernel oil is twice as saturated as lard.

It's not clear who is supposed to be eating 40-30-30 bars. And that's one secret to their success.

A bar that isn't for anyone in particular is for everyone. They're for athletes (real or would-be) who want to stay "in the zone." (Long before —and one reason why—Barry Sears' diet book became a best seller, that term applied to athletes at the top of their game.) They're for people who want to lose weight. And they're for people who want the "sustained energy" that the bars promise in order to get them through the day.

Of course, no published studies show how 40-30-30 bars like Balance or Ironman affect performance or weight loss for any of those groups. One small study concluded that an Ironman bar didn't raise blood sugar levels as rapidly or as much as a (high-carbohydrate) PowerBar.[2] Of course, a quick rise in blood sugar is precisely what an athlete wants.

"A 40-30-30 bar doesn't have enough carbohydrate for an athlete," says Ball State's Pearson. "But if you're sitting behind a desk and you want a bar instead of a Big Mac for lunch, you're better off with a 40-30-30 bar than a high-carbohydrate bar, because it's closer to what you'd get in a typical American diet."

That's not to say that the highly processed milk and soy protein, high-fructose corn syrup, oils, vitamins, and minerals are anything approaching an ideal food. Missing are the vegetables, beans, low-fat dairy, and other real foods that can cut the risk of cancer, heart disease, and stroke.

"If you're using bars in place of a meal, look for at least 10 to 15 grams of protein," says Applegate. "I also recommend eating at least one real food—like a piece of fresh fruit or some carrots or low-fat cheese sticks—with the bar."

Ads boast that the new Balance Gold bars "taste like a candy bar!" That's because they *are* candy bars... with some extra soy or milk protein and vitamins. Balance Outdoor bars use more natural ingredients, like soy pieces, fruit, and nuts. But watch out.

"You can still get a lot of calories from these bars," says Pearson. The 200-odd calories may not seem like much, but 200 calories in roughly two ounces of food means that bars are calorie-dense.

For a quick snack, you're better off with an apple, a handful of grape tomatoes, or some other fruit or vegetable that fills you up with fewer calories.

## High-Protein Bars

They've got names like Ultimate Lo Carb, Met-Rx Protein Plus, Promax, Protein Fuel, Protein Revolution, Pure Protein, Solid Protein, and Steel. They're often bigger in calories (250 or so) and size (as much as three ounces), for people who want bigger muscles. Body builders—not dieters, soccer moms, or busy Yuppies—are the typical target audience.

Do they work?

"Protein needs increase with exercise, whether it's strength training or endurance," says Applegate. But that doesn't mean that people need protein bars.

"You can easily get the protein from food," she explains. "The bars are more expensive and it's just food protein they put in there. People are surprised to hear that. They think, 'it's exactly what my muscles need.'"

Few companies have studies to show that their "proprietary blends" of milk or soy protein and other ingredients like "growth factors" and glutamine trump the competition.

Take Met-Rx's blend, which is called metamyosyn. Two published studies have tested its impact in healthy people in exercise programs. One found that overweight policemen gained more muscle mass and strength on metamyosyn than they did on another protein supplement, but the measurements were outdated and inexact.[3]

"The results of this study are interesting, but it needs to be repeated using more sophisticated methods of body composition assessment before definitive conclusions can be made," says Rick Kreider of the University of Memphis.

The other study, using more exact measures, found that Met-Rx was no better than a high-carbohydrate supplement at increasing muscle mass and strength in college football players.[4]

## Supplement Bars

"Just taste these delicious, satisfying *new* energy sources for women," say ads for Viactiv. "Boost bars are the ideal snack and help give you the energy to do the things you want to do," says the company's Web site.

Yes, you do get calories from these bars. You also get the same vitamins and minerals that you'd find in a vitamin pill. The main difference is that someone might take a pill along with a bowl of lentil soup, a plate of stir-fried vegetables and chicken, or a fruit salad. But Mead Johnson's clever marketing for its Boost bars persuades people—especially women—to eat a fortified candy bar *instead* of real food... and to think they're healthier and more energetic as a result.

Soy protein bars like GeniSoy and Soy Sensations may help lower your cholesterol. But it's too early to say if their phytoestrogens can cut the risk of breast and prostate cancers. In fact, some preliminary studies suggest that consuming more soy may *raise* the risk of breast cancer in some people (see *Nutrition Action*, Sept. 1999 and Jan./Feb. 2000).

And soy isn't the only new twist. Think! bars sell nothing less than brain power. As if the name weren't enough, the labels and the company Web site (www.thinkproducts.com) note that the bars have "ginkgo biloba to stay sharp" and other "mind-enhancing" ingredients, which have an "impact on brain and nerve cell function." But don't expect the company to supply evidence to back up its claims.

"We're not claiming it helps you think," insists Garrett Jennings, the inventor of Think!, the "Food for Thought" bar. Think! bars contain Jennings's secret blend of amino acids, fatty acids, and herbs.

Good published studies show no significant impact on thought or memory in people given the amounts of ginkgo or ginseng (60 mg each) or the other ingredients in Think! Bars. (A recent study found that 160 mg of a proprietary blend of ginseng and ginkgo modestly improved the "quality' of memory in middle-aged men and women, but until it's published, we can't draw any conclusions.)

"But if somebody feels great after a Think! bar," asks Jennings, "who cares if that's just a placebo effect?"

---

*The information for this article was compiled by Jackie Adriano.*

## Notes

1. *J. Strength Cond. 10*:1996.
2. *J. Amer. Diet. Assoc. 100*: 97, 2000.
3. *Ann. Nutr. Metab. 44*: 21, 2000.
4. *J. Exercise Physiol. (online) 2*: 24, 1999.

BRAND-NAME RATING

# Raising the Bar

We had no Best Bites because most people—endurance athletes aside—are better off eating healthy whole foods than energy bars. Since some people are going to rely on bars anyway, we gave Better Bites to those with no more than two grams of saturated fat and at least three grams of fiber. The sat-fat limit means the bars won't threaten your blood vessels, and the fiber usually means the bars have some oats, nuts, fruit, or other real food. Within each category, bars are ranked from best to worst (least to most saturated fat, then most to least fiber, then least to most calories).

| | **High-Carbohydrate Bars** *(weight of one bar, in ounces)* | **Calories** | **Total Fat** *(grams)* | **Saturated Fat** *(grams)* | **Protein** *(grams)* | **Carbohydrates** *(grams)* | **Fiber** *(grams)* |
|---|---|---|---|---|---|---|---|
| ✔ | ProZone Cashew Almond Crunch *(1.8)* | 190 | 5 | 1 | 7 | 29 | 5 |
| ✔ | Nutra-Fig Cheetah *(2.3)*[1] | 200 | 2 | 1 | 3 | 44 | 5 |
| ✔ | You Are What You Eat *(2.0)*[1*] | 200 | 4 | 1 | 4 | 40 | 5 |
| ✔ | Clif *(2.4)*[1*] | 230 | 4 | 1 | 10 | 41 | 5 |
| ✔ | Boulder *(2.5)*[1] | 210 | 4 | 1 | 10 | 42 | 4 |
| ✔ | PowerBar Harvest *(2.3)*[1*] | 240 | 4 | 1 | 7 | 45 | 4 |
| ✔ | PowerBar Performance *(2.3)*[1*] | 230 | 2 | 1 | 10 | 45 | 3 |
| | Tiger's Milk *(1.2)*[1*] | 140 | 4 | 1 | 5 | 22 | 1 |
| ✔ | PowerBar Essentials, except Chocolate Raspberry Truffle *(1.9)*[1*] | 180 | 4 | 2 | 10 | 28 | 3 |
| | PowerBar Essentials Chocolate Raspberry Truffle *(1.9)*[*] | 180 | 4 | 3 | 10 | 28 | 3 |

| | **40/30/30 Bars** *(weight of one bar, in ounces)* | **Calories** | **Total Fat** *(grams)* | **Saturated Fat** *(grams)* | **Protein** *(grams)* | **Carbohydrates** *(grams)* | **Fiber** *(grams)* |
|---|---|---|---|---|---|---|---|
| ✔ | Balance Outdoor Honey Almond *(1.8)* | 200 | 6 | 1 | 15 | 21 | 3 |
| | Balance Outdoor Crunchy Peanut *(1.8)* | 200 | 6 | 1 | 15 | 21 | 2 |
| | Balance Outdoor Nut Berry *(1.8)* | 200 | 6 | 1 | 15 | 21 | 2 |
| ✔ | Balance Outdoor Chocolate Crisp *(1.8)* | 200 | 6 | 2 | 15 | 21 | 3 |
| | TwinLab Ironman *(2.0)*[1*] | 230 | 7 | 2 | 16 | 24 | 0 |
| | Balance *(1.8)*[1*] | 200 | 6 | 3 | 14 | 22 | 1 |
| | Balance + *(1.8)*[1*] | 200 | 6 | 4 | 14 | 22 | 1 |
| | Balance Gold *(1.8)*[*] | 210 | 7 | 4 | 15 | 23 | 0 |
| | ProZone, except Cashew Almond Crunch *(1.8)*[1] | 190 | 6 | 5 | 14 | 18 | 5 |

| | **High-Protein Bars** *(weight of one bar, in ounces)* | **Calories** | **Total Fat** *(grams)* | **Saturated Fat** *(grams)* | **Protein** *(grams)* | **Carbohydrates** *(grams)* | **Fiber** *(grams)* |
|---|---|---|---|---|---|---|---|
| | Met-RX Natural Krunch *(1.1)*[1*] | 110 | 2 | 1 | 6 | 18 | 0 |
| | Biochem Ultimate Lo Carb *(20.)*[1*] | 240 | 7 | 1 | 22 | 2 | 0 |
| | EAS Myoplex Deluxe *(3.2)*[1*] | 340 | 7 | 2 | 24 | 44 | 1 |
| | Premier Elite *(1.5)*[1] | 150 | 3 | 2 | 18 | 2 | 0 |

*(continued on next page)*

| | | Calories | Total Fat (grams) | Saturated Fat (grams) | Protein (grams) | Carbohydrates (grams) | Fiber (grams) |
|---|---|---|---|---|---|---|---|
| | Protein Revolution *(2.1)*[1*] | 230 | 8 | 2 | 22 | 3 | 0 |
| | PowerBar Protein Plus *(2.8)*[1*] | 290 | 5 | 3 | 24 | 38 | 2 |
| | EAS Myoplex Lite *(2.0)*[1*] | 190 | 4 | 3 | 15 | 27 | 1 |
| | SportPharma Extra Protein *(2.8)*[1*] | 280 | 5 | 3 | 31 | 11 | 1 |
| | TwinLab Protein Fuel *(2.9)*[1*] | 330 | 5 | 3 | 35 | 12 | 1 |
| | Nature's Best Perfect Solid Protein *(2.8)*[1*] | 270 | 5 | 3 | 32 | 11 | 0 |
| | Worldwide Sport Nutrition Pure Protein *(2.8)*[1*] | 280 | 5 | 3 | 33 | 13 | 0 |
| | Biochem Ultimate Protein *(2.8)*[1*] | 290 | 5 | 3 | 31 | 19 | 0 |
| | American Body Building Hi-Protein Steel Bar *(3.0)*[1*] | 330 | 6 | 3 | 16 | 52 | 0 |
| | Nature's Best Perfect Isopure *(2.1)*[1*] | 220 | 6 | 4 | 11 | 36 | 3 |
| | EAS Myoplex HP *(2.3)*[1*] | 250 | 5 | 4 | 20 | 30 | 2 |
| | Premier Protein *(2.5)*[1] | 290 | 8 | 4 | 31 | 14 | 2 |
| | MLO BioProtein *(2.9)*[1*] | 300 | 6 | 4 | 21 | 40 | 2 |
| | Met-RX SourceOne *(2.1)*[1*] | 170 | 5 | 4 | 16 | 20 | 1 |
| | SportPharma Promax *(2.6)*[1*] | 280 | 5 | 4 | 20 | 37 | 1 |
| | EAS Simply Protein *(2.8)*[1*] | 310 | 7 | 4 | 33 | 16 | 1 |
| | Premier Eight *(2.5)*[1] | 270 | 6 | 4 | 31 | 7 | 0 |
| | Think! Protein *(2.3)*[1*] | 270 | 9 | 5 | 22 | 19 | 0 |
| | Met-RX Protein Plus Food Bar *(3.0)*[1*] | 250 | 8 | 6 | 34 | 13 | 0 |
| ***Supplement Bars*** *(weight of one bar, in ounces)* | | | | | | | |
| ✔ | GeniSoy Nature Grains *(2.3)*[1] | 230 | 3 | 0 | 11 | 41 | 3 |
| | Viactiv Energy Fruit Crispy *(1.1)*[1*] | 120 | 2 | 0 | 4 | 21 | 0 |
| ✔ | TwinLab Soy Sensations, except Chocolate Fondue *(1.8)*[1*] | 180 | 5 | 1 | 15 | 23 | 6 |
| ✔ | Odwalla *(2.4)*[1*] | 240 | 4 | 1 | 7 | 48 | 4 |
| ✔ | Think! Chocolate Mocha *(2.0)*[1*] | 210 | 4 | 1 | 9 | 36 | 3 |
| | Ensure *(1.2)*[1*] | 130 | 3 | 1 | 6 | 21 | 2 |
| | Luna *(1.7)*[1*] | 180 | 4 | 2 | 10 | 25 | 2 |
| | Think!, except Chocolate Mocha *(2.0)*[1*] | 220 | 7 | 2 | 10 | 33 | 2 |
| | GeniSoy Soy Protein *(2.2)*[1*] | 220 | 3 | 2 | 14 | 33 | 1 |
| | TwinLab Soy Sensations Choc. Fondue *(1.8)*[*] | 180 | 6 | 3 | 15 | 22 | 5 |
| | Boost *(1.6)*[1*] | 190 | 6 | 4 | 5 | 30 | 1 |

***(continued)***

| | Calories | Total Fat *(grams)* | Saturated Fat *(grams)* | Protein *(grams)* | Carbohydrates *(grams)* | Fiber *(grams)* |
|---|---|---|---|---|---|---|
| Viactiv Hearty Energy *(1.6)*[1*] | 180 | 5 | 4 | 6 | 29 | 0 |
| Think! Divine *(1.9)*[1*] | 210 | 8 | 6 | 6 | 32 | 1 |
| **For Comparison** *(weight of one bar, in ounces)* | | | | | | |
| Quaker Chewy Granola *(1.0)*[1] | 120 | 3 | 1 | 2 | 21 | 1 |
| Kellogg's Nutri-Grain *(1.3)*[1*] | 140 | 3 | 1 | 2 | 27 | 1 |
| Snickers *(2.1)* | 280 | 14 | 5 | 4 | 35 | 1 |
| Hershey's Milk Chocolate *(1.6)* | 230 | 13 | 9 | 3 | 25 | 1 |

**✔ Better Bite. [1]Average of the entire line. *Fortified with vitamins and minerals.**



**SOURCE: MANUFACTURERS.**

From *Nutrition Action Healthletter,* December 2000, pp. 10-13. © 2000 by Center for Science in the Public Interest. Reprinted with permission.

# UNIT 6

# Food Safety

## Unit Selections



## Key Points to Consider

- What are the main causes of food-borne diseases?
- What are some of the best methods for avoiding or minimizing disease from contaminated foods?

**Links: www.dushkin.com/online/**
These sites are annotated in the World Wide Web pages.

**American Council on Science and Health (ACSH)**
*http://www.acsh.org/food/*

**Centers for Disease Control and Prevention**
*http://www.cdc.gov*

**FDA Center for Food Safety and Applied Nutrition**
*http://vm.cfsan.fda.gov*

**Food Safety Information from North Carolina**
*http://www.ces.ncsu.edu/depts/foodsci/agentinfo/*

**Food Safety Project (FSP)**
*http://www.extention.iastate.edu/foodsafety/*

**Gateway to Government Food Safety Information**
*http://www.foodsafety.gov*

**National Food Safety Programs**
*http://vm.cfsan.fda.gov/~dms/fs-toc.html*

**USDA Food Safety and Inspection Service**
*http://www.fsis.usda.gov*

Food-borne disease constitutes an important public health problem in the United States. The U.S. Centers for Disease Control has reports 76 million cases of food-borne illness each year out of which 5,000 end in death. The annual cost of losses in productivity ranges from $20 to $40 billion. Food-borne disease results primarily from microbial contamination but also from naturally occurring toxicants, environmental contaminants, pesticide residues, and food additives.

The first Food and Drug Act was passed in 1906 and was followed by tighter control on the use of additives that might be carcinogenic. In 1958, the Delaney Clause was passed and a list of additives that were considered as safe for human consumption (GRAS list) was developed. The Food and Drug Administration (FDA) controls and regulates procedures dealing with food safety, including food service and production. The FDA has established rules (Hazard Analysis and Critical Control Points) to improve safety control and to monitor the production of seafood, meat, and poultry. Even though there have been outbreaks of food poisoning traced to errors at the commercial processing stage, the culprit is usually mishandling of food at home, in a food service establishment, or other noncommercial setting. Surveys show that over 95 percent of the time people do not follow proper sanitation methods when working with food. The U.S. government, therefore, launched the Food Safety Initiative to minimize food-borne disease and to educate the public about safe food handling practices. Additionally, for the first time this year, the newest edition of the U.S. government's *Dietary Guidelines* includes guidelines for food safety.

Some of the articles in Unit 6 review the seven highly effective habits that help cooks decrease food-borne illness as established by the Food Safety and Inspection Service (FSIS) and the U.S. Department of Agriculture (USDA). The most common food-borne illnesses come from bacterial infestation of food such as *Salmonella, Campylobacter,* hemorrhagic *E. coli* and *Listeria. Staphylococcus* and *Clostridium botulinum* produce toxins that cause illness. Outbreaks of food poisoning can be very serious and many times even deadly. Pasteurization and irradiation by the processing industry and using preventive techniques at home, such as avoiding cross-contamination, can prevent and contain these outbreaks. Still, people adopt many unsafe practices when it comes to preparing and storing food. The American Dietetic Association's (ADA) Nutrition Hot Line is staffed by registered dietitians who will provide you with reliable, timely, and objective answers to your questions.

The recent scare in Europe about "mad cow" disease, which killed over 100 people during the last few years, has increased awareness of the disease in the United States and has forced the government to look at the gaps in its system so that the disease might be prevented here. Animals get the disease by eating contaminated animal food. Humans get the disease by eating "mechanically separated" meats that contain infectious spinal cord tissues of the animals. Tips for how American tourists in Europe may avoid contracting the disease are offered in "How Now, Mad Cow?"

Another threat to our food safety is dioxin, a potent carcinogen found in incinerator emissions and spills from electrical transformers. It may end up in our cheeseburgers, chicken, and pizza to name a few. Dioxin accumulates in our bodies and may trigger cancers such as lung, especially in people who consume a diet high in animal fat. It may also decrease learning ability, affect reproduction, decrease sperm production, cause birth defects, and impair the immune system.

Food additives have been used for a long time to provide or maintain consistency, improve nutritive value, prevent spoilage, provide leavening, control acidity, and enhance flavor or color. Food additives, though, have caused concern and confusion among consumers especially because of their long chemical names and the lack of long-term research studies of their effects on health. The sixth article in this unit explains what the functions of some additives are in our food and informs the consumer of positive effects of additives in our food supply.

Food irradiation has been a controversial topic for quite a while. The government's position is offered in the last article of this unit, which presents evidence for the importance of food irradiation to combat food-borne illness and reduce food spoilage. The author of the article also cautions that irradiation should not be a substitute for proper food handling.

# AMERICA'S DIETARY GUIDELINE ON FOOD SAFETY: A PLUS, OR A MINUS?

Kathleen Meister

Imagine a delicious, inexpensive convenience food that is low in fat, cholesterol, sodium, and calories—and provides all essential nutrients and dietary fibers in optimum quantities. This may seem the ideal food—but it would be far from ideal if it were contaminated with pathogenic bacteria.

The idea that a food must be microbiologically safe to be healthful may seem obvious. And addressing the issue of microbiological safety might seem integral to any guide to healthy eating. Until this year, however, the U.S. government's principal guide of this sort, the "Dietary Guidelines" document, did not so much as allude to the issue. The 2000 edition gives this issue a distinct Guideline, called "Keep food safe to eat."

## WHAT ARE THE DIETARY GUIDELINES?

The Dietary Guidelines, which are issued as a brochure, are official recommendations concerning healthy eating for all Americans who are at least two years old. The document was first published in 1980, and groups of experts have updated it every five years. A draft of the latest edition was released in February 2000.

**The Dietary Guidelines affect even Americans who don't know what they are—70 percent of the U.S. population.**

The Dietary Guidelines affect even Americans who don't know what they are—70 percent of the U.S. population. They represent a crucial federal policy statement—one that sets the nationwide agenda on food-related issues. Not only do they constitute the basis for federal food and nutrition programs; they are also in extensive educational use by nonfederal groups—including state and local-government agencies, voluntary organizations, professional associations, and food-industry groups.

## FOODBORNE DISEASE

"Foodborne disease" refers to any disease that results from eating food contaminated with a pathogen, most often a bacterium. Such diseases constitute an important public health problem. The U.S. Centers for Disease Control and Prevention (CDC) has estimated that, each year in the U.S., there are 76 million cases of foodborne disease, with 325,000 cases involving subsequent hospitalization and 5,000 ending in death. Moreover, it has been estimated that the annual cost of related decreases in productivity ranges from $20 billion to $40 billion.

But, in the U.S., foodborne disease is almost always preventable. Most cases trace to improper handling of food between its initial production and its ingestion. In 1997 the U.S. government launched the Food Safety Initiative—a program whose goal is to minimize foodborne disease in the U.S. Integral to this program is educating the public about safe food-handling practices.

The emphasis on food safety has increased in recent years. One reason for this is that the proportion of the American population especially vulnerable to foodborne disease, such as the elderly and persons whose immune systems are compromised, has increased. Another is that scientists have become aware that changes in how food is produced and distributed have led to changes in susceptibilities to mishandling and contamination.

Some foodborne-disease hazards have diminished in recent decades in the U.S.—for example, unpasteurized milk, improper home canning, and lack of a home refrigerator. But, meanwhile, the number of centralized, large-scale food-processing operations has increased considerably, and one slip in such an operation can result in the sickening of numerous consumers.

**The U.S. Centers for Disease Control and Prevention (CDC) has estimated that, each year in the U.S., there are 76 million cases of foodborne disease . . .**

There have been changes in food handling at the end-user level as well. Half of every dollar that American consumers spend is spent on food prepared outside the home. Keeping such foods safe requires measures different from those that apply to dishes prepared at home.

## LOOKING OUT FOR NUMBER ONE

Although chemicals can cause foodborne disease, it is most commonly associated with microorganisms. As the food safety Guideline implies, in the U.S. at least, microbial food contamination is far more of a public health problem than is chemical food contamination. Yet many Americans evidently believe the fallacy that manmade additives and pesticides and other such chemicals make their food supply dangerous. The U.S. Food and Drug Administration has ranked diet related hazards in descending order of dangerousness:

1. microbial contamination
2. naturally occurring toxicants
3. environmental contaminants (e.g., metals)
4. nutritional problems (i.e., malnutrition, undernutrition)
5. pesticide residues
6. food additives

By focusing on microbial contamination, the Dietary Guideline called "Keep food safe to eat" facilitates making it center stage in terms of public food-safety education.

## THE CONSUMER'S PART IN FOOD SAFETY

The Dietary Guidelines document states: "Farmers, food producers, markets, and food preparers have a legal obligation to keep food safe, but we also need to keep foods safe in the home." For instance, although in the last few years the egg industry has impressively reduced *Salmonella enteritidis* contamination of whole chicken eggs, eating raw or undercooked eggs remains somewhat risky. Even the safest food purchase can quickly become unsafe. Foodservice establishments must try to ensure that takeout foods, such as roast chickens or prepared salads, are safe at purchase—but it is in any case incumbent on the buyer to ensure that, within two hours of its purchase, the food is eaten or appropriately refrigerated.

## THE ALCOHOL GUIDELINE

Since its introduction, in 1980, the Dietary Guidelines document has called for moderateness in alcoholic-beverage consumption. Three changes in this Guideline, however, are present in the 2000 edition. Two of these are desirable: First, both the 1995 edition and the 2000 edition acknowledge that moderate alcohol consumption may reduce the risk of developing coronary heart disease (CHD), but unlike the previous edition, the 2000 edition states that this holds "mainly among men over age 45 and women over age 55." CHD is rare among young men and premenopausal women. Thus, moderate drinking is associated with lower death rates only among persons who are at least middle-aged.

Second, a mistake in the 1995 edition has been corrected. In that edition a list of "people who should not drink alcoholic beverages at all" included "individuals using prescription and over-the-counter medications." This was an overstatement: Some medications are quite compatible with alcohol. The new edition implies this and advises persons on medication to request "advice about alcohol intake" from their "health care professional."

But one of the three changes present in the 2000 edition is problematic: It states that "even one drink/day can slightly raise the risk of breast cancer." The claim that the positive statistical association of moderate alcohol intake and breast-cancer risk is causal is doubtful. The scientific evidence on this point is not consistent. Moreover, the possibility that this alcohol–cancer association is merely a result of confounders—in this event, non-alcohol related factors accompanying both drinking and the development of cancer—has not been ruled out. In any case, the association is weak, and if it proves causal, it would have to be weighed against the much stronger relationship between alcohol consumption and heart disease in women.

In recent years, several well-publicized outbreaks of food poisoning have been traced to errors at the

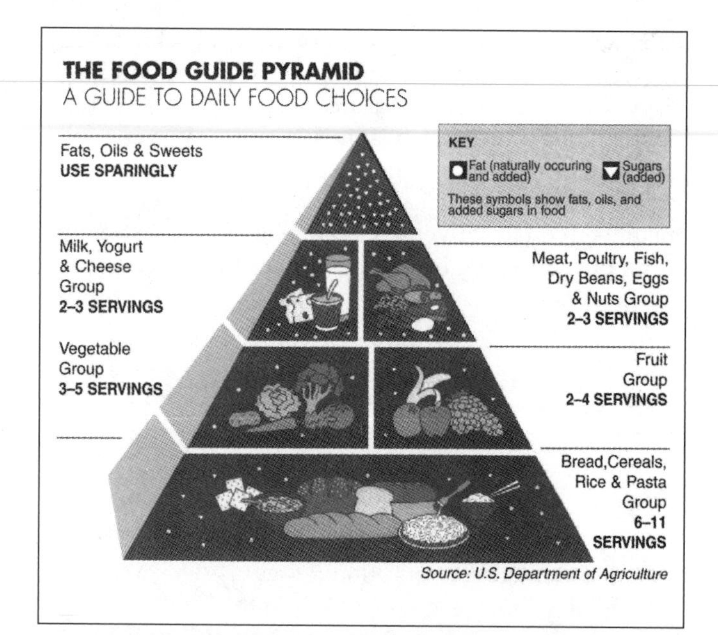

*Source: U.S. Department of Agriculture*

commercial-processing stage. For example, a large food-poisoning outbreak was traced to an ice-cream mix that had been transported in inadequately disinfected tankers previously used to transport shelled raw eggs. But most cases of foodborne disease in the U.S. result not from errors related to commercial processing, but from the mishandling of food in a foodservice establishment, at home, or in another noncommercial setting, such as a picnic.

While government regulation is crucial to keeping down foodborne disease in the U.S., it has little effect on the committing of food safety mistakes in noncommercial settings. No American governmental agency can pressure households to wash their cutting boards or to refrigerate the food in their doggie bags. The only non-intrusive way to improve food-handling practices in noncommercial settings is to instruct the public on food safety hows and whys. Therein lies the utility of the food safety aspect of the Dietary Guidelines document.

According to government surveys, behavior that is risky in terms of foodborne disease is common among Americans, of whom:

- 50 percent eat raw or undercooked eggs,
- 23 percent eat undercooked hamburger,
- 17 percent eat raw clams or oysters,
- 28 percent leave perishable foods unrefrigerated for more than two hours,
- 26 percent do not wash cutting boards after they have cut raw meat or poultry on them, and
- 20 percent do not wash their hands after they have handled raw meat or poultry.

## THE DIETARY GUIDELINES

### NOW

The U.S. Department of Agriculture (USDA) and the U.S. Department of Health and Human Services have jointly issued the Dietary Guidelines document every five years since 1980. The 2000 edition differs substantially from the 1995 edition. The number of Guidelines, for example, has increased from 7 to 10:

- Aim for a healthy weight.
- Be physically active each day.
- Let the Pyramid guide your food choices.
- Choose a variety of grains daily, especially whole grains.
- Choose a variety of fruits and vegetables daily.
- Keep food safe to eat.
- Choose a diet that is low in saturated fat and cholesterol and moderate in total fat.
- Choose beverages and foods to moderate your intake of sugars.
- Choose and prepare foods with less salt.
- If you drink alcoholic beverages, do so in moderation.

### AND THEN

The statements below represent the 1995 Guidelines.

- Eat a variety of foods.
- Balance the food you eat with physical activity—maintain or improve your weight.
- Choose a diet with plenty of grain products, vegetables, and fruits.
- Choose a diet low in fat, saturated fat, and cholesterol.
- Choose a diet moderate in sugars.
- Choose a diet moderate in salt and sodium.
- If you drink alcoholic beverages, do so in moderation.

Each of the seven messages that amount to the food safety Guideline is consistent with established principles of food handling:

- Clean. Wash hands and surfaces often.
- Separate. Separate raw, cooked, and ready-to-eat foods while storing and preparing.
- Cook. Cook foods to a safe temperature.
- Chill. Refrigerate perishable foods promptly.
- Check and follow the label.
- Serve safely.
- When in doubt, throw it out.

## CONTROVERSY OVER THE FOOD SAFETY GUIDELINE

No one can reasonably deny that the message of the food safety Guideline is scientifically well-grounded, but some qualified professionals have objected to the inclusion of this message in the Dietary Guidelines document. Some nutrition scientists say that adding messages on new topics to the document may distract the public from the guide's thrust: discussion of food choices that are better in terms of specific food constituents. For example, the January 25, 2000, edition of *The New York Times* quoted Marion Nestle, Ph.D., of New York University: "What this has done is shift the focus of the guidelines from food to other factors. The deemphasis on food and increased emphasis on other factors is not a step forward."

**[M]ost cases of foodborne disease in the U.S. result . . . from the mishandling of food in a food service establishment, at home, or in another noncommercial setting. . . .**

Healthy eating entails many considerations—for example, energy intake versus energy expenditure, intakes of protein and essential nutrients, and intakes of saturated fat. It requires attention to the principles of moderation, variety, and balance. Above all, however, it requires that whatever is eaten be harmless with respect to bacterial and similarly acting pathogens. If it isn't, none of the other factors matter. Thus, the food safety Guideline is perhaps the most fundamental.

---

KATHLEEN MEISTER, M.S., IS A FREELANCE MEDICAL WRITER AND A FORMER ACSH RESEARCH ASSOCIATE.

# Don't Mess With Food Safety Myths!

## *A food safety educator shares seven highly effective habits for food safety.*

*by Alice Henneman, M.S., R.D.*

True or false? The best way to decide if a food is safe to eat is to taste it.

That belief, and others like it, focuses our thoughts on food safety. Misconceptions about food safety abound and can make consumers sick! Once a food leaves the grocery store, the consumer becomes an important link in the food safety chain. Safely processed foods can become unsafe if mishandled in the home. Check your food safety savvy against the statements that follow. Have you—or consumers you know—been misled by any of the following food safety myths?

### *Three Myths That Make Consumers Sick*

#### Myth No. 1

"If it tastes okay, it's safe to eat."

Fact: If you trust your taste buds to detect unsafe food, you may be in trouble.

Many consumers believe a food is safe to eat if it tastes, smells, or looks all right. The Council for Agricultural Science and Technology estimated in its 1994 report, Food-borne Pathogens: Risks and Consequences, that as many as 6.5 million to 33 million illnesses yearly are food related.[1*] You can't always rely on your sense of taste, smell, or sight to determine if a food is safe. Taking even a tiny bite to test the safety of a questionable food can be dangerous.

#### Myth No. 2

"We've always handled our food this way and nothing has ever happened."

Fact: If you use past experiences to predict whether a food is safe, you may have a food-borne illness in your future.

Many incidents of food-borne illness went undetected in the past. Food-borne illness signs and symptoms of nausea, vomiting, cramps, and diarrhea were often and still are blamed on the "flu." Also, both the nature of our food supply and the virulence of food-borne pathogens has changed.

In the past, the chicken served at night might have been walking around the backyard that afternoon! Today, your food may travel halfway around the world before it arrives at your table. Food often passes from producer to processor to retailer before it reaches you. The opportunities for mishandling are higher.

More potent forms of bacteria present further problems. For example, in 1990 the US Public Health Service cited *Escherichia coli* 0157:H7, *Salmonella*, *Listeria monocytogenes*, and *Campylobacter jejuni* as the four most serious food-borne pathogens in the United States. Twenty years ago, three of these—*Campylobacter*, *Listeria*, and *E. coli*

0157:H7—were not even recognized as sources of food-borne disease![2]

Myth No. 3

"I sampled it a couple of hours ago and never got sick, so it should be safe to eat."

Fact: Your timing may be way off if you believe this myth!

Although you may feel all right a few hours after eating a food, the food may still be unsafe for you and others to consume. A food-borne illness may develop within a half hour to a few days; some may occur as long as 2 or more weeks after a contaminated food is eaten. If sickness occurs 24 hours or longer after a food is eaten—which is often the case—it is frequently blamed on other causes.

Another consideration: While you might safely eat a food, someone with a weaker immune system could be more susceptible to a food-borne illness. Young children, older individuals, pregnant women, and persons with an illness are more vulnerable and would be more likely to get sick.

Finally, if you guess wrong about the safety of a food, you—and those you serve—may feel more than a few hours of discomfort! Some food-borne illnesses can last several weeks or longer and require hospitalization. Some can be fatal.

## Seven Highly Effective Habits for Home Food Safety

How can food safety educators reach people with valid food safety information? One tactic cited by McNutt in Nutrition Today[3] for making food safety messages memorable is to use "a rap song or a 'little ditty' like the old Chiquita Banana song." This was one of several suggestions that consumers made as part of a focus group conducted by the Food Safety and Inspection Service (FSIS) of the US Department of Agriculture (USDA) in conjunction with the Food and Drug Administration.[3]

Based on my personal experience in providing consumer food safety information through an international e-mail newsletter, one of my most popular articles—according to reader response—used a ditty-type approach. Here are my seven highly effective habits for home food safety, based on recommendations of the USDA/FSIS.[4-8] These are offered as an example of one possible strategy to consider as you develop and deliver food safety messages.

***These seven habits help cooks to do it right!***

*Habit 1: Hot or Cold Is How to Hold*

Keep hot foods hot and cold foods cold. Avoid the "danger zone" between 40 and 140°F. Food-borne bacteria multiply rapidly in this zone, doubling in number in as little as 20 minutes.

Take perishable foods—such as meat, poultry, and seafood products—home immediately after purchase. Place them in the refrigerator (40°F or below) or freezer (0°F) on arrival. Buy a refrigerator/freezer thermometer at a variety, hardware, grocery, or department store. Monitor temperatures on a regular basis. When holding hot foods, keep them at an internal temperature of 140°F or higher. At events such as buffets at which food is set out for guests, serve smaller bowls of food and set out fresh food bowls as needed. For added safety, put foods on ice or over a heat source to keep them out of the temperature danger zone. Replace serving dishes with a new plate of fresh food; do not add fresh food to food that has been sitting out for a while.

*Habit 2: Don't Be a Dope—Wash with Soap*

Wash hands with soap and warm water for 20 seconds before and after handling food. This is especially important when handling raw meat, poultry, or seafood products. Bacteria can be spread all over your kitchen if you neglect to wash your hands properly.

*Habit 3: Watch That Plate—Don't Cross-Contaminate*

Cross-contamination occurs when bacteria are transferred from one food to another through a shared surface. Don't let juices from raw meat, poultry, or seafood come in contact with already cooked foods or foods that will be eaten raw. For example, when grilling, avoid putting cooked meat on the plate that held the raw meat. After cutting a raw chicken, clean the cutting board with hot, soapy water. Follow with hot rinse water before cutting greens for a salad. Place packages of raw meat, poultry, or fish on plates on the lower shelves of refrigerators to prevent their juices from dripping on other foods.

*Habit 4: Make It a Law—Use the Fridge to Thaw*

Never thaw (or marinate) meat, poultry, or seafood on the kitchen counter. It is best to plan ahead for slow, safe thawing in the refrigerator. Small items may thaw overnight. Larger foods may take longer—allow approximately 1 day for every 5 pounds of weight. For faster thawing, place food in a leak-proof plastic bag and immerse the bag in cold water. Change the water every 30 minutes to be sure it stays cold. After thawing, refrigerate the food until it is ready to use. Food thaws in cold water at a rate of approximately 1 pound per half hour. If food is thawed in the microwave, cook it right away. Unlike food thawed in a refrigerator, microwave-thawed foods reach temperatures that encourage bacterial growth. Cook immediately to kill any bacteria that may have developed and to prevent further bacterial growth.

*Habit 5: More Than Two Is Bad for You*

Never leave perishable foods at room temperature for longer than 2 hours. Perishable foods include raw and cooked meat, poultry, and seafood products. If perishable food is left at room temperature for longer than 2 hours, bacteria can grow to harmful levels and the food may no longer be safe. The 2-hour limit includes preparation time as well as serving time. Once fruits and vegetables are cut, it is safest to limit their time at room temperature as well. On a hot day with temperatures at 90°F or higher, your "safe use time" decreases to 1 hour.

*Habit 6: Don't Get Sick—Cool It Quick*

One of the most common causes of food-borne illness is improper cooling of cooked foods. Remember—bacteria are everywhere. Even after food is cooked to a safe internal temperature, bacteria can be reintroduced to food from many sources and then can reproduce. Put leftovers in the refrigerator or freezer promptly after eating. As Habit 5 stresses, refrigerate perishable foods within 2 hours. Put foods in shallow containers so they cool faster. For thicker foods—such as stews, hot puddings, and layers of meat slices—limit food depth to 2 inches.

*Habit 7: Cook It Right Before You Take a Bite*

Always cook perishable foods thoroughly. If harmful bacteria are present, only thorough cooking will destroy them. Freezing or rinsing foods in cold water is not enough to destroy bacteria.

USDA recommends using a food thermometer to assure that meat and poultry reaches a safe internal temperature. There are many types of food thermometers. Some thermometers are inserted at the start of cooking and others are used for testing at the end. The depth of required penetration and the time it takes to register a temperature also vary. Although some thermometers are suitable for measuring the temperature of thin foods such as hamburger patties or chops, others are not. Read the manufacturer's instructions before selecting and using a food thermometer. In general, the thermometer should be placed in the thickest part of the food, away from bone, fat, or gristle. It may be necessary to insert the thermometer sideways for some foods. When the food being cooked is irregularly shaped, the temperature should be checked in several places. It is important to wash the thermometer probe with hot, soapy water after each insertion to prevent cross-contamination.

Cook beef, veal, and lamb to 160°F internally for medium doneness. Cook all cuts of fresh pork to 160°F. Large cuts of beef, veal, and lamb—like roasts and steaks—can be cooked to an internal temperature of 145°F (medium rare) if they have never been pierced in any way during slaughter, processing, or preparation, which can force surface bacteria into the center. Cook pierced beef, veal, and lamb to 160°F. It is especially important that ground meat, in which bacteria can spread during processing, is cooked thoroughly (160°F for ground red meat and 165°F for ground poultry). New research indicates that judging red meat by whether it is "brown inside" is not always a reliable indicator of a safe internal temperature.

Although "no pink in the juices" when you cut into a piece of meat is a visual sign of doneness, a consumer looking for a visual sign of doneness might continue cooking meat until it is overcooked and dry. Using a thermometer is an inexpensive way to help assure a safe and flavorful product.

Cook whole poultry to 180°F and poultry breasts and roasts to 170°F; cooked-out juices should appear clear rather than pink when poultry is pierced with a fork. Fish should be opaque and flake easily with a fork when done.

If raw meat and poultry have been mishandled (left in the danger zone too long—see Habit 1), bacteria may grow and produce heat-resistant toxins that can cause food-borne illness. Warning: If meat and poultry are mishandled when raw, they may not be safe to eat even after proper cooking.

## When in Doubt, Throw It Out!

Remember this phrase whenever you have a question about food safety and are unsure if the seven safe food habits have been followed.

## And for Those Who Still Believe in Food Safety Myths

Many people will not change their minds about food safety misconceptions until they—or a family member—become sick. This is somewhat like saying "I'll buy insurance after my house burns down." You only need an extra minute or two to wash hands, clean a cutting board, cook a food to a recommended temperature, and so on. This is a small price to pay to help ensure that you, family members, and friends avoid food-borne illness!

## REFERENCES

1. *Food Safety from Farm to Table. Report to the President, Environmental Protection Agency, Department of Health and Human Services, and United States Department of Agriculture. May 1997:8.
2. The Partnership for Food Safety Education. Foodborne illness: a constant challenge (cited on the FightBAC Web site: http://www.fightbac.org/). November 1997.
3. McNutt K. Common sense advice to food safety educators. Nutr Today 1997;32:132.
4. USDA/FSIS. Basics for handling food safely (prepared by the Food Safety and Consumer Education Office). September 1997.
5. USDA/FSIS. Kitchen thermometers (prepared by the Food Safety Education and Communications Staff). October 1997.

6. USDA/FSIS. How Temperatures Affect Food (prepared by the Food Safety Education and Communications Staff). May 1997.
7. USDA/FSIS. Food safety in the kitchen: a "HACCP" approach (prepared by the Food Safety Education and Communications Staff). November 1996.
8. USDA/FSIS. The big thaw: safe defrosting methods (prepared by the Food Safety Education and Communications Staff). July 1996.


---

*AUTHOR'S UPDATE, 11/09/00

The Centers for Disease Control and Prevention estimated in their September 1999 article, *Food-Related Illness and Death in the United States*, that food-borne diseases cause approximately 76 million illnesses, 325,000 hospitalizations, and 5,000 deaths in the United States each year.[1a]

1a. Mead PS, Slutsker L, Dietz V, McCaig LS, Bresce JS, Shapiro C, Griffin PM, Tauxe RV. Food related illness and death in the United States. Emerg Infect Dis 1999;5(5). Available online at: http://www.cdc.gov/ncidod/cid/vol5no5/mead.htm.

---

*Alice Henneman is an extension educator with the University of Nebraska Cooperative Extension in Lancaster County. She is actively involved in developing and delivering consumer programs in the areas of food safety and nutrition. This article is adapted from information presented by Henneman in her international e-mail newsletter,* Food Talk *(http://www.ianr.unl.edu/ianr/lanco/family/FoodTalk.htm), and her food safety game,* Don't Get Bugged by a Food-borne Illness. *Address correspondence to Alice Henneman, University of Nebraska Cooperative Extension in Lancaster County, 444 Cherrycreek Road, Lincoln, NE 68528-1507. Fax: (402) 441-7148. E-mail: ahenneman1@unl.edu.*

# Bacterial Food-Borne Illness

*by P. Kendall*

Food-borne infection is caused by bacteria in food. If bacteria become numerous and the food is eaten, bacteria may continue to grow in intestines and cause illness. *Salmonella, Campylobacter*, hemorrhagic *E. coli* and *Listeria* all cause infections.

> **Quick Facts...**
>
> Bacterial food-borne illness is the result of mishandling food. It includes food infection and food intoxication.
>
> *Salmonella, Campylobacter, E. coli* and *Listeria* bacteria in food cause food infection.
>
> *Staphylococcus* and *Clostridium botulinum* bacteria produce a toxin (or poison) as a by-product of growth and multiplication in food and cause food intoxication.
>
> *Clostridium perfringens* can multiply in foods to sufficient numbers to cause food poisoning.
>
> Sanitation and proper heating and refrigeration practices will help prevent food-borne illness.

Food intoxication results from consumption of toxins (or poisons) produced in food by bacterial growth. Toxins, not bacteria, cause illness. Toxins may not alter the appearance, odor or flavor of food. Common kinds of bacteria involved are *Staphylococcus aureus* and *Clostridium botulinum*. (See fact sheet 9.305, *Botulism*, for more information on its prevention.) In the case of *Clostridium perfringens*, illness is caused by toxins released in the gut when large numbers of vegetative cells are eaten.

## Salmonellosis

Salmonellosis is a form of food infection that may result when foods containing *Salmonella* bacteria are consumed. Once eaten, the bacteria may continue to live and grow in the intestine, set up an infection and cause illness. The possibility and severity of the illness depends in large part on the size of the dose, the resistance of the host and the type of organism causing the illness.

The bacteria are spread through indirect or direct contact with the intestinal contents or excrement of animals, including humans. For example, they may be spread to food by hands that are not washed after using the toilet. They also may be spread to raw meat during processing so that it is contaminated when brought into the kitchen. Because of this, it is important to make sure hands and working surfaces are thoroughly washed after contact with raw meat, fish and poultry before working with foods that require no further cooking.

*Salmonella* bacteria thrive at temperatures between 40 and 140 degrees F. They are readily destroyed by cooking to 165 F and do not grow at refrigerator or freezer temperatures. They do survive refrigeration and freezing, however, and will begin to grow again once warmed to room temperature.

Symptoms of salmonellosis include headache, diarrhea, abdominal pain, nausea, chills, fever and vomiting. These usually occur within 12 to 36 hours after eating contaminated food and may last two to seven days. Arthritis symptoms may follow three to four weeks after onset of acute symptoms. Infants, the elderly or people already ill have the least resistance to disease effects.

> *Preventive measures for campylobacter infections include pasteurizing milk; avoiding post-pasteurization contamination; cooking raw meat, poultry and fish; and preventing cross-contamination between raw and cooked or ready-to-eat foods.*

Foods commonly involved include eggs or any egg-based food, salads (such as tuna, chicken or potato), poultry, pork, processed meats, meat pies, fish, cream desserts and fillings, sandwich fillings, and milk products. These foods may be contaminated at any of the many points where the food is handled or processed from the time of slaughter or harvest until it is eaten.

## Campylobacteriosis

Campylobacteriosis or campylobacter enteritis is caused by consuming food or water contaminated with the bacteria *Campylobacter jejuni*. Considered a pathogen principally of veterinary significance until recently, this bacteria is now thought to be responsible for 2.5 times more food poisoning outbreaks per year than *Salmonella*.

*C. jejuni* commonly is found in the intestinal tracts of healthy animals (especially chickens) and in untreated surface water. Raw and inadequately cooked foods of animal origin and non-chlorinated water are the most common sources of human infection (e.g. raw milk, undercooked chicken, raw hamburger, raw shellfish). The organism grows best in a reduced oxygen environment, is easily killed by heat (120 F), is inhibited by acid, salt and drying, and will not multiply at temperatures below 85 F.

Diarrhea, nausea, abdominal cramps, muscle pain, headache and fever are common symptoms. Onset usually occurs two to five days after eating contaminated food. Duration is two to seven days, but can be weeks with such complications as urinary tract infections and reactive arthritis. Meningitis, recurrent colitis, acute cholecystitis, and Guillain-Barre syndrome are rare complications. Deaths, also rare, have been reported.

> *Preventive measures for listeriosis include maintaining good sanitation, pasteurizing milk, avoiding post-pasteurization contamination and cooking foods thoroughly.*

## Listeriosis

Prior to the 1980s, listeriosis, the disease caused by *Listeria monocytogenes*, was primarily of veterinary concern, where it was associated with abortions and encephalitis in sheep and cattle. As a result of its wide distribution in the environment, its ability to survive for long periods under adverse conditions, and its ability to grow at refrigeration temperatures, *Listeria* has since become recognized as an important food-borne pathogen. *L. monocytogenes* is frequently carried by humans and animals. The organism grows in the pH range of 5.0 to 9.5. It is salt tolerant and relatively resistant to drying, but easily destroyed by heat. (It grows between 34 F and 113 F.)

Listeriosis primarily affects newborn infants, pregnant women, the elderly and those with compromised immune systems. In a healthy non-pregnant person, listeriosis may occur as a mild illness with fever, headaches, nausea and vomiting. Among pregnant women, intrauterine or cervical infections may result in spontaneous abortion or stillbirth. Infants born alive may develop meningitis. The mortality rate in diagnosed cases is 20 to 35 percent. The incubation period is a few days to three weeks. Recent cases have involved cole slaw, raw milk and cheeses made with raw milk.

> *Foods commonly involved in staphylococcal intoxication include protein foods such as ham, processed meats, tuna, chicken, sandwich fillings, cream fillings, potato and meat salads, custards, milk products and creamed potatoes. Foods that are handled frequently during preparation are prime targets for staphylococci contamination.*

## Staphylococcal Intoxication

*Staphylococcus* bacteria are found on the skin and in the nose and throat of most people; people with colds and sinus infections are special carriers. Infected wounds, pimples, boils and acne are generally rich sources. *Staphylococcus* also are widespread in untreated water, raw milk and sewage.

When *Staphylococcus* get into warm food and multiply, they produce a toxin or poison that causes illness. The toxin is not detectable by taste or smell. While the bacteria itself can be killed by temperatures of 120 F, its toxin is heat resistant; therefore, it is important to keep the staph organism from growing. Keep food clean to prevent its contamination, keep it either hot (above 140 F) or cold (below 40 F) during serving time, and as quickly as possible refrigerate or freeze leftovers and foods to be served later. (See Figure 1.)

Symptoms include abdominal cramps, vomiting, severe diarrhea and exhaustion. These usually appear within one to eight hours after eating staph-infected food and last one or two days. The illness seldom is fatal.

> *Foods commonly involved in clostridium illnesses include cooked, cooled, or reheated meats, poultry, stews, meat pies, casseroles and gravies. Holding foods at warm (110 F) rather than hot (140 F) temperatures and cooling foods too slowly are the primary causes of* perfringens *contamination.*

## Clostridium Perfringens Food-Borne Illness

*Clostridium perfringens* belong to the same genus as the botulinum organism. However, the disease produced by *C. perfringens* is not as severe as botulism and few deaths have occurred. Spores are found in soil, nonpotable water, unprocessed foods and the intestinal tract of animals and humans. Meat and poultry are frequently contaminated with these spores from one or more sources during processing.

Spores of some strains are so heat resistant that they survive boiling for four or more hours. Furthermore, cooking drives off oxygen, kills competitive organisms and heat-shocks the spores, all of which promote germination.

Once the spores have germinated, a warm, moist, protein-rich environment with little or no oxygen is necessary for growth. If such conditions exist (i.e., holding meats at warm room temperature for several hours or cooling large pots of gravy or meat too slowly in the refrigerator), sufficient numbers of vegetative cells may be produced to cause illness.

Symptoms occur within eight to 24 hours after contaminated food is eaten. They include acute abdominal pain and diarrhea. Nausea, vomiting and fever are less common. Recovery usually is within one to two days, but symptoms may persist for one or two weeks.

*Preventive strategies for* E. coli *infections include thorough washing and other measures to reduce the presence of the microorganism on raw food, through cooking of raw animal products, and avoiding recontamination of cooked meat with raw meat. To be safe, cook ground meats to 160 F.*

## E. Coli Hemorrhagic Colitis

*Escherichia coli* belong to a family of microorganisms called coliforms. Many strains of *E. coli* live peacefully in the gut, helping keep the growth of more harmful microorganisms in check. However, one strain, *E. coli* 0157:H7, causes a distinctive and sometimes deadly disease.

Symptoms begin with nonbloody diarrhea one to five days after eating contaminated food, and progress to bloody diarrhea, severe abdominal pain and moderate dehydration. In young children, hemolytic uremic syndrome (HUS) is a serious complication that can lead to renal failure and death. In adults, the complications sometimes lead to thrombocytopenic purpura (TPP), characterized by cerebral nervous system deterioration, seizures and strokes.

Ground beef is the food most associated with *E. coli* 0157:H7 outbreaks, but other foods also have been implicated. These include raw milk, unpasteurized apple juice and cider, dry-cured salami, homemade venison jerky, sprouts, and untreated water. Infected food handlers and diapered infants with the disease likely help spread the bacteria.

## Preventing Food-Borne Illness

Food-borne illness can be prevented. The following food handling practices have been identified by the Food Safety Inspection Service of USDA as essential in preventing bacterial food-borne illness.

### Purchase and Storage

- Keep packages of raw meat and poultry separate from other foods, particularly foods to be eaten without further cooking. Use plastic bags or other packaging to prevent raw juices from dripping on other foods or refrigerator surfaces.
- Buy products labeled "keep refrigerated" only if they are stored in a refrigerated case. Refrigerate promptly.
- Buy dated products before the label sell-by, use-by or pull-by date has expired.

### Preparation

- Wash hands (gloved or not) with soap and water for 20 seconds before preparing foods and after handling raw meat or poultry, touching animals, using the bathroom, changing diapers, smoking or blowing your nose.
- Thaw only in refrigerator, under cold water changed every 30 minutes, or in the microwave (followed by immediate cooking).
- Scrub containers and utensils used in handling uncooked foods with hot, soapy water before using with ready-to-serve foods. Use separate cutting boards to help prevent contamination between raw and cooked foods.
- Stuff raw products immediately before cooking, never the night before.
- Don't taste raw meat, poultry, eggs, fish or shellfish. Use pasteurized milk and milk products.
- Do not eat raw eggs. This includes milk shakes with raw eggs, Caesar salad, Hollandaise sauce, and other foods like homemade mayonnaise, ice cream or eggnog made from recipes that call for uncooked eggs.
- Use a meat thermometer to judge safe internal temperature of meat and poultry over 2 inches thick (160 F or higher for meat, 180 F or higher for poultry). If your microwave has a temperature probe, use it.
- For meat or poultry less than 2 inches thick, look for clear juices as signs of "doneness."
- When using slow cookers or smokers, start with fresh rather than frozen, chunks rather than roasts or large cuts, and recipes that include a liquid. Check internal temperature in three spots to be sure food is thoroughly cooked.
- Avoid interrupted cooking. Never partially cook products, to refrigerate and finish later. Also, don't put food in the oven with a timer set to begin cooking later in the day.
- If microwave cooking instructions on the product label are not appropriate for your microwave, increase microwave time to reach a safe internal temperature. Rotate, stir and/or cover foods to promote even cooking.
- Before tasting, boil all home-canned vegetables and meats 10 minutes plus one minute per 1,000 feet.

## Figure 1: Temperature of food for control of bacteria.

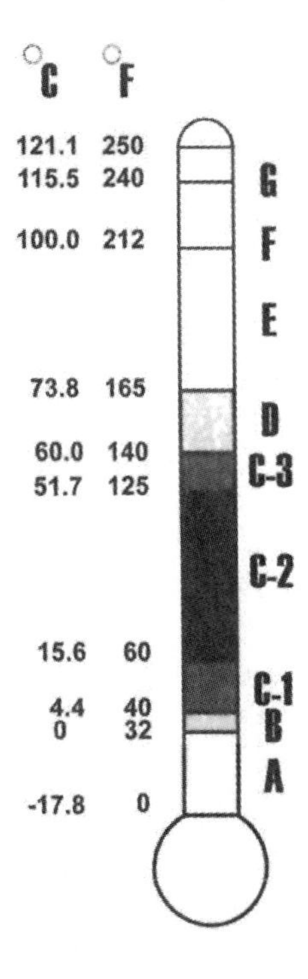


A. Freezing temperatures stop growth of bacteria, but may allow bacteria to survive. Set freezer to 0 F.

B. Cold temperatures permit slow growth of some bacteria. Do not store raw meats for more than five days or poultry, fish or ground meat for more than two days in the refrigerator.

C. DANGER ZONE.

C-1. Some growth of food poisoning bacteria may occur.

C-2. Temperatures in this zone allow rapid growth of bacteria and production of toxins by some bacteria. Do not hold foods in this zone for more than two hours.

C-3. Some bacterial growth may occur. Many bacteria survive.

D. Warming temperatures prevent growth but allow survival of some bacteria.

E. Cooking temperatures destroy most bacteria. Time required to kill bacteria decreases as temperature increases.

F. Canning temperatures for fruits, tomatoes and pickles in water-bath canner.

G. Canning temperatures for low-acid vegetables, meat and poultry in pressure canner.

### Serving

- Wash hands with soap and water before serving or eating food. Serve cooked products on clean plates with clean utensils and clean hands.
- Keep hot foods hot (above 140 F) and cold foods cold (below 40 F).
- In environmental temperatures of 90 F or warmer, leave cooked food out no longer than one hour before reheating, refrigerating or freezing. At temperatures below 90 F, leave out no more than two hours.

### Handling Leftovers

- Wash hands before handling leftovers and use clean utensils and surfaces.
- Remove stuffing before cooling or freezing.
- Refrigerate or freeze cooked leftovers in small, covered shallow containers (2 inches deep or less) within two hours after cooking. Leave air-space around containers to help ensure rapid, even cooling.
- Do not taste old leftovers to determine safety.
- If reheating leftovers, cover and reheat to appropriate temperature before serving (a rolling boil for sauces, soups, gravies, "wet" foods; 165 F for all others).
- If in doubt, throw it out. So they cannot be eaten by people or animals, discard outdated, unsafe or possibly unsafe leftovers in the garbage disposal or in tightly-wrapped packages.

### References


*Buchanan, R. L., and Doyle, M. P. Foodborne disease significance of Escherichia coli 0157:H7 and other enterohemorrhagic Escherichia coli.* Food Technology, *51(10)69–76, 1997.*

*USDA. Food Safety Inspection Service.* A Margin of Safety: The HACCP Approach to Food Safety Education. *Government Printing Office, Washington, D.C. June, 1989.*



Issued in furtherance of Cooperative Extension work, Acts of May 8 and June 30, 1914, in cooperation with the U.S. Department of Agriculture, Milan A. Rewerts, director of Cooperative Extension, Colorado State University, Fort Collins, Colorado. Cooperative Extension programs are available to all without discrimination. No endorsement of products mentioned is intended nor is criticism implied of products not mentioned.



*P. Kendall, Colorado State University Cooperative Extension foods and nutrition specialist and professor, food science and human nutrition.*

# HOW NOW, MAD COW?

They're disoriented, irritable, apprehensive, and unable to stand or walk properly. You can see why the British press called them "mad cows" in 1986, when the first cases of the mysterious ailment surfaced. And the name has stuck. In part, that's because "bovine spongiform encephalopathy" (BSE) is a mouthful. But mad cow also conjures up the mysterious nature of the frightening new disease.

The fear crystalized in the spring of 1996, when British health officials identified ten people with a new and devastating brain affliction. It seemed to resemble Creutzfeldt-Jakob Disease (CJD), a rare, invariably fatal neurological condition.

But unlike CJD, which seldom strikes those under age 50, the newly christened *variant* Creutzfeldt-Jakob Disease (vCJD) was turning up in young men and women. While it often started with leg pain and difficulty walking, the progressive brain damage eventually left them hallucinating, their memories destroyed, unable to see, speak, or feed themselves. Within a year or two, it left them dead. In 1996, vCJD killed ten people; last year it killed 27. Just over 100 people have died from the disease, all of them in Europe. No one knows how many more are already infected and will develop vCJD, which may take five to ten years to emerge.

**No cases of mad cow disease or human vCJD have ever been detected here.**

BSE in cows and vCJD in humans are both caused by prions gone awry. The brains of all mammals (including humans) contain harmless proteins called prions (pronounced PREE-ons). In BSE and vCJD, infectious, deformed prions somehow induce harmless prions to become deformed. Scientists aren't certain how deformed prions do their damage. One possibility: as the prions accumulate in the brain, brain cells start to die, leaving holes where thoughts and emotions, speech and coordination once resided.

It's no coincidence that the disease in cattle resembles the disease in humans. "The evidence is now quite strong that exposure to cattle with BSE causes vCJD in people," says Ermias Belay of the Centers for Disease Control and Prevention (CDC) in Atlanta.

And that raises an unsettling question: Even though no cases of mad cow disease or human vCJD have ever been discovered here, how susceptible is the beef-loving, barbecuing, meat-and-potatoes, McDonald's-on-every corner United States?

## How's the Beef?

On the surface, the news is good. Since 1990, the U.S. Department of Agriculture (USDA) has analyzed the brains of more than 12,000 cattle, most of them chosen because they showed signs of neurological disease or other health problems before they died.

"Not a single case of BSE has ever been detected in any of those animals," says Linda Detwiler, a veterinarian who heads the USDA's anti-BSE efforts.

"Beef produced in the U.S. is free from BSE, so consumers shouldn't worry," says Paul Brown, an epidemiologist at the National Institute of Neurological Disorders and Stroke. Brown chairs a panel that advises the Food and Drug Administration on BSE.

Some of the credit goes to the USDA's 1989 ban on importing ruminants (cattle, sheep, and goats) and most ruminant by-products from the United Kingdom. (Ruminants have several stomachs, which allows them to regurgitate their food and chew it a second time.) The ban has been gradually extended to cover all of Europe.

In Great Britain, "the first cows with BSE probably got it from eating sheep with scrapie," says Will Hueston, Chair of Veterinary Medicine at the Virginia-Maryland Regional College of Veterinary Medicine in College Park, Maryland. Scrapie (pronounced SCRAY-pee) is a disease that has afflicted sheep, especially in the United Kingdom, for more than 300 years. Like BSE, it's caused by prions.

We don't think of farm animals eating other animals, but eat them they do... usually in the form of meat-and-bonemeal protein supplements, which are made by rendering (boiling and grinding up) the carcasses of sheep, cattle, pigs, poultry, road kill, whatever. Just about anything not removed at the slaughterhouse—bones, brains, internal organs—goes into the renderer's pot. It would have been easy for infected brain tissue from sheep with

## WHEN YOU TRAVEL

The mad cow epidemic in the United Kingdom appears to have peaked (although the number of human vCJD cases hasn't). At its worst, in early 1993, veterinarians were diagnosing about 1,000 new cases each week, mostly in Great Britain. Now, it's down to less than 30 cases a week in the UK and to less than ten a week in the rest of Europe, to which Britain exported contaminated feed until 1996. Part of the reason for the decline: the British government has destroyed more than four million cows, many of them healthy, to prevent new outbreaks. (It has also destroyed hundreds of thousands of animals to halt the spread of foot-and-mouth disease, which poses no threat to humans.)

**Is it safe to eat meat in Europe?** Your odds of contracting variant Creutzfeldt-Jakob Disease (vCJD) from eating a serving of British beef is about one in ten billion, says the U.S. Centers for Disease Control and Prevention. You'd have the same chance of getting sick from eating at McDonald's if only one of the ten billion or so hamburgers it has sold since it opened in 1955 were infected.

If that still ruins your appetite, steer clear of beef entirely when you travel (milk, cheese, and other dairy foods are fine). If you are going to eat beef, stay away from burgers, hot dogs, and sausages, which are more likely to be contaminated with infected nervous-system tissue than boneless steaks, roasts, and other whole cuts. Cuts like the T-bone, porterhouse, standing rib roast, prime rib with bone, bone-in rib steak, and bone-in chuck blade roast may contain spinal cord tissue or tiny nerves called dorsal root ganglia, which are infectious if they come from a cow with BSE.

**And don't assume that you're out of danger if you're traveling outside of Europe.** For well over a decade, England exported its tainted animal feed to more than 70 countries. Some scientists believe that the next epidemic of mad cow disease—and the next wave of human vCJD victims—could occur in places like Russia and Asia, which have few if any safeguards.

So far, cattle with mad cow disease have turned up in Belgium, Denmark, France, Germany, Great Britain, Ireland, Italy, Liechtenstein, Luxembourg, the Netherlands, Portugal, Spain, and Switzerland.

scrapie to have gotten into a meat-and-bonemeal supplement that was fed to cattle.

"The cattle got BSE from this feed," says Hueston, "and then their remains were recycled as meat-and-bonemeal, which infected more cattle."

Could the same thing happen here? All it may take is one infected sheep or cow or one contaminated batch of animal feed.

The government has set up several "firewalls" to keep mad cow disease out. One protects cattle from BSE; another prevents people from getting sick if the first one fails. So far, both seem to be working, but both have gaps in them.

### Preventing BSE in Animals

In 1997, the FDA prohibited animal-feed mills from mixing meat-and-bonemeal made from rendered cows and sheep into feed for cows or sheep. (The supplements *can* be fed to pigs and poultry, because they don't get BSE-like diseases from food.)

**Normal, harmless prions are proteins that occur in the brains of all mammals, including humans. Abnormal, deformed prions can start a chain reaction that turns normal prions into abnormal ones.**

But that ban isn't foolproof. In 1998 and 1999, the FDA inspected 63 plants that render both ruminants (cattle and sheep) and non-ruminants (pigs and poultry). Ten of them had no system in place to keep the two apart. Thirty-seven of the 300 feed mills that handle both ruminant and non-ruminant meat-and-bonemeal also had no system to keep them apart.

The problem made headlines last January, when a Texas feedlot inadvertently fed meat-and-bonemeal intended for pigs and poultry to more than 1,200 cattle. A clerk at Purina Mills in St. Louis had mistakenly mixed the supplement into the company's cattle feed. Although the meal was produced from BSE-free cattle, Purina Mills purchased the animals and turned them into pig and poultry feed.

The FDA's inspection results were a real eye-opener for the rendering and feed industries, which are scrambling to police themselves before the Feds step in. Or before Ronald McDonald does.

The restaurant chain that buys more beef than any other has been stung by sharply lower sales at its European outlets. It doesn't want to see the same happen here. So McDonald's has told its U.S. suppliers to document that their cattle haven't been fed meat-and-bonemeal made from cows or sheep.

"The U.S. has always been BSE-free," says McDonald's spokesman Walt Riker. "McDonald's has the world's big-

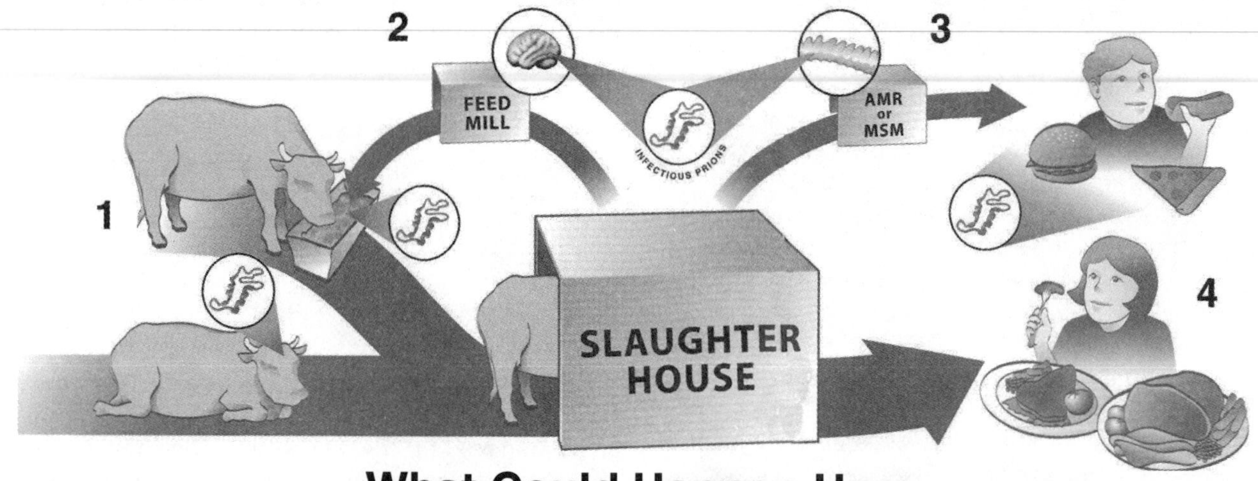


## What Could Happen Here

**Mad Cow Disease has never been found in the U.S. The government has tried to create several "firewalls" to halt its spread in case the disease does appear. Here are some potential gaps in those firewalls.**

**1.** A cow could get BSE from eating contaminated animal feed that was imported accidentally… or illegally.
**2.** The brains and spinal cords of infected cows could accidentally end up in cow feed. That's illegal, but the rules aren't always enforced.
**3.** Infectious spinal cord tissue could accidentally end up in beef from advanced meat recovery (AMR) or mechanically separated meat (MSM). Both can be used in foods like burgers, hot dogs, and the meat in pizza toppings and taco fillings.
**4.** Boneless steaks, roasts, and other whole cuts of beef do not contain infectious prions.

gest shopping cart, and we try to use that leverage for good."

When McDonald's talks, the beef industry listens.

"We're calling for the complete removal of ruminant-derived meat-and-bonemeal from those plants that make feed for cattle," says Richard Sellers of the American Feed Industry Association, which represents nearly 700 feed companies. "that should prevent the accidental mixing of the two kinds of feed."

"We've already set up an independent third-party certification program to verify that our members are following all FDA regulations about the proper labeling of their products," adds Sellers.

The rendering industry is doing likewise. "On April 1, we began to have outside inspectors verify that renderers are following all government regulations," says Tom Cook of the National Renderers Association.

Another potential breach in the BSE firewall has already been plugged. Up until 1998, many slaughterhouses stunned their cattle with an air-injection rifle before killing them. The explosive blast of air to the head often scattered brain tissue throughout the carcass (see July/August 1997, cover story). In cows with BSE, brain tissue is highly infectious.

"The beef industry has eliminated air-injection stunning because of the potential for contamination," says Janet Riley of the American Meat Institute, an industry group. "No one is even manufacturing the equipment any more."

### Preventing vCJD in People

Prions mostly infect an animal's brain and spinal cord, not its meat. So how did 101 people (so far) in Europe become infected with vCJD? "Most likely from eating inexpensive beef products that contained mechanically separated meat," says the NIH's Paul Brown.

"Mechanically separated meat is a paste produced by compressing carcasses, much like a used car is crushed into a dense block of metal," he explains. The British meat industry used this extruded paste, which could have included spinal cords, in hot dogs, sausages, and burgers.

"So, while a filet mignon was safe to eat," says Brown, "a hot dog made with mechanically separated meat was not at all safe."

This year, the European Union banned mechanically separated meat made from cattle and sheep, though as of April the ban hadn't fully taken effect.

Unfortunately, the U.S. hasn't done the same. Mechanically separated beef—spinal cords and all—is still allowed here, though it's hard to get a handle on how common it is.

## A METHIONINE TO THEIR MADNESS

Why do some people who eat BSE-infected meat develop variant Creutzfeldt-Jakob Disease while others don't seem to? To find out, scientists have tested tissue samples from 76 of the 101 people who have died from vCJD. Remarkably, all 76 "were homozygous for methionine at codon 129 on the prion protein gene," as the National Institutes of Health's Paul Brown puts it.

Translation: they inherited from each of their parents a gene that substitutes one amino acid (methionine) for another (valine) in one portion of the prion protein that the gene tells the body to make. For some reason, the methionine form of the protein seems to make people more susceptible to vCJD," says Brown.

Four out of every ten people inherit a copy of the gene from each of their parents, it's always possible that people who don't have two copies of the gene also develop vCJD, but that "it just takes them longer to become ill," cautions Brown.

"In the U.S., mechanically separated beef is rarely used any more," says Janet Riley of the American Meat Institute. "The machinery was expensive and there were too many restrictions on how the produce could be used," adds the USDA's Bob Brewer. Yet neither the AMI nor the USDA can say how much—if any—mechanically separated beef Americans eat each year.

The good news: Any food that contains mechanically separated beef has to say so on the label. The bad news: There are no labels when you eat out. So it's possible that hot dogs, sausages, hamburgers, and some other restaurant foods made with ground meat could contain spinal cord tissue. If mad cow disease ever shows up in the U.S., that could spell trouble.

Many U.S. meat processors have switched from mechanically separated beef to advanced meat recovery (AMR), which also extrudes meat from carcasses under pressure, but without crushing the bones. That alone makes it less risky than mechanically separated beef. More than 60 percent of cattle are now processed using AMR, which has a huge competitive advantage over mechanically separated meat. It's not a paste, and labels don't have to identify it. AMR meat often ends up in hamburgers, hot dogs, sausages, and the meat in pizza toppings and taco fillings.

Companies are supposed to remove the animals' brains and spinal cords before putting the carcasses through the AMR machinery, but getting out all of the spinal cord isn't easy. "It requires special tools and skills," says Glenn Schmidt, a meat scientist at Colorado State University. "The workers have to reach down to the neck region of the carcass to remove the spinal cord by scraping or suction, and sometimes they don't get all of it."

Sometimes is right. Since 1996, USDA surveys have turned up spinal cord tissue in four of 70 samples of AMR meat. That worries the U.S. beef industry, which has seen its European counterpart decimated by the mad cow scare. The National Cattlemen's Beef Association has hired Schmidt to test the meat produced at the eight major AMR plants.

"We're finding that some companies are succeeding at keeping spinal cord tissue out, while other companies are still working toward that goal," says Schmidt.

The only way to guarantee that AMR meat is free of nervous-system tissue is to require meat processors to remove the entire spinal *Column* (bones and all), not just the spinal *cord*, before sending cattle carcasses through their machinery (see "Making Meat Safe").

## The Scorecard

What's the risk of getting variant Creutzfeldt-Jakob Disease from eating meat?

• **Beef** is safe to eat in countries where the cattle don't have BSE. In countries where BSE has been found, it's safe to eat boneless steaks, roasts, and other muscle meats (see "When You Travel"). But you'd be smart to avoid processed meats like burgers, sausages, and the meat toppings on pizzas. (McDonald's, Burger King, and Wendy's, the three chains we contacted, say that they have never used advanced meat recovery or mechanically separated meat in any of their outlets in the U.S. or abroad.)

• **Pork and poultry** are safe, even in countries where cattle have BSE. "We can produce a BSE-like disease in pigs in the lab by injecting infected tissue into their brains," says the National Institutes of Health's Paul Brown, "but not by putting it into their food." Poultry don't seem to get BSE-like diseases.

• **Fish and shellfish** caught in the wild are safe, even in countries where cattle have BSE. Farm-raised fish should also be okay, since they're mostly fed fish meal and soybean meal, neither of which carries infectious prions.

• **Lamb and mutton** are safe, even in countries where cattle have BSE. "There's never been any evidence that humans can get a brain disease from eating the meat from sheep or goats with scrapie," says Paul Brown.

• **Diary products** are safe, even if they come from cows with BSE. Milk and other dairy products don't carry infectious prions.

• **Game meat** like wild elk and deer can suffer from "chronic wasting disease," which occurs naturally and belongs to the same family of prion diseases as scrapie, BSE, CJD, and vCJD. "No cases of humans getting a brain disease from eating wild game with chronic wasting dis-

## MAKING MEAT SAFE

You can help urge the government to strengthen the firewall against mad cow disease by sending this coupon or a letter or e-mail in your own words.

**To:** USDA Secretary Ann M. Veneman
U.S. Department of Agriculture, Suite 200A
14th St. & Independence Ave., S.W.
Washington, D.C. 20250
e-mail: ann.veneman@usda.gov
Fax: (202) 720-2166

**From:**____________________________________

**As a member of the Center for Science in the Public Interest, I urge you to help protect the public from mad cow disease by requiring companies to remove the neck bones and spinal *columns* (including the spinal cords) from cattle carcasses before processing them through mechanically separated meat (MSM) or advanced meat recovery (AMR) systems.**

ease have ever been documented," says the NIH's Paul Brown. Still, he adds, "you'd have to be crazy to eat the brain of a wild animal."

- **Gelatin** is an animal protein that comes from the hides and bones of cows and pigs. It's what makes Jell-O gel and gummy bears soft and pliable. It's used as a thickener in some yogurts, ice creams, and other foods. And it's in the capsules, gel caps, and coatings of many over-the-counter supplements and prescription drugs.

Is gelatin infectious if it's made from animals that have mad cow disease? Probably not. Skin and hides don't seem to carry any risk, while bones have a "low infectivity" (because they contain bone marrow), according to the World Health Organization.

In 1997 the FDA prohibited gelatin manufacturers from using hides and bones from cows with any signs of neurological disease.

"Many confectioners do not use beef gelatin," says Susan Smith of the National Confectioners Association. "But some do." (You can't tell from the label.) "We use mostly pork gelatin to make our Jell-O," says Claire Regan of Kraft Foods.

Few if any scientists see a problem. "Gelatin is off my radar screen," concludes BSE expert Will Hueston of the Virginia-Maryland Regional College of Veterinary Medicine.

- **Vaccines** are often made using cattle by-products that could be infectious. But there is no evidence that any of the world's 101 cases of variant Creutzfeldt-Jakob Disease were caused by contaminated vaccines. Nevertheless, in 1993 the FDA asked vaccine manufacturers to stop importing animal products from countries "where BSE is known to exist or may exist." Last year the government learned that five vaccine-makers hadn't complied and ordered them to do so. Clearly, the benefits of vaccination outweigh a risk that the government considers "theoretical and remote."

- **Glandular supplements** are often made from animal parts that could be infectious. Nature's Plus Ultra Male, for example, contains cow tissue from the brain, eyes, pituitary, and spleen.

The major supplement-makers say that they're complying with a 1993 FDA request that they not use cow tissue from countries where BSE exists or may exist.

"We've found that almost all of our suppliers use only domestic cattle as sources, and that those that do import bovine-derived materials do so from non-European countries," says Phillip Harvey of the industry's National Nutritional Foods Association. That's based on a NNFA survey of its members.

But the FDA has no system in place to monitor what companies actually put into their supplements. Our advice: avoid any supplements that contain animal brains, eyes, or glands, especially since there's little evidence that they work.

---

*For links to the most useful Web sites with information on mad cow disease, see www.cspinet.org/nah/06_01/bselinks.html.*

# Dioxin for Dinner?

by Richard Clapp

## Q: *What is dioxin?*

**A:** It's a complicated family of 75 chemicals, including dioxins, furans, and PCBs. One of the worst dioxins is 2,3,7,8-tetrachlorodibenzo-p-dioxin (TCDD). The molecule binds particularly strongly to intracellular receptors in the nuclei of animal and human cells. So dioxin can easily get into the nucleus, where the cell's DNA is located, and wreak havoc. If it damages the DNA, that could cause cancer or birth defects. It could also alter the DNA's instructions to make normal enzymes, hormones, and other proteins, which could lead to any of a number of diseases.

## Q: *Are the receptors there to admit things the cell needs?*

**A:** We're not sure exactly what the receptors do. But we know that they allow the cell to respond to signals and reproduce genes and that they pick up other toxins, like benzopyrene from diesel fuel or tobacco smoke.

## Q: *What about dioxin's cousins?*

**A:** The polychlorinated dibenzofurans—often called furans—are closely related to dioxin. So are PCBs, or polychlorinated biphenyls [see "All in the Dioxin Family"]. There are 135 furans and 209 PCBs. Of the 419 chemicals from all three families, 30 have dioxin-like toxicity, but we're usually exposed to a mixture of toxic and non-toxic members of each family at the same time.

## Q: *How do they get into the environment?*

**A:** PCBs were used as insulators in electrical equipment, but their production was banned in 1977. Today, they're mainly found in electrical transformers in large office or apartment buildings. When there's a fire in an old building, they're released into the atmosphere. That's unfortunate because when you burn PCBs, it produces furans, which are more toxic than PCBs.

Dioxins and furans can be produced when almost anything is burned under the right conditions. So two big sources have been municipal waste incinerators and hospital incinerators, though recently, government regulations appear to have cut those emissions dramatically.

Bleaching wood pulp with free chlorine to make paper white has been another major source. Dioxin is released into the waste water, although the amounts have declined because most plants no longer use free chlorine.

## Q: *How does dioxin get from incinerators to people?*

**A:** It goes into the air. People can breathe in the particles, but a bigger problem is that the particles can settle on grazing land. Cows eat the grass and the dioxin gets concentrated in the fat in their meat and milk. It also gets concentrated in cattle and hogs that are fed dioxin-tainted grain.

Dioxin particles can also fall into rivers, streams, and other bodies of water—or get there in runoff. It settles on the bottom. When fish and shellfish ingest small particles of sediment, dioxin builds up in their fat or organs. In Maine, pregnant women are advised not to eat the green stuff in lobsters because it's high in dioxin. People call it the "tomalley," but it's actually a combined liver and pancreas—a hepatopancreas.

## Q: *So the dioxins get concentrated as they move up the food chain?*

**A:** Yes. More than 90 percent of our exposure comes from food, mostly fish, meat, poultry, and non-skim dairy products. Fattier fish have more than leaner fish. Shellfish like lobsters are low in fat, but the dioxin may be in their hepatopancreas or organs, not the meat.

## All in the Dioxin Family

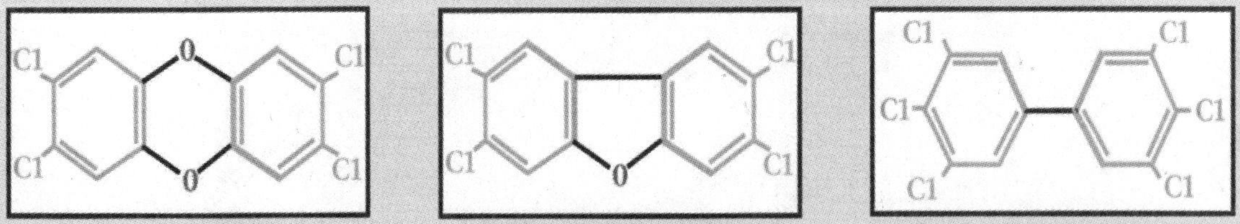

2,3,7,8 - Tetrachlorodibenzo-p-dioxin
**DIOXINs**

2,3,7,8 - Tetrachlorodibenzofuran
**FURANs**

3,3',4,4',5,5' - Hexachlorobiphenyl
**PCBs**

**Dioxin has two benzene rings—that is, two rings of carbon atoms (green)—joined by two oxygen atoms (red). Furans have only one oxygen linking the two benzene rings. PCBs have two benzene rings joined without any oxygen atoms.**

Source: U. S. Environmental Protection Agency.

**Q:** *And it accumulates in our bodies?*

**A:** Yes. It's like the daily newspaper. It comes into the house every day but you don't notice it. It has a cumulative effect.

**Q:** *Can you get rid of dioxin?*

**A:** Yes. There's a dynamic within the body of accumulation and excretion of toxic substances. Dioxin is accumulated in fat, so if you lose weight, you lose some with the fat. If you're breastfeeding, you get rid of it through the breast milk. Humans get their greatest dose of dioxin during breastfeeding because it's concentrated in breast milk and because the infant is so small that the dose per pound of body weight is quite high. The benefits of breastfeeding still outweigh the risks of dioxin, though we'd rather not have to make such a choice.

**Q:** *How long does it take to get rid of dioxin?*

**A:** Its half-life is about seven years—in other words, it takes seven years for half of it to be excreted by the body. The average levels of dioxin in the U.S. population are declining, according to the Environmental Protection Agency [EPA]. So a 40-year-old today has less than a 40-year-old would have had 15 years ago.

### One in a Hundred

**Q:** *What harm does dioxin cause?*

**A:** First of all, it's a known carcinogen. TCDD is the most potent animal carcinogen ever tested. It causes tumors in both genders of every species and every strain of animal that's been tested. And the animals get different types of tumors, so it doesn't just initiate tumors, it also promotes the growth of tumors caused by other initiators.

**Q:** *And it's more potent than we thought?*

**A:** Yes. The EPA recently released a draft report that projected an excess cancer risk of one in 100 for the most sensitive people who consume a diet high in animal fats. In other words, the risk of getting cancer from dioxin—over and above the risk of cancer from other sources—is one in 100 for some people. That's a worst-case scenario. It's for the most sensitive responders among the five percent of the population who consume the most dioxin. It's an upper bound estimate—the lower bound is zero. But it's still shocking.

And the EPA's draft estimates that the upper bound risk for the most sensitive responders to *average* exposure is one in 1,000. That's not a small risk.

**Q:** *Are the EPA's draft estimates reliable?*

**A:** They're the most reliable ones we have. The estimates now go to the EPA's Scientific Advisory Board, which includes outside consultants to the agency. I was a consultant on the Board five years ago, when it reviewed the EPA's last estimates. But there are also representatives from the American Paper Institute and consultants from industry-funded groups like Harvard's Center for Risk Analysis.

## Q: *What happened at the Advisory Board's last review?*

**A:** In 1995, the Board told the EPA to redo parts of the risk estimates. That led the agency to gather more science to justify its final draft. But the evidence led the agency to increase its risk estimates, so it backfired on the industry folks. Since then, several studies have looked at workers who sprayed or manufactured herbicides that contained dioxin, and data showing how much harm was caused by each level of exposure to the herbicides were added to the animal data.

## Q: *What kind of cancer does dioxin cause in people?*

**A:** Some studies suggest that it promotes soft-tissue sarcomas, which are cancers of the fat and muscle, and lung cancer. Most of the studies indicate an increased risk of all cancers. They don't focus on one because there are so few individual cancers in small studies of exposed populations.

## Q: *How powerful is dioxin compared to other carcinogens?*

**A:** It doesn't cause as much cancer as smoking. It may be in the same ballpark as radon or second-hand tobacco smoke. But that's based on mathematical projections from models, and all of the projections are shaky.

# Beyond Cancer

## Q: *Do dioxins impair learning behavior?*

**A:** PCBs appear to lower IQ or cause developmental delays in the children of women who ate large quantities of PCB-tainted fish during pregnancy. The studies that monitor these children are still going on, so we don't know for how long the adverse effects last. Up until age seven, researchers are still finding measurable developmental delays. Over time, those delays may become imperceptible, but we don't know about IQ.

It's also possible that PCB exposure may only affect learning in a minority of children who, for some reason, are more vulnerable. In one study, a majority of highly exposed children scored in the normal range on a memory scale. But a minority was also twice as likely as other kids to score in the "poor" range.

## Q: *How does dioxin affect reproduction?*

**A:** Dioxins seem to impair the development of the human reproductive system. There have been case reports of hypospadias—a birth defect in which the urethra opens on the underside of the penis—in populations exposed to dioxin.

Researchers have also found a decrease in the number of male babies born in Seveso, Italy, since July 10, 1976, when there was an explosion at a chemical plant making pesticides like 2,4,5-T—the "T" stands for trichlorophenoxyacetic acid. The containment vessel exploded, sending a black plume of smoke into the sky. Black dust and particles of the dioxin-contaminated pesticide fell on people who lived miles downwind from the explosion. The dioxin killed pets and contaminated the soil.

A recent study of former Seveso residents compared the ratio of males to females born in Zone A, which was closest to the explosion, and Zone B, which was further away, to ratios elsewhere. Usually, 51 percent of newborns are male and 49 percent are female. But among children of men who lived in Seveso, only 44 percent were male in the years since 1976. And among children of men who were younger than 19 when the explosion occurred, only 38 percent were male.

Zone A is still evacuated, 24 years after the explosion. In the U.S., dioxin was the most worrisome contaminant at Times Beach in Missouri and at Love Canal in New York State.

## Q: *How might dioxin harm males?*

**A:** We don't know. One theory is that it's toxic to the male fetus. Another is that it damages the Y chromosome, so sperm with Y chromosomes don't fertilize eggs. It's the Y chromosome that makes a fertilized egg develop into a male.

## Q: *Does dioxin have other effects on males?*

**A:**Yes. In animal studies, we see decreased testicular size and decreased sperm production. That's in adult rats who were exposed to dioxins before they were born. Dioxin also lowers testosterone levels in men.

## Q: *And it causes birth defects?*

**A:** Yes. During the Vietnam War, the U.S. military used an herbicide called Agent Orange to defoliate the jungles of Southeast Asia. The herbicide is 50 percent 2,4,5-T. Small amounts of dioxin are produced when 2,4,5-T is made, so it's an unavoidable contaminant. Studies on Vietnam vets exposed to Agent Orange suggest that their children have an increased risk of spina bifida.

That's a birth defect that occurs when the neural tube—which develops into the spinal cord—fails to close during the first six weeks of gestation. Children born with spina bifida often lack bowel and bladder control, and many are paralyzed from the waist down or suffer from mental retardation. The evidence that dioxin causes the defect is strong enough that Vietnam vets are compensated if their children are born with spina bifida.

## DODGING DIOXIN

It starts out as emissions from incinerators and spills from electrical transformers. It ends up in cheeseburgers, chicken wings, and pizza.

Dioxin and its chemical cousins, the furans and the dioxin-like PCBs, make their way from the air, water, soil, and sediment into plants. As animals eat the plants, and people eat the animals, the concentration of dioxin climbs.

Clearly, one way to minimize your exposure to dioxin is to avoid animal foods, including dairy products. A more targeted approach is to eat less animal fat, since that's where dioxin and its fat-soluble relatives reside.

"In most instances, anyone who reduces the amount of animal fat in their diet will reduce the amount of dioxin they consume," says Dwain Winters of the U.S. Environmental Protection Agency (EPA). "Vegans—who eat no animal products—should get the lowest levels, but ovo-lacto-vegetarians who substitute full-fat dairy products and eggs for meat can be exposed to levels similar to those found in a typical diet."

The EPA recently released draft estimates of dioxin, furan, and PCB levels in beef, pork, poultry, milk, and seafood (see "The Dioxin is Cast"). The seafood numbers aren't as bad as they seem. The EPA's draft estimates for dioxin levels in fish and shellfish are higher than for other animal foods, but they're the least certain because only limited information is available.

### Seafood Uncertainty

Dioxin levels in fish and shellfish are the toughest to estimate "because it's much harder to get representative samples of the seafood we eat," says Winters. "And the levels of dioxin depend on where the fish live, what they have eaten, and where they are on the food chain."

Most of the seafood people eat is marine or farm-raised freshwater fish, which have lower levels of dioxin than wild freshwater fish. Two of the most commonly eaten fish are pollock—the white fish that ends up in most fish sticks and fried fish sandwiches—and tuna. "They tend to have lower levels of dioxin because they live in open marine waters that are cleaner," says Winters.

Catfish is the most popular freshwater fish, thanks to restaurants like Red Lobster and Cracker Barrel. Most catfish and trout are now farm-raised and fed largely plant meal, which means that they tend to have lower dioxin levels than their wild-caught, carnivorous cousins.

"EPA's draft freshwater fish numbers are taken from wild-caught fish in the late 1980s," says Winters. "They're not necessarily indicative of wild fish caught today or farm-raised freshwater fish." As for salmon, "much of it is farm-raised in the ocean, but you'd expect even wild-caught salmon to be lower in dioxin, because they spend their adult life in the ocean."

Other fish, like rockfish, striped bass, snapper, and redfish, might have more dioxin, because they often breed in estuarine waters. That's where the ocean meets freshwater, so it's more contaminated than the oceans.

"Seafood in the marketplace is harvested from all over the globe, not just from our local waters," says Winters, "which means that overall you're less likely to get dioxin-contaminated seafood. There's a great leveling."

And because dioxin in the environment keeps dropping, older data may not reflect current levels. "More effort is going to be put into measuring dioxin levels in fish and shellfish," says Winters, "and we also want to periodically go back and do beef, pork, poultry, and other foods because everything's changing."

### Smart Strategies

It's not seafood, but the animal fat from meat, poultry, seafood, and dairy foods that boosts the average person's dioxin burden the most. But you can't take the EPA's draft estimates at face value.

The beef, pork and poultry numbers represent averages for all cuts. If you eat leaner cuts of meat (like sirloin, round steak, or pork tenderloin) or poultry (like breast or drumstick), you get less dioxin. Trimming fat and skin is a key strategy, and that goes for the skin of fish, too.

And you can avoid much of the dioxin in milk, cheese, yogurt, and ice cream by buying fat-free or low-fat versions. Likewise, egg whites or the egg substitutes made out of egg whites (like Egg Beaters) should have less dioxin.

But there's a catch: For middle-aged or older adults, eating less dioxin now doesn't mean you've cut the amount of dioxin in your body proportionately.

"If you cut your dioxin intake in half, you haven't reduced your overall risk in half," says Winters. "It's not that you are what you eat; you are what you ate. Your body burden is a product of your lifetime consumption, and adults who make radical shifts in their diets don't get immediate results. But reducing the intake for children for their lifetimes is going to have more of an effect.

"Many of us are still carrying the exposure from the 1950s and '60s, when levels in the environment were much higher. My three-year-old daughter will have much lower levels than mine when she grows up."

### The Good News

Today's children will be exposed to less dioxin because the EPA has cracked down on the major sources.

"Our regulations will reduce the dioxin emitted from municipal and medical waste incinerators and from pulp and paper facilities by at least 95 percent," says Winters. Most of these regulations will be fully in effect by 2002, but most incinerators and paper-making plants are already meeting the levels set by the regulations.

"For instance, in the late 1980s, municipal incinerators were emitting more than 8,000 grams of dioxin a year in the U.S.," says Winters. "Under the new regulations, they'll emit less than 12 grams.

"Now that we've addressed the major industrial sources, we're shifting our focus to better understand how uncontrolled combustion, like backyard trash-burning and forest fires, contributes dioxin to our food supply."

---

For more information, see www.epa.gov/NCEA/dioxin.htm.

Other than that, we don't have strong evidence that dioxin causes specific birth defects in humans. But in animal studies, it's a powerful teratogen—something that causes birth defects. Its teratogenic effects in animals are as dramatic as its carcinogenic effects. It causes different defects in different organs in different species and strains of animals. For example, it causes cleft palate in mice, malformed kidneys in rats, and extra ribs in rabbits.

**Q:** *Does dioxin impair the immune system?*

**A:** Yes. One of the EPA's dioxin experts, Linda Birnbaum, calls dioxin an "immune modulator," because it makes the immune systems of animals both under-reactive and over-reactive to stimuli. An over-reactive immune system may raise the risk of auto-immune diseases like lupus. An under-reactive immune system is less able to respond to an antigenic challenge—that is, it makes vaccines less effective and leaves the animal less able to fight off infections and possibly diseases like cancer.

**The Dioxin is Cast**

The numbers for dioxin in freshwater fish do not reflect current levels in the most popular farm-raised fish, like catfish, salmon, and trout. What's more, the numbers are averages. Lower-fat versions of these foods have less dioxin—and higher-fat versions have more—than shown here.

| Food *(4 oz. unless otherwise indicated)* | Dioxins, PCBs, & Furans *(picograms)*[1] |
|---|---|
| Freshwater fish | 274 |
| Marine shellfish | 95 |
| Marine fish | 70 |
| Beef | 33 |
| Pork | 26 |
| Poultry | 18 |
| Eggs *(2)* | 13 |
| Milk *(1 cup)* | 11 |
| Vegetable oil *(1 Tbs.)* | 1 |

[1]Because all foods contain a mixture of dioxins, furans, and PCBs, the Environmental Protection Agency's draft estimates give greater weight to the most harmful contaminants.
Source: Adapted from "Draft Exposure and Human Health Reassessment of 2,3,7,8-Tetrachlorodibenzo-p-Dioxin (TCDD) and Related Compounds," Volume 3, Chapter 3, Table 3-56, U.S. Environmental Protection Agency (www.epa.gov/ncea/ pdfs/dioxin/part1and2.htm, click on Volume 3, Chapter 3).

The evidence in humans is limited. But after the residents of Quail Run, Missouri, were exposed to dioxin-contaminated oil and debris from Agent Orange manufacturing plants, they had a large number of welts on a skin-prick test, which is designed to detect allergies. That meant that they were allergic to many things—it's a sign of an over-reactive immune system—though the welts diminished over time.

## Q: *Does dioxin cause diabetes?*

**A:** The risk of diabetes seems to be elevated in the Ranch Hands—the Air Force troops who had the job of spraying Agent Orange in Vietnam. Researchers recently studied Ranch Hands who *weren't* exposed to Agent Orange, which means that their dioxin levels were similar to most Americans'. They found that those with higher dioxin levels—within the normal range—had a higher risk of diabetes than those with lower dioxin levels.

## Q: *Does dioxin have any other long-term effects?*

**A:** It has been shown to cause either endometriosis or a proliferation of endometrial tissue in monkeys, mice, and rats. In humans, the evidence is less clear, but one small study found higher levels of PCBs in infertile women with endometriosis than in infertile women without the disease.

## Q: *Which of dioxin's adverse effects are conclusive?*

**A:** Everyone, except perhaps some industry groups, accepts that dioxin is a human carcinogen. IARC, the International Agency for Research on Cancer, which is part of the World Health Organization, reclassified it as a human carcinogen in 1997. The studies on veterans are strong enough that they get compensated if their children are born with spina bifida. We have animal evidence for developmental delays and reproductive hormonal effects. The human evidence is not as strong for endometriosis and immunotoxic effects.

---

Epidemiologist Richard Clapp is an associate professor of Environmental Health at the Boston University School of Public Health. He has done extensive research on veterans and workers who have been exposed to dioxin. Clapp spoke to *Nutrition Action*'s Bonnie Liebman.

# What's This Doing In My Food?

## A Guide to Food Ingredients

*Although many of us never give them a thought, we count on a variety of food ingredients to make food more appealing to the senses, provide nutritional benefits and keep food fresh longer, among other things. These ingredients can cause concern and confusion among consumers—especially if they have chemical names. Actually, many of these additives are quite familiar, they just go by more scientific names when used on food labels. For example, ascorbic acid is another name for vitamin C and alpha-tocopherol is vitamin E.*

Here, in part one of a two-part *Food Insight* series on food ingredients, you'll learn the "what and why" of common food ingredients—what they are and why they're added to our food supply. Part two will cover the "how" aspect of additives—how different food ingredients allow food manufacturers to develop the innovative food products that today's consumers seek.

## What Do They All Do?

There are approximately 3,000 food additives used in this country, and many of them are common food ingredients we use at home every day, such as sugar or baking soda. Food additives are divided into categories based on function. Some of the basic categories are: acidulants, antioxidants, colors, emulsifiers, flavors and flavor enhancers, gums, preservatives, sweeteners and vitamins/minerals.

### *Acidulants*

A lemon-lime beverage or food product wouldn't have that refreshing tartness without an acidulant ingredient. Basically, acidulants are acids that are used for flavoring, as preservatives, for gelling and coagulation, and to help prevent oxidation of fats and oils. Examples of acidulants include citric acid, tartaric acid, lactic acid, adipic acid, and malic acid.

### *Antioxidants*

Many of us are familiar with the term "antioxidants" from a health perspective. In this context, however, the antioxidants are added to delay or prevent rancidity. Over time, fats and oils that come in contact with oxygen from the air can become rancid—developing unpleasant off-flavors and odors. Two of the most commonly used antioxidants are BHA, or butylated hydroxyanisole, and BHT, or butylated hydroxytoluene. Natural antioxidants such as tocopherols (forms of vitamin E) and guaiac gum are also used. Foods to which antioxidants are added include fats and oils, cereals, and high-fat foods such as doughnuts and chips.

### *Colors*

Almost everyone has had fun mixing up colored frosting or coloring homemade play-clay with food colors. Food colors, dyes and pigments used in food, drugs and cosmetics are regulated by the U.S. Food and Drug Administration (FDA), and require testing similar to that required for other food additives. Colors are either classified as "certified" or "exempt from certification." All nine certified colors are artificial, and most are named with the color name and number, (e.g., Red #2, Yellow #5). Exempt colors are frequently derived from natural sources such as vegetables, and also must meet certain criteria for purity and safety. Examples of exempt colors include substances such as annatto extract (yellow), dehydrated beets (bluish-red to brown), caramel (yellow to tan), beta-carotene (yellow to orange) and grape skin extract (red, green).

### *Emulsifiers*

In food science classes, making salad dressing or mayonnaise is the classic lesson for teaching what emulsions are. With proper mixing, fat or oil and water will combine to become an emulsion. In food products, emulsifiers are added to keep emulsified products stable, reduce stickiness, control crystallization, keep ingredients dispersed (such as spices within a salad dressing) and to help products dissolve more easily (such as powdered coffee creamer). They work because their chemical structure attracts fats on one end and water on the other, thereby letting the two substances combine easily. Common emulsifiers include lecithin (often made from soybeans), alginates (chemical salts found in algae) and mono- and diglycerides (syrup- or fat-like substances found in alcohols).

### *Flavors and Flavor Enhancers*

We all like our food to have pleasing flavors, and the food industry relies on various substances to provide the flavors that consumers demand. Spices and herbs, essential oils and their extracts, fruits and fruit juices and manufactured (also called "artificial") compounds are classified as flavors. Often, both natural and artificial flavors are used together in one food item.

Somewhat less understood are flavor enhancers, the most common of which is probably monosodium glutamate, or MSG. Since 1909 when it was first manufactured, MSG has been used in a variety of foods, including meat and poultry items, soups and broths, salad dressings and sauces. MSG is the sodium salt of glutamic acid (glutamate), which is one of the most common amino acids found in nature. Although it has no true taste of its own, MSG works to enhance the flavors already present in foods. The overall taste effect contributed by glutamate is savory or meaty.

### *Gums*

Gums provide thickness to foods and help form gels in products such as frozen desserts, candies, salad dressings, puddings and whipped toppings. They're also used to keep ingredients suspended in a food and to inhibit crystallization, among other functions. Gums are classified by source, such as seaweed (which includes agar, alginates, carrageenan), plant seed gums (which include guar, locust bean, psyllium), plant extracts (which include pectin), fermentation gums (which include xanthan gum), plant exudates (which include gum arabic) and cellulose derivatives.

### *Preservatives*

Because of preservatives, bread does not grow mold overnight, but remains fresh for several days. Preservatives can be antimicrobials, antioxidants, or both. As antioxidants, they keep foods from becoming rancid and turning brown. As antimicrobials, they inhibit the growth of bacteria, yeast and mold.

Food additives are very tightly regulated. The Food Additives Amendment to the U.S. Food, Drug and Cosmetic Act, implemented in 1958, assigned proof for additive safety to the food industry. The degree of safety testing necessarily became very high because the industry had to prove additives were safe before they could be used.

Consumers can easily see which food additives are present in a food by reading the ingredient statement on the product label—the FDA requires all additives and ingredients to be listed. Food additives play many important roles in our food supply, helping to ensure that the wide array of foods we eat are safe, wholesome and tasty.

## What is a GRAS ingredient?

A list of GRAS (or "generally recognized as safe") ingredients was created in 1959 by the U.S. Food and Drug Administration (FDA). The roughly 700 additives on this list are believed by experts to be safe, based on their extensive history of use in foods, or based on published scientific evidence. Salt, sugar, spices, vitamins and monosodium glutamate are examples of GRAS ingredients. The FDA and the U.S. Department of Agriculture routinely reexamine GRAS ingredients in order to evaluate their safety in light of new scientific information, and to re-approve, reclassify or remove them from the list.

## Food Additive Functions and Examples*

### Provide or Maintain Consistency

Lecithin, mono- and diglycerides, methyl cellulose, carrageenan, glycerine, pectin, guar gum, sodium aluminosilicate

### Improve or Maintain Nutritive Value

Vitamins A and D, thiamine, niacin, riboflavin, pyridoxine, folic acid, cyanocobalamin (vitamin B12), ascorbic acid, calcium carbonate, zinc oxide, iron

### Maintain Wholesomeness and Prevent Spoilage

Propionic acid and its salts, ascorbic acid, butylated hydroxyanisole (BHA), butylated hydroxytoluene (BHT), benzoates, sodium nitrite, citric acid, erythrobates

### Provide Leavening and Control Acidity

Yeast, sodium bicarbonate, citric acid, fumaric acid, phosphoric acid, lactic acid, tartrates

### Enhance Flavor or Color

Cloves, ginger, fructose, aspartame, saccharin, sucralose, acesulfame potassium, FD&C colors, monosodium glutamate, caramel, annatto, limonene, turmeric

**Adapted from "Common Uses of Additives," Food and Drug Administration and IFIC Foundation Food Additives brochure.*

# Food Irradiation: A Safe Measure

Food safety is a subject of growing importance to consumers. One reason is the emergence of new types of harmful bacteria or evolving forms of older ones that can cause serious illness. A relatively new strain of *E. coli*, for example, has caused severe, and in some cases life-threatening, outbreaks of food-borne illness through contaminated products such as ground beef and unpasteurized fruit juices.

Scientists, regulators and lawmakers, working to determine how best to combat food-borne illness, are encouraging the use of technologies that can enhance the safety of the nation's food supply.

***"Irradiation should be our next step in food safety and should play an integral part in our continued demand for safer food."***

**—David Kessler, M.D., dean of Yale Medical School and former FDA commissioner**

Many health experts agree that using a process called irradiation can be an effective way to help reduce food-borne hazards and ensure that harmful organisms are not in the foods we buy. During irradiation, foods are exposed briefly to a radiant energy source—such as gamma rays or electron beams—within a shielded facility. Irradiation is not a substitute for proper food manufacturing and handling procedures. But the process, especially when used to treat meat and poultry products, can kill harmful bacteria, greatly reducing potential hazards.

The Food and Drug Administration has approved irradiation of meat and poultry and allows its use for a variety of other foods, including fresh fruits and vegetables, and spices. The agency determined that the process is safe and effective in decreasing or eliminating harmful bacteria. Irradiation also reduces spoilage bacteria, insects and parasites, and in certain fruits and vegetables it inhibits sprouting and delays ripening. For example, irradiated strawberries stay unspoiled up to three weeks, versus three to five days for untreated berries.

Food irradiation is allowed in nearly 40 countries and is endorsed by the World Health Organization, the American Medical Association and many other organizations.

Irradiation does not make foods radioactive, just as an airport luggage scanner does not make luggage radioactive. Nor does it cause harmful chemical changes. The process may cause a small loss of nutrients but no more so than with other processing methods such as cooking, canning, or heat pasteurization. Federal rules require irradiated foods to be labeled as such to distinguish them from non-irradiated foods.

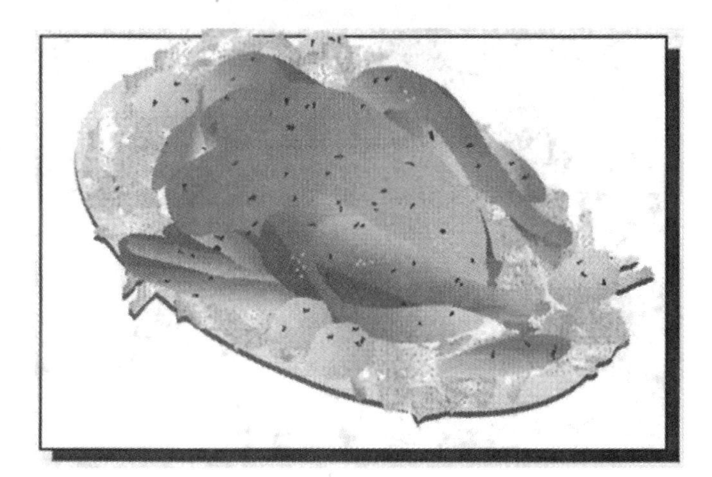

Studies show that consumers are becoming more interested in irradiated foods. For example, the University of Georgia created a mock supermarket setting that explained irradiation and found that 84 percent of participating consumers said irradiation is "somewhat necessary" or "very necessary." And consumer research conducted by a variety of groups—including the American Meat Institute, the International Food Information Council, the Food Marketing Institute, the Grocery Manufacturers of America, and the National Food Processors Association—has found that a large majority of consumers polled would buy irradiated foods.

Some special interest groups oppose irradiation or say that more attention should be placed on food safety in the early stages of food processing such as in meat plants. Many food processors and retailers reply that irradiation can be an important tool for curbing illness and death from food-borne illness. But it is not a substitute for comprehensive food safety programs throughout the food distribution system. Nor is irradiation a substitute for good food-handling practices in the home.

***" The American Medical Association affirms food irradiation as a safe and effective process that increases the safety of food when applied according to governing regulations. Irradiation can be a beneficial addition to the techniques available to maintain and increase the safety of the U.S. food supply."***

**—Thomas R. Reardon, M.D., AMA president**

## Questions and Answers About Irradiation

**Q.** What is food irradiation?

**A.** Food irradiation is a process in which food products are exposed to a controlled amount of radiant energy to kill harmful bacteria such as *E. coli* O157:H7, *Campylobacter*, and *Salmonella.* The process also can control insects and parasites, reduce spoilage, and inhibit ripening and sprouting.

**Q.** Is irradiated food safe?

**A.** Yes. The Food and Drug Administration has evaluated the safety of this technology over the last 40 years and has found irradiation to be safe under a variety of conditions and has approved its use for many foods. Scientific studies have shown that irradiation does not significantly reduce nutritional quality or significantly change food taste, texture or appearance. Irradiated foods do not become radioactive. Irradiation can produce changes in food, similar to changes caused by cooking, but in smaller amounts.

**Q.** How does irradiation work?

**A.** Food is packed in containers and moved by conveyer belt into a shielded room. There the food is exposed briefly to a radiant-energy source—the amount of energy depends on the food. Energy waves passing through the food break molecular bonds in the DNA of bacteria, other pathogens, and insects. These organisms die or, unable to reproduce, their numbers are held down. Food is left

## Proper Food Handling Still Needed

Experts emphasize that though food irradiation can reduce food-borne illness risk, the process *complements*, but doesn't replace, proper food handling practices by producers, processors and consumers. For example, a few bacteria may survive the irradiation process in meats and poultry and could multiply if the meat is left unrefrigerated. Also, bacteria from other foods can be carried to irradiated foods if care isn't taken to avoid cross-contamination. So consumers should continue to follow these food safety precautions:

- **Clean**—Wash hands in hot, soapy water before preparing food and after using the bathroom, changing diapers and handling pets. Wash cutting boards, knives, utensils and countertops in hot, soapy water after preparing each food item and before going on to the next one.
- **Separate**—Avoid cross-contamination by keeping raw meat, poultry and seafood separate from other foods in the grocery cart and in the refrigerator. If possible, use one cutting board for raw meat products and another for salads and other foods that are ready to be eaten. Don't place cooked food on a plate that has held raw meat, poultry, seafood, or uncooked marinades.
- **Cook**—Use a meat thermometer to measure the internal temperature of cooked meat and poultry to ensure thorough cooking. Ground poultry should be cooked to at least 165 degrees F; ground meat, 160 degrees F; roasts and steaks, 145 degrees F; and poultry (whole bird), 180 degrees F. Cook eggs until the yolk and white are firm, and cook fish until it is opaque and flakes easily. Boil sauces, soups and gravy when reheating, and heat other leftovers to 165 degrees F.
- **Chill**—Refrigerate or freeze perishables, prepared foods, and leftovers within two hours.

Never defrost or marinate foods on the counter. Use the refrigerator, cold running water, or a microwave oven. Divide large amounts of leftovers into small, shallow containers for quick cooling in the refrigerator. Remove stuffing from poultry and other stuffed meats after cooking and refrigerate in a separate container. Don't pack the refrigerator full. Cool air must circulate to keep food safe.

virtually unchanged, but the number of harmful bacteria, parasites and fungi is reduced and may be eliminated.

**Q.** How do I know if food has been irradiated?

**A.** FDA currently requires that irradiated foods include labeling with either the statement "treated with radiation" or "treated by irradiation" and the international symbol for irradiation, the radura .

*The Radura*

**Q.** Are irradiated foods available now?

**A.** Not widely yet. Some stores have sold irradiated fruits and vegetables since the early 1990s. Irradiated poultry is available in some grocery stores—mostly small, independent markets—and on menus of a few restaurants.

On the other hand, some spices sold wholesale in this country are irradiated, which eliminates the need for chemical fumigation to control pests. American astronauts have eaten irradiated foods in space since the early 1970s. Patients with weakened immune systems are sometimes fed irradiated foods to reduce the chance of a life-threatening infection.

**Q.** Are food irradiation facilities safe for workers and surrounding communities?

**A.** Yes. The transport and handling of radioactive material is strictly regulated, and irradiation facilities are made to withstand natural disasters such as earthquakes. The radioactive cobalt commonly used is made specially to serve as a safe radiation source for hospitals and irradiation facilities. Workers in irradiation plants are protected by thick walls surrounding the radiation source. If workers need to enter the irradiating room, the energy source is lowered into a pool of water that absorbs the radiation and protects the workers from any exposure. In electron beam facilities, the energy source is turned off. There are about 30 licensed irradiation facilities in the United States, used mainly to sterilize medical equipment, many consumer products, and, in some cases, food.

***"When the public finally sees a need for irradiation and realizes its value, I think people will accept it, maybe even demand it."***
**—George Pauli, food irradation safety coordinator, U.S. Food and Drug Administration.**

**Q.** Will irradiated foods cost more?

**A.** Irradiated products sold to date have cost slightly more than their conventional counterparts. Some industry experts estimate the increase at two to three cents per pound for fruits and vegetables and three to five cents a pound for meat and poultry products. But these costs may be offset by advantages such as keeping a product fresh longer and enhancing its safety. Food trade groups say that as irradiated foods become more widespread, their cost is likely to drop.

This brochure is based on an article that appeared in *FDA Consumer*, the official magazine of the U.S. Food and Drug Administration. It is intended to serve as a

consumer education tool on the process of food irradiation.

"Food Irradiation: A Safe Measure" is also available on the FDA Website at *http://www.fda.gov/*. Or you can call 1-888-SAFEFOOD for more information on food safety.

The organizations listed below have contributed to the content and printing of this brochure:

American Meat Institute
Department of Health and Human Services
(U.S. Food and Drug Administration)
Food Marketing Institute
Grocery Manufacturers of America
National Cattlemen's Beef Association
National Food Processors Association
The American Dietetic Association

# UNIT 7

# World Hunger and Malnutrition

## Unit Selections

45. **Hunger and Food Insecurity**, Katherine L. Cason
46. **The Challenge of Feeding the World**, *Food Insight*
47. **World Food Prospects: Critical Issues for the Early Twenty-First Century**, *International Food Policy Research Institute*
48. **Nutrition and Infection: Malnutrition and Mortality in Public Health**, Gro Harlem Brundtland
49. **Agricultural Growth, Poverty Alleviation, and Environmental Sustainability: Having It All**, Peter Hazell
50. **Will Frankenfood Feed the World?** Bill Gates
51. **Biotechnology and the World Food Supply**, *Union of Concerned Scientists*

## Key Points to Consider

- How extensive is the malnutrition-infection combination globally?
- What are some of the causes of global malnutrition?
- To what extent can agricultural development alleviate poverty and malnutrition?
- What sort of role will genetically modified food have in the future in feeding people in developing countries?

**Links: www.dushkin.com/online/**
These sites are annotated in the World Wide Web pages.

**Population Reference Bureau**
*http://www.prb.org*

**World Health Organization**
*http://www.who.ch*

**WWW Virtual Library: Demography & Population Studies**
*http://demography.anu.edu.au/VirtualLibrary/*

The cause of malnutrition worldwide is poverty. The United Nations Food and Agriculture Organization (FAO) determined that a body mass index (BMI) (body weight divided by the square root of height) of 18.5 is indicative of a chronic energy deficit in an adult. Approximately 840 million people are malnourished in the developing world: Asia has the largest number of them and children under 5 years of age are the most susceptible. Infectious disease kills approximately 10 million children each year. Thus, the director general of FAO launched, in 1994, a special Programme for Food Security (SPFS) for low-income food-deficit countries (LIFDCs), which was endorsed by the World Food Summit held in Rome in 1996. They pledged to increase food production and access to food in LIFDCs so that the number of malnourished people would be reduced by half. They set goals to increase sustainable agricultural production within the cultural, political, and economic milieu of the country to improve access to food, to increase the role of trade, and to deal effectively with food emergencies.

Malnutrition is also the main culprit for lowered resistance to disease, infection, and death, especially in children. The malnutrition-infection combination results in stunted growth, lowered mental development in children, and lowered productivity and higher incidence of degenerative disease in adulthood. This directly affects the economies of developing countries.

According to Gro Harlem Brundtland, director general of the World Health Organization, diet-related areas that we need to focus on to stop this vicious cycle of malnutrition and infection are vitamin A and iron deficiencies that occur simultaneously with protein-energy deficits. Nutrient deficiencies magnify the effect of disease and result in more severe symptoms and greater complications of the disease. For example, vitamin A deficiency leads to blindness in about 250,000–300,000 children annually, and exacerbates the symptoms of measles. Iron deficiency, which is widespread among pregnant women and those in the child-bearing years in developing countries, increases the risk of death from hemorrhage in their offspring and reduces physical productivity and learning capacity. Finally, iodine deficiency causes brain damage and mental retardation. It is estimated that 1.5 billion people are at risk for iodine deficiency disorders (IDD).

Malnutrition does not only affect children and adults in developing countries, but it is also prevalent in this country. Thirty million Americans, of whom 11 million are children, experience food insecurity and hunger. In a country where one-fifth of the food is wasted and 130 pounds of food per person is disposed of, it is unacceptable that Americans go hungry.

In a survey conducted by the U.S.D.A. in 1989, approximately 66 percent of low-income children did not consume the Recommended Dietary Allowance (RDA) for calories. The primary nutrient-related problems in this country, as in developing countries, are iron deficiency anemia, common in infants, young children, and teens, and lead poisoning. Undernourished pregnant women give birth to low-weight babies who suffer developmental delays and increases in mortality rate. Another group in the United States that experiences health problems due to hunger are the elderly. Articles about food assistance programs that are available in the United States to combat hunger and new initiatives for policy changes that may eradicate hunger and ensure food security for all citizens are included in this unit.

Even though some developing countries have increased agricultural growth, it still has failed to benefit the poor. Environmental problems may slow down production in the future. Future strategies should focus on increasing agricultural growth without endangering the natural resources and on alleviating poverty equitably. To positively influence the world food situation in the early years of this century, the International Food Policy Research Institute proposes investing in women's education, pursuing better access to markets of industrial countries, supporting the agroecological approach for farming, as well as creating access to information and communication technology. It questions whether modern biotechnology will contribute to the achievement of food security.

Biotechnologists believe that genetically modified (GM) foods, such as rice that is fortified with beta-carotene and iron, may not only help feed the world, but they could also eradicate nutritional deficiencies. Additionally, GM foods may decrease damage to crops from pests, viruses, bacteria, and drought. Yet the existence of GM foods is not enough. If farmers cannot afford to grow GM crops or people cannot afford to buy the food, if the infrastructure for transport and distribution is not available, the same products may never reach consumers. Since the safety of humans and the efficacy for the environment of GM crops have not been adequately studied, the Union of Concerned Scientists believes that genetic engineering is by no means the panacea for hunger. They propose that educating the farmer to increase production, limiting environmentally destructive practices, and promoting sustainable intensification of agricultural production will solve many of the problems connected to hunger and malnutrition.

# HUNGER AND FOOD INSECURITY


**ABSTRACT**

*Approximately 30 million Americans, including 11 million children, currently experience hunger and food insecurity. Assistance programs and policies help alleviate poverty and food insecurity; however, the rate of hunger and malnutrition has increased. Recent welfare reform legislation decreases funding for assistance. Approaches are needed to achieve long-term food security in our communities. Family and consumer scientists can help through education, food-recovery programs, cost-effectiveness program assessments, and public issues education.*



**KATHERINE L. CASON, Ph.D, R.D.**
Associate Professor, Department of Family and Youth Development, Clemson University


According to data released by the U.S. Census Bureau in September 1997, 36.5 million Americans, or 13.7% of the population, lived in poverty in 1996. Poverty is a high priority on the agendas of many economists and politicians; yet no one has been able to overcome the problems and obstacles associated with this social disease.

**Hunger and the broader issue of food security have been a public concern in the United States since our nation's inception.**

Living in poverty often means that individuals are victims of hunger (Clancy & Bowering, 1992). Living below the poverty line puts tremendous strains on a household budget, adversely affecting the ability to purchase a nutritionally adequate diet (Clancy & Bowering, 1992). Hunger and the broader issue of food security have been a public concern in the United States since our nation's inception. One of the earliest underlying goals of public policy (still in effect) is to assure an adequate supply of safe, nutritious food at reasonable cost (Voichick & Drake, 1994). Recent studies suggest at least 30 million Americans, including 11 million children, currently experience food insecurity (Wehler, Scott & Anderson, 1996).

Food security can be defined as access by all people at all times to enough food for an active, healthy life. Food security includes a ready availability of nutritionally adequate and safe foods and an ability to acquire acceptable foods in socially acceptable ways (Hamilton et al., 1997). The complex issues surrounding food insecurity encompass physiological, social, and economic dimensions. Food, or lack of it, is a determinant of human development, health, and behavior. Its absence affects a community's economy, taxes its resources, and influences its social policies (Breglio, 1992).

Those who experience food insecurity may try to avoid hunger by decreasing the size of meals, skipping meals, or not eating any food for one or more days. When food is severely limited, these methods for avoiding hunger are ineffective (Klein, 1996).

Lack of food, and the subsequent undernutrition, affects physiological functioning in every stage of the life cycle. Most adversely affected are the fetus, pregnant and lactating women, children, and older adults. According to the Community Childhood Hunger Identification Project (CCHIP), hungry children suffer from two to four times as many individual health problems as low-income children whose families do not experience food shortages. Only 44% of low-income children consumed at or above 100% of the Recommended Dietary Allowance (RDA) for calories (USDA, 1989).

Failure to grow over time is a consequence of undernutrition. Inadequate food intake limits the ability of children to learn about the world around them (Center on Hunger, Poverty and Nutrition Policy, 1993). When children are chronically undernourished, their bodies attempt to conserve energy by shutting down "nonessential" bodily functions, leaving energy available for vital organs and growth. If any energy remains, it can be used for social activity and cognitive development. When the body conserves energy, decreased activity levels and increased apathy soon follow. This in turn affects social interactions, inquisitiveness, and overall cognitive functioning. In comparison to nonhungry children, hungry children are more than four times as likely to suffer from irritability; more than 12 times as likely to report dizziness; and almost three times as likely to suffer from concentration problems (Food Research and Action Center [FRAC], 1991).

In the United States, iron deficiency anemia is still common in infants and young children between 6 months and 3 years, and again during adolescence. About twice as many 4- to 5-year-old African American children have iron deficiency as Mexican American or Caucasian children. The most common causes of anemia in childhood are inadequate intakes of iron, infection, and lead poisoning. Among children 12 to 36 months of age with iron deficiency anemia, 20.6% were from low-income families (Fomon, 1993).

Pregnant women who are undernourished are more likely to experience low birth weight babies. These infants are more likely to suffer delays in their development and are more likely to experience behavior and learning problems later in life. The infant mortality rate is closely linked to inadequate quantity of quality in the diet of the infant's mother (U.S. Department of Health and Human Services [USDHHS], 1994).

**Anxiety, negative feelings about self-worth, and hostility toward the outside world can result from chronic hunger and food insecurity**

Older adults are also at increased risk of suffering health consequences as a result of food insecurity and hunger. Older adults have a number of risk factors that place them at an increased risk for developing malnutrition. Among these risk factors are diseases such as chronic lung disease, heart disease, neurological diseases; disabilities, functional impairments; sensory losses; poor dental health; multiple medication use; therapeutic diets; and social isolation. Malnutrition in older adults can result in loss of muscle mass, which can lead to disabilities that affect levels of independence. Malnutrition can also compromise the immune function, increasing susceptibility to infections (Codispoti & Bartlett, 1994).

Insecurity about whether a family will be able to obtain enough food to avoid hunger also ha[s] an emotional impact on children and their parents. Anxiety, negative feelings about self-worth, and hostility toward the outside world can result from chronic hunger and food insecurity (World Hunger Year, 1994).

## FOOD ASSISTANCE PROGRAMS

During the 1960s, food security became a high-priority issue at all levels of the government. Government officials and influential leaders, the media, and the general public could no longer ignore the issue of hunger (Egan, 1980).

Several programs were implemented in the 1960s and early 1970s, including the Food Stamp Program; the Special Supplemental Program for Women, Infants and Children (WIC); the Community Food and Nutrition Program; and the Expanded Food and Nutrition Education Program (EFNEP) within the Cooperative Extension Service Program. The media has labeled these years the "War on Hunger" (Voichick & Drake, 1994).

During the 1980s, hunger increased primarily due to a combination of economic factors and resulting cuts in federal assistance programs (FRAC, 1991). In the early 1990s, advocates were hopeful about the renewed interest among elected leaders in improving programs that feed people. The historic passage of the Mickey Leland Childhood Hunger Relief Act in August 1993 helped to improve benefits to food stamp families and improve access for those who had been unable to participate in the Food Stamp Program. The president and Congress committed to place the Special Supplemental Nutrition Program for Women, Infants, and Children (WIC) on track for full funding by 1996, and Congress made funding available to start and expand the School Breakfast and Summer Food Programs (Uvin, 1994).

### *Food Stamp Program*

The Food Stamp Program puts food on the table for some 9 million households and 22 million individuals each day. It provides low-income households with coupons or electronic benefits used like cash at most grocery stores to ensure access to a healthy diet. The current program structure was implemented in 1977 with a goal of alleviating hunger and malnutrition by permitting low-income households to obtain a more nutritious diet through normal channels of trade. It provided more than $19 billion in benefits in 1997 (FRAC, 1997).

The Food Stamp Program began as a federal assistance program designed to help farmers dispose of surplus food products. While assistance to farmers remains a part of the program, the current objective is to help low-income families increase their food purchasing power and achieve a nutritionally adequate diet (Social Security, 1996). However, CCHIP data and other sources indicate that food stamps are not used by millions of people who appear eligible to participate in them due to barriers to participation, lack of information about eligibility, and inadequate funding. Survey results consistently show food stamp benefits are not sufficient to protect many low-income families from experiencing hunger (FRAC, 1998). The *Third Report on Nutrition Monitoring in the United States (1995)* indicates that individuals receiving food stamps have less than adequate diets than those low-income individuals who do not receive food stamps. The report suggests that such risk factors as obesity, hypertension, and high serum cholesterol are major concerns for low-income individuals and place them at higher risk for developing chronic diseases due to inadequate diets. The lack of improvement in adequacy of the diets of food stamp recipients suggests that food stamp recipients would benefit from nutrition education; yet nutrition education is not a mandatory component of the program (Joy & Doisy, 1996).

Since 1986, USDA funds have been available for development and implementation of nutrition education programs; however, only 21 states have instituted such programs. Evaluation of the program is at the discretion of each state (Joy & Doisy, 1996).

### *National School Lunch Program (NSLP)*

The National School Lunch Program was created by Congress 50 years ago as a measure of national security, to safeguard the health and well-being of the nation's children. The NSLP provided meals to 25.1 million children in 1997. Of the more than 26 million children participating in the lunch program, 14.6 million low-income children receive free or reduced price lunches daily (FRAC, 1997).

### *School Breakfast Program*

The School Breakfast Program was established by Congress, initially as a temporary measure through the Child Nutrition Act of 1966 in areas where children had long bus rides to school and in areas where mothers were in the workforce. Permanent authorization in 1975 assisted schools in the provision of a nutritious morning meal to children. In 1997, more than 7 million children and 67,063 schools participated in the School Breakfast Program; 86% were from families with low incomes (FRAC, 1997).

### *Summer Food Service Program*

The Summer Food Service Program was created by Congress in 1968. It is an entitlement program designed to provide funds for eligible sponsoring organizations to serve nutritious meals to low-income children when school is not in session. In the summer of 1996, the program served more than 2.2 million children at more than 28,000 sites operated by more than 3,400 sponsoring organizations nationwide (FRAC, 1997).

### *Child and Adult Care Feeding Program (CACFP)*

The CACFP was founded in 1968 to provide federal funds for meals and snacks to licensed public and nonprofit child-care centers and family and group child-care homes for preschool children. Funds are also provided for meals and snacks served at after-school programs for school-age children, and to adult day-care centers serving chronically impaired adults or people over the age of 60. In 1966, CACFP served more than 2.6 million children daily, providing approximately 1.5 billion meals and snacks; and served more than 40,000 elderly persons in the Adult Day Care portion of the program (FRAC, 1997).

### *The Special Supplemental Program for Women, Infants, and Children (WIC)*

WIC was established by Congress as a pilot program in 1972 and authorized as a national program in 1975. WIC is a federally funded, preventive nutrition program that provides nutritious foods, nutrition education, and access to health care to low-income pregnant women, new mothers, and infants and children at nutritional risk. The WIC program appropriation in fiscal year 1997 was $3.7 billion, which the USDA estimated would serve approximately 7.4 million participants (FRAC, 1997).

### *The Expanded Food and Nutrition Education Program (EFNEP)*

EFNEP is administered by the Cooperative State Research Education and Extension Service of the U.S. Department of Agriculture, in cooperation with state Cooperative Extension Services in the 55 U.S. states and territories. In 1968, EFNEP was federally initiated by the USDA Extension Service with $10 million (from Section 32 of An Act to Amend the Agricultural Adjustment Act). In 1970, EFNEP received funding under the Smith-Lever Act; in 1977, under the Food and Agriculture Act; and in 1981, under the Agriculture and Food Act.

Since the program's inception, EFNEP paraprofessionals have taught limited-resource families how to improve dietary practices and become more effective managers of their available resources. The paraprofessionals provide intensive nutrition education to individuals and groups in a variety of nonformal education settings, including homes, community centers, housing complexes, WIC offices, and churches.

While EFNEP is not a food-assistance program, it is an effective educational program with a mission to reduce food insecurity. EFNEP teaching is tailored to the needs, interests, financial resources, age, ethnic backgrounds, and learning capabilities of participants.

EFNEP's objectives are to improve diets and nutritional welfare for the total family; to increase knowledge of the essentials of human nutrition; to increase the ability to select and buy food that satisfies nutritional needs; to improve practices in food production, storage, preparation, safety, and sanitation; to increase ability to manage food budgets and related resources such as food stamps.

### *Personal Responsibility and Work Opportunity Reconciliation Act of 1996*

The Personal Responsibility and Work Opportunity Reconciliation Act of 1996 (PRWORA) is the most comprehensive welfare reform program since the Social Security Act of the 1930s. The PRWORA has far-reaching implications in a number of programs. The act fundamentally reforms the Food Stamp Program, Supplemental Security Income (SST) for children, the Child Support Enforcement Program, and benefits for legal immigrants. The act modifies the child nutrition programs and provides cuts in the Social Service Block Grants (SSBG).

The act features decreases in funding for programs for low-income children and families and requires structural changes in the Aid to Families with Dependent Children (AFDC) program. The act converts AFDC and Job Opportunities and Basic Skills (JOBS) into the Temporary Assistance to Needy Families (TANF) block grant. Family assistance is limited to 5 years, while granting states the option to limit assistance for a shorter time period.

The PRWORA significantly reduced funding for food assistance programs and represented a sharp reversal from the trends of the early 1990s. This 1996 legislation contains numerous, significant structural changes to the Food Stamp Program, public assistance programs in general, to the Summer Food Program, and the Child and Adult Care Food Program. Start-up and expansion funds for the School Breakfast and Summer Food Programs were eliminated by this legislation. Entire classes of people have been eliminated from eligibility for the Food Stamp Program. For example, unemployed, childless individuals aged 18 to 50 years can receive food for only 3 of every 36 months.

Cuts in food assistance programs are likely to cause an increase in hunger and food insecurity. State and local governments and private charities, enlisted to make up for federal cutbacks and budget restraints, are increasingly unable to shoulder the burden. Many states, in financial crisis, have previously made severe cuts in human services programs.

## RECOMMENDATIONS AND IMPLICATIONS FOR FAMILY AND CONSUMER SCIENTISTS

The physical, psychological, social, and economic tolls of food insecurity are both interconnected and interdependent. While important work has been conducted to redefine and clarify terms related to hunger and food security, redefinition of the solution to food insecurity is needed.

Family and consumer scientists understand the complexity of food security issues and their interrelatedness with other social, economic, and environmental problems that affect the individual, the family, and society.

### *Strengthen the Safety Net*

The most immediate and direct way to reduce hunger and food insecurity is to strengthen the array of food assistance programs in place. The benefits of food assistance programs such as Food Stamps, WIC, School Breakfast Program, and the Summer Food Service Program have not been fully realized because a large percentage of eligible households are not participating. Barriers exist that prevent those needing and wanting assistance from receiving the services. Little research has been conducted that identifies the barriers and possible methods to reduce them. Extensive needs assessment, which includes addressing the social diagnosis phase of Green and Kreuter's PRECEDE-PROCEED planning framework (1991) is needed. Social diagnosis allows the researcher to determine the target population's perceptions of its own needs or quality of life through multiple information-gathering activities. There are only a few methodologies that allow the emic point of view emphasized in social diagnosis. The focus group method provides an ideal venue for eliciting emic data, and it is proven to be effective in collecting this type of information (Dignan, 1995). Family and consumer scientists can work to increase awareness, identify barriers through focus group techniques, and make recommendations to policy makers and program directors on ways to reduce barriers to participation.

**Up to one fifth of America's food goes to waste each year, with an estimated 130 pounds of food per person ending up in landfills.**

### *Education*

The importance of education in resolving the food security issue has been recognized by researchers as well as policy makers. Education is necessary to elicit changes in behavior that will lead to improved food security. While nutrition and family food economics education is provided by some states as a part of the food assistance programs, it is not a mandatory component of all of the available programs. The nutrition education programs offered through the Food Stamp Program, EFNEP, and WIC need to be enhanced and adequately funded to meet the needs of all low-income families and youth. Family and consumer scientists have a direct role in the provision of innovative nutrition education targeted at health promotion and disease prevention. Professionals serve as advocates to provide support for public policy and legislation that promotes cost-effective food assistance programs that require nutrition education for participants.

### *Food Recovery*

Food recovery is a creative way to decrease hunger in America. It supplements the federal food assistance programs by making better use of a food source that already exists. Up to one fifth of America's food goes to waste each year, with an estimated 130 pounds of food per person ending up in landfills. The annual value of this wasted food is approximately $31 billion. It is estimated that about 49 million people could have been fed by these lost resources (USDA, 1996).

Food recovery is the collection of wholesome food for distribution to those who are hungry. Gleaning, the gathering of food after harvest, dates back to biblical times. Today the terms gleaning and food recovery cover a variety of different efforts. Gleaning refers to the collection of crops from farmers' fields that have been mechanically harvested or from fields where it is not economically profitable to harvest. Food rescue refers to the collection of perishable food from wholesale and retail stores, and prepared and processed food from the food processors and food service industry. Family and consumer scientists can actively support and participate in food recovery programs. They can assist diverse agencies and community-based groups to work together to establish local hunger programs, administer food-recovery programs, and coordinate gleaning efforts. Family and consumer scientists provide a national network of practical science-based knowledge; an important contribution may be education and training for recipients, staff, and volunteers working with food recovery. Information may be provided on food preparation and handling, nutrition, food preservation and safety, dietary guidance, and balanced meal planning.

### *Cost Effectiveness Analysis and Impact Assessment*

The cost effectiveness of food assistance programs must be assessed so that program directors can modify the programs to best meet the needs of those receiving benefits. Family and consumer scientists are positioned to conduct or participate in research on the cost effectiveness of food assistance programs, to assist in the evaluation of nutrition education programs designed to alleviate food insecurity, and to monitor the effects of welfare reform in their communities.

The PRWORA is in its early stages of implementation, and scholars and policy makers have not assessed its impact on welfare recipients. Examination of how the PRWORA and subsequent changes in policies and programs affect food security is important research. Assessment of the impacts of PRWORA implementation on food security of families and children will provide a better understanding of program benefits as well as adverse effects on those in poverty. This information is crucial for program planning and management. These issues are very important in making public policy decisions that address the food security problems associated with poverty.

### *Public Issues Education*

Public policy shapes and directs actions to achieve defined societal goals. It may be adopted and implemented formally through government action or adopted informally through common practice and assumptions. Public policy provides direction for personal and group behavior based on values and beliefs as well as government and economic systems. Public policy decisions affect food security and nutritional well-being of the population. There is a need for broad public participation in policy decisions that affect food security. Family and consumer scientists can assist communities in this process through building societal capacity to understand and address this critical issue. The democratic political process works when citizens believe that they have sufficient power to negotiate for their own rights and interests. As people develop their public leadership skills and gain access to information, they are better able to achieve food security for themselves and their communities. Family and consumer scientists can facilitate a greater awareness and understanding of the food security situation in communities throughout the nation.

## SUMMARY

Despite all the programs implemented and legislation designed to reduce poverty and its consequences, hunger and food insecurity will continue to be critical issues in the next century. Hunger and food insecurity have serious, complex effects. Clearly, new approaches are necessary to achieve long-term food security in our communities.

Family and Consumer Science professionals can work for policy changes that would increase cost effectiveness and decrease barriers to participation in food assistance programs, provide intensified education about hunger, and help to shape public policy at the local, state, and national levels. Aggressive action is needed to bring an end to hunger and to achieve food security for all citizens.

## *References*


Breglio, V. J. (1992). *Hunger in America: The voter's perspective*. Lanham, MD: Research/Strategy/Management (RMS).

Center for Hunger, Poverty and Nutrition Policy. (1993). *The link between nutrition and cognitive development in children.* Medford, MA: Tufts University.

Clancy, K. L., & Bowering, J. (1992). The need for emergency food: Poverty problems and policy responses. *J Nutr Ed., 24,* 12S–17S.

Codispoti, C. L., & Bartlett, B. J. (1994). *Food and nutrition for life: Malnutrition and older Americans.* Washington, DC: National Aging Information Center. (Publication No. NAIC–12).

Dignan, M. B. (1995). *Measurement and evaluation of health education.* Springfield, IL: C. C. Thomas Publisher.

Egan, M. (1980). Public health nutrition services: Issues today and tomorrow. *JADA, 77,* 423–427.

Federation of American Societies for Experiment Biology, Life Sciences Research Office. (1995). *Third Report on nutrition monitoring in the United States.* Washington, DC: U.S. Government Printing Office.

Fomon, S. J. (1993). *Normal nutrition of infants.* St. Louis, MO: Mosby.

Food Research and Action Center (FRAC). (1991). *Community Childhood Hunger Identification Project: A survey of childhood hunger in the United States.* Washington, DC.

Food Research and Action Center (FRAC). (1997). *Community Childhood Hunger Identification Project: A survey of childhood hunger in the United States.* Washington, DC.

Green, L. W., & Kreuter, M. W. (1991). *Health promotion planning: An educational and environmental approach* (2nd ed.). Mountain View, CA: Mayfield.

Hamilton, W. L., Cook, J. T., Thompson, W. W., Buron, L. F., Frongillo, E. A., Olson, D. M., & Wehler, C. A. (1997). *Household food security in the United States in 1995.* Washington, DC: U.S. Department of Agriculture Food and Consumer Service.

Joy, A. B., & Doisy, C. (1996). Food stamp nutrition education program: Assisting food stamp recipients to become self-sufficient. *J Nutr Ed., 28,* 123–126.

Klein, B. W. (1996). Food security and hunger measures: Promising future for state and local household surveys. *Family Econ Nutr Rev., 9,* 31–37.

U.S. Department of Agriculture. (1989). *Nationwide Food Consumption Survey, continuing survey of food intakes by individuals, low income women 19–50 years and their children, 1–5 years, 4 days.* (NFCF, CSFII Report 85-4). Hyattsville, MD: U.S. Government Printing Office.

U.S. Department of Agriculture. (1996). *A citizen's guide to food recovery.* Washington, DC: U.S. Government Printing Office.

U.S. Department of Health and Human Services. (1994). *Healthy People 2000 review 1993.* (DHHS Publication No. PHS 94-1232-1). Hyattsville, MD: U.S. Government Printing Office.

Uvin, P. (1994). The state of world hunger. *Nutr Rev., 52,* 151–1161.

Voichick, J., & Drake, L. T. (1994). Major stages of U.S. Food and Nutrition Policy Development Related to Food Security. *In: Food security in the United States: A guidebook for public issues education.* Washington, DC: USDA Cooperative Extension System.

Wehler, C. A., Scott, R. I., & Anderson, J. J. (1996). *The Community Childhood Hunger Identification Project: A survey of childhood hunger in the United States.* Washington, DC: Food Research and Action Center.

World Hunger Year. (1994). *Reinvesting in America: Hunger and poverty wheel.* New York: Reinvesting in America.

New York Academy of Sciences:

# The Challenge of Feeding the World

Mahatma Gandhi once said, "Honest disagreement is often a sign of progress." This is certainly true of agricultural biotechnology. This past year there have been numerous forums discussing the finer points of agricultural biotechnology. Both pros and cons of the issue have been raised in an effort to bring the facts about this issue to the forefront of public discourse. As is expected, some of the public debates have been productive, increasing understanding of and clarifying some of the misinformation about the issues surrounding agricultural biotechnology. Others have been more along the lines of a public venting of anger, myths, and dire predictions.

All of these discussions are necessary to move the important issue forward. Of note, a meeting this summer at the New York Academy of Sciences (NYAS) raised the level of discourse on the evolving issue of food biotechnology beyond misinformation and distrust, to looking at what is truly critical—the impact of the technology on the developing world. The NYAS press background briefing titled "Agricultural Biotechnology and the Developing Countries," held on June 20, 2000, was a forum for honest discussion, debate and resolution in the area of agricultural biotechnology and its real value to the world.

On October 12, 1999, the world celebrated the birth of its six billionth human being, a doubling of the world's population since 1960. Today, however, an estimated 800 million people do not have enough to eat. By 2050 the earth's population is expected to grow by a minimum of 50 percent with little additional land suitable for farming. What does all of this mean?

With an ever-growing number of mouths to feed and with the even more limited means to feed those persons, a more sustainable, more economical, and more environmentally friendly method of producing food is needed. "There is no question about the demand for food and the need to eat. The problem comes in the means of meeting the demand," Rodney W. Nichols, president and chief executive officer (CEO) of the New York Academy of Sciences (NYAS), stated during a recent press event held by the Academy.

Among the possible solutions, many people see agricultural biotechnology as one solution to the problem of feeding the world's inhabitants. Agricultural biotechnology is the use of modern genetics in the age-old process of improving plants and microorganisms for food production.

Although many see the benefits and potential of agricultural biotechnology, others do not. Nichols worries that "hyperbole is driving solid evidence out of public view." In turn, this creates a sense of distrust of science in the minds of the public and causes the evidence concerning agricultural biotechnology to become politicized.

The briefing began with an introduction by Rodney Nichols as well as presentations from Per Pinstrup-Andersen of the International Food Policy Research Institute and Charles Arntzen, Ph.D., president and CEO of the Boyce Thompson Institute for Plant Research. After the presentations, Ira Flatow of *National Public Radio* moderated a six-member panel discussion.

Dr. Per Pinstrup-Andersen captured the growing concerns of developing nations with a review of the disturbing numbers concerning worldwide population growth, food insecurity and the demand for food worldwide. He noted that several years ago, during the World Food Summit, numerous heads of state determined that the number of food-insecure people needed to drop to 400 million by 2015. In reality, the decline in food insecurity is happening at a much slower rate and the total number of food-insecure people by 2010 is expected to fall to only 680 million.

**Agricultural biotechnology is merely one piece of the solution: it has the potential to develop crops that are drought tolerant and self-fertilizing, thereby increasing overall yield. It is also capable of fortifying crops with nutrients needed for basic health and for delivering much needed vaccines to people living in developing countries.**

He also suggests that developed countries are part of the problem for the much slower than anticipated decline and stated that "reducing hunger, food insecurity and child death due to malnutrition is not a high priority in very many countries around the world."

Pinstrup-Andersen reported that not every country needs to be self-sufficient in food production if they have other sources of income to afford the importation of staple items. For instance, many countries rely on the manufacturing capabilities of their large urban populations to compensate for a lack in rural farming production.

Agricultural biotechnology is merely one piece of the solution: it has the potential to develop crops that are drought tolerant and protected from pests, thereby increasing overall yield. It is also capable of fortifying crops with nutrients needed for basic health and for delivering much needed vaccines to people living in developing countries.

According to Dr. Arntzen our ancestors were the original experimenters; they domesticated plants such as the tomato and the potato. Originally, potatoes contained alkaloids that are harmful to humans, but our ancestors removed them through crop breeding. The downfall was that the alkaloids were also natural pesticides and fungicides. Thus, the potatoes were safe for human consumption, but were more susceptible to pests and spoilage.

For years the potato crop has been treated with a series of insecticide sprays to kill off the insects and prevent disease, but such treatments are costly and potentially damaging to the environment. Through the use of biotechnology, we have the ability to add the Bacillus thuringiensis (Bt) gene to the plant. The incorporation of the Bt gene naturally wards off pests and spoilage that result in crop loss in many developing countries. Another advantage to using the Bt gene is that it encodes a host-specific protein that is not harmful to humans and causes adverse effects only in a certain population of insect pests.

"The one key thing we have to emphasize with biotechnology [is that] the technology has a high cost up-front, but once it is created, it is captured in the seed and only the seed needs to be distributed," emphasized Arntzen. He also believes that there is a great deal of opportunity in agricultural biotechnology, especially in developing countries—to stabilize food costs and add nutrients to food.

In contrast to the many people who believe in and discuss the benefits of agricultural biotechnology, Rebecca Goldberg, Ph.D., of the Environmental Defense Fund expressed the view that environmental questions need to be answered through research and studies. She also suggested that biotechnology as a whole needs greater and more long-term examination as well as stricter governmental regulation.

"While biotechnology can enable scientists to do some unusual things, it is not the panacea it is often advertised to be," stated Goldberg. She believes that the shortcomings in feeding the world are the result of social and political issues involving food distribution, not the technology used to grow the food or the amount of food grown. In conclusion, Goldberg stated, "Some efforts are well-intentioned, but I see the role of biotechnology as being very limited."

Dr. Calestous Juma of Harvard University is in agreement with Goldberg in terms of the fact that countries and politics get in the way of feeding the world, but sees the problem as a lack of international cooperation. The root of the problem is that "some countries are reluctant to include a biotechnology component in their development assistance because they are afraid the Green parties will attack them," according to Juma.

**"The one key thing we have to emphasize with biotechnology [is that] the technology has a high cost up-front, but once it is created, it is captured in the seed and only the seed needs to be distributed," emphasized Arntzen.**

This political division places developing countries in a tough position because conventional research and biotechnology research often take place in the same laboratory. Some developed countries are reluctant to take part in or to help fund this research, because it might have a biotechnology component. "This has an overall negative impact on the development cooperation in general and developing countries in particular," states Juma.

Juma believes there is a future for biotechnology; however, there needs to be an explanation of the technology, a debate on the subject, development from private enterprise and interaction from the public sector to allow the use of biotechnology in the developing world.

"The problem is not with the potential of biotechnology to feed the world; it is with the gap between the potential and the current reality of how the technology is developing," according to Tony Laviña, Ph.D., of the World Resources Institute. He also believes that agricultural biotechnology can help with the resolution of food security and environmental issues within the next 10 to 15 years.

Laviña states that "the challenge is how to make the technology available to developing countries. We need to create biotechnology solutions to deal with problems relevant to developing nations and to make it affordable to their farmers."

Terry Medley, vice president of Biotechnology Regulatory and External Affairs of DuPont and former administrator of the Unites States Department of Agriculture's Animal and Plant Health Inspection Service stated, "We face a number of challenges... one of which is food security." Biotechnology is a tool with many applications and is capable of solving food insecurity problems in a safe way. For this to happen there needs to be cooperation among the scientific community, regulatory agencies and public policy makers. Medley also emphasized that cooperation must raise public confidence through an integration of technology and science-based information as well as a right to choose when it comes to food.

There is no doubt that there is a problem concerning food insecurity. There is also no doubt that solutions need to be found. The question is how agricultural biotechnology will best fit into the puzzle and help contribute to much needed solutions.

---

*The NYAS program was supported in part by grants from the International Food Information Council, the Richard Lounsbery Foundation, and Pfizer, Inc.*

From *Food Insight,* September/October 2000, pp. 1, 4-5. © 2000. Reprinted with permission of the International Food Information Council Foundation.

# World Food Prospects

## Critical Issues for the Early Twenty-First Century

By the year 2020 the world's population is projected to grow by some 30 percent, become more urban, and have more income. Meeting the world's food needs under these conditions will have profound implications for the world's agricultural production and trading systems in coming decades. World Food Prospects: Critical Issues for the Early Twenty-first Century, a recent Food Policy Report by Per Pinstrup-Andersen, Rajul Pandya-Lorch, and Mark W. Rosegrant, presents the most recent IFPRI projections of the future world food situation and identifies six recent developments and emerging issues that will influence the prospects for global food security.

### Prospects for Food Security

Almost all of the increase in world food demand will take place in developing countries. Developing countries will account for about 85 percent of the increase in the global demand for cereals and meat between 1995 and 2020. However, a developing-country person in 2020 will consume less than half the amount of cereals consumed by a developed-country person and slightly more than one-third of the meat products.

A demand-driven "livestock revolution" is under way in the developing world. Between the early 1970s and the mid-1990s, the volume of meat consumed in the developing world grew almost three times as fast as it did in the developed countries. Demand for meat in the developing world is projected to double between 1995 and 2020. In response to the strong demand for meat products, demand for cereals for feeding livestock will double in developing countries. Demand for maize in developing countries will increase much faster than for any other cereal and will overtake demand for rice and wheat by 2020.

To meet demand, the world's farmers will have to produce 40 percent more grain in 2020. Increases in cultivated area are expected to contribute only about one-fifth of the increase in global cereal production between 1995 and 2020, so improvements in crop yields will be required to bring about the necessary production. However, growth in farmers' cereal yields is slowing from the heyday of the Green Revolution during the 1970s. Without substantial and sustained additional investment in agricultural research, it will become more and more difficult to maintain, let alone increase, cereal yields in the long run.

Food production is increasing much faster in the developing world than in the developed world. By 2020, the developing world will be producing 59 percent of the world's cereals and 61 percent of the world's meat. Nevertheless, cereal production in the developing world will not keep pace with demand, and net cereal imports by developing countries will almost double between 1995 and 2020 to fill the gap between production and demand. Net meat imports by developing countries will increase eightfold during this period to 6.6 million tons.

About 60 percent of the developing world's net cereal imports in 2020 will come from the United States. Eastern Europe and the former Soviet Union are forecast to emerge as major net exporters, and the European Union and Australia are projected to increase their net exports as well.

Food prices will remain steady or fall slightly between 1995 and 2020. The much slower decrease in food prices compared with past trends is due to the continued slowdown in crop yield increases, as well as strong growth in demand for meat in developing countries. In the scenario described in the report, food insecurity and malnutrition will persist in 2020 and beyond. It projects that 135 million children under five years of age will be malnourished in 2020, a decline of only 15 percent from 160 million in 1995. With more than 77 percent of the developing world's malnourished children in 2020, Sub-Saharan Africa and South Asia will remain "hot spots" of child malnutrition and food insecurity.

### Emerging Issues

A number of emerging issues could significantly influence the outlook for the world food situation in the early years of the next century.

- First, new IFPRI research finds that improvements in four critical areas helped improve child nutrition in the developing world between 1970 and 1995: women's education, per capita food availability, the health environment, and women's status relative to men. This research suggests that investments in these four areas could significantly reduce child malnutrition.
- Second, world market prices for wheat, maize, and rice, adjusted for inflation, are the lowest they have been in the last century. This situation may threaten

producer incomes and future food production and stocks. Although increased climatic variations may cause larger production fluctuations in the future, current large grain stocks and continued productivity increases make it difficult to believe that another significant price spike will occur in the next few years.

- Third, the next round of world trade negotiations will begin in November 1999. To gain from trade talks, developing countries must participate effectively in the negotiations. Among other things, developing countries should pursue better access to markets in industrial countries for their agricultural commodities.
- Fourth, the desire to help poor farmers, combined with concerns about excessive dependence on fertilizers, pesticides, and irrigation water, has stimulated interest in an "agroecological approach" to agricultural production. The agroecological approach aims to reduce the amount of external inputs that farmers use, relying instead on available farm labor and organic material, as well as on improved knowledge and farm management. It has tremendous potential to promote sustainable productivity increases in small-scale agriculture.
- Fifth, the extent to which modern biotechnology will contribute to the achievement of food security for all is still an open question. While molecular biology-based science is moving at great speed, its application to agriculture has been mostly limited to solving problems facing farmers in the industrial countries and large farmers in a few developing countries. If focused on solving small farmers' problems, biotechnology may help these farmers reduce production risks and increase productivity, which will, in most developing countries, result in both higher incomes for small farmers and lower food prices for poor consumers. Biotechnology to make foodgrains more nutritious could help combat widespread nutritional problems among the poor in developing countries.
- Sixth, the recent revolutionary developments in information and communication technology (ICT) have dramatically reduced the cost of processing and transmitting information. In developing countries, access to ICT can open up new opportunities for education, primary health care, and agricultural extension as well as for conveying information on markets, transport options, road conditions, employment opportunities, and other issues important to the rural poor.

## Conclusion

IFPRI projections suggest that, under the most likely scenario, food insecurity and child malnutrition will remain widespread in 2020. Many millions of people will suffer from hunger and its debilitating consequences. This does not have to be so. If we can harness the political will to adopt policies and make investments that will eradicate poverty, foster food security, and protect natural resources, then a food-secure world—a world in which each and every person is assured of access at all times to the food required to lead healthy and productive lives—will be within our reach.

# Nutrition and Infection: Malnutrition and Mortality in Public Health

Gro Harlem Brundtland, M.D., M.P.H.

Earlier this century a number of eminent nutrition scientists recognized that nutrition deficiency, particularly with respect to vitamin A, was likely to be responsible for a large number of infectious conditions, but the biological mechanisms were entirely unknown. Thirty-one years ago, WHO published a historic monograph by Scrimshaw, Taylor, and Gorden that comprehensively reviewed the slowly mounting evidence of the interaction of nutrition and infection. This review marked a decisive turning point in research, epidemiologic investigation, and the management of malnutrition and infectious disease.

An important implication of this work is that, by working together—in science, in policy formulation and implementation, in nutrition and in infectious diseases, and in health and economic development—we are likely to raise the quality of life more than we do by working independently. In partnership, we can achieve more than we can separately.

In repeating this message today, I would like to give you a number of concrete examples, and look to a future where these partnerships must be routinely created because there is still much work to be done.

The combination of malnutrition and infectious disease is deadly. Separately, the effect of each is huge. Together, their impact is far greater than the sum of their parts. Both are conditions of poverty. They arise from poverty and they keep people in poverty, not just for one generation, but for many generations.

In a well-nourished child, a common infectious disease is usually a passing illness. In a malnourished child, the same disease can precipitate life-long disabilities such as blindness. A rapid sequence of common infection and malnutrition too often leads to death.

A slow sequence of disease followed by malnutrition leads to stunting and wasting, and affects mental development, decisively handicapping the affected millions that do not die. The survivors have special difficulties in terms of their cognitive and physical development. Their handicap, though invisible, is lasting. And when they reach adulthood, they are less productive and they earn less.

The malnutrition-infection complex is a drain on human resources. One condition aggravates the other. Infections lead to malnutrition, and malnutrition exacerbates infections, increasing their duration and severity. A look at the figures for each condition helps us to understand the true magnitude of this interaction.

Worldwide, infectious diseases kill approximately 10 million children each year before they reach the age of 5. Fifty percent of these deaths are associated with malnutrition. Seven of 10 of these deaths are due to diarrheal diseases, pneumonia, malaria, and measles, in combination with malnutrition. This is not counting tuberculosis, intestinal parasitic infestations, and HIV—which also comprise huge numbers in terms of ill-health and death—and are also associated with malnutrition.

Globally, children who are poorly nourished have up to 160 days of illness each year, with 3–4 episodes of diarrhea and 4–5 illnesses owing to severe respiratory infections. They often come from large poor families whose mothers are not well educated, who have, or will have, many dependent children, who themselves are not well nourished, and who produce low-birth-weight infants. Such women are themselves likely to have been born with low birth weight; their time and energy are stretched to the limit.

A large proportion of the world's population is affected by at least one of the several major forms of malnutrition. I am referring to low-birth-weight infants, wasted and stunted children, people who are brain-damaged from iodine deficiency, pre-schoolers who die or become blind from vitamin A deficiency and who are intellectually impaired as a result of iron deficiency, mothers who die in childbirth because of anemia, and the large numbers of malnourished elderly who are largely overlooked.

This is how malnutrition kills, maims, cripples, blinds, and retards, thereby impairing human and national development on a massive scale.

Now, let us examine the interaction of malnutrition and infectious disease. Malnutrition magnifies the effect of disease. A malnourished person has more severe disease episodes, more complications, and spends more time ill for each episode.

Because they aggravate one another, we cannot partition deaths into those owing to malnutrition and those owing to infection. In any population, the impact of malnutrition depends on the prevalence of infection, and the impact on infection—in terms of severity and duration—depends upon the nutrition base. Both need to be vigorously tackled.

Historically, despite its magnitude and obvious importance for morality, the prevention and management of malnutrition took a back seat, both clinically and programmatically, to the prevention and management of infectious diseases. Clinicians in developing countries still find it much easier to deal with diarrhea, pneumonia, measles, or tuberculosis than to mange severe protein-energy malnutrition. In many health-care centers there is still a 30% mortality rate in children with severe malnutrition, compared with only 5% in those receiving proper management. Similarly, in developing countries, most national health services pour resources into combating communicable diseases, whereas relatively meager resources are fed into national nutrition programs. Yet, where malnutrition prevails, the incidence of infectious disease, and its associated mortality, remains high.

Death rates increase exponentially with the degree of malnutrition. We have consistently found this to be so in all countries for which data are available. Any deterioration in nutrition status carries with it an increased risk of death. Thus, a severely malnourished child is 11 times more likely to die than a well-nourished child, a moderately malnourished child is 3 times more at risk of death, and a mildly malnourished child is twice as likely to die than a well-nourished child.

This reality has serious policy implications. The volume of malnutrition globally is in the mild and moderate category. And as long as half or greater (45–83%) of all malnutrition-related deaths occur to children in the mild to moderate category, we need to focus on this group. We shall not be making a dent in mortality if our policies and programs focus only on the severely malnourished.

It is true that there are many children who are severely malnourished but we need to think on a still broader front. For every child that is severely malnourished, there are many more who are moderately or mildly malnourished. Indeed, this is precisely how all severely malnourished children started out! Severe malnutrition is but the tip of an exceedingly great iceberg. We need to pay attention to the base. And we can expect to achieve the greatest impact by tackling the base.

Poor nutrition, however, is not the whole story. The more infectious disease there is in a population, the higher the death rate at any level of malnutrition; the bigger the burden of disease, the bigger the iceberg. This has profound policy implications. It means that we can reduce deaths by improving nutrition and we can reduce deaths by reducing infection but the greatest impact is likely to be achieved by addressing both at the same time.

Malnutrition, however, should be regarded as not just a single disease, but a range of conditions, many life-threatening or irreversibly disabling, resulting from an imbalance in availability or use of nutrients. Poverty and lack of education, which are so often the effects of underdevelopment, are usually the primary causes of hunger and malnutrition. There are poor people in most societies who do not have adequate access to food, care, safe water and sanitation, health services, and education. All of these are basic requirements for proper nutrition, and they require both short-term and long-term sustainable solutions and strategies.

There are several critical strategic approaches of proven effectiveness for preventing, reducing, and eliminating malnutrition. Whereas not all approaches are the primary mandate, the health sector has the overall leadership role in combating malnutrition. This is most likely because of its unique diagnostic contribution in assessing, measuring, and monitoring the different forms of malnutrition and alerting other sectors to its magnitude, trends, consequences, and the population groups affected.

These strategies include incorporating nutrition objectives into national development policies and programs; ensuring household food security, including food and nutrition as a human right; preventing and managing infectious diseases; promoting breastfeeding; caring for the socioeconomically deprived and nutritionally vulnerable; preventing and eliminating micronutrient malnutrition; promoting healthful diets and lifestyles; and assessing, analyzing, and monitoring nutrition status. Not all of these are completely or primarily within the domain of the health sector. However, they all affect health and nutrition well-being. This means that we must look outside of our sector and into other sectors that affect our goals in order to make the difference.

There are three major areas on which I would focus. The first is pregnancy and early nutrition. The sequence that begins with fetal malnutrition and results in a low-birth-weight baby is well known. One-third of low-birth-weight babies are moderately and severely malnourished by 6 months of age, and half are malnourished by 1 year. The poorer the start babies have in life, the more likely they are to become sick and malnourished and to die.

The antecedent of the sick malnourished child is low birth weight. Low birth weight results from pregnancies that are too short, too close together, too many, or too long. Pregnancies that are too close together do the most damage, especially among teenage or young mothers. Births that are spaced too closely do not give time for mothers to recover. Those who have not recovered cannot provide adequate nutrition for their fetus and fetal growth is retarded.

To improve the nutrition status of children, we must give them a healthy start. We must increase birth spacing and the rate of exclusive early breastfeeding of infants. We must ensure that mothers are adequately nourished before and during pregnancy.

A special issue in pregnancy is anemia. The prevalence of anemia in pregnant women is high: 63% in Africa, 80% in South Asia, and 30% in Latin America. It is increased when the mother lives in a malaria-endemic area, and is pregnant for the first time. Severe anemia in pregnancy is a major obstetric problem in malaria-endemic areas and a primary cause of maternal morbidity and mortality. The risk for underweight babies is twice as high in a malaria-endemic area as for an area without malaria. Five hundred million people live in malaria-endemic areas. Stillbirths are more common there as is the risk for miscarriage. Half of the pregnant women who develop cerebral malaria die.

One of the most important factors in reducing child deaths and the vicious cycle between nutrition, infection, and poverty is female education and literacy. Female education determines infant (and child) health and is statistically more significant than rural-urban differentials, income differentials, or ethnic origin.

Malnutrition and infection in children is the outcome of poverty, ignorance, and, among other factors, high-risk pregnancies. The responsibility for improving them lies with those dealing with economic development, education, social affairs, and agriculture, as well as with health. We need to be able to convince those dealing with education and economic development that their efforts affect health outcomes. To do this we must be backed by evidence.

The evidence can only come from interventions that are undertaken on a large enough scale to measure impact and that are done well enough to be generally applicable. Armed with such convincing evidence, we need to ensure that food and nutrition objectives are adequately incorporated into national development policies and programs. We need to ensure that sustainable improvement of nutrition and health, particularly of the most deprived and vulnerable population groups, goes hand in hand with permanent reduction of poverty and sustainable national development.

The role of health in development has been underestimated. The role of economic development in health is also underestimated. Poverty, poor female education, and rapid birth spacing give babies a poor start in life. A healthy start makes good economic sense.

The second point is related to repairing immune function. One of the most important interventions in interrupting the link between malnutrition and infection is the use of vitamin A supplementation. Since the 1920s we knew that an important function of vitamin A is its ability to repair immune function, and that the body is unable to properly resist infection without this micronutrient. Vitamin A supplementation is therefore a crucial immediate intervention that can break the malnutrition-infection complex in areas where vitamin A deficiency is prevalent. By increasing resistance to infection, it reduces case fatality rates when the infection does occur, as in diarrheal disease and measles.

Large supplementation trials show that routine vitamin A supplements given between 6–72 months of age can reduce overall mortality by at least 23% where vitamin A deficiency exists in a population. The impact of this single supplementation on childhood mortality is therefore as great as, or greater than, that of any single vaccine and it only costs a couple of cents per dose. Given to breastfeeding mothers postpartum, it protects infants from vitamin A deficiency.

The combined approach to nutrition and infection has achieved more. In the last 3 years we established that a combination of the two most cost-effective tools, vitamin A supplementation and vaccines, achieves more than the sum of their benefits. An example of the power of this combined approach is the case of the measles vaccine and vitamin A.

The measles vaccine, developed in the 1960s, is safe and effective, and provides long lasting immunity to measles infection. The priority target group for protection against vitamin A deficiency and measles is the same: infants and young children of poor families living in overcrowded housing who are already at risk of malnutrition.

Measles infection claimed 7–8 million of these lives per year before the vaccine became available. Measles causes loss of vitamin A, frequently precipitating acute vitamin A deficiency and blindness. Of children who become blind, half die within one year. Measles also leads to long-term complications including deafness, chronic lung disease, poor growth, and recurrent infections. Given the measles vaccine at approximately 9 months of age with vitamin A enables infants to receive both interventions for the addition of only a few cents per child.

Today, approximately 900,000 infants die from measles each year. These deaths are preventable. When vitamin A is introduced as part of measles management, the case fatality rate can be reduced by greater than 50%.

Last year, of those countries classified by WHO as having clinical signs or severe, moderate, or mild subclinical symptoms of vitamin A deficiency, over 40 countries administered vitamin A with their National Immunization Day vaccines. Now, many other countries include vitamin A in their routine immunization services.

We must also be clear that the ultimate battle to reduce and eliminate vitamin A deficiency and effectively combat malnutrition will not and cannot be won simply through short-term interventions such as providing vitamin A supplements, nor through clinic and hospital-based improved management systems, even though these are important and effective for saving lives.

These short-term interventions must be backed up by long-term enduring sustainable solutions to vitamin A deficiency and malnutrition in general. These include food-based dietary approaches, breastfeeding, appropriate complementary feeding, and fortification of appropriate foods with vitamin A.

The third area in which we can make a difference is iron supplementation. The nutrition science community is no doubt aware of the importance placed upon rolling back malaria. The effect of this disease upon iron status was, until recently, unquantified. Iron deficiency is, of course, the most common nutrition disorder in the world, affecting more than 1 billion people, particularly reproductive women and preschool children in tropical areas. Uncorrected, it leads to severe anemia, reduced work capacity, diminished learning ability, increased susceptibility to infection, and increased risk of death associated with pregnancy and childbirth.

Because the adverse affects of iron deficiency are preventable, iron supplementation has been WHO's policy in all areas where there is iron deficiency, except in malaria-endemic areas. In areas where there is malaria, efforts were hampered by conflicting evidence on the effects of iron deficiency (some studies show that iron supplementation triggers latent malaria or increases severe malaria episodes). As a result of this controversy, which has prevented the 500 million people in malaria-endemic areas with iron deficiency anemia from obtaining iron supplementation, WHO funded a study to establish whether or not iron supplementation increased risk of malaria or protected against severe iron deficiency anemia.

These results are now well known. Iron supplementation protects a child who is at high risk of dying from severe anemia in the first 2 years of life. However, antimalarial prophylaxis protects against severe anemia much more. The work, published recently, has provided us with evidence that malaria is the single largest contributor to the etiology of severe iron deficiency anemia in malaria-endemic areas.

In short, in areas of intense malaria transmission, reducing malaria makes more of a difference than iron supplementation in preventing severe anemia. By rolling back malaria, a major cause of iron deficiency anemia will be removed.

There is so much more that could be said in examining the nutrition-infection relationship and exploring its implications for public health policy. The World Health Organization is committed to reducing the mortality caused by malnutrition and infectious diseases. The impact we are likely to achieve to give children a healthy nutrition start in life is not likely to be made through the health sector alone. Solid evidence of strategies that are as good for health as for development is needed, as are the price tag and the impact.

We have a greater chance of making a difference, of getting programs implemented, when the benefits and costs are apparent to all the stakeholders. We depend upon evidence not only on the nutrition and health cost/benefit relationship of a program, but projections of these calculations into broader benefits for the economy. Making every child a wanted child, a healthier child, a more productive child and adult, through female education and better birth spacing, has implications for human development as well as for economic growth.

I count on the scientific community to join forces with the World Health Organization in this task, so that together we can make a difference.

---

Dr. Brundtland is the Director-General of the World Health Organization, CH-1211, Geneva, Switzerland. This paper was originally presented in a slightly different form as an address.

# AGRICULTURAL GROWTH, POVERTY ALLEVIATION, AND ENVIRONMENTAL SUSTAINABILITY: Having It All

**by Peter Hazell**

Many developing countries have achieved impressive growth rates in agriculture in recent decades. Asia, for example, was threatened by hunger and mass starvation in the 1960s but is now self-sufficient in staple foods, even though its population has more than doubled. Despite this success, serious concerns remain for the future. Hunger and malnutrition persist in many countries, often because past patterns of agricultural growth were insufficient or failed to adequately benefit the poor. Expected increases in agricultural demand associated with population growth and rising per capita incomes will require continuing increases in agricultural productivity, although evidence indicates that yield growth is slowing and prospects for further expansion of cropped and irrigated areas are limited. And environmental problems associated with agriculture could, if not checked, threaten future levels of agricultural productivity and impose severe health and environmental costs at the national and international levels.

Continued agricultural growth is a necessity, not an option, for most developing countries. But this growth must not jeopardize the underlying natural resource base or impose costly externalities on others. It must also be equitable if it is to help alleviate poverty and food insecurity. These three goals—agricultural growth, poverty alleviation, and environmental sustainability—are not necessarily complementary, and achieving all three simultaneously cannot be taken for granted. Although much depends on the specific social, economic, and agroecological circumstances, a high degree of complementarity is more likely to be achieved when agricultural development is (1) broadly based and involves small- and medium-sized farms, (2) market driven, (3) participatory and decentralized, and (4) driven by technological change that enhances factor productivity but does not degrade the resource base. Such growth can reduce food prices while increasing farm incomes; is employment intensive; and increases the effective demand for nonfood goods and services, particularly in small towns and market centers. By reducing poverty and promoting economic diversification in rural areas, it also relieves livelihood demands on the natural resource base.

## THE FIVE I's FOR AGRICULTURAL GROWTH

The requirements for broad-based agricultural development are reasonably well understood and should not be forgotten in the contemporary quest for environmental sustainability. Since they are so important, they are briefly reviewed here.

Back in the 1950s and 1960s, policymakers and agricultural development experts were primarily interested in growth, and the lessons that emerged from that experience can be summarized as the five I's for agricultural growth.

*Innovation.* Strong national agricultural research and extension systems (both public and private) to generate and disseminate productivity-enhancing technologies.

*Infrastructure*, particularly good road and transport systems.

*Inputs.* Efficient delivery systems for agricultural services, especially for modern farm inputs, agroprocessing, irrigation water, and credit.

*Institutions.* Efficient, liberalized markets that provide farmers with ready access to domestic and international markets and effective public institutions to provide key services where these cannot be developed to the private sector.

*Incentives.* Conducive macro, trade, and sector policies that do not penalize agriculture.

## EQUITY MODIFIERS: HOW AGRICULTURAL DEVELOPMENT CAN REDUCE POVERTY

In the 1970s and 1980s, policymakers and development experts began to focus on ways of using agricultural development to reduce poverty and food security as well as contribute to growth. The lessons that emerged from that era can be summed up in six "equity modifiers" to agricultural growth:

1. Promote broad-based agricultural development. There are few economies of scale in agricultural production in developing countries (unlike processing and marketing). Hence, targeting family farms is attractive on both equity and efficiency grounds. But small- and medium-sized farms must receive priority in publicly funded agricultural research and extension and in marketing, credit, and input supplies.
2. Undertake land reforms, where necessary. Such reforms, particularly market-assisted redistribution programs, may be needed where productive land is too narrowly concentrated among large farms.
3. Invest in human capital, such as rural education, clean water, health, family planning, and nutrition programs, to

improve the productivity of poor people and increase their opportunities for gainful employment.

4. Ensure that agricultural extension and education, as well as credit and small business assistance programs, reach rural women, since women play a key role in farming and ancillary activities.

5. Let all rural stakeholders (not just the rich and powerful) participate in setting priorities for public investments that they expect to benefit from or to help finance.

6. Actively encourage the rural nonfarm economy. It is not only an important source of income and employment in rural areas, especially for the poor, but it benefits from powerful income and employment multipliers when agriculture grows. In many countries, these potential multiplier effects are constrained by investment codes and related legislation that discriminate against small, rural nonfarm firms.

## ENVIRONMENTAL MODIFIERS FOR SUSTAINABLE AGRICULTURAL DEVELOPMENT

The new priority of environmental sustainability that has emerged in the 1990s does not negate the need for agriculture to continue to contribute to growth, poverty alleviation, and increased food security; it is just that agriculture is now required to accomplish all of these in ways that do not degrade the environment. In addition to the five I's and the six equity modifiers (there are no shortcuts here), eight environmental modifiers are now required for sustainable agricultural development. These modifiers have yet to be fully worked out and tested through development experience. In many ways the process is still at the research and design stage.

1. Give higher priority to backward regions in agricultural development, even though many of these may be resource poor. Considering the rapid population growth and limited nonfarm opportunities, agricultural growth is the only viable means of meeting the food and livelihood needs of growing populations in many backward areas for the next few decades. Failure to do so will lead to excessive outmigration, which will add to the problems of already overloaded urban slums. It will also lead to worsening poverty and further degradation of hillsides, forests, and soils. The development of backward regions will require additional resources for agricultural development, not diversion of resources from favorably endowed agricultural regions, where productivity increases are still important.

2. Pay more attention in agricultural research to sustainability features of recommended technologies, to broader aspects of natural resource management at the watershed and landscape levels, and to the problems of resource-poor areas.

3. Ensure that farmers have secure property rights over their resources. This does not necessarily imply that governments should invest in ambitious land registration programs. In many cases (in Sub-Saharan Africa, for example), the indigenous tenure systems still work surprisingly well. They are better able to meet equity needs and to recognize the rights of multiple users than are fully privatized property rights systems.

4. Privatize common property resources, or where this is not desirable (because of externality benefits or for equity reasons), strengthen community management systems.

5. Resolve externality problems through optimal taxes on polluters and degraders, regulation, empowerment of local organizations, or appropriate changes in property rights. But note that free market prices are not always the best; externalities may require optimal tax or subsidy interventions.

6. Improve the performance of relevant public institutions that manage and regulate natural resources (such as irrigation and forestry departments). Devolve management decisions to resource users, or groups of users, wherever possible. This also requires transfer of secure property or use rights.

7. Correct price distortions that encourage excessive use of modern inputs in intensive agriculture. That is, remove subsidies on fertilizers and pesticides and charge the full costs of irrigation water and electricity. It may still be necessary to subsidize fertilizer in backward regions where current use is low and soil fertility is being mined.

8. Establish resource monitoring systems to track changes in the condition of key resources, educate farmers about the environment effects of their actions, and delineate and protect sites of particular environmental value.

## CONCLUSIONS

Past patterns of agricultural growth have sometimes harmed the environment and exacerbated poverty and food insecurity among rural people, even as agriculture has met national food needs and contributed to export earnings. But poverty and environmental degradation are not an inevitable outcome of agricultural growth. Rather, these negative effects reflect inappropriate economic incentives for managing modern inputs in intensive farming systems, insufficient investment in many heavily populated backward areas, inadequate social and poverty concerns, and political systems that are often biased against rural people. With appropriate government policies and investments, institutional development, and agricultural research, there is no reason why agricultural development cannot simultaneously contribute to growth, poverty alleviation, and environmental sustainability.

---

For more information, see Peter Hazell and Ernst Lutz, "Integrating Environmental and Sustainability Concerns into Rural Development Policies," in *Agriculture and the Environment: Perspectives on Sustainable Rural Development*, ed. Ernst Lutz, with the assistance of Hans Binswanger, Peter Hazell, and Alexander McCalla (Washington, D.C.: World Bank, 1998).

---

*Peter Hazell is director of the Environment and Production Technology Division at the International Food Policy Research Institute.*

# WILL FRANKENFOOD FEED THE WORLD?

**Genetically modified food has met fierce opposition among well-fed Europeans, but it's the poor and the hungry who need it most**

**BY BILL GATES**

If you want to spark a heated debate at a dinner party, bring up the topic of genetically modified foods. For many people, the concept of genetically altered, high-tech crop production raises all kinds of environmental, health, safety and ethical questions. Particularly in countries with long agrarian traditions—and vocal green lobbies—the idea seems against nature.

In fact, genetically modified foods are already very much a part of our lives. A third of the corn and more than half the soybeans and cotton grown in the U.S. last year were the product of biotechnology, according to the Department of Agriculture. More than 65 million acres of genetically modified crops will be planted in the U.S. this year. The genetic genie is out of the bottle.

Yet there are clearly some very real issues that need to be resolved. Like any new product entering the food chain, genetically modified foods must be subjected to rigorous testing. In wealthy countries, the debate about biotech is tempered by the fact that we have a rich array of foods to choose from—and a supply that far exceeds our needs. In developing countries desperate to feed fast-growing and underfed populations, the issue is simpler and much more urgent: Do the benefits of biotech outweigh the risks?

The statistics on population growth and hunger are disturbing. Last year the world's population reached 6 billion. And by 2050, the U.N. estimates, it will probably near 9 billion. Almost all that growth will occur in developing countries. At the same time, the world's available cultivable land per person is declining. Arable land has declined steadily since 1960 and will decrease by half over the next 50 years, according to the International Service for the Acquisition of Agri-Biotech Applications (ISAAA).

The U.N. estimates that nearly 800 million people around the world are undernourished. The effects are devastating. About 400 million women of childbearing age are iron deficient, which means their babies are exposed to various birth defects. As many as 100 million children suffer from vitamin A deficiency, a leading cause of blindness. Tens of millions of people suffer from other major ailments and nutritional deficiencies caused by lack of food.

How can biotech help? Biotechnologists have developed genetically modified rice that is fortified with beta-carotene—which the body converts into vitamin A—and additional iron, and they are working on other kinds of nutritionally improved crops. Biotech can also improve farming productivity in places where food shortages are caused by crop damage attributable to pests, drought, poor soil and crop viruses, bacteria or fungi.

Damage caused by pests is incredible. The European corn borer, for example, destroys 40 million tons of the world's corn crop annually, about 7% of the total. Incorporating pest-resistant genes into seeds can help restore the balance. In trials of pest-resistant cotton in Africa, yields have increased significantly. So far, fears that genetically modified, pest-resistant crops might kill good insects as well as bad appear unfounded.

Viruses often cause massive failure in staple crops in developing countries. Two years ago, Africa lost more than half its cassava crop—a key source of calories—to the mosaic virus. Genetically modified, virus-resistant crops can reduce that damage, as can drought-tolerant seeds in regions where water shortages limit the amount of land under cultivation. Biotech can also help solve the problem of soil that contains excess aluminum, which can damage roots and cause many staple-crop failures. A gene that helps neutralize aluminum toxicity in rice has been identified.

Many scientists believe biotech could raise overall crop productivity in developing countries as much as 25% and help prevent the loss of those crops after they are harvested.

Yet for all that promise, biotech is far from being the whole answer. In developing countries, lost crops are only one cause of hunger. Poverty plays the largest role. Today more than 1 billion people around the globe live on less than $1 a day. Making genetically modified crops available will not reduce hunger if farmers cannot afford to grow them or if the local population cannot afford to buy the food those farmers produce.

Nor can biotech overcome the challenge of distributing food in developing countries. Taken as a whole, the world produces enough food to feed everyone—but much of it is simply in the wrong place. Especially in countries with undeveloped transport infrastructures, geography restricts food availability as dramatically as genetics promises to improve it.

Biotech has its own "distribution" problems. Private-sector biotech companies in the rich countries carry out much of the leading-edge research on genetically modified crops. Their products are often too costly for poor farmers in the developing world, and many of those products won't even reach the regions where they are most needed. Biotech firms have a strong financial incentive to target rich markets first in order to help them rapidly recoup the high costs of product development. But some of these companies are responding to the needs of poor countries. A London-based company, for example, has announced that it will share with developing countries technology needed to produce vitamin-enriched "golden rice."

More and more biotech research is being carried out in developing countries. But to increase the impact of genetic research on the food production of those countries, there is a need for better collaboration between government agencies—both local and in developed countries—and private biotech firms. The ISAAA, for example, is successfully partnering with the U.S. Agency for International Development, local researchers and private biotech companies to find and deliver biotech solutions for farmers in developing countries.

Will "Frankenfoods" feed the world? Biotech is not a panacea, but it does promise to transform agriculture in many developing countries. If that promise is not fulfilled, the real losers will be their people, who could suffer for years to come.

---

*Bill Gates is chairman and chief software architect of Microsoft and co-founder of the Bill and Melinda Gates Foundation*

# Biotechnology and the World Food Supply

Today, in a world with abundant food, more than 700 million people are chronically undernourished. Over the next 20 years, the world's population will probably double. The global food supply would need to double just to stay even, but to triple for the larger population to be fed adequately. Meanwhile, we are approaching limits in arable land and productivity and are employing practices that are destroying the soil's capacity to produce food.

Some see biotechnology as the answer to the problem of enabling this much larger population to feed itself. But biotechnology, if by this we mean crops engineered to contain new genes, is not *essential*. It could play a minor and useful role in developing new agricultural products, but other factors—including other kinds of breeding technologies—will be much more important than transgenic crops in determining whether we meet this challenge. It would be a tragedy if other necessary actions were not taken because of a mistaken belief that genetic engineering is some sort of a panacea for hunger. Some of the reasons biotechnology should not be relied on to enable the world to feed itself are outlined below.

### More productive crops are only part of the solution to the world's food crisis.

There are many reasons for the current and projected food crisis. Among the most important are lack of income to buy food, lack of infrastructure like roads to get products to market, trade policies that disadvantage farmers in the developing world, lack of inputs such as fertilizer, lack of information, and low-yield farming practices. More productive crops will do little to alleviate hunger if deficiencies in those areas are not addressed as well.

### Where more productive crops are needed, there is little reason to believe that genetic engineering will be better than other technologies—in particular, sophisticated traditional breeding—at producing higher yielding crops.

Many technologies can increase the yields of crops. These include traditional breeding, production of hybrids, so-called marker-assisted breeding (a sophisticated way of enhancing traditional breeding by knowing which plant cultivars carry which trait), and tissue culture methods for propagating virus-free root stocks. All of these could help improve the productivity of crops in the developing world, but currently only limited resources are available for applying them there.

So far, there no reason to believe that genetic engineering would be markedly better than these more traditional technologies in improving crops. Early "gene dreams" were of nitrogen-fixing crops, higher intrinsic yield, and drought tolerance. But so far none of these seems realistic because most involve complex multigene traits. For the most part, genetically engineered crops are limited to one or two gene transfers and have relative few applications of use to hungry people. Those that are of use, such as insect resistance and virus tolerance, do not increase intrinsic yield and vary in effectiveness. In addition, they appear to be short lived due to the almost certain evolution of resistant pests.

Currently, there is no reason to believe that the limited resources for agricultural development would be better spent on producing genetically engineered crops rather than on applying breeding technologies.

### For the most part, genetic engineering techniques are being applied to crops important to the industrialized world, not crops on which the world's hungry depend.

Most genetic engineering in agriculture is being done by large transnational corporations that need to sell their products at premium prices to cover the cost of research. These companies are developing products for farmers in rich countries who can afford to pay high prices for seed. Such farmers are interested in field crops like corn, soybeans, and cotton and fruits like tomatoes and cantaloupes. And that is what the agricultural biotechnology industry is providing. In many cases, genetically engineered fruits are sold at premium prices and seeds are sold with an added technology fee to cover the costs of research. These products are of virtually no value to hungry farmers in Africa, who cannot afford the products of traditional technology, much less these expensive genetically engineered products. In addition, these products are often inappropriate for the developing world because, among other things, they require large amounts of fertilizers, pesticides, and water.

In sum, more productive crops are only part of the solution to the world hunger problem and transgenic crops are not uniquely capable of increasing food production. While some genetically engineered crops will undoubtedly prove useful, there is no reason at this time to invest huge sums in them, especially at the expense of traditional breeding.

## What can be done to increase the food supply, particularly for the poor?

Many, many things. At bottom, we need more and better targeted agricultural research. Unlike the past, research can no longer concentrate exclusively on increased production—it must find ways to minimize the soil erosion, degradation of lakes and rivers, and groundwater pollution that can result from industrial agricultural practices. Growing appreciation of environmentally destructive impacts has led to a renewed interest in agroforestry, intercropping, mixed crop-livestock operations as systems that can increase production with minimal chemical fertilizers and pesticides and a high degree of environmental protection.

Much can be done to promote the sustainable intensification of agricultural production. Most of it should be done in developing countries to enable people to feed themselves so that they do not become dependent on commodities from abroad. All of it depends on local climates, cultures, and economic conditions. Rice farmers in Southeast Asia, for example, are in a far different situation from farmers living at the edge of the Sahara desert. Among the many research areas important for increasing production are the efficient use of irrigation water, crop improvement through traditional plant breeding, and new ways to manage crop-pest interactions, such as integrated pest management.

There is every reason to expect that research along these lines will lead to increased yields. Recently, agricultural scientists working in the Philippines announced that they had used sophisticated traditional breeding techniques to develop a rice variety that increased the proportion of the plant devoted to rice grains in ways that improved rice yields by 20 percent, a stunning achievement considering the importance of rice in the human diet. (Interestingly, the announcement was not accompanied by headlines like "Traditional Crop Breeding Can Feed the World!")

Improvements in other parts of the agricultural system are also essential. These include building and maintaining roads so that farmers can get their crops to market, organizing cooperatives so that farmers can purchase equipment and fertilizer, and reducing post-harvest losses of crops.

Finally, meeting the world food crisis will require changes outside of agriculture like improving the incomes of the poor through microenterprises and shifting the diet of the rich away from excessive dependence on grain-fed livestock. Growing corn to feed cows and chickens is a much less efficient use of limited arable land than growing corn for humans to eat directly.

# Glossary

**Absorption** The process by which digestive products pass from the gastrointestinal tract into the blood.
**Acid/base balance** The relationship between acidity and alkalinity in the body fluids.
**Amino acids** The structural units that make up proteins.
**Amylase** An enzyme that breaks down starches; a component of saliva.
**Amylopectin** A component of starch, consisting of many glucose units joined in branching patterns.
**Amylose** A component of starch, consisting of many glucose units joined in a straight chain, without branching.
**Anabolism** The synthesis of new materials for cellular growth, maintenance, or repair in the body.
**Anemia** A deficiency of oxygen-carrying material in the blood.
**Anorexia nervosa** A disorder in which a person refuses food and loses weight to the point of emaciation and even death.
**Antioxidant** A substance that prevents or delays the breakdown of other substances by oxygen; often added to food to retard deterioration and rancidity.
**Arachidonic acid** An essential polyunsaturated fatty acid.
**Arteriosclerosis** Condition characterized by a thickening and hardening of the walls of the arteries and a resultant loss of elasticity.
**Ascorbic acid** Vitamin C.
**Atherosclerosis** A type of arteriosclerosis in which lipids, especially cholesterol, accumulate in the arteries and obstruct blood flow.
**Avidin** A substance in raw egg white that acts as an antagonist of biotin, one of the B vitamins.

**Basal metabolic rate (BMR)** The rate at which the body uses energy for maintaining involuntary functions such as cellular activity, respiration, and heartbeat when at rest.
**Basic four** The food plan outlining the milk, meat, fruits and vegetables, and breads and cereals needed in the daily diet to provide the necessary nutrients.
**Beriberi** A disease resulting from inadequate thiamin in the diet.
**Beta-carotene** Yellow pigment that is converted to vitamin A in the body.
**Biotin** One of the B vitamins.
**Bomb calorimeter** An instrument that oxidizes food samples to measure their energy content.
**Buffer** A substance that can neutralize both acids and bases to minimize change in the pH of a solution.

**Calorie** The energy required to raise the temperature of one gram of water one degree Celsius.
**Carbohydrate** An organic compound composed of carbon, hydrogen, and oxygen in a ratio of 1:2:1.
**Carcinogen** A cancer-causing substance.
**Catabolism** The breakdown of complex substances into simpler ones.
**Celiac disease** A syndrome resulting from intestinal sensitivity to gluten, a protein substance of wheat flour especially and of other grains.
**Cellulose** An indigestible polysaccharide made of many glucose molecules.
**Cheilosis** Cracks at the corners of the mouth, due primarily to a deficiency of riboflavin in the diet.
**Cholesterol** A fat-like substance found only in animal products; important in many body functions but also implicated in heart disease.
**Choline** A substance that prevents the development of a fatty liver; frequently considered one of the B-complex vitamins.
**Chylomicron** A very small emulsified lipoprotein that transports fat in the blood.
**Cobalamin** One of the B vitamins ($B_{12}$).
**Coenzyme** A component of an enzyme system that facilitates the working of the enzyme.
**Collagen** Principal protein of connective tissue.
**Colostrum** The yellowish fluid that precedes breast milk, produced in the first few days of lactation.
**Cretinism** The physical and mental retardation of a child resulting from severe iodine or thyroid deficiency in the mother during pregnancy.

**Dehydration** Excessive loss of water from the body.
**Dextrin** Any of various small soluble polysaccharides found in the leaves of starch-forming plants and in the human alimentary canal as a product of starch digestion.
**Diabetes (diabetes mellitus)** A metabolic disorder characterized by excess blood sugar and urine sugar.
**Digestion** The breakdown of ingested foods into particles of a size and chemical composition that can be absorbed by the body.
**Diglyceride** A lipid containing glycerol and two fatty acids.
**Disaccharide** A sugar made up of two chemically combined monosaccharides, or simple sugars.
**Diuretics** Substances that stimulate urination.
**Diverticulosis** A condition in which the wall of the large intestine weakens and balloons out, forming pouches where fecal matter can be entrapped.

**Edema** The presence of an abnormally high amount of fluid in the tissues.
**Emulsifier** A substance that promotes the mixing of foods, such as oil and water in a salad dressing.
**Enrichment** The addition of nutrients to foods, often to restore what has been lost in processing.
**Enzyme** A protein that speeds up chemical reactions in the cell.
**Epidemiology** The study of the factors that contribute to the occurrence of a disease in a population.
**Essential amino acid** Any of the nine amino acids that the human body cannot manufacture and that must be supplied by the diet, as they are necessary for growth and maintenance.
**Essential fatty acid** A fatty acid that the human body cannot manufacture and that must be supplied by the diet, as it is necessary for growth and maintenance.

**Fat** An organic compound whose molecules contain glycerol and fatty acids; fat insulates the body, protects organs, carries fat-soluble vitamins, is a constituent of cell membranes, and makes food taste good.
**Fatty aci** dA simple lipid—containing only carbon, hydrogen, and oxygen—that is a constituent of fat.
**Ferritin** A substance in which iron, in combination with protein, is stored in the liver, spleen, and bone marrow.
**Fiber** Indigestible carbohydrate found primarily in plant foods; high fiber intake is useful in regulating bowel movements, and may lower the incidence of certain types of cancer and other diseases.
**Flavoprotein** Protein containing riboflavin.
**Folic acid (folacin)** One of the B vitamins.
**Fortification** The addition of nutrients to foods to enhance their nutritional values.
**Fructose** A six-carbon monosaccharide found in many fruits as well as honey and plant saps; one of two monosaccharides forming sucrose, or table sugar.

**Galactose** A six-carbon monosaccharide, one of the two that make up lactose, or milk sugar.
**Gallstones** An abnormal formation of gravel or stones, composed of cholesterol and bile salts and sometimes bile pigments, in the gallbladder; they result when substances that normally dissolve in bile precipitate out.
**Gastritis** Inflammation of the stomach.
**Glucagon** A hormone produced by the pancreas that works to increase blood glucose concentration.
**Glucose** A six-carbon monosaccharide found in sucrose, honey, and many fruits and vegetables; the major carbohydrate found in the body.

**Glucose tolerance factor (GTF)** A hormone-like substance containing chromium, niacin, and protein that helps the body to use glucose.
**Glyceride** A simple lipid composed of fatty acids and glycerol.
**Glycogen** The storage form of carbohydrates in the body; composed of glucose molecules.
**Goiter** Enlargement of the thyroid gland as a result of iodine deficiency.
**Goitrogens** Substances that induce goiter, often by interfering with the body's utilization of iodine.

**Heme** A complex iron–containing compound that is a component of hemoglobin.
**Hemicellulose** Any of various indigestible plant polysaccharides.
**Hemochromatosis** A disorder of iron metabolism.
**Hemoglobin** The iron-containing protein in red blood cells that carries oxygen to the tissues.
**High-density lipoprotein (HDL)** A lipoprotein that acts as a cholesterol carrier in the blood; referred to as "good" cholesterol because relatively high levels of it appear to protect against atherosclerosis.
**Hormones** Compounds secreted by the endocrine glands that influence the functioning of various organs.
**Humectants** Substances added to foods to help them maintain moistness.
**Hydrogenation** The chemical process by which hydrogen is added to unsaturated fatty acids, which saturates them and converts them from a liquid to a solid form.
**Hydrolyze** To split a chemical compound into smaller molecules by adding water.
**Hydroxyapatite** The hard mineral portion (the major constituent) of bone, composed of calcium and phosphate.
**Hypercalcemia** A high level of calcium in the blood.
**Hyperglycemia** A high level of "sugar" (glucose) in the blood.
**Hypocalcemia** A low level of calcium in the blood.
**Hypoglycemia** A low level of "sugar" (glucose) in the Blood.

**Incomplete protein** A protein lacking or deficient in one or more of the essential amino acids.
**Inorganic** Describes a substance not containing carbon.
**Insensible loss** Fluid loss, through the skin and from the lungs, that an individual is unaware of.
**Insulin** A hormone produced by the pancreas that regulates the body's use of glucose.
**Intrinsic factor** A protein produced by the stomach that makes absorption of $B_{12}$ possible; lack of this protein results in pernicious anemia.

**Joule** A unit of energy preferred by some professionals instead of the heat energy measurements of the calorie system for calculating food energy; sometimes referred to as "kilojoule."

**Keratinization** Formation of a protein called keratin, which, in vitamin A deficiency, occurs instead of mucus formation; leads to a drying and hardening of epithelial tissue.
**Ketogenic** Describes substances that can be converted to ketone bodies during metabolism, such as fatty acids and some amino acids.
**Ketone bodies** The three chemicals—acetone, acetoacetic acid, and betahydroxybutyrie—that are normally involved in lipid metabolism and accumulate in blood and urine in abnormal amounts in conditions of impaired metabolism (such as diabetes).
**Ketosis** A condition resulting when fats are the major source of energy and are incompletely oxidized, causing ketone bodies to build up in the bloodstream.
**Kilocalorie** One thousand calories, or the energy required to raise the temperature of one kilogram of water one degree Celsius; the preferred unit of measurement for food energy.
**Kilojoule** *See* Joule.
**Kwashiorkor** A form of malnutrition resulting from a diet severely deficient in protein but high in carbohydrates.

**Lactase** A digestive enzyme produced by the small intestine that breaks down lactose.
**Lactation** Milk production/secretion.
**Lacto-ovo-vegetarian** A person who does not eat meat, poultry, or fish but does eat milk products and eggs.
**Lactose** A disaccharide composed of glucose and galactose and found in milk.
**Lactose intolerance** The inability to digest lactose due to a lack of the enzyme lactase in the intestine.
**Lacto-vegetarian** A person who does not eat meat, poultry, fish, or eggs but does drink milk and eat milk products.
**Laxatives** Food or drugs that stimulate bowel movements.
**Lignins** Certain forms of indigestible carbohydrate in plant foods.
**Linoleic aci dAn** essential polyunsaturated fatty acid.
**Lipase** An enzyme that digests fats.
**Lipid** Any of various substances in the body or in food that are insoluble in water; a fat or fat-like substance.
**Lipoprotein** Compound composed of a lipid (fat) and a protein that transports both in the bloodstream.
**Low-density lipoprotein (LDL)** A lipoprotein that acts as a cholesterol carrier in the blood; referred to as "bad" cholesterol because relatively high levels of it appear to enhance atherosclerosis.

**Macrocytic anemia** A form of anemia characterized by the presence of abnormally large blood cells.
**Macroelements (also macronutrient elements)** Those elements present in the body in amounts exceeding 0.005 percent of body weight and required in the diet in amounts exceeding 100 mg/day; include sodium, potassium, calcium, and phosphorus.
**Malnutrition** A poor state of health resulting from a lack, excess, or imbalance of the nutrients needed by the body.
**Maltose** A disaccharide whose units are each composed of two glucose molecules, produced by the digestion of starch.
**Marasmus** Condition resulting from a deficiency of calories and nearly all essential nutrients.
**Melanin** A dark pigment in the skin, hair, and eyes.
**Metabolism** The sum of all chemical reactions that take place within the body.
**Microelements (also micronutrient elements; trace element s)** Those elements present in the body in amounts under 0.005 percent of body weight and required in the diet in amounts under 100 mg/day.
**Monoglyceride** A lipid containing glycerol and only one fatty acid.
**Monosaccharide** A single sugar molecule, the simplest form of carbohydrate; examples are glucose, fructose, and galactose.
**Monosodium glutamate (MSG)** An amino acid used in flavoring foods, which causes allergic reactions in some people.
**Monounsaturated fatty aci dA** fatty acid containing one double bond.
**Mutagen** A mutation-causing agent.

**Negative nitrogen balance** Nitrogen output exceeds nitrogen intake.
**Niacin (nicotinic acid)** One of the B vitamins.
**Nitrogen equilibrium (zero nitrogen balanc e N)**trogen output equals nitrogen intake.
**Nonessential amino acid** Any of the 13 amino acids that the body can manufacture in adequate amounts, but which are nonetheless required in the diet in an amount relative to the amount of essential amino acids.
**Nutrients** Nourishing substances in food that can be digested, absorbed, and metabolized by the body; needed for growth, maintenance, and reproduction.
**Nutrition** (1) The sum of the processes by which an organism obtains, assimilates, and utilizes food. (2) The scientific study of these processes.

**Obesity** Condition of being 30 percent above one's ideal body weight.
**Oleic acid** A monounsaturated fatty acid.
**Organic foods** Those foods, especially fruits and vegetables, grown without the use of pesticides, synthetic fertilizers, etc.
**Osmosis** Passage of a solvent through a semipermeable membrane from an area of higher concentration to an area of lower concentration until the concentration is equal on both sides of the membrane.
**Osteomalacia** Condition in which a loss of bone mineral leads to a softening of the bones; adult counterpart of rickets.
**Osteoporosis** Disorder in which the bones degenerate due to a loss of bone mineral, producing porosity and fragility; normally found in older women.
**Overweight** Body weight exceeding an accepted norm by 10 or 15 percent.

**Ovo-vegetarian** A person who does not eat meat, poultry, fish, milk, or milk products but does eat eggs.
**Oxidation** The process by which a substrate takes up oxygen or loses hydrogen; the loss of electrons.

**Palmitic acid** A saturated fatty acid.
**Pantothenic acid** One of the B vitamins.
**Pellagra** Niacin deficiency syndrome, characterized by dementia, diarrhea, and dermatitis.
**Pepsin** A protein-digesting enzyme produced by the stomach.
**Peptic ulcer** An open sore or erosion in the lining of the digestive tract, especially in the stomach and duodenum.
**Peptide** A compound composed of amino acids that are joined together.
**Peristalsis** Motions of the digestive tract that propel food through the tract.
**Pernicious anemia** One form of anemia caused by an inability to absorb vitamin $B_{12}$, owing to the absence of intrinsic factor.
**pH** A measure of the acidity of a solution, based on a scale from 0 to 14: a pH of 7 is neutral; greater than 7 is alkaline; less than 7 is acidic.
**Phenylketonuria (PKU)** A genetic disease in which phenylalanine, an essential amino acid, is not properly metabolized, thus accumulating in the blood and causing early brain damage.
**Phospholipid** A fat containing phosphorus, glycerol, two fatty acids, and any of several other chemical substances.
**Polypeptide** A molecular chain of amino acids.
**Polysaccharide** A carbohydrate containing many monosaccharide subunits.
**Polyunsaturated fatty acids** A fatty acid in which two or more carbon atoms have formed double bonds, with each holding only one hydrogen atom.
**Positive nitrogen balance** Condition in which nitrogen intake exceeds nitrogen output in the body.
**Protein** Any of the organic compounds composed of amino acids and containing nitrogen; found in the cells of all living organisms.
**Provitamins** Precursors of vitamins that can be converted to vitamins in the body (e.g., beta-carotene, from which the body can make vitamin A).
**Pyridoxine** One of the B vitamins ($B_6$).
**Pull date** Date after which food should no longer be sold but still may be edible for several days.

**Recommended Daily Allowances (RDAs)** Standards for daily intake of specific nutrients established by the Food and Nutrition Board of the National Academy of Sciences; they are the levels thought to be adequate to maintain the good health of most people.
**Rhodopsin** The visual pigment in the retinal rods of the eyes which allows one to see at night; its formation requires vitamin A.
**Riboflavin** One of the B vitamins ($B_2$).
**Ribosome** The cellular structure in which protein synthesis occurs.
**Rickets** The vitamin D deficiency disease in children characterized by bone softening and deformities.

**Saliva** Fluid produced in the mouth that helps food digestion.
**Salmonella** A bacterium that can cause food poisoning.
**Saturated fatty acid** A fatty acid in which carbon is joined with four other atoms; i.e., all carbon atoms are bound to the maximum possible number of hydrogen atoms.
**Scurvy** A disease characterized by bleeding gums, pain in joints, lethargy, and other problems; caused by a deficiency of vitamin C (ascorbic acid).
**Standard of identity** A list of specifications for the manufacture of certain foods that stipulates their required contents.
**Starch** A polysaccharide composed of glucose molecules; the major form in which energy is stored in plants.
**Stearic acid** A saturated fatty acid.
**Sucrose** A disaccharide composed of glucose and fructose, often called "table sugar."
**Sulfites** Agents used as preservatives in foods to eliminate bacteria, preserve freshness, prevent browning, and increase storage life; can cause acute asthma attacks, and even death, in people who are sensitive to them.

**Teratogen** An agent with the potential of causing birth defects.
**Thiamin** One of the B vitamins ($B_1$).
**Thyroxine** Hormone containing iodine that is secreted by the thyroid gland.
**Toxemia** A complication of pregnancy characterized by high blood pressure, edema, vomiting, presence of protein in the urine, and other symptoms.
**Transferrin** A protein compound, the form in which iron is transported in the blood.
**Triglyceride** A lipid containing glycerol and three fatty acids.
**Trypsin** A digestive enzyme, produced in the pancreas, that breaks down protein.

**Underweight** Body weight below an accepted norm by more than 10 percent.
**United States Recommended Daily Allowance (USRDA)** The highest level of recommended intakes for population groups (except pregnant and lactating women); derived from the RDAs and used in food labeling.
**Urea** The main nitrogenous component of urine, resulting from the breakdown of amino acids.
**Uremia** A disease in which urea accumulates in the blood.

**Vegan** A person who eats nothing derived from an animal; the strictest type of vegetarian.
**Vitamin** Organic substance required by the body in small amounts to perform numerous functions.
**Vitamin B complex** All known water-soluble vitamins except C; includes thiamin ($B_1$), riboflavin ($B_2$), pyridoxine ($B_6$), niacin, folic acid, cobalamin ($B_{12}$), pantothenic acid, and biotin.

**Xerophthalmia** A disease of the eye resulting from vitamin A deficiency.

# Index

## F



## G



## H



## I



## J



## K



## L



## M



## N

# Test Your Knowledge Form

We encourage you to photocopy and use this page as a tool to assess how the articles in *Annual Editions* expand on the information in your textbook. By reflecting on the articles you will gain enhanced text information. You can also access this useful form on a product's book support Web site at *http://www.dushkin.com/online/*.

NAME: DATE:

TITLE AND NUMBER OF ARTICLE:

BRIEFLY STATE THE MAIN IDEA OF THIS ARTICLE:

LIST THREE IMPORTANT FACTS THAT THE AUTHOR USES TO SUPPORT THE MAIN IDEA:

WHAT INFORMATION OR IDEAS DISCUSSED IN THIS ARTICLE ARE ALSO DISCUSSED IN YOUR TEXTBOOK OR OTHER READINGS THAT YOU HAVE DONE? LIST THE TEXTBOOK CHAPTERS AND PAGE NUMBERS:

LIST ANY EXAMPLES OF BIAS OR FAULTY REASONING THAT YOU FOUND IN THE ARTICLE:

LIST ANY NEW TERMS/CONCEPTS THAT WERE DISCUSSED IN THE ARTICLE, AND WRITE A SHORT DEFINITION:

# We Want Your Advice

ANNUAL EDITIONS revisions depend on two major opinion sources: one is our Advisory Board, listed in the front of this volume, which works with us in scanning the thousands of articles published in the public press each year; the other is you—the person actually using the book. Please help us and the users of the next edition by completing the prepaid article rating form on this page and returning it to us. Thank you for your help!

## ANNUAL EDITIONS: Nutrition 02/03

### ARTICLE RATING FORM

Here is an opportunity for you to have direct input into the next revision of this volume. We would like you to rate each of the articles listed below, using the following scale:

1. **Excellent: should definitely be retained**
2. **Above average: should probably be retained**
3. **Below average: should probably be deleted**
4. **Poor: should definitely be deleted**

Your ratings will play a vital part in the next revision. Please mail this prepaid form to us as soon as possible. Thanks for your help!

| RATING | ARTICLE |
|---|---|
| ________ | 1. The 2000 Dietary Guidelines for Americans: What Are the Changes and Why Were They Made? |
| ________ | 2. Picture This! Communicating Nutrition Around the World |
| ________ | 3. The New American Plate |
| ________ | 4. Food Portions and Servings: How Do They Differ? |
| ________ | 5. Americans Ignore Importance of Food Portion Size |
| ________ | 6. In the Drink: When it Comes to Calories, Solid Is Better Than Liquid |
| ________ | 7. Food Industry Is Making America Fat |
| ________ | 8. Supermarket Psych-Out |
| ________ | 9. Dietary Protein and Weight Reduction |
| ________ | 10. Fats: The Good, the Bad, the Trans |
| ________ | 11. Omega-3 Fatty Acids and Health |
| ________ | 12. Building Healthy Bones |
| ________ | 13. Vitamins & Minerals: How Much Is Too Much? |
| ________ | 14. Can Taking Vitamins Protect Your Brain? |
| ________ | 15. When (and How) to Take Your Vitamin and Mineral Supplements |
| ________ | 16. Nutrient-Drug Interactions and Food |
| ________ | 17. Diet and Health: The Issues |
| ________ | 18. The Human Genome: A Master Code for Better Health |
| ________ | 19. Diabetes: How to Cut Your Risk |
| ________ | 20. Homocysteine: "The New Cholesterol"? |
| ________ | 21. DASH Diet May Prevent Heart Attacks |
| ________ | 22. What We Still Don't Know About Soy |
| ________ | 23. Aging Well With Good Nutrition |
| ________ | 24. The Female Athlete Triad: Nutrition, Menstrual Disturbances, and Low Bone Mass |
| ________ | 25. Healthy People 2010: Overweight and Obesity |
| ________ | 26. Why We Get Fat |
| ________ | 27. Size Acceptance, Alternative to Fat Phobia |
| ________ | 28. Diet vs. Diet: Battle of the Bulge Doctors |
| ________ | 29. Weight Loss Diets and Books |
| ________ | 30. A Guide to Rating the Weight-Loss Websites |
| ________ | 31. Nondiet Approach to Treatment of Binge Eating Disorder |
| ________ | 32. The Mouse That Roared: Health Scares on the Internet |
| ________ | 33. Herbals for Health? |
| ________ | 34. Functional Foods: An Overview |
| ________ | 35. Nutrition Supplements: Science vs. Hype |
| ________ | 36. Does the Supplement You Buy Contain What Its Label Says? |
| ________ | 37. Bar Exam: Energy Bars Flunk |
| ________ | 38. America's Dietary Guideline on Food Safety: A Plus, or a Minus? |
| ________ | 39. Don't Mess With Food Safety Myths! |
| ________ | 40. Bacterial Food-Borne Illness |
| ________ | 41. How Now, Mad Cow? |
| ________ | 42. Dioxin for Dinner? |
| ________ | 43. What's This Doing in My Food? A Guide to Food Ingredients |
| ________ | 44. Food Irradiation: A Safe Measure |
| ________ | 45. Hunger and Food Insecurity |
| ________ | 46. The Challenge of Feeding the World |
| ________ | 47. World Food Prospects: Critical Issues for the Early Twenty-First Century |
| ________ | 48. Nutrition and Infection: Malnutrition and Mortality in Public Health |
| ________ | 49. Agricultural Growth, Poverty Alleviation, and Environmental Sustainability: Having It All |
| ________ | 50. Will Frankenfood Feed the World? |
| ________ | 51. Biotechnology and the World Food Supply |

*(Continued on next page)*

NO POSTAGE NECESSARY IF MAILED IN THE UNITED STATES

**BUSINESS REPLY MAIL**

FIRST-CLASS MAIL PERMIT NO. 84 GUILFORD CT

POSTAGE WILL BE PAID BY ADDRESSEE

**McGraw-Hill/Dushkin**
**530 Old Whitfield Street**
**Guilford, Ct 06437-9989**

## ABOUT YOU

Name                                                                 Date

Are you a teacher ?☐ A student? ☐
Your school's name

Department

Address                    City                    State                    Zip

School telephone #

## YOUR COMMENTS ARE IMPORTANT TO US!

Please fill in the following information:
For which course did you use this book?

Did you use a text with this ANNUAL EDITION? ☒ yes ☐ no
What was the title of the text?

What are your general reactions to the *Annual Editions* concept?

Have you read any pertinent articles recently that you think should be included in the next edition? Explain.

Are there any articles that you feel should be replaced in the next edition? Why?

Are there any World Wide Web sites that you feel should be included in the next edition? Please annotate.

May we contact you for editorial input? ☐ yes ☐ no
May we quote your comments ?☐ yes ☐ no